歐洲卷

中國攝影藝術年鑒

European - Chinese Photographic Art Yearbook 2022-2023

《中國攝影藝術年鑒-歐洲卷》2022-2023
European - Chinese Photographic Art Yearbook

ISBN 978-1-7392839-0-2

This hardback edition published in the United Kingdom in 2023.
By Sino European Arts (Europen - Chinese Photographic Art Yearbool Editiorial Committee London, UK)
此精裝版由英國華歐藝術文化中心 – 中國攝影藝術年鑒英國倫敦編委會，于 2023 年在英國出版。

admin@sinoeuropeanarts.co.uk
www.sinoeuropeanarts.co.uk

British Library Cataloguing-in-Publication Data.
A catalogue record for this book is available from the British Library.
本書已記録在大英圖書館出版目録中。

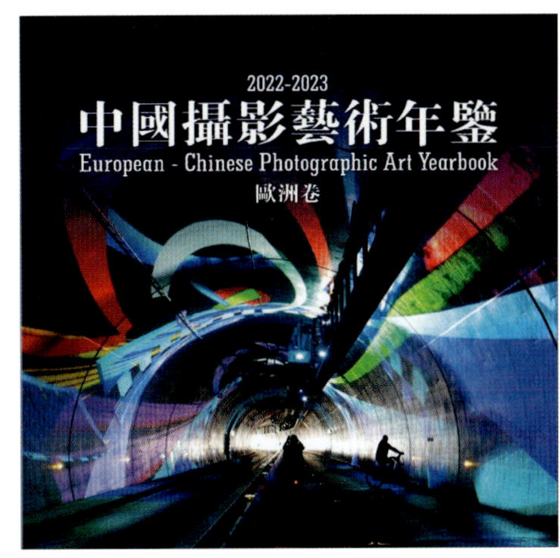

封面: 法國裏昂時光遂道 / 攝影:黄松辉
Cover: Time Tunnel in Lyon, France
by Huang Songhui FRPS

専家委員會
Committee of Experts

編輯委員会
Editorial Board

目錄
TABLE OF CONTENTS

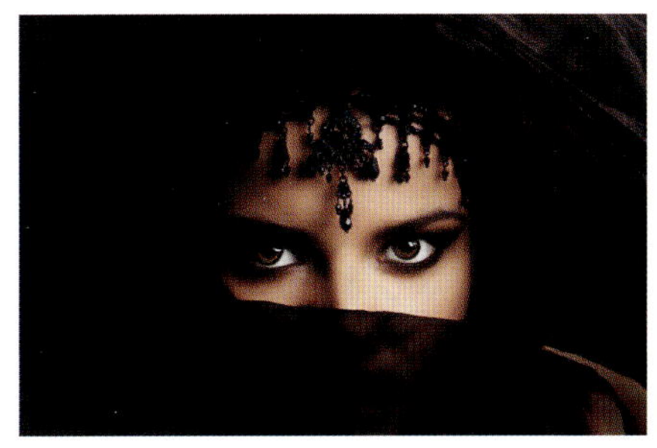

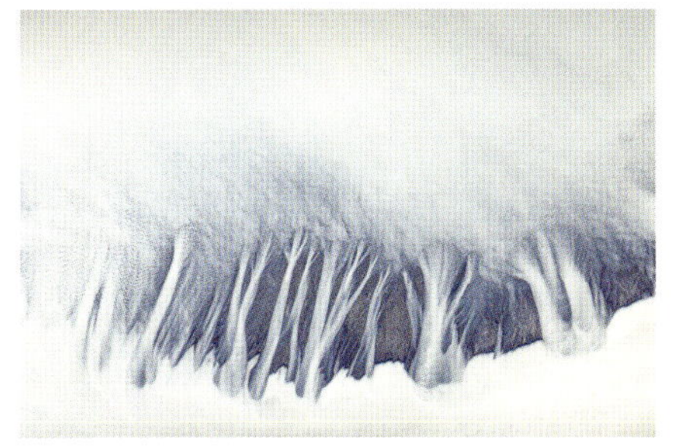

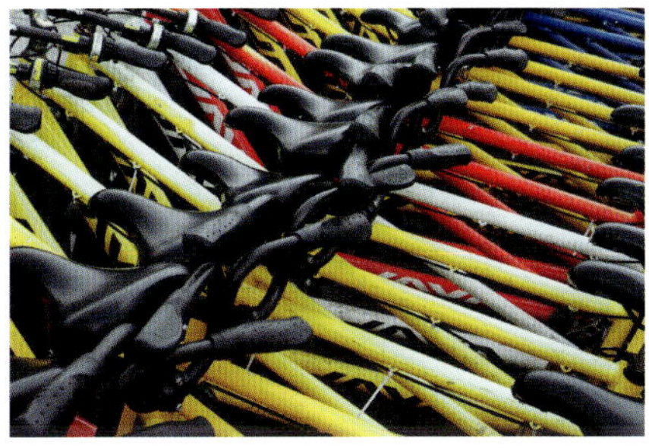

介紹

《中國攝影藝術年鑒》是一部深具權威性及影響力的史籍畫册，作爲中國唯一一部具有文化公益性質的大型攝影出版物，不僅是攝影藝術的作品集成，更是中國影像乃至世界華人影像的時代記録，有着巨大的文化傳播和文明承載作用。該書由中國文化和旅游部–中國藝術研究院 創辦于2006年，至今已連續出版16年。

隨着《中國攝影藝術年鑒》影響在海内外的不斷擴大，《年鑒》總編輯高健生先生以其寬闊的國際視野、深厚的文化底蘊及藝術情懷， 决定在英國倫敦設立《中國攝影藝術年鑒–歐洲卷》編輯部，授權英國華歐藝術文化中心負責徵集歐洲地區的優秀作品，設計，編輯及出版。

值此中英建立大使級外交關系50周年之際，爲慶祝中英兩國建交後在藝術與文化領域半個世紀交流合作，隆重推出《中國攝影藝術年鑒 – 歐洲卷》，攝影是一種不需要翻譯的通用語言: 强大的圖像可以表達攝影師的想法和情感。這部書的推出，對進一步促進東西藝術文化的溝通與交流將具有深遠的影響。

歷年的攝影年鑒是以中國攝影師爲主，但這部《中國攝影藝術年鑒 – 歐洲卷》首次包括歐洲攝影師，本書的亮點在于匯聚了東西方多個視角，通過這些杰出攝影師的鏡頭，表達了在各自文化語境下對當今世界的理解，以及東西方藝術家不同的思維方式和獨特表達。

本書首次在倫敦出版，中英文對照精裝彩印，并編輯出版限量版，是中西文化交流的有效平臺。目標讀者爲攝影藝術收藏家、攝影師、商業投資者和藝術愛好者。

該年鑒將由大英圖書館和其他歐洲藝術大學圖書館收藏。

本年鑒編委會致敬所有對影像有貢獻的藝術家，并分享精彩絶倫的影像藝術世界。

《中國攝影藝術年鑒–歐洲卷》編輯委員會

INTRODUCTION

This *Chinese Photographic Art Yearbook* is a highly authoritative and influential historical book. It is the only large-scale photographic publication in China associated with a cultural public charitable institution, but it is not just a collection of photographic artworks, it is also a record of an entire era of Chinese image-making and a record of images from the whole world. As a result, it has a huge role in cultural dissemination and as a record of the progress of civilisation. The book was founded in 2006 by the Ministry of Culture and Tourism of China - the China Academy of Arts and has now been published continuously for 16 years.

With the consistent expansion of the influence of the *Chinese Photographic Art Yearbook* at home and abroad, Mr. Gao Jiansheng, the editor-in-chief of the Yearbook, used his broad international vision, profound cultural background and artistic insight and decided to establish the *Chinese Photographic Art Yearbook* in London, UK, The Editorial Committee of the Yearbook - European Volume has authorised Sino European Arts Ltd., UK, to be responsible for sourcing equally excellent artworks in Europe, as well as editing, designing and publishing this edition.

This year marks the 50th anniversary of the establishment of ambassadorial diplomatic relations between China and the UK and – by way of celebrating the half century of exchanges and cooperation in the fields of art and culture following that agreement-the *European - Chinese Photographic Art Yearbook 2022* is proudly launched. Photography is a universal language that needs no translation: a powerful image can express the ideas and the emotions of the photographer. Through the launch of this Yearbook we aim to greatly promote ongoing communication between Eastern and Western art and culture

Previous Yearbooks were dominated by Chinese photographers, but this one includes European photographers for the first time. Showing the two side-by-side will promote artistic exchange and symbiosis between China and Europe.

The intention of this Yearbook is to bring together a variety of visions, through the lenses of these outstanding photographers, to show their unique views on visual art in their different cultural contexts. Through this Yearbook, we aim to promote the world's photographic culture to create a new dialogue and develop the exchange of ideas across space and time. Western and Eastern perspectives are both represented, providing an effective platform for cultural exchange between the two regions.

This book is being published in London for the first time. It is edited and published in a limited edition and aims to create an effective platform for cultural exchanges between East and the West. Target readers are photographic art collectors, photographers, business investors and art lovers around the world.

The Yearbook will be collected by the British Library and many other European art institutions as well as university libraries. The editorial board of this yearbook pays tribute to all the artists who have contributed to the images, sharing the wonderful world of art. We hereby thank them all for their many and varied contributions.

European - Chinese Photographic Art Yearbook Editorial Committee

前言

《中國攝影藝術年鑒》自2006年出版以來，在中國大陸影響巨大，隨着中國改革開放的步伐，其影響力逐漸傳達至海外。2017年我們在香港設立編輯部，負責編輯出版《中國攝影藝術年鑒–港澳卷》，2018年又在倫敦設立編輯部，負責編輯出版《中國攝影藝術年鑒–歐洲卷》。

今年是中英兩國建立大使級外交關系50周年，半個世紀的人員交往、半個 世紀的文化交流，讓兩國人民相互了解到了對方更多的生活方式和文化觀念， 找到了更多的共同點。世界就是這樣，了解的越深，相處的就越好，求同存异，共同發展。從這個意義上來講《中國攝影藝術年鑒–歐洲卷》的出版爲增進中英、中歐之間的友好與理解是有貢獻的。

《歐洲卷》的出版爲我們提供了一個比較東西方文化的獨特視角。本卷的獨特之處在于作者大部分是來自歐洲各國的攝影家和旅居歐洲的華人攝影家，這兩部分人從各自文化的角度觀看當今的世界，同一種事務，不同的表達，相同或相异。相同之處是人性，相异之處是文化，這也正是我們這個世界統一性和多樣性的存在。各美其美，美美與共，和而不同，天下大同。

攝影家眼中的世界就是他們心中的世界，無論是歌頌光明，還是鞭笞陰暗，其終極目的都是讓我們生活的世界更加美好。

在本書的編輯過程中遭遇新冠病毒大流行，爲徵集稿件和出版發行帶來了許多困難，但倫敦編輯部的各位同仁在牟樺主編的帶領下依然出色地完成了本書的編輯出版，在此我表示誠摯的敬意和由衷的感謝。

《中國攝影藝術年鑒》是一部圖片形式的史籍，攝影家記録了歷史，我們的責任就是讓歷史記住這些攝影家。

《中國攝影藝術年鑒》總編輯: 高健生
2022年12月30日
中國・北京

FOREWORD

Since the first publication of *Chinese Photographic Art Yearbook* in 2006, the work has had great influence in mainland China. With the pace of China's reform and opening up, its influence has gradually spread overseas. In 2017, we set up an editorial department in Hong Kong, responsible for editing and publishing the *Chinese Photographic Art Yearbook-Hong Kong and Macau Volume* and in 2018 we followed up with an editorial department in London, to produce the Chinese Photographic Art Yearbook - European Volume. It is called *European - Chinese Photographic Art Yearbook.*

Now is the occasion of the 50th of anniversary of the establishment of diplomatic relations at ambassadorial level between China and the UK. Half a century of personal and cultural exchanges have enabled the people of the two countries to learn more about each other's lifestyles and cultural concepts, and to find more common ground. The point to take from this is that the world is like this, the deeper we understand, the better we get along, seeking common ground while reserving differences, and all the while developing together. In this sense, the publication of the *European - Chinese Photographic Art Yearbook 2022* has contributed to the promotion of friendship and understanding between China and Britain, and between China and Europe.

The publication of the *European - Chinese Photographic Art Yearbook 2022* provides us with a unique perspective to compare Eastern and Western cultures. The uniqueness of this volume is that the authors are photographers from various European countries and Chinese. These two groups view the world today from the perspective of their respective cultures. The commonality of things happening, different expressions. The universality of human nature, and the difference in culture, the experience of unity and diversity in our world. Each has its own beauty, and that beauty can be shared, in a united vision.

The world in the eyes of photographers is the world in their hearts. Whether it is singing the praises of the light or attacking the darkness, the ultimate goal is to make the world we live in a better place.

During the editing process of this book the coronavirus pandemic presented many difficulties in the collection of photographs and publication. However, under the able leadership of editor-in-chief Suzanna Mu, the London editorial department still managed to complete the editing and publication of this book brilliantly. Here I express my sincere respect and heartfelt thanks.

The *Chinese Photographic Art Yearbook* & *European - Chinese Photographic Art Yearbook* are historical books in the form of pictures. Photographers have recorded history, and our responsibility is to let history remember these photographers.

Editor-in-chief: Mr. Gao Jiansheng
Chinese Photographic Art Yearbook
December 30, 2022
Beijing, China

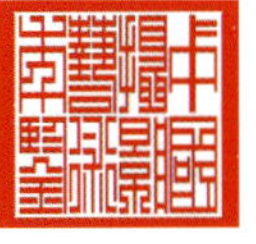

一鏡走天涯

一圖勝千言

一書連東西

A lens travels the world
A picture is worth a thousand words
A book connects East and West through Photographic Art

唉乃一聲山水綠 / 攝影: 高占祥
A Sound of Green Mountains and Rivers
by Gao Zhanxiang

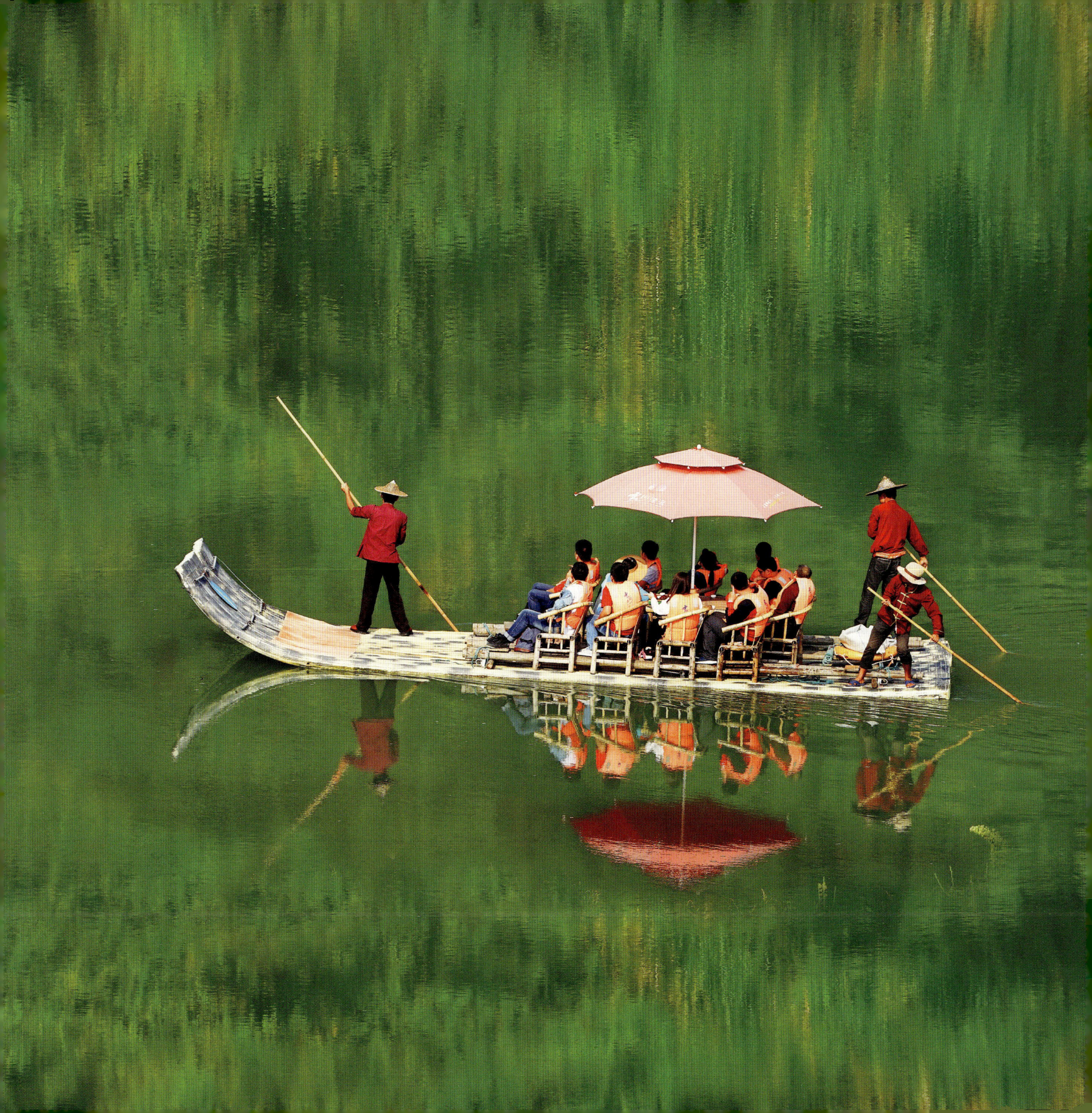

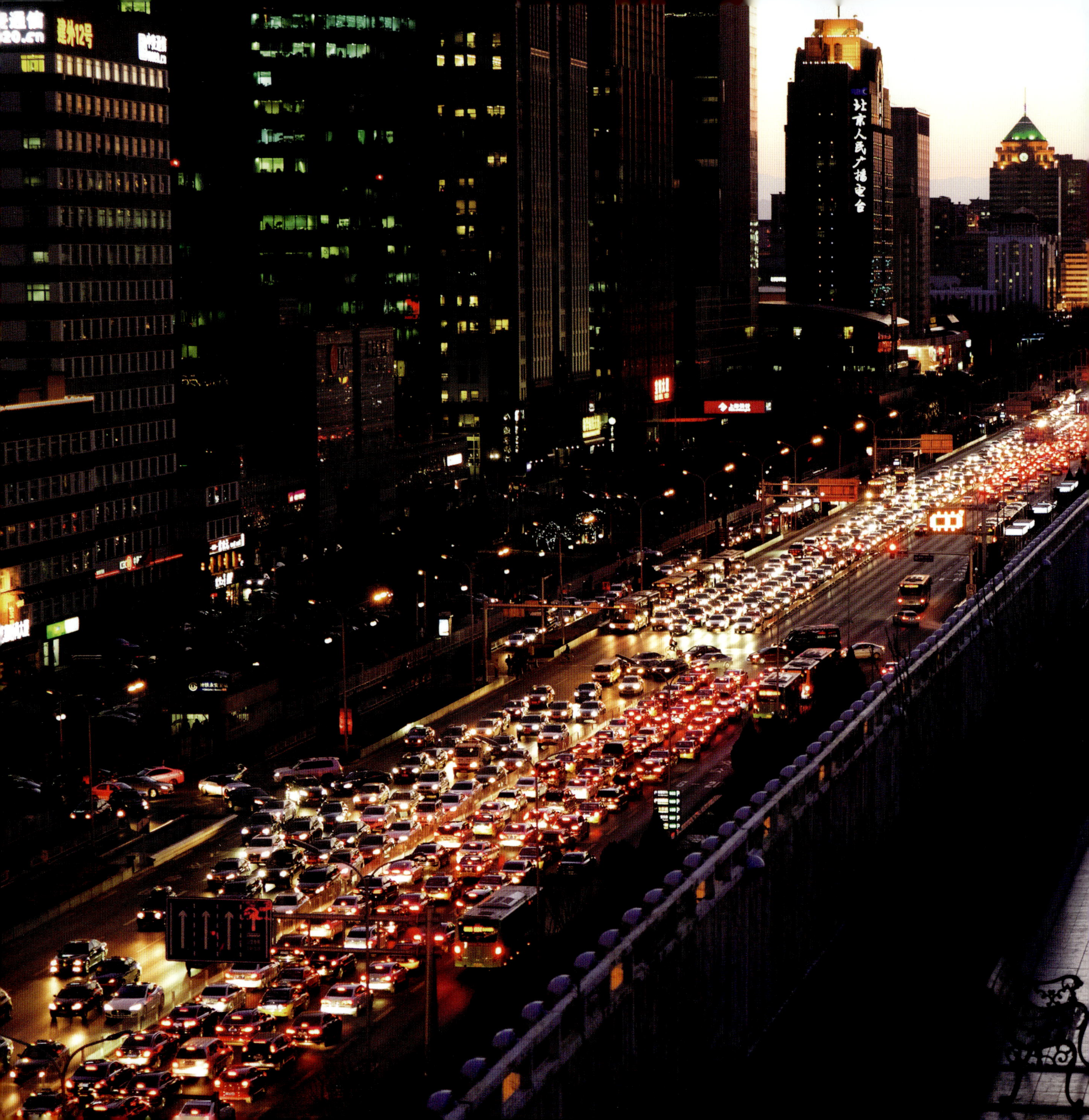
建外12号
北京人民广播电台

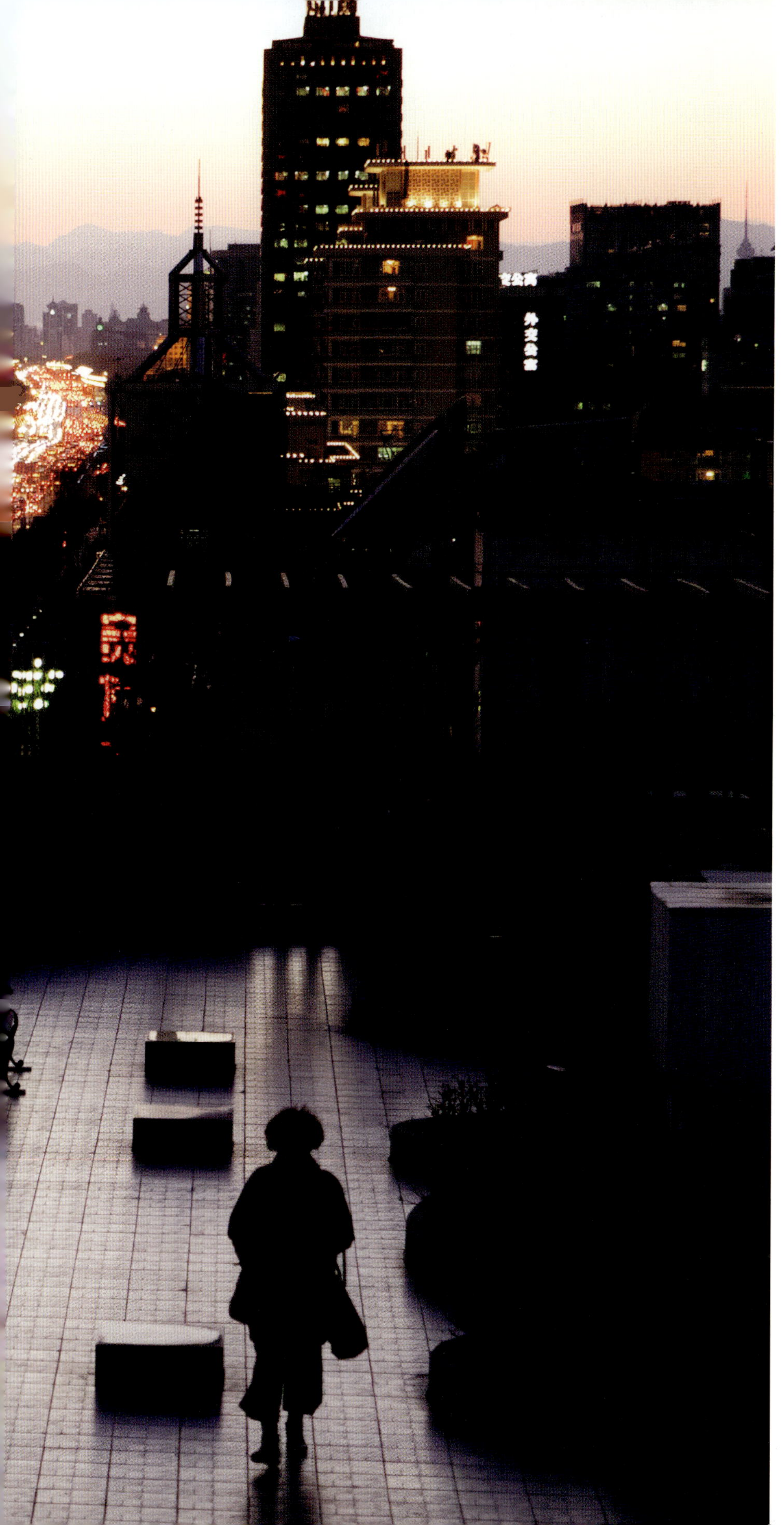

時空-北京 / 攝影: 朱憲民
Time and Space–Beijing by Zhu Xianmin

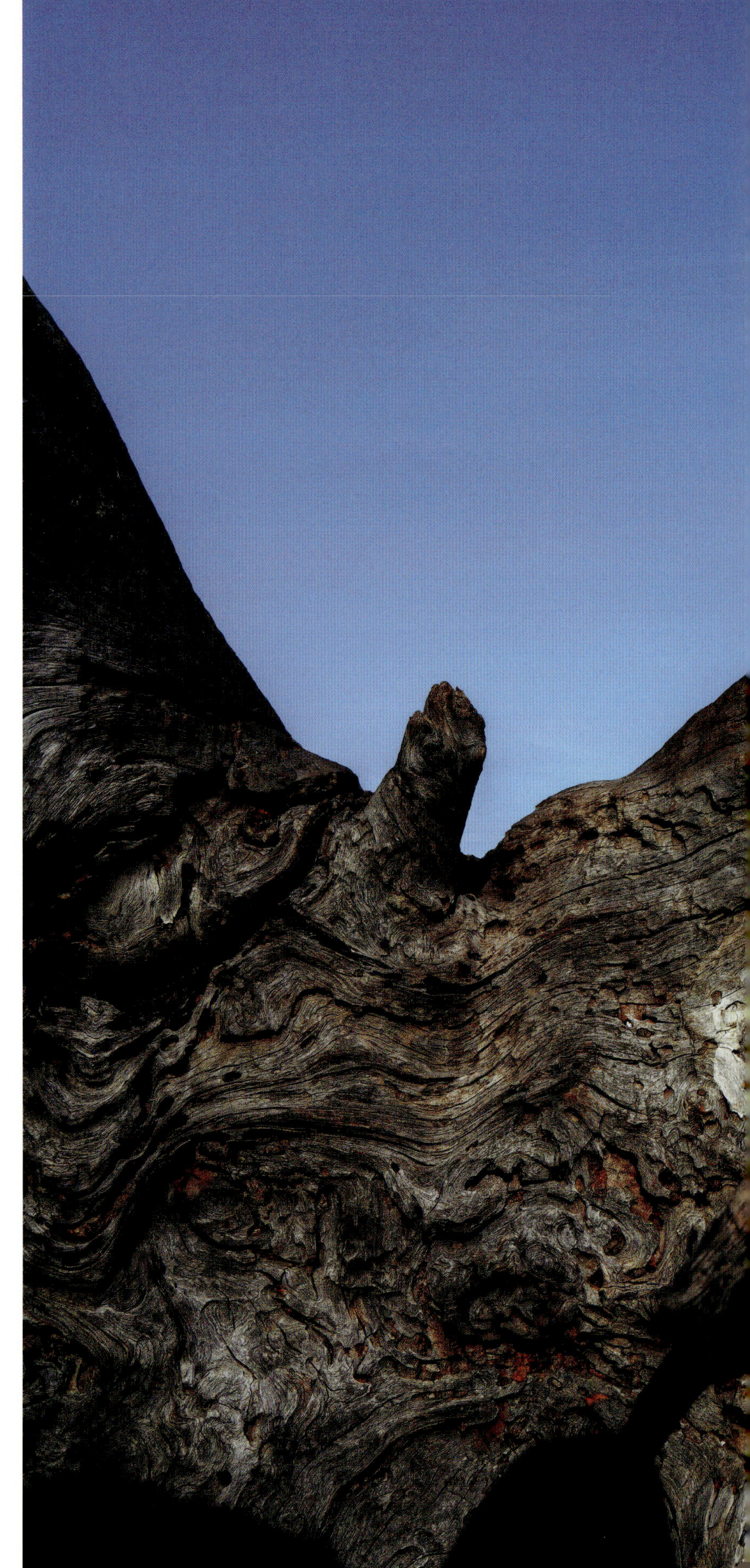

新疆赛里木湖畔的打草人 / 攝影: 高健生
Grassmen by the Sailimu Lake in Xinjiang
by Gao Jiansheng

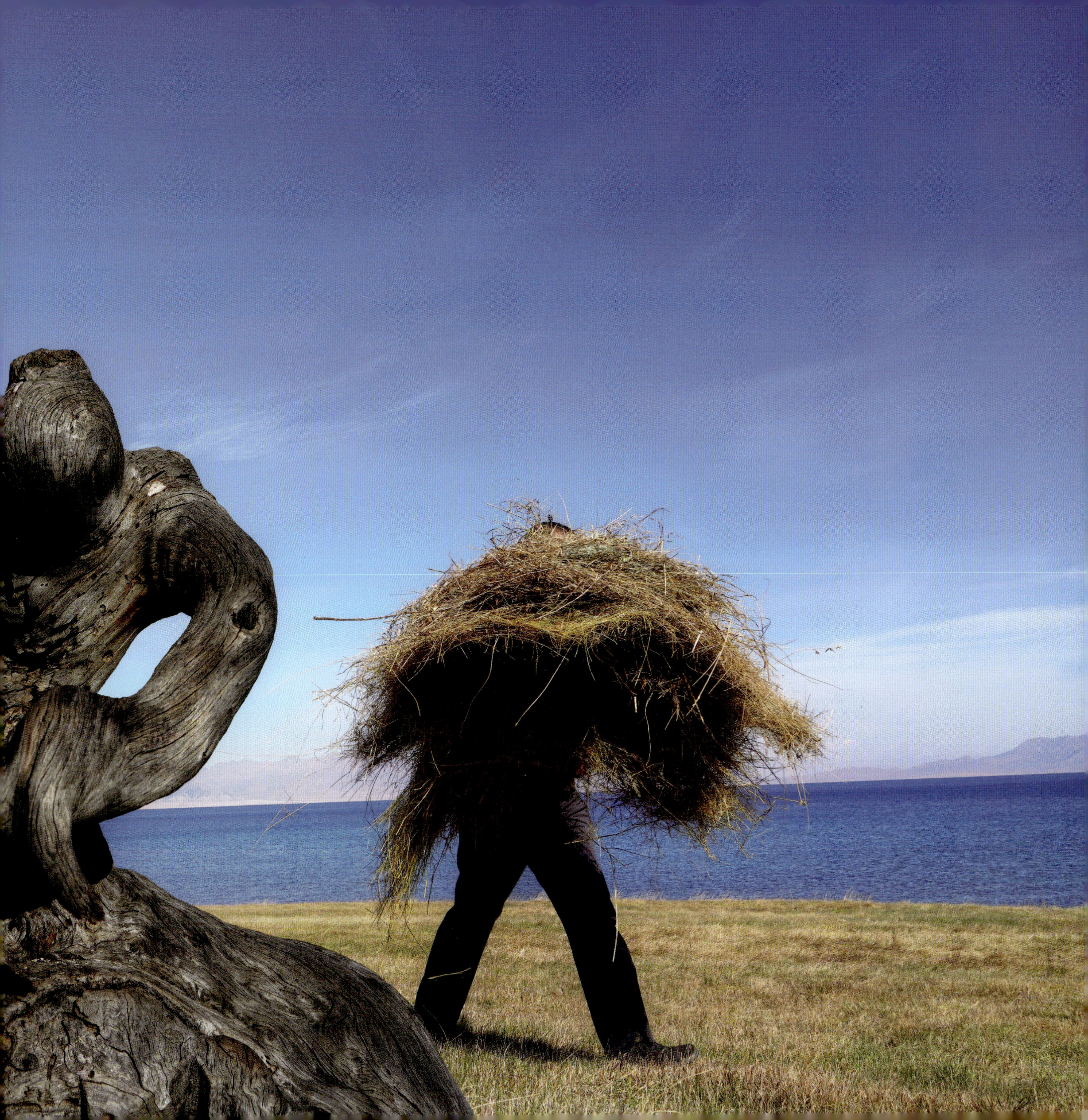

LANDSCAPE 風景

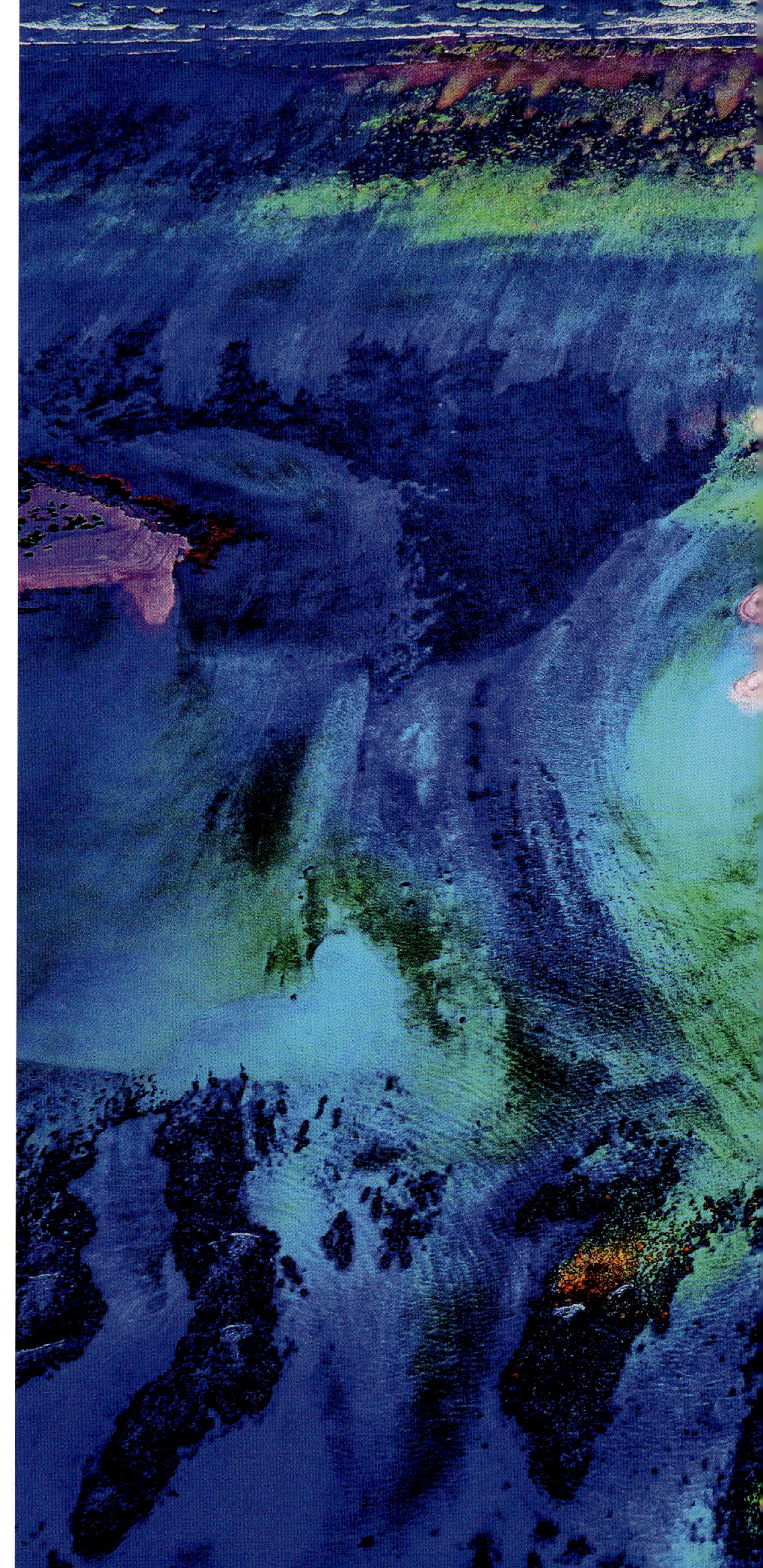

南海島礁 / 攝影: 牟健爲
South China Islands by Mou Jianwei

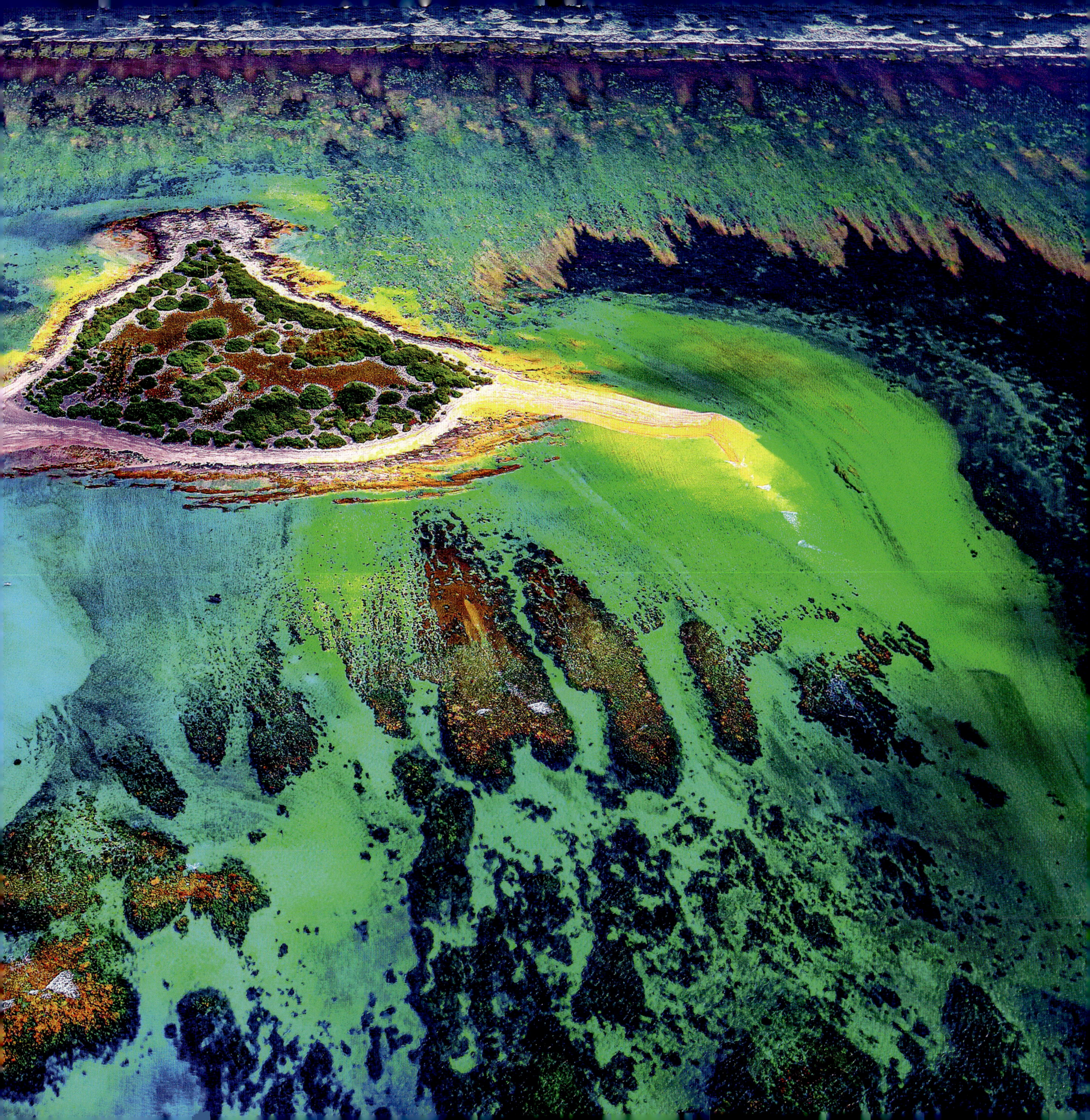

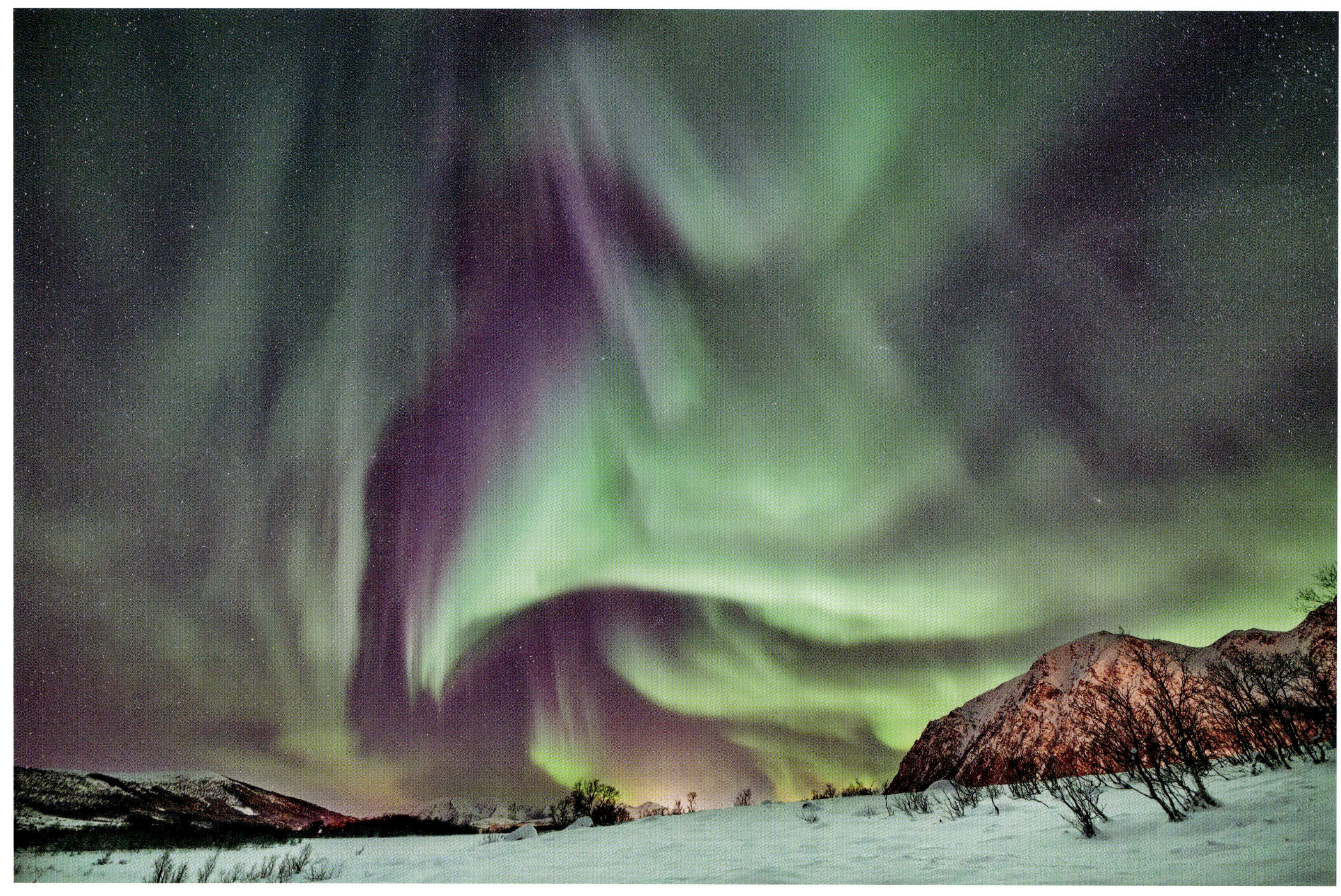

北極光
Northern Lights by Martin Gandy LRPS

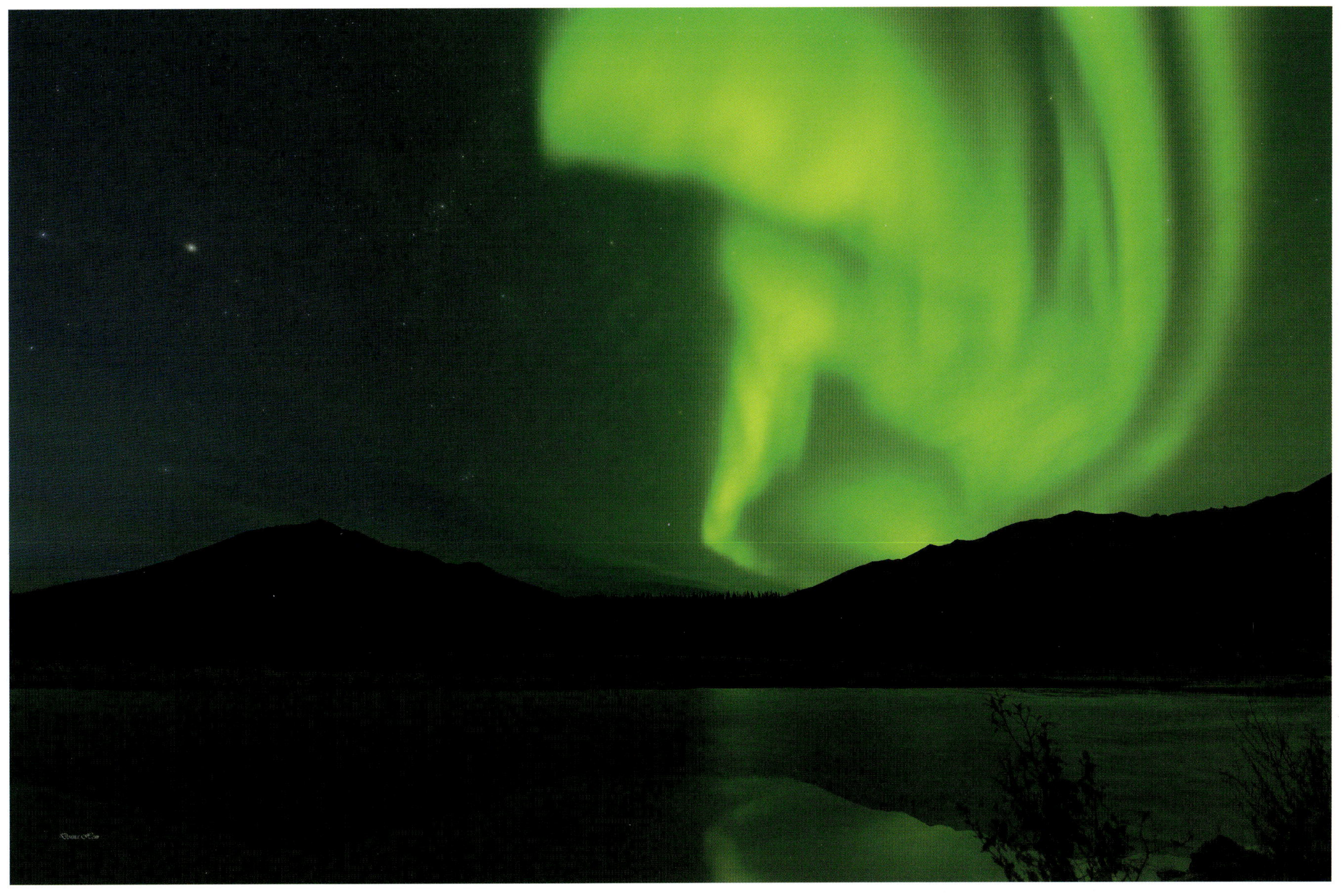

碧龍騰空 / 攝影: 丹菁
Green Dragon in the Sky by Donna Hom

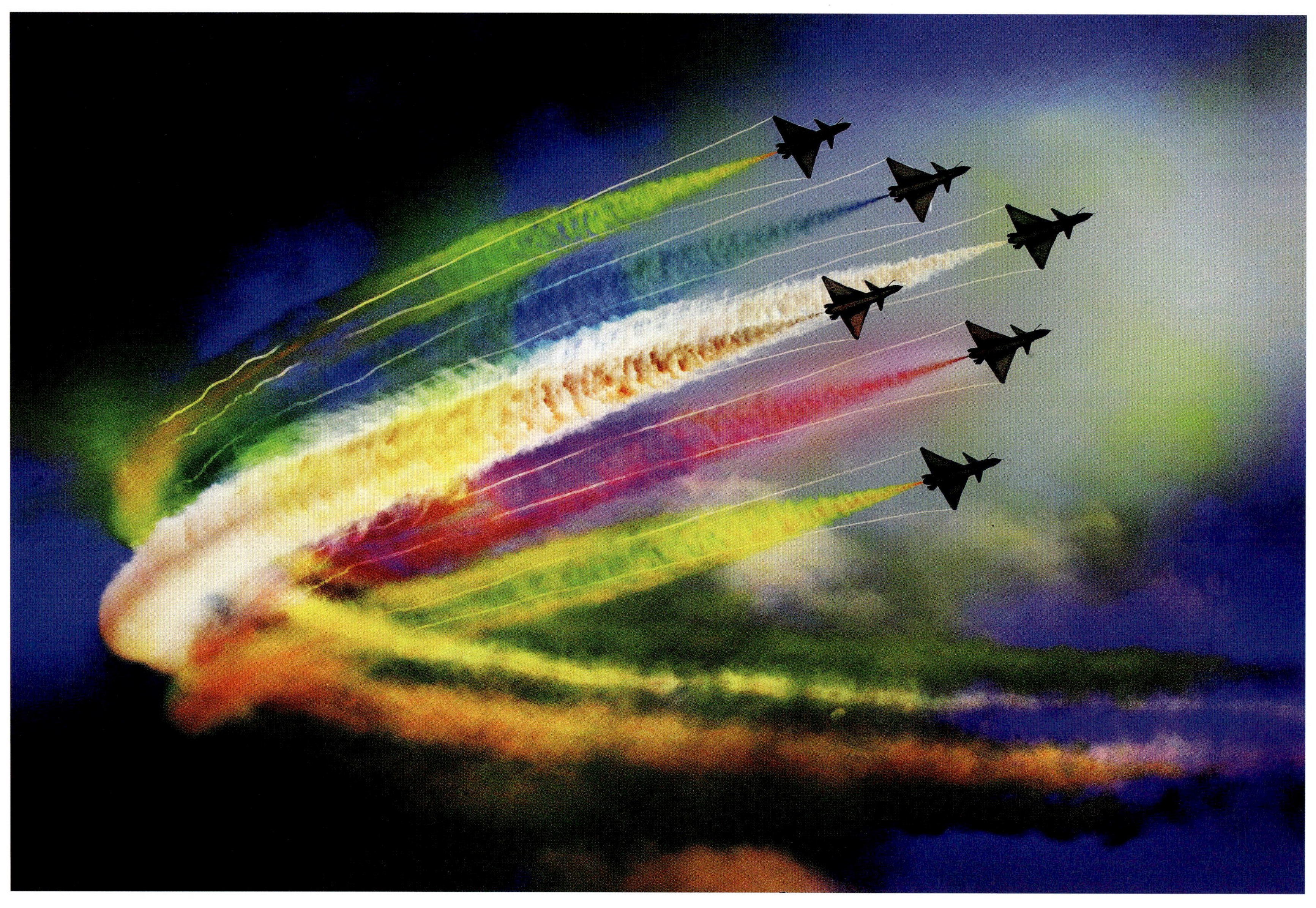

彩練當空舞 / 攝影: 牟健爲
Colorful Practice Dancing in the Sky by Mou Jianwei

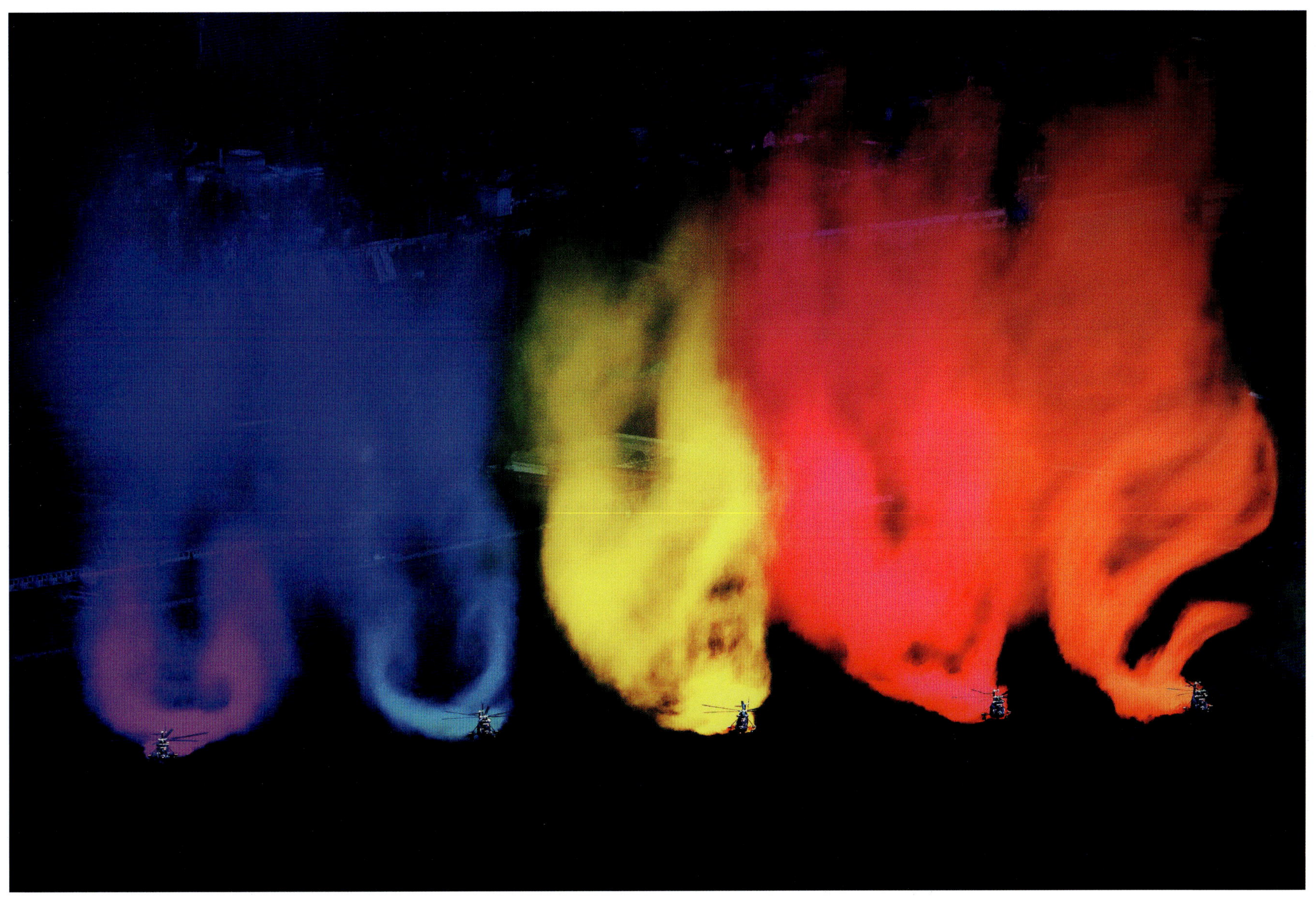

五彩航路 / 攝影: 牟健爲
Colorful Voyage by Mou Jianwei

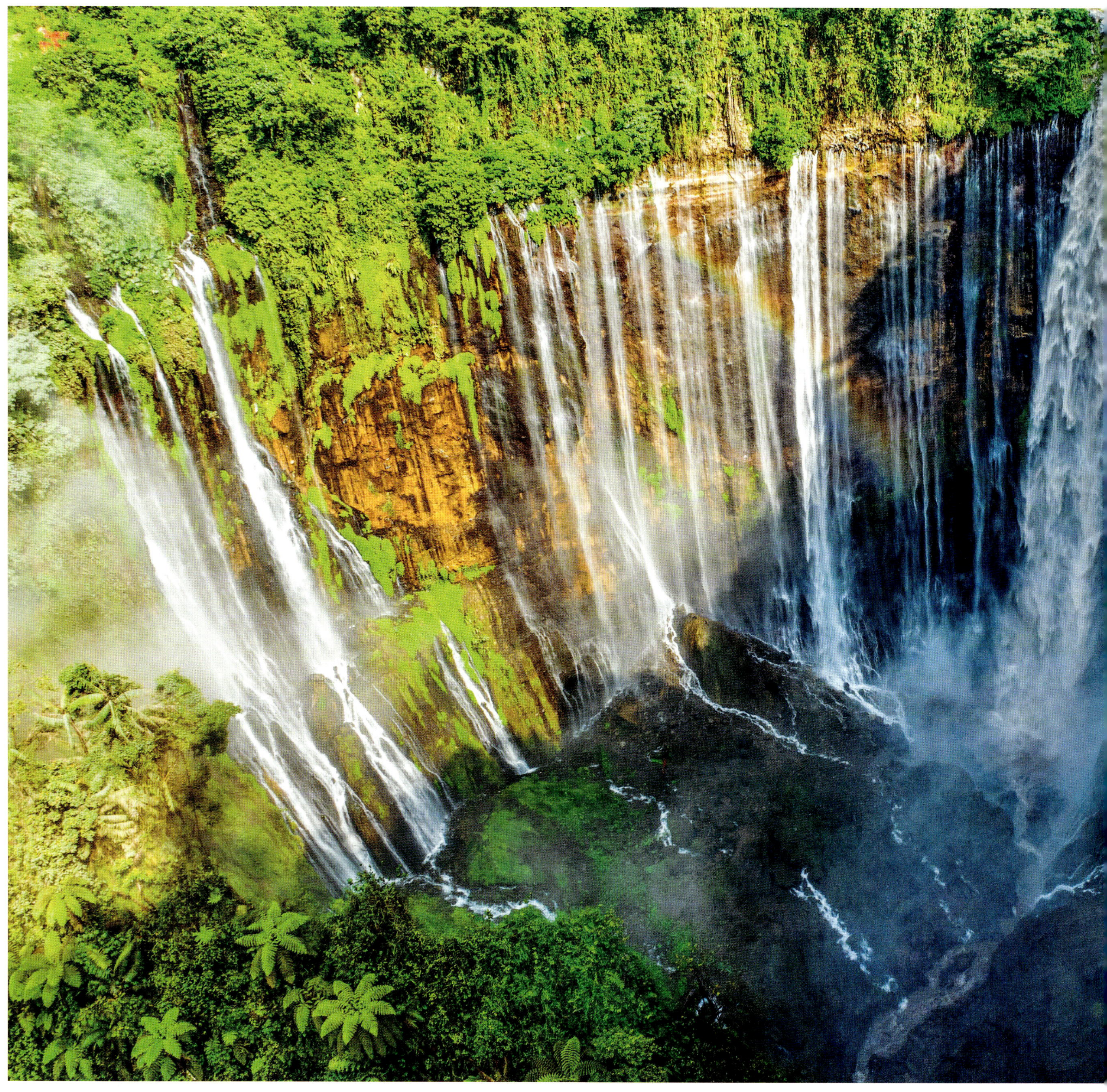

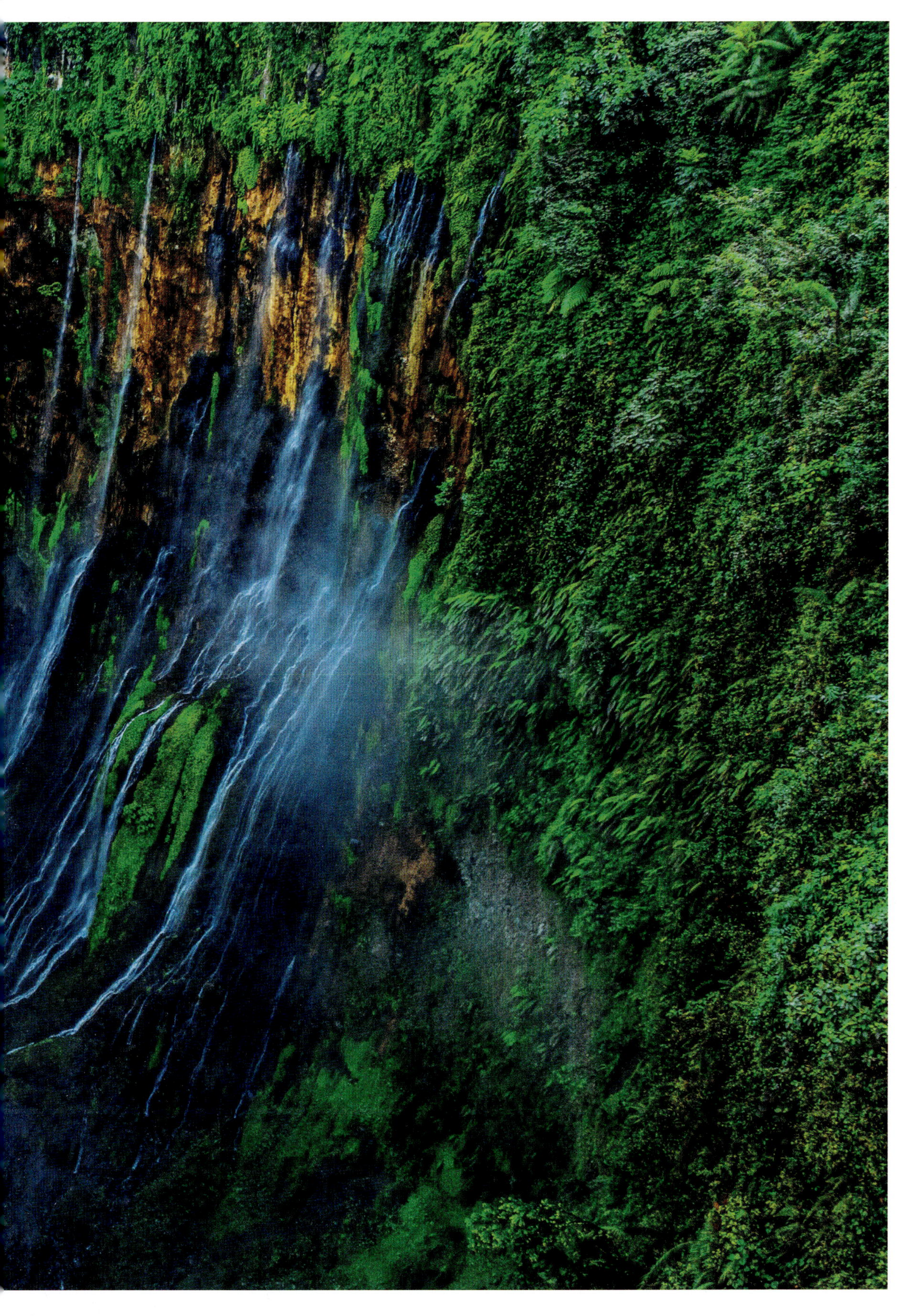

大自然的秘密 / 攝影: 王朝盛
Nature's Secret
by Wang Zhaosheng

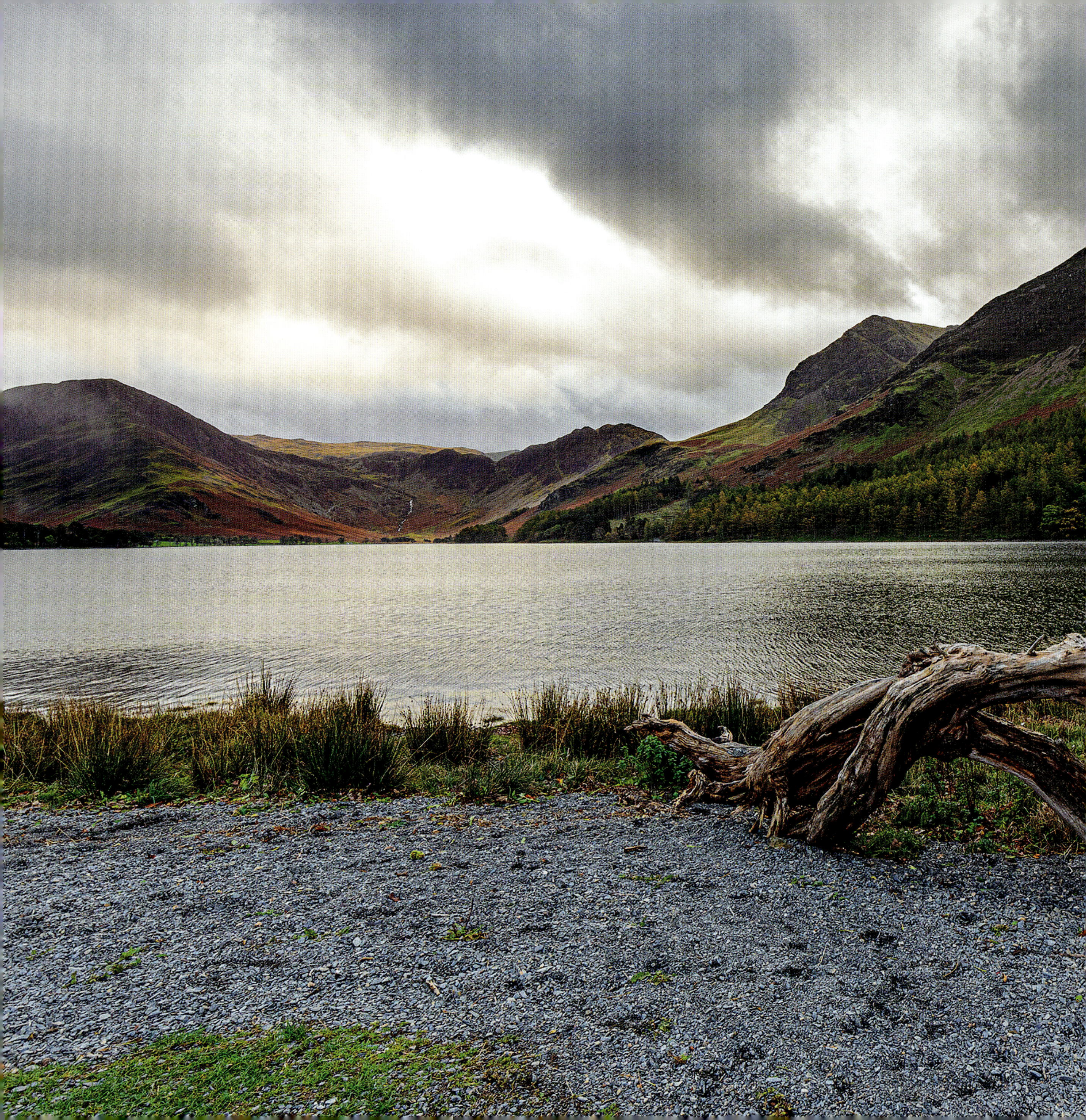

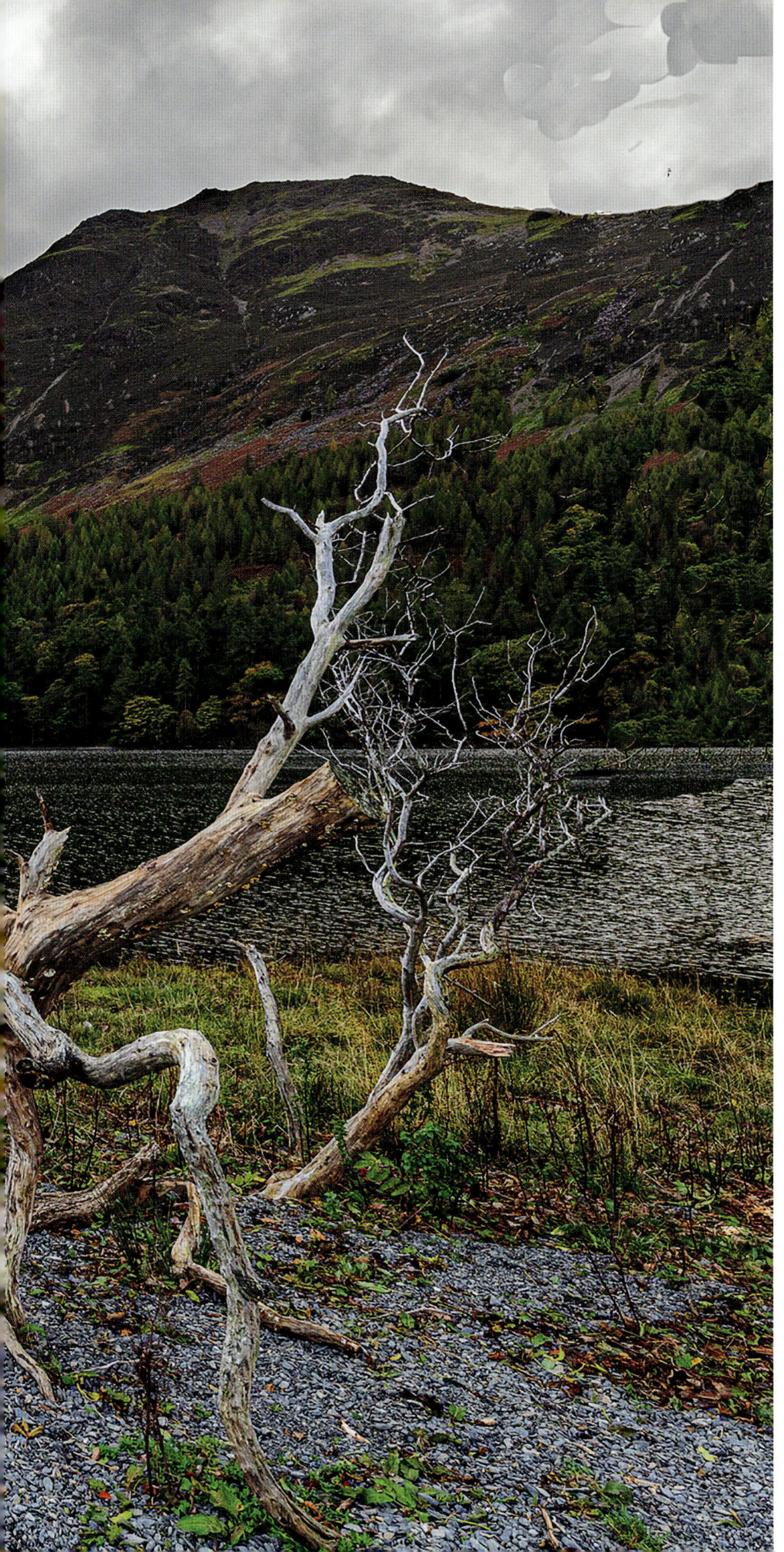

布特梅爾湖和幹草堆山丘
Buttermere Lake and Haystacks Fell
by Mike Psyllides ARPS

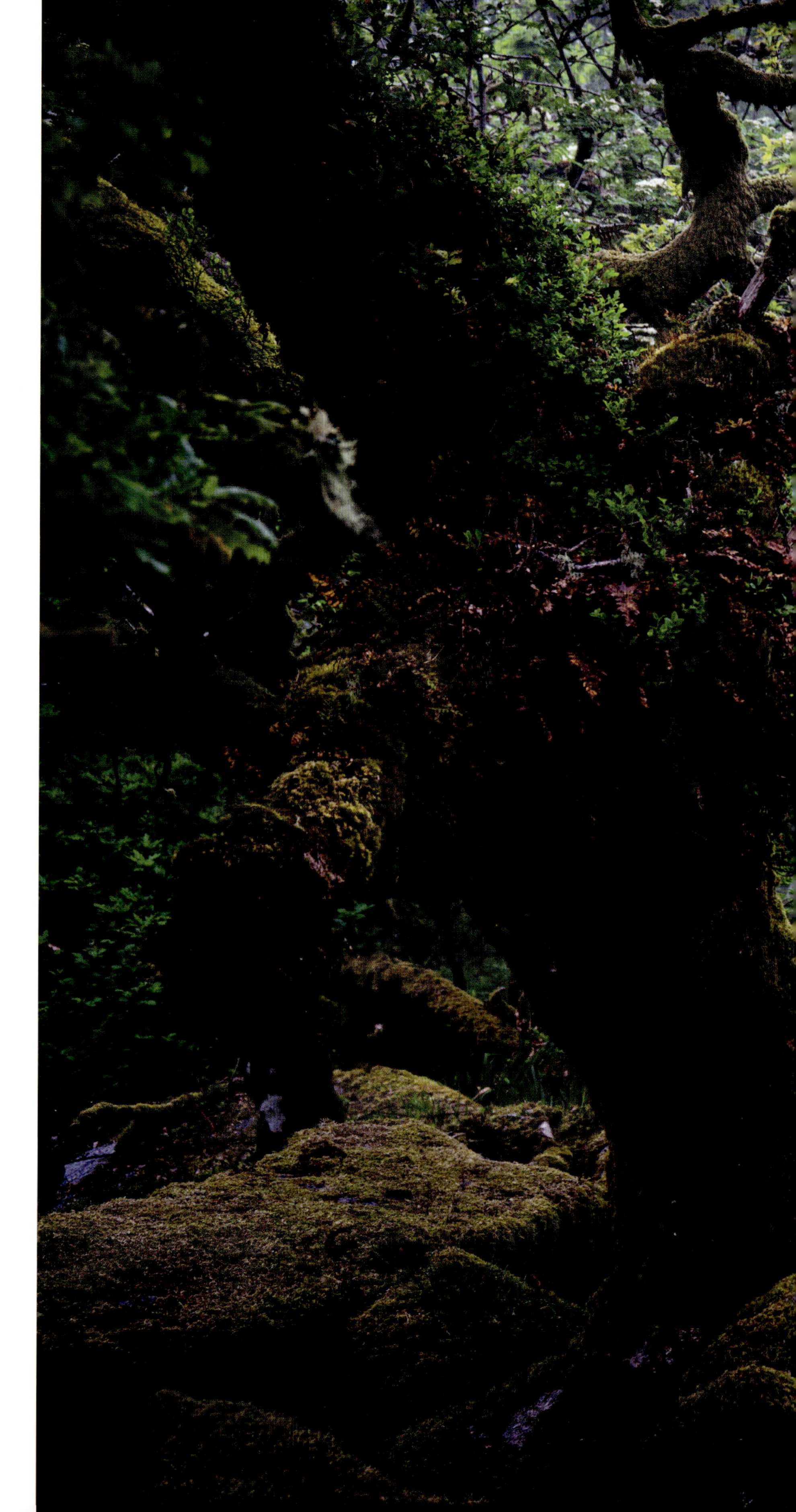

神秘的惠斯曼
Mysterious Whistmans by Susi Petherick ARPS

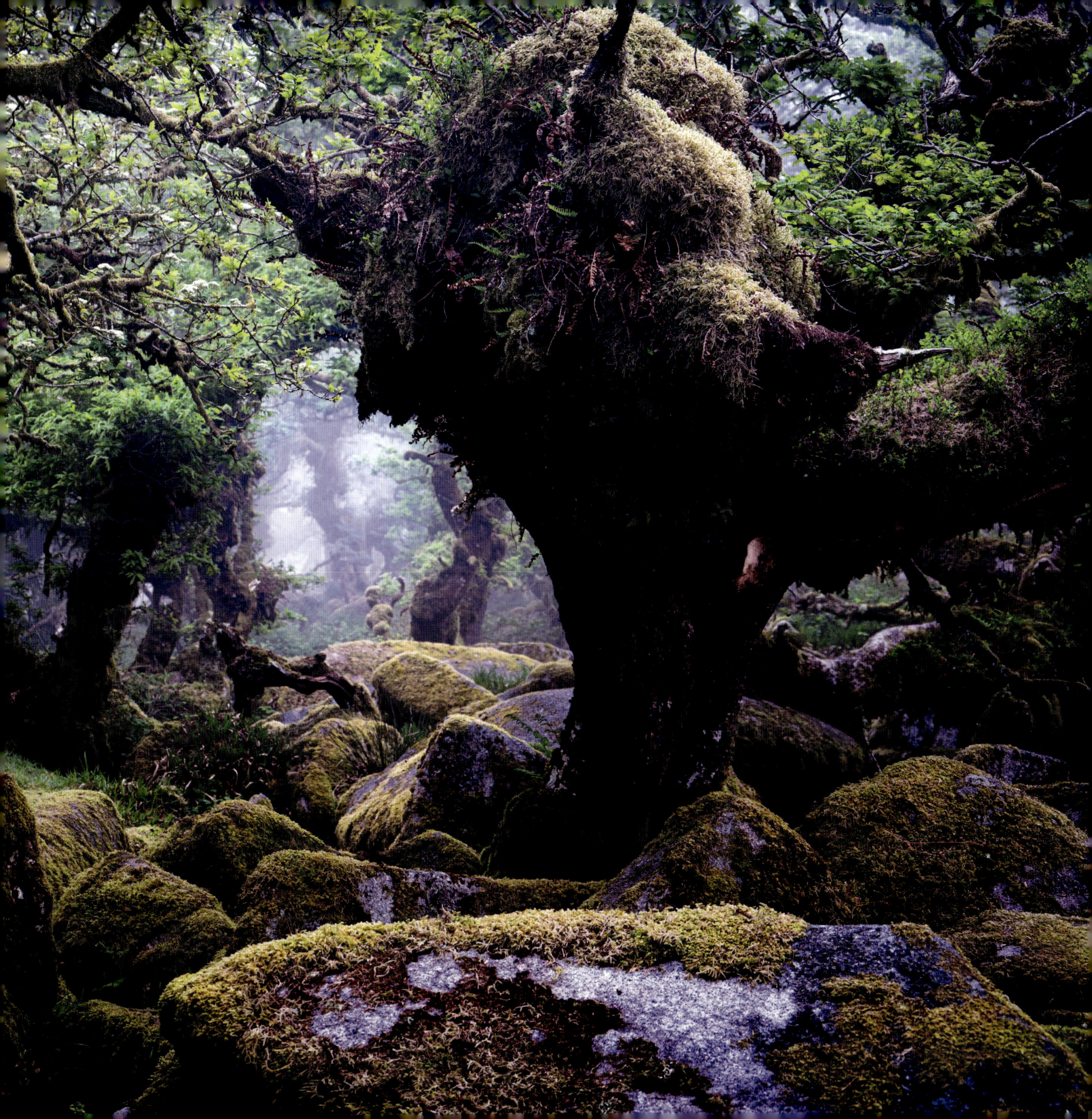

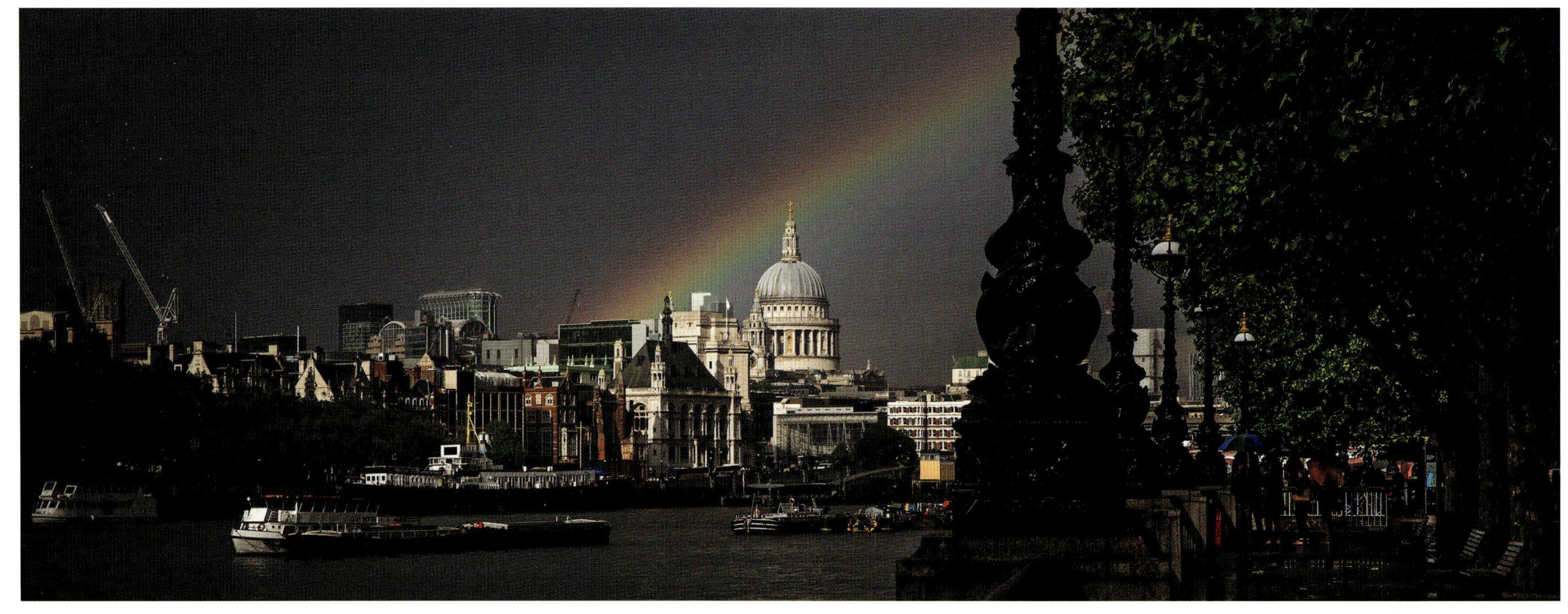

暴風雨後的彩虹
Heavy Weather on Kings Reach by Colin Clarke ARPS

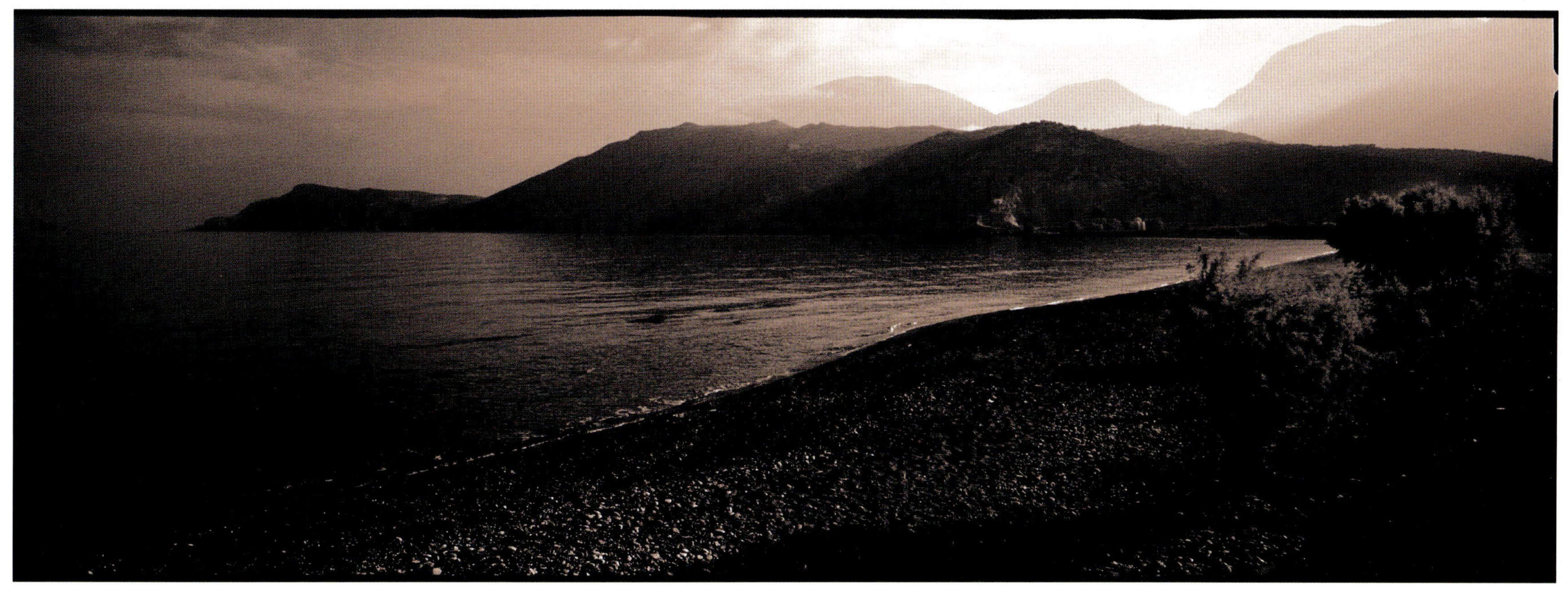

寧静
Serenity by Anthony Karydis

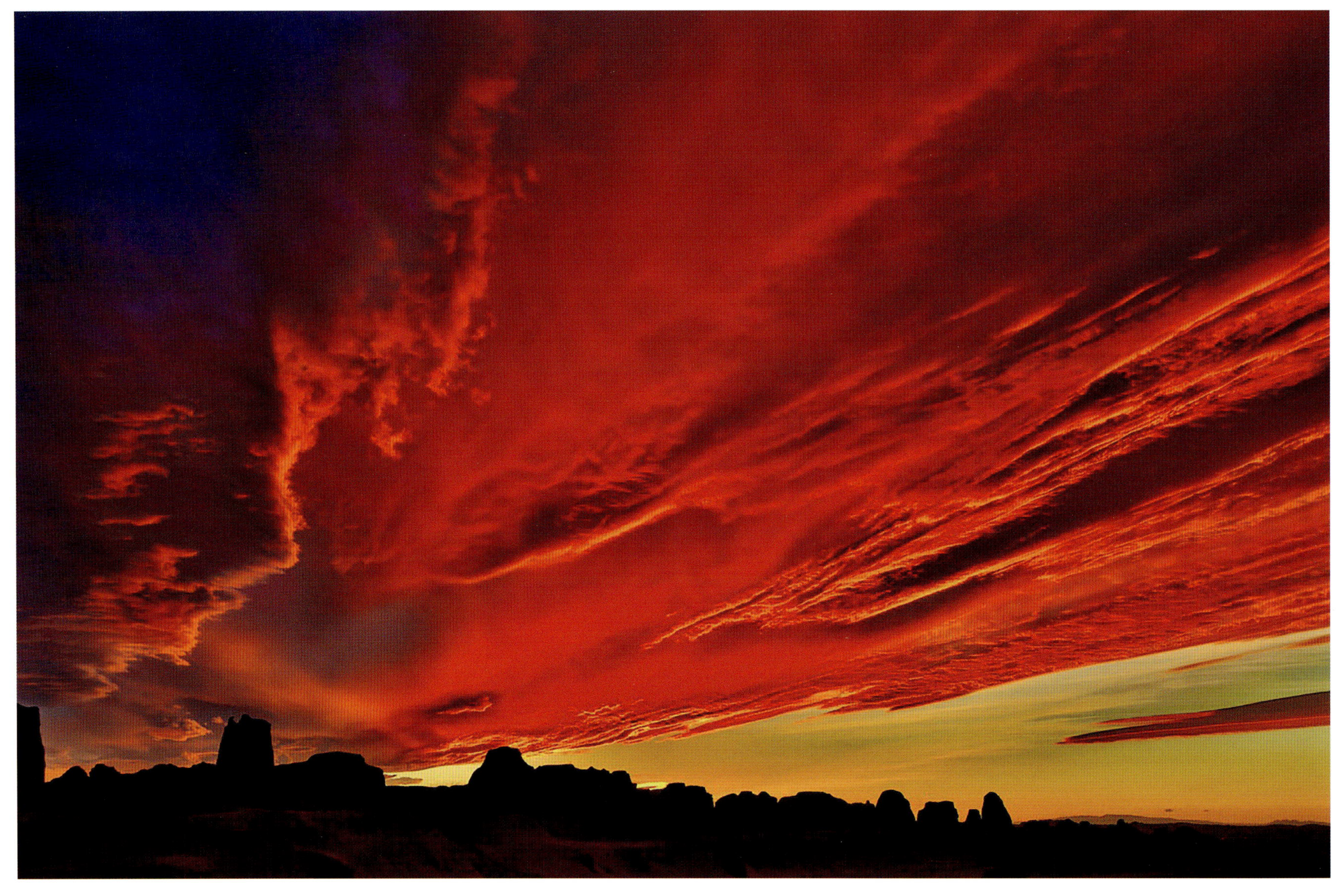

魔鬼紅霞 / 攝影: 崔明浩
Sunset Glow over the Ghost by Cui Minghao

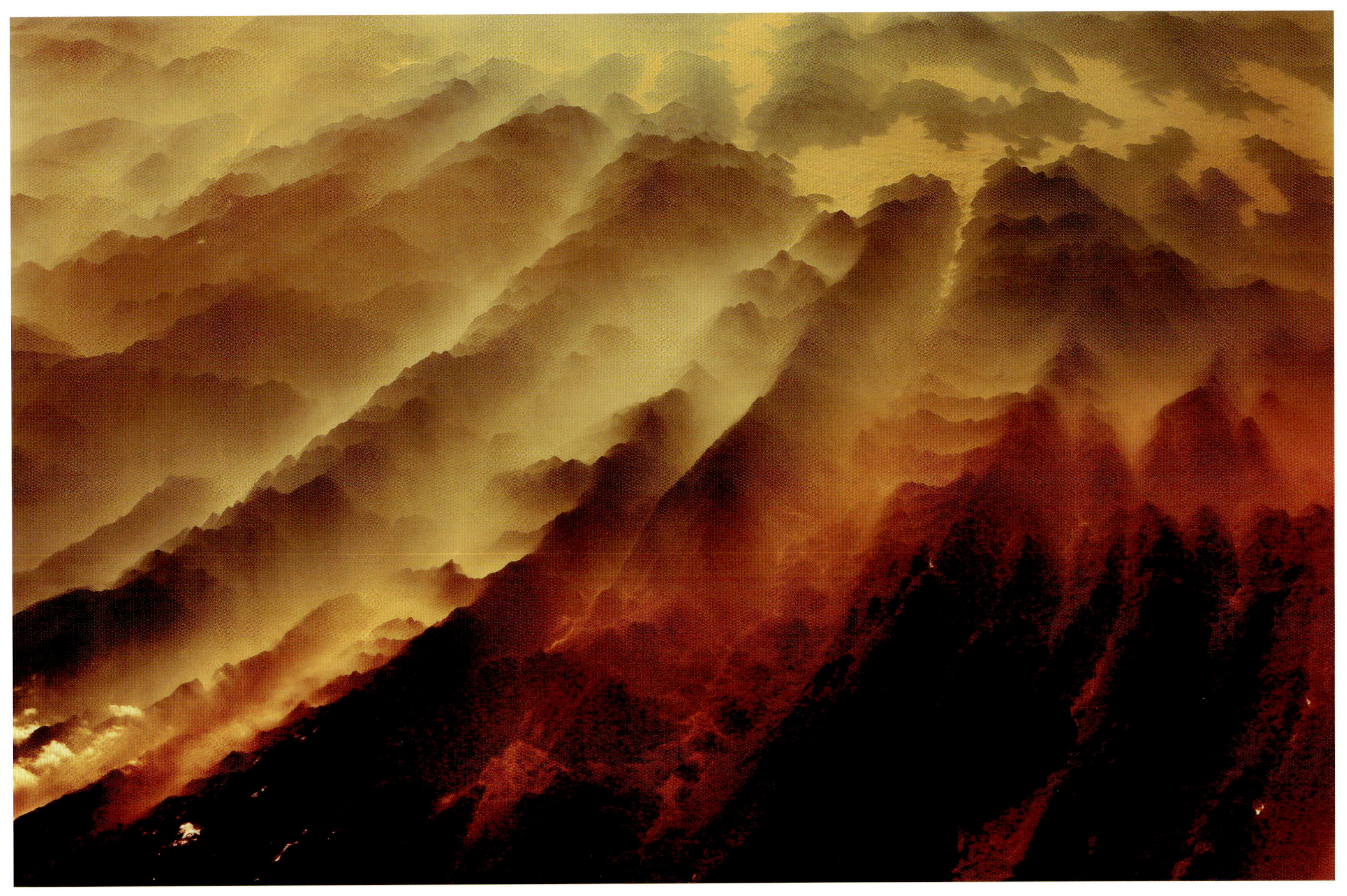

巴山幽靈 / 攝影: 牟健爲
The Ghost of Bashan by Mou Jianwei

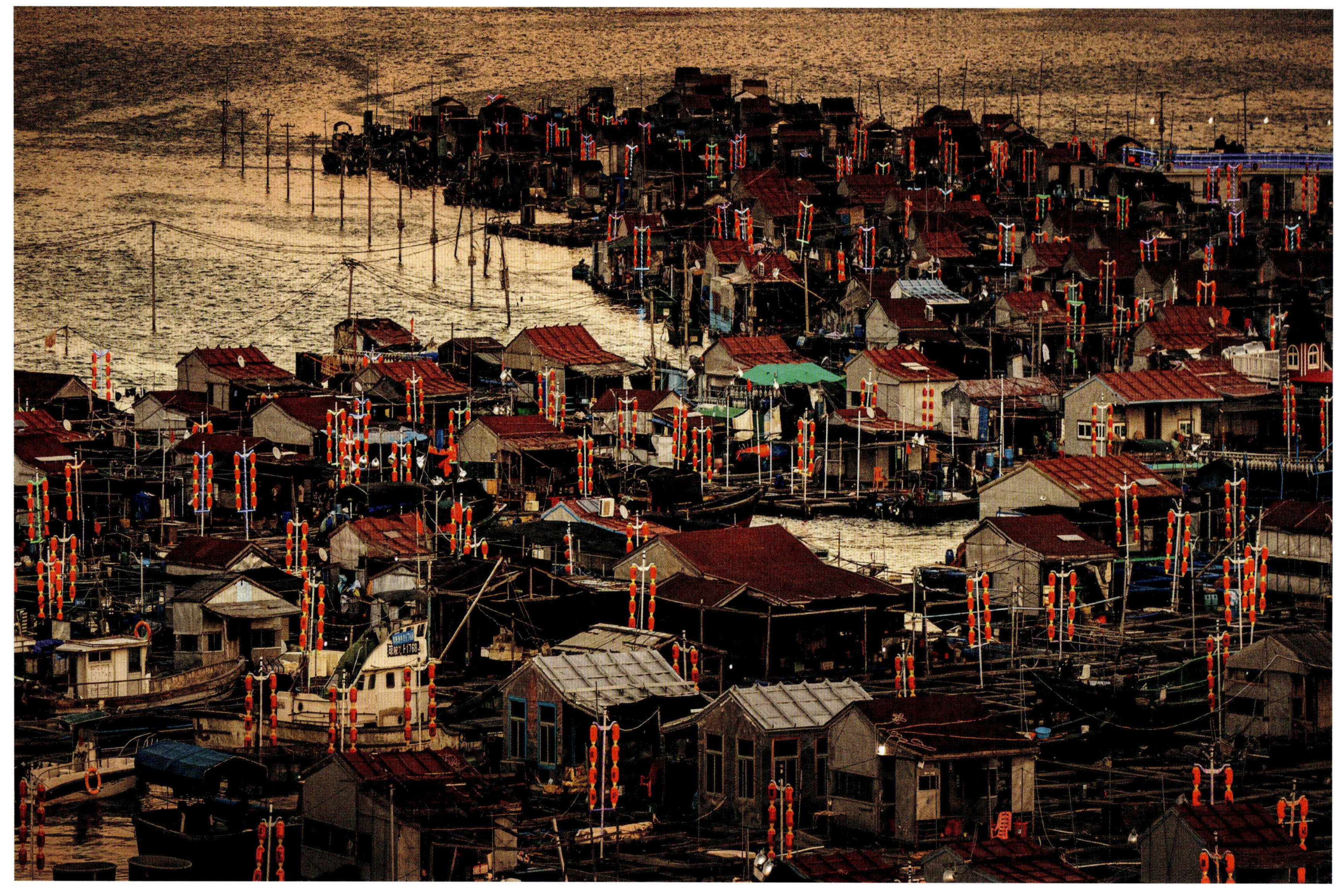

水上漁家 / 攝影: 牟健爲
Fisherman Family on the Water by Mou Jianwei

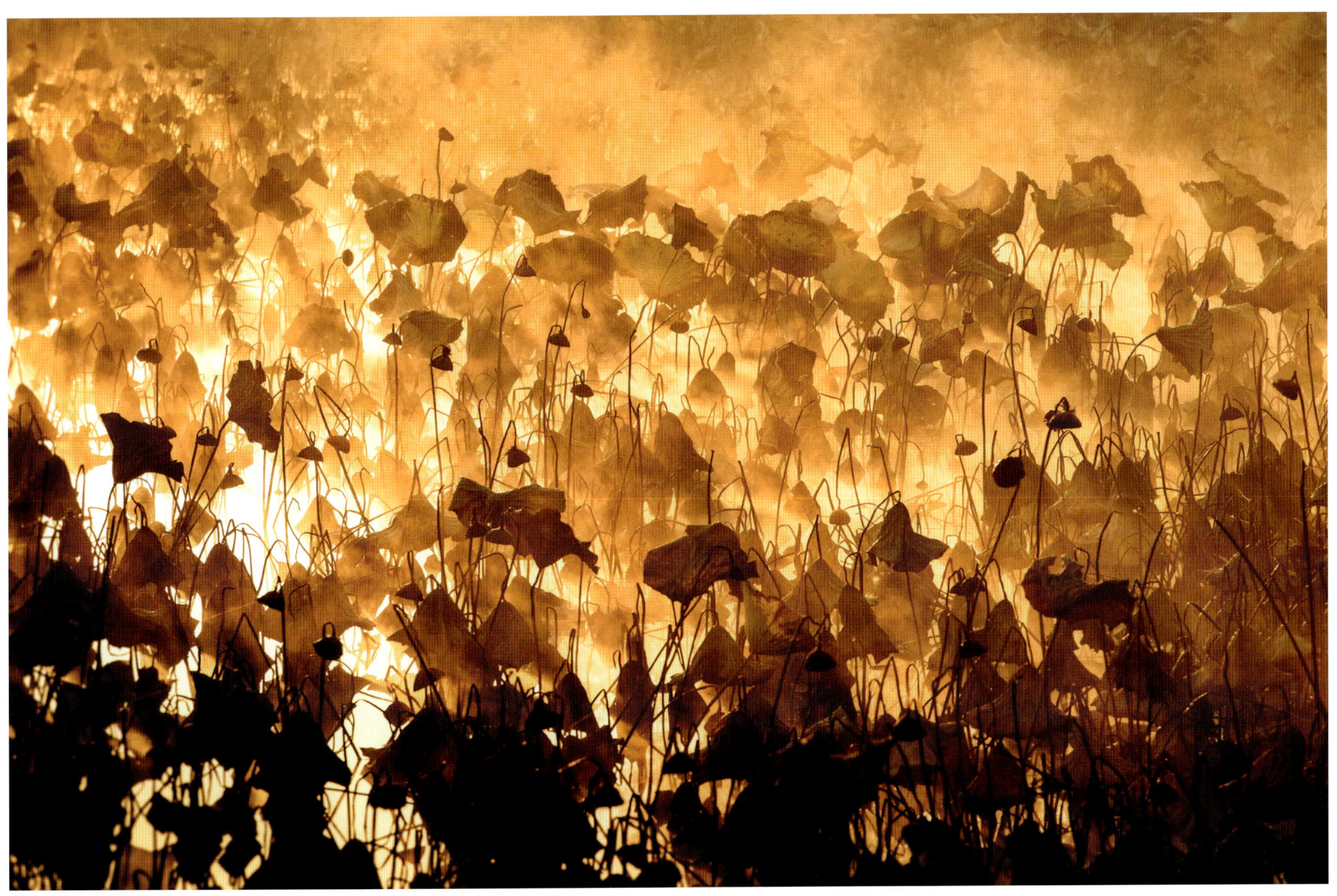

荷塘秋色 / 攝影: 喬仲林
Autumn in the Lotus Pond by Qiao Zhonglin

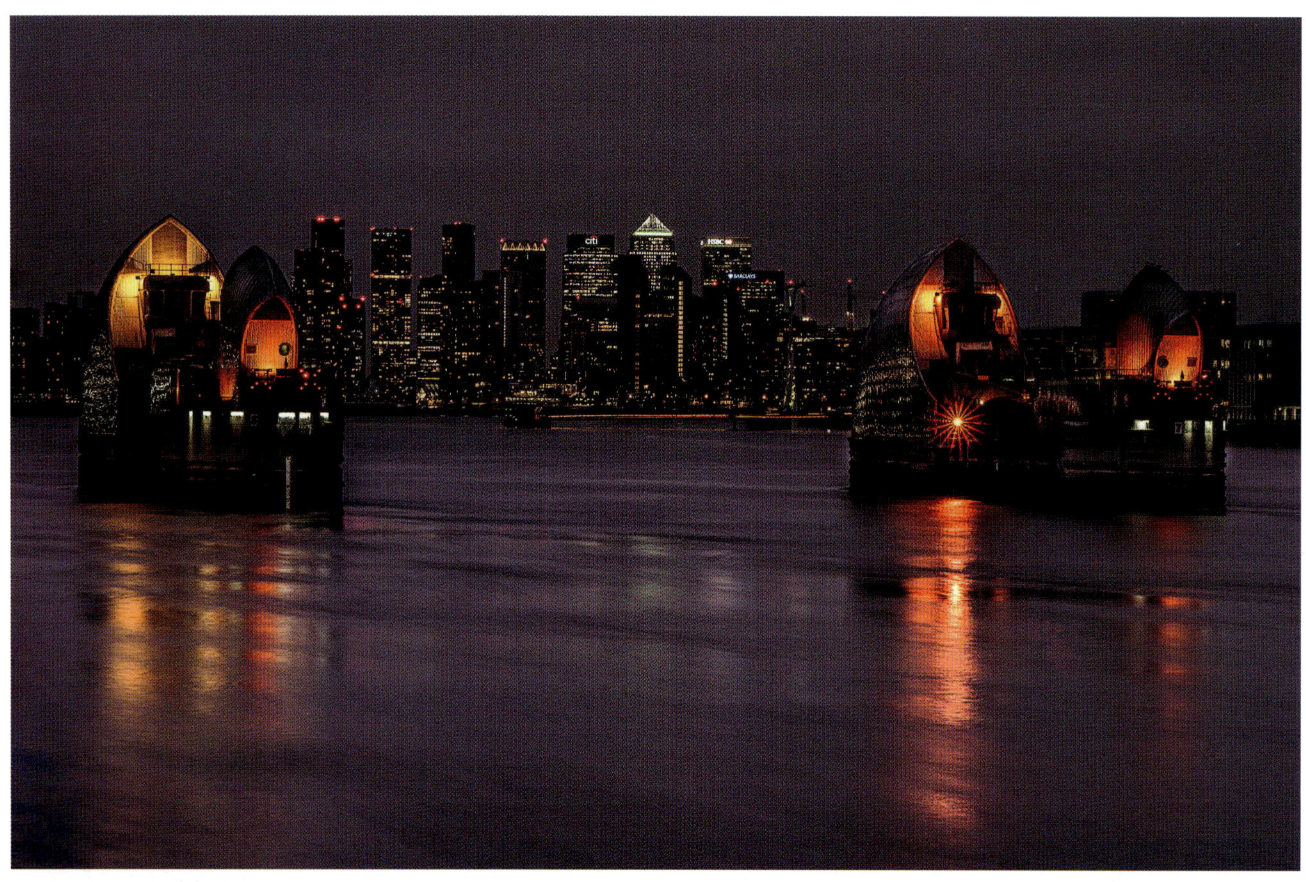

泰晤士河的屏障
Thames Barrier
by Julian Rouse LRPS

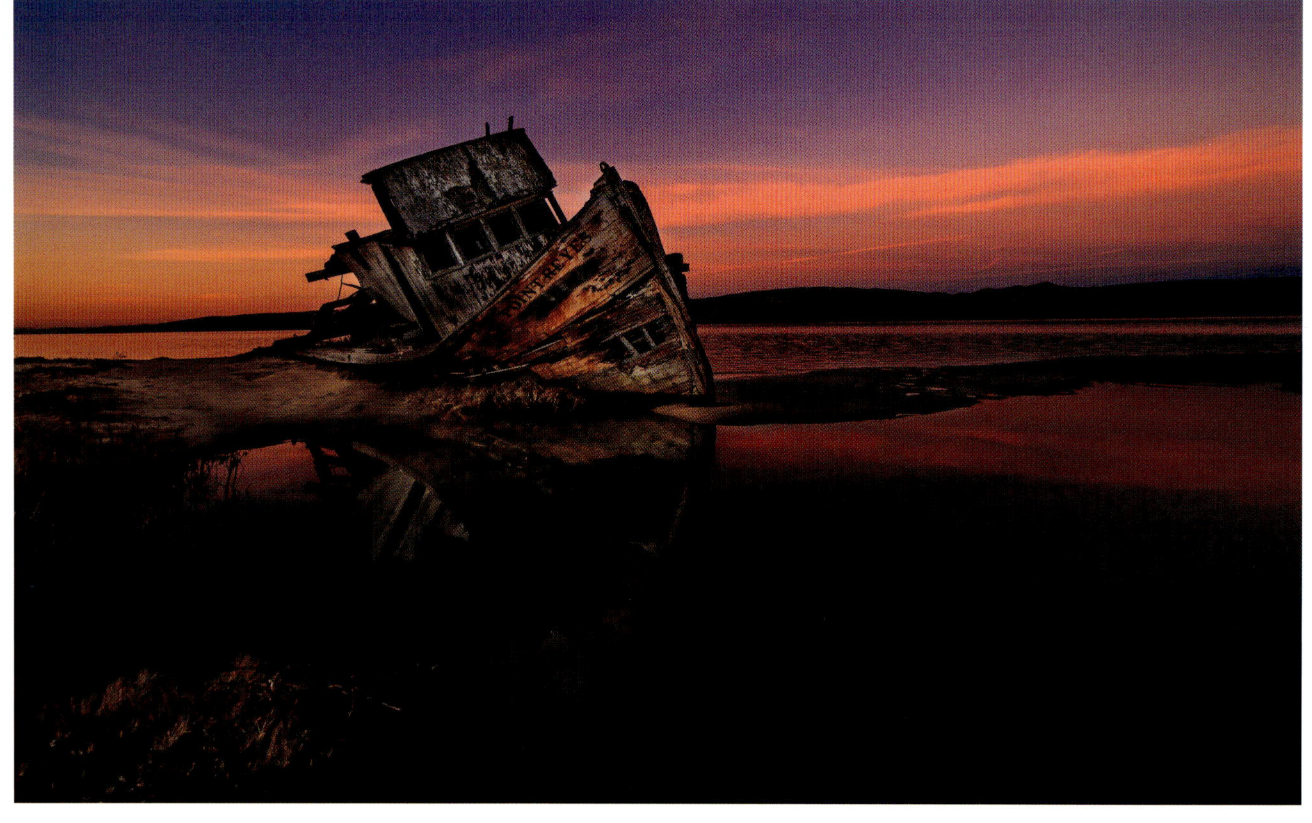

加州海岸綫 / 攝影: 黃立亞
California Coastline
by Huang Liya

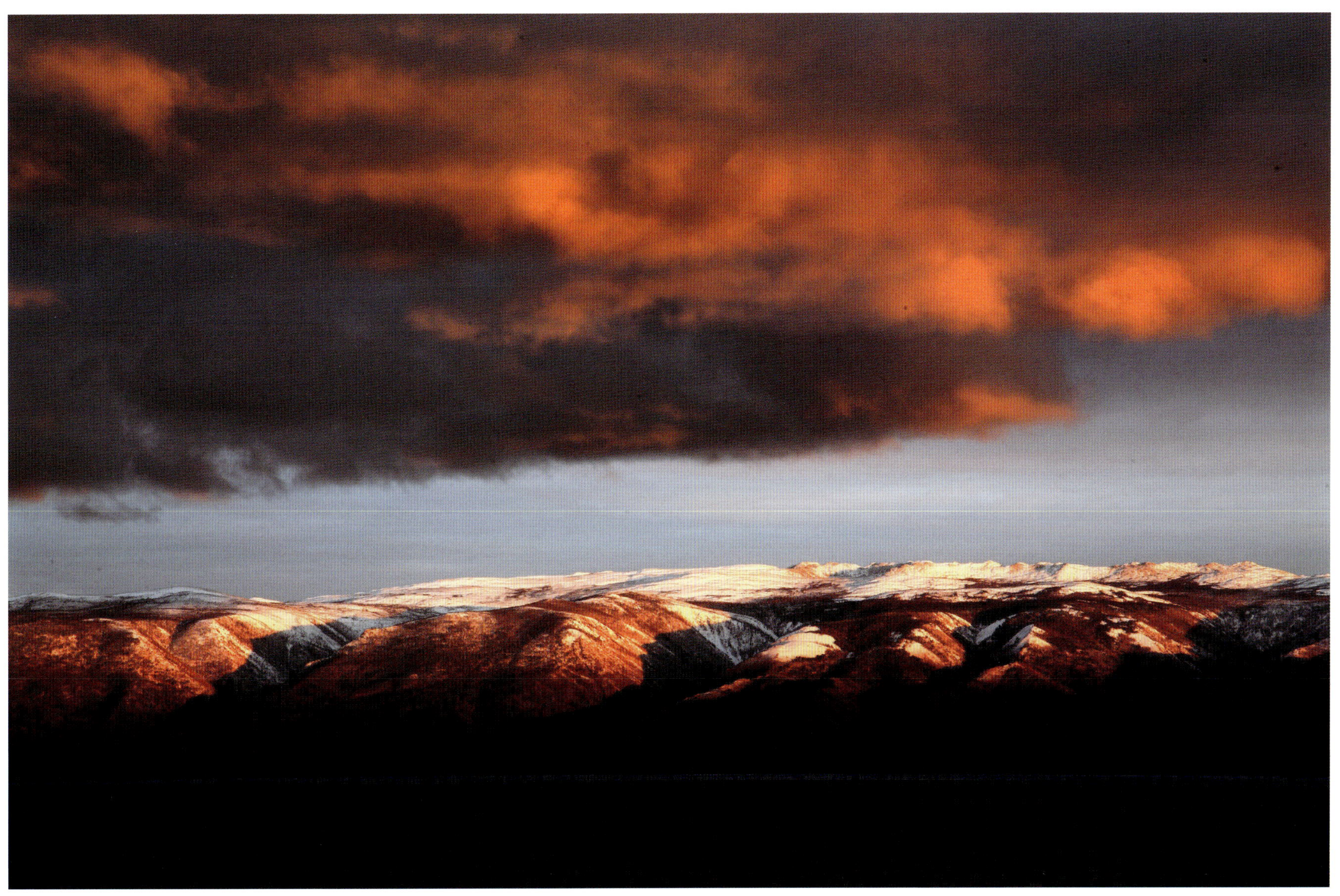

霞光 / 攝影: 幹登榮
Twilight by Gan Dengrong

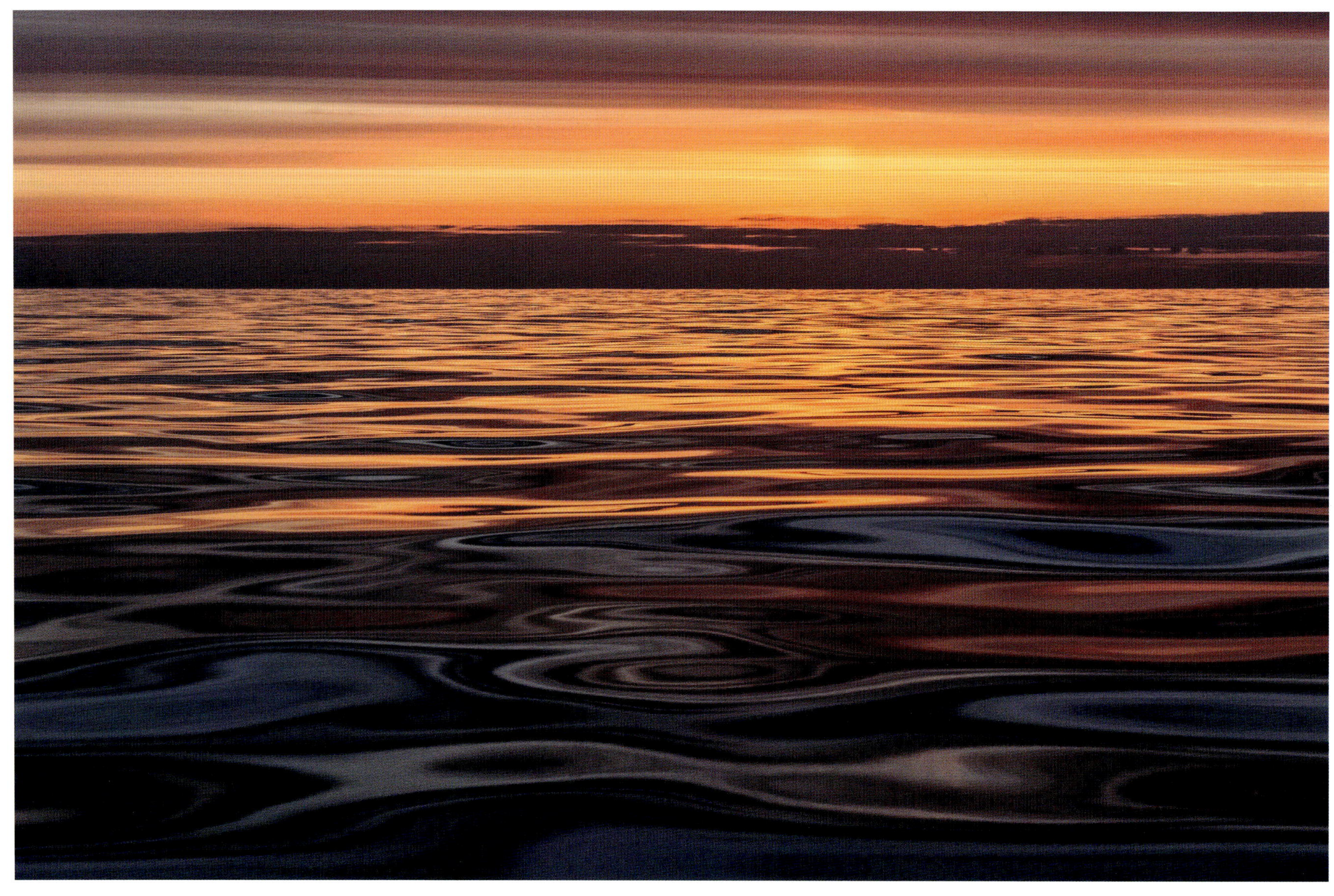

凱爾特海的日出
Sunrise in the Celtic Sea by Colin Clarke ARPS

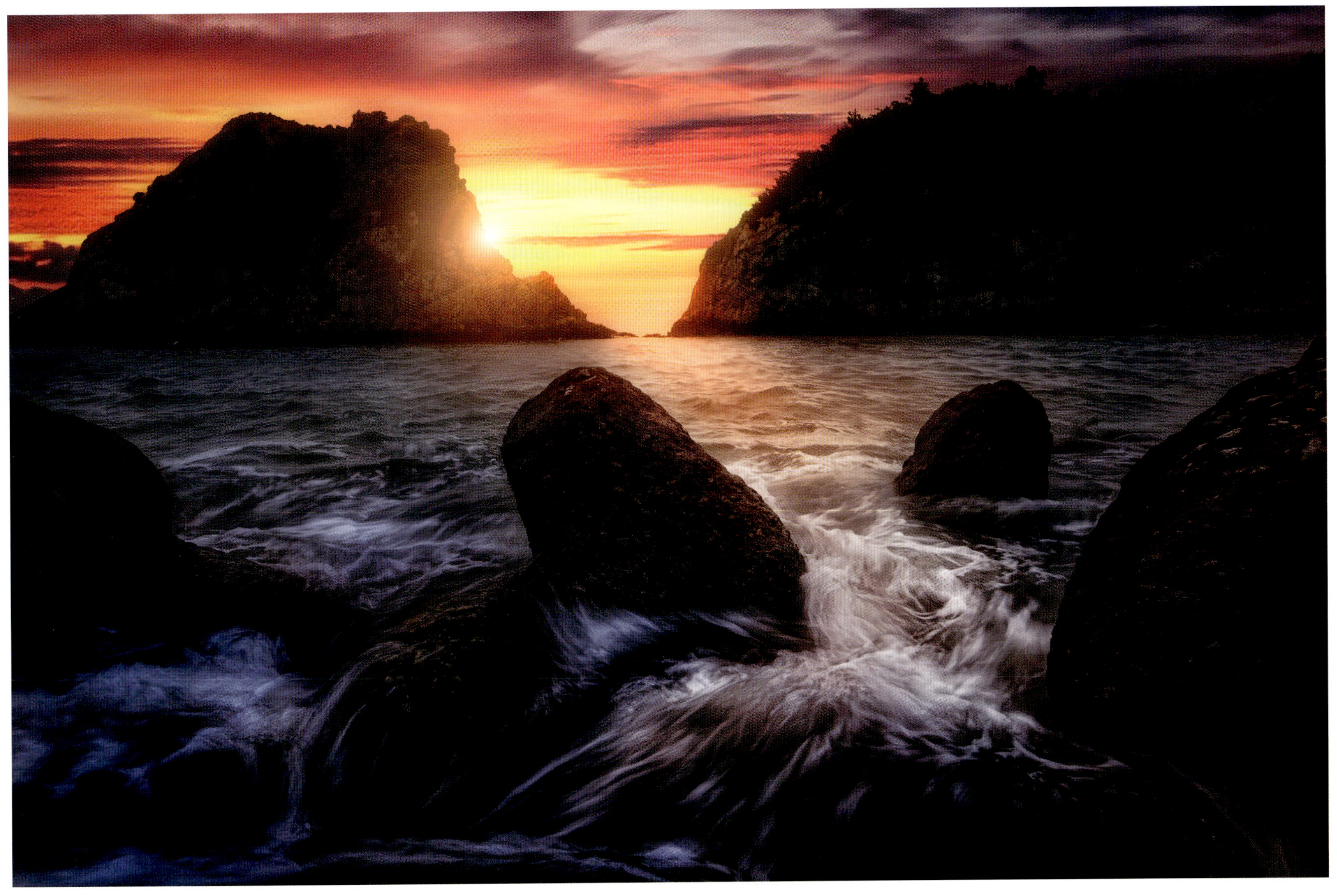

海邊 / 攝影: 陸佳敏
Seaside by Lu Jiamin

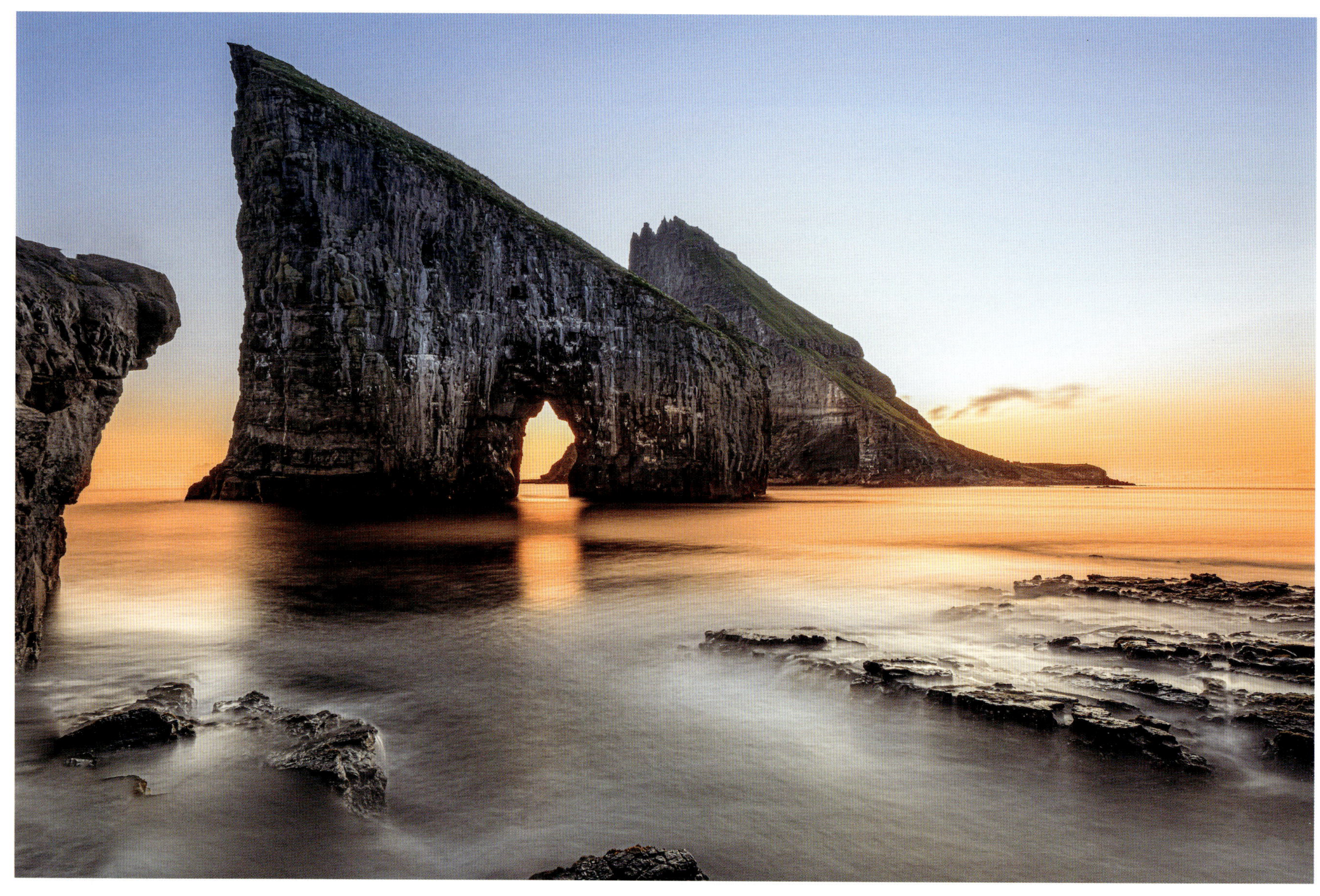

德蘭卡尼爾海棧
Drangarnir Sea Stacks by Esther Serrano

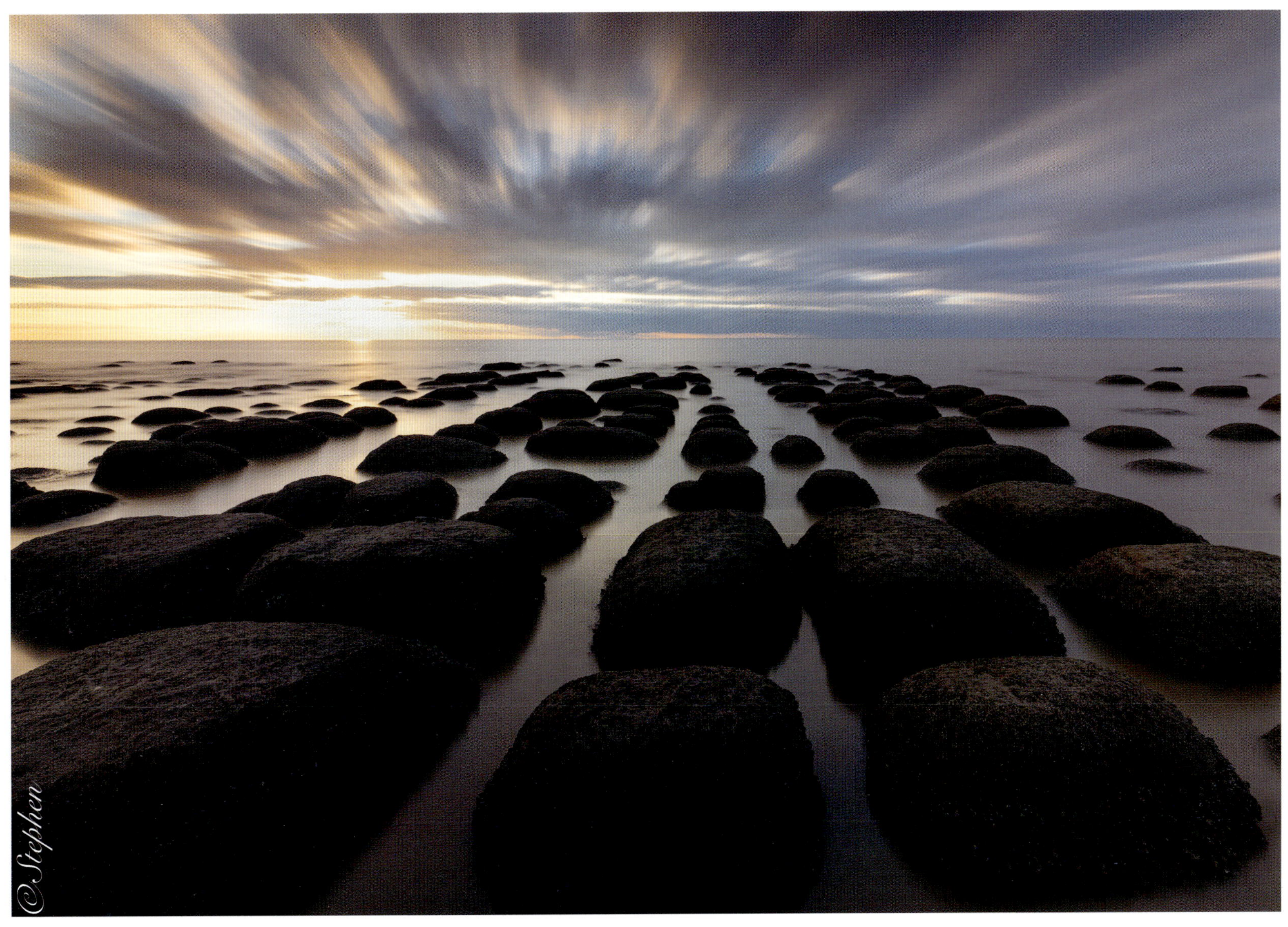

北諾福克海岸
North Norfolk Coast by Stephen Roberts

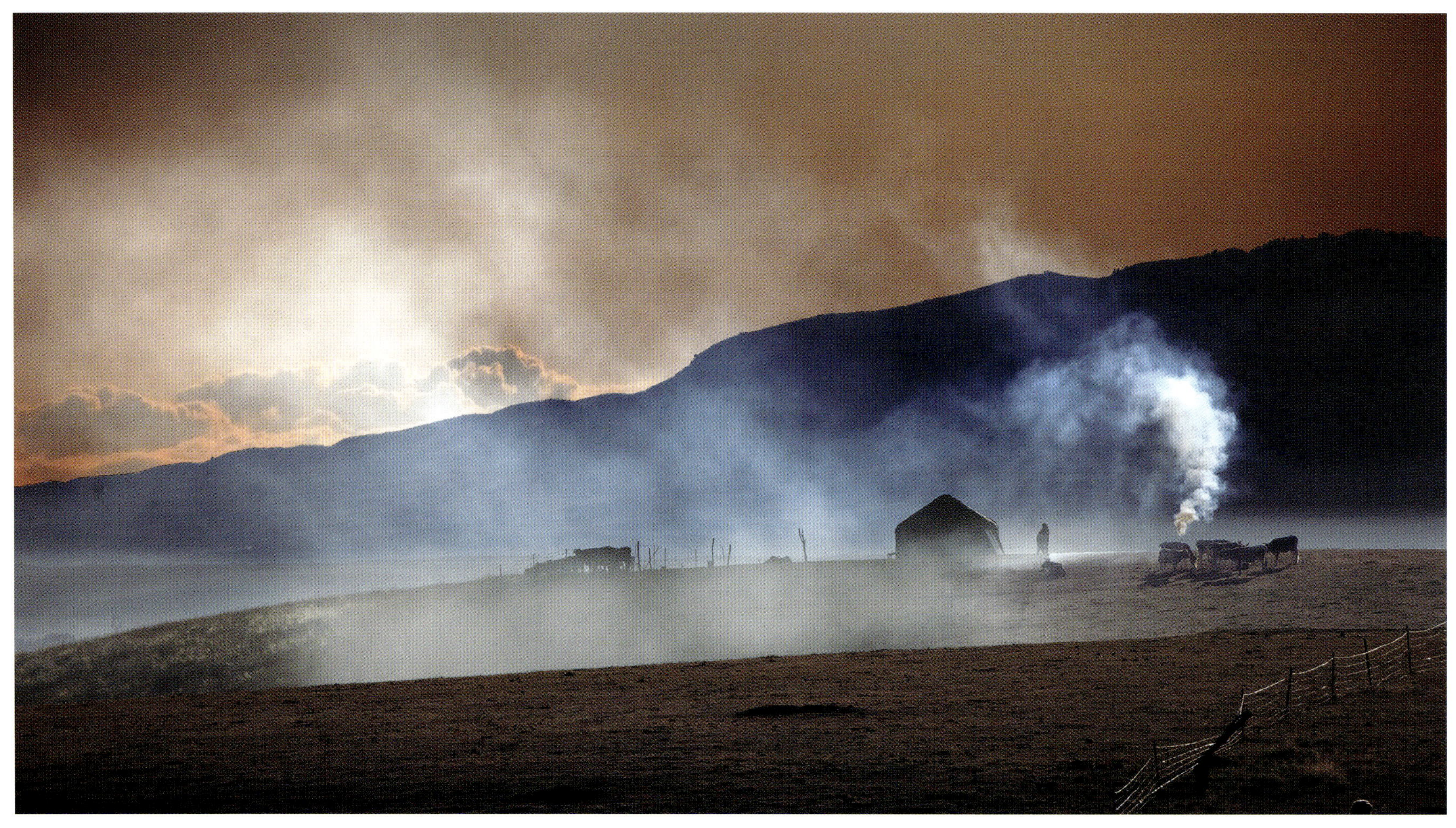

又見炊烟 / 攝影: 盧寒
Seeing the Smoke Again by Lu Han

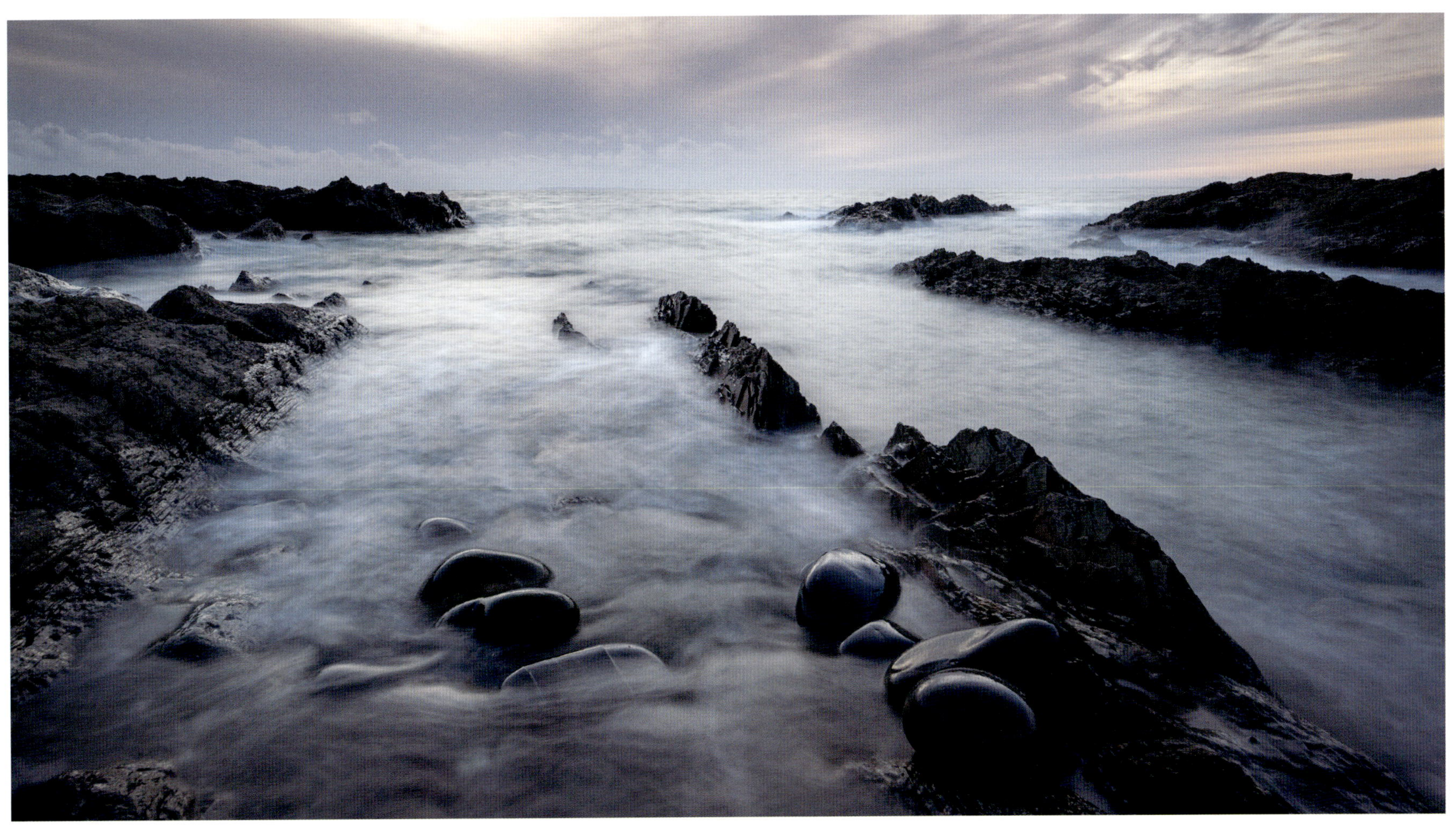

西游記
Westward Ho! by Richard Ellis ARPS

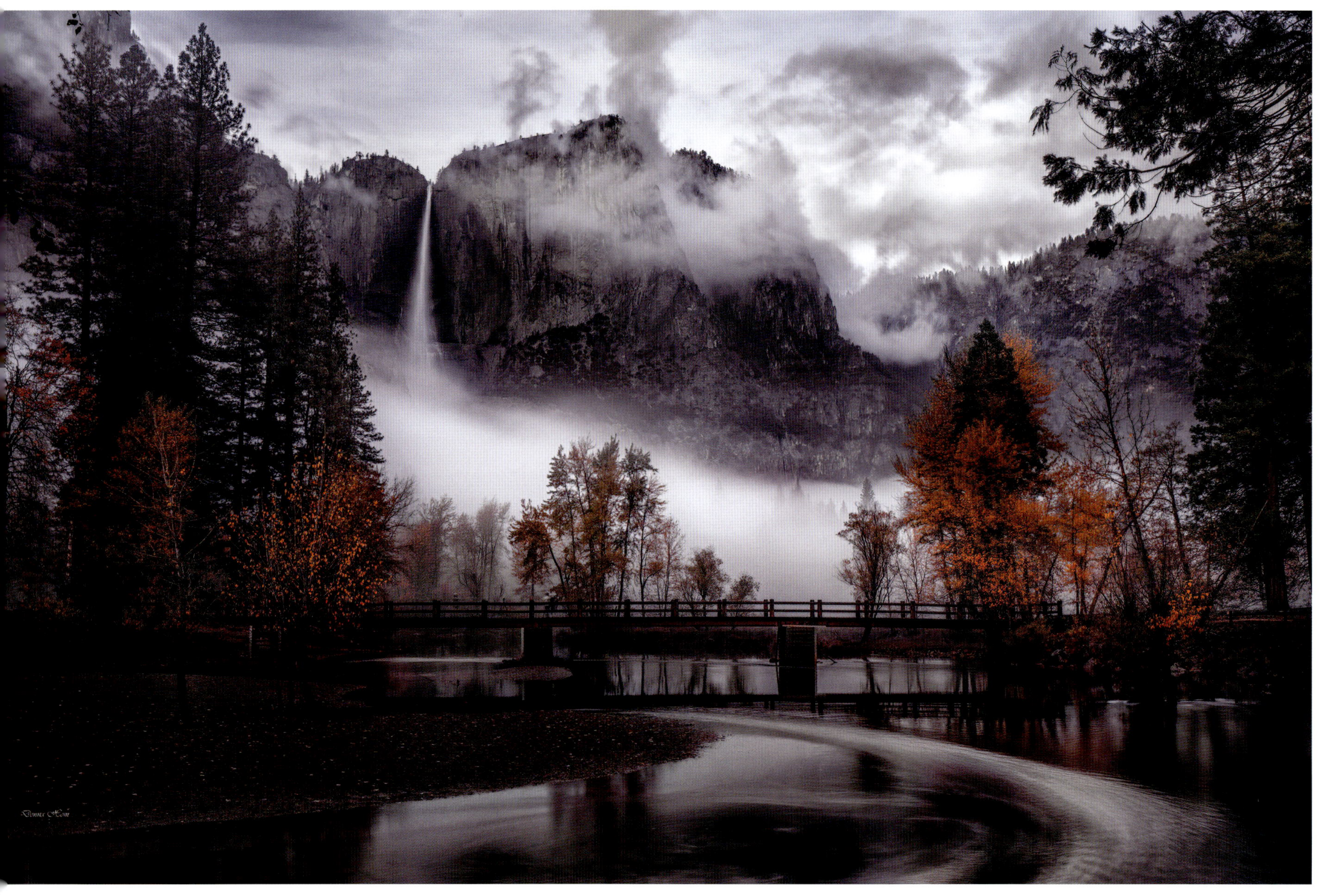

優山美地的秋色 / 攝影: 丹菁
Amazing Autumn by Donna Hom

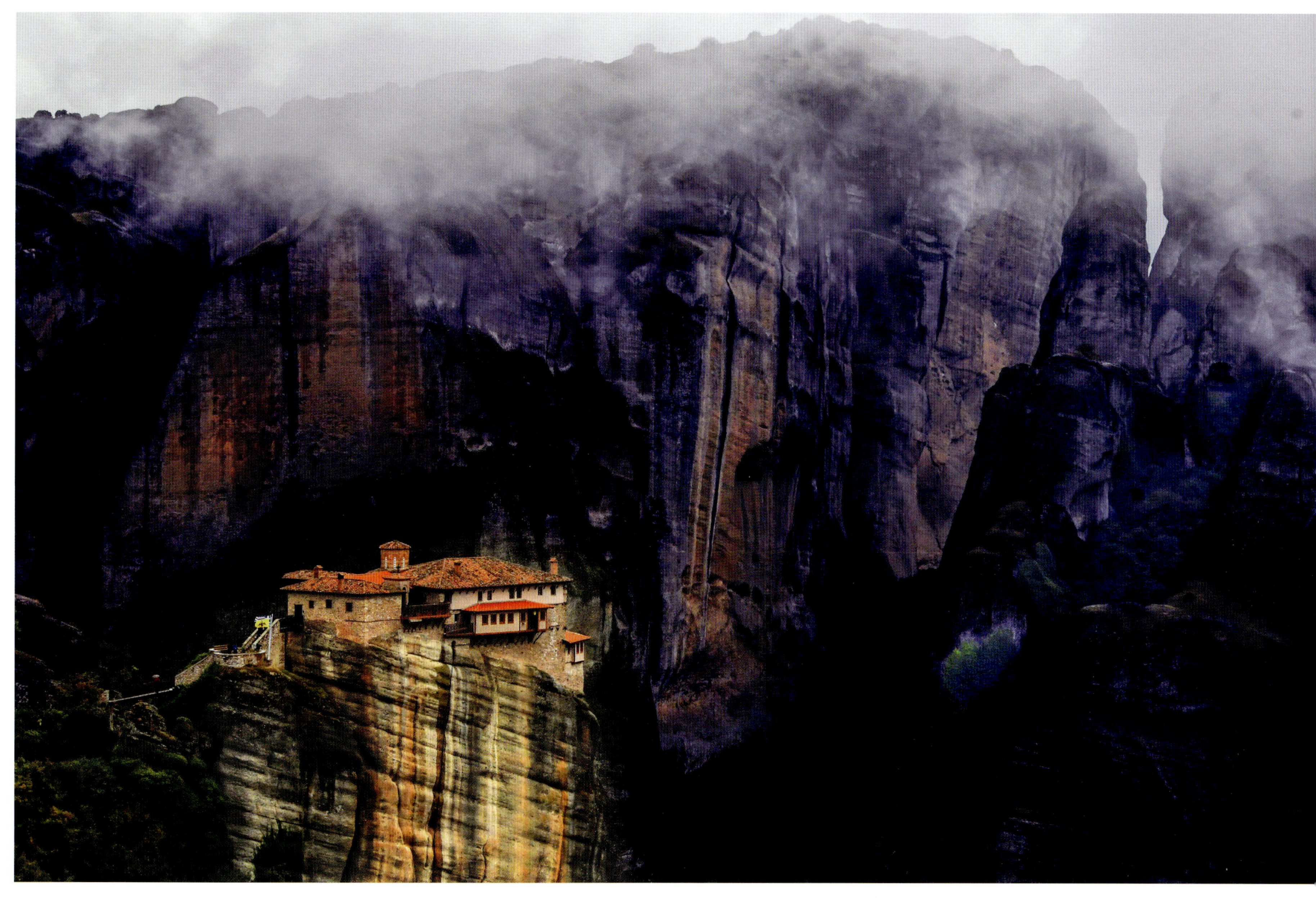

空中修道院 / 攝影: 尹宏
Air Monastery by Yin Hong

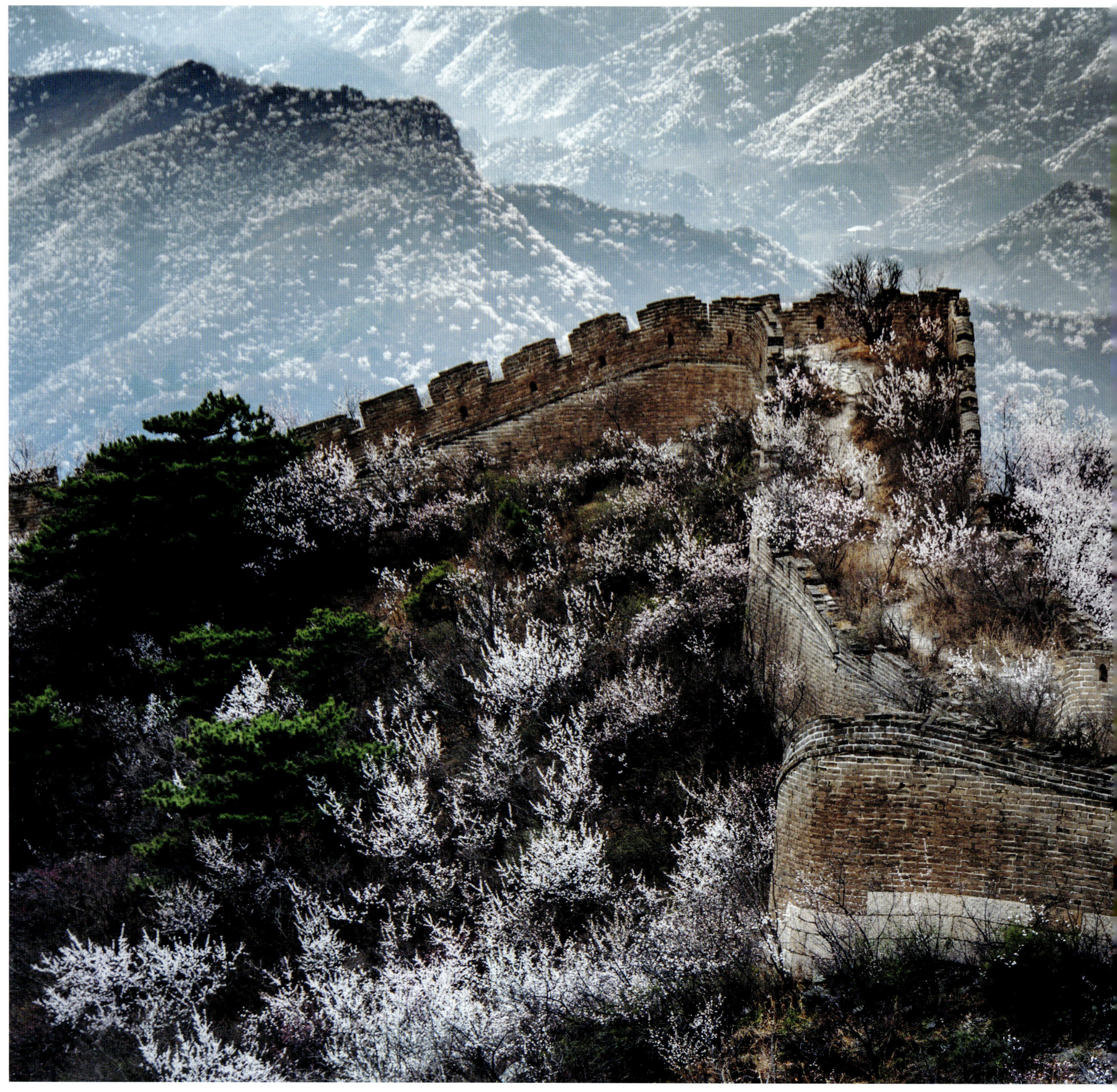

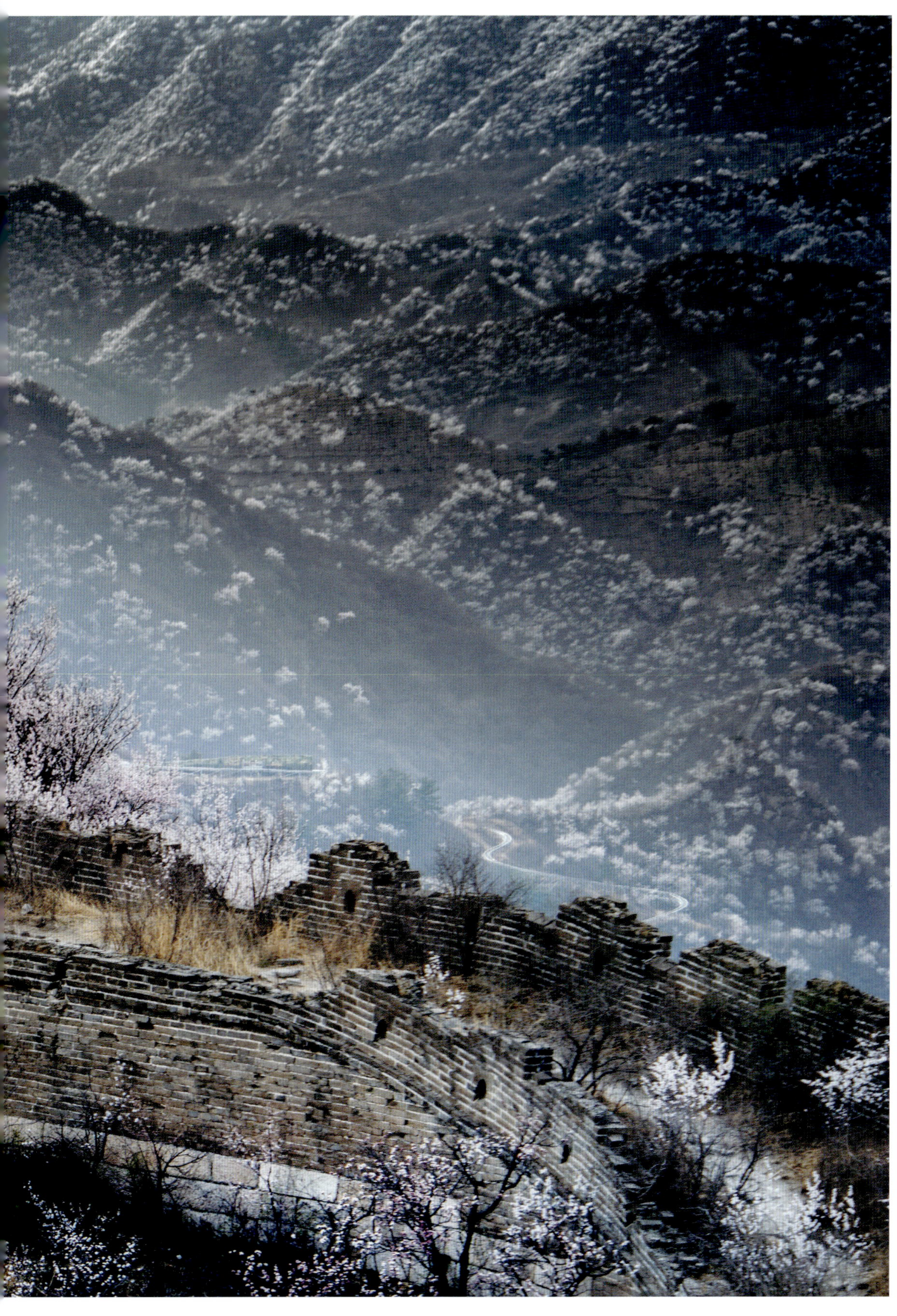

春滿長城 / 攝影: 杜海東
Spring in the Great Wall
by Du Haidong

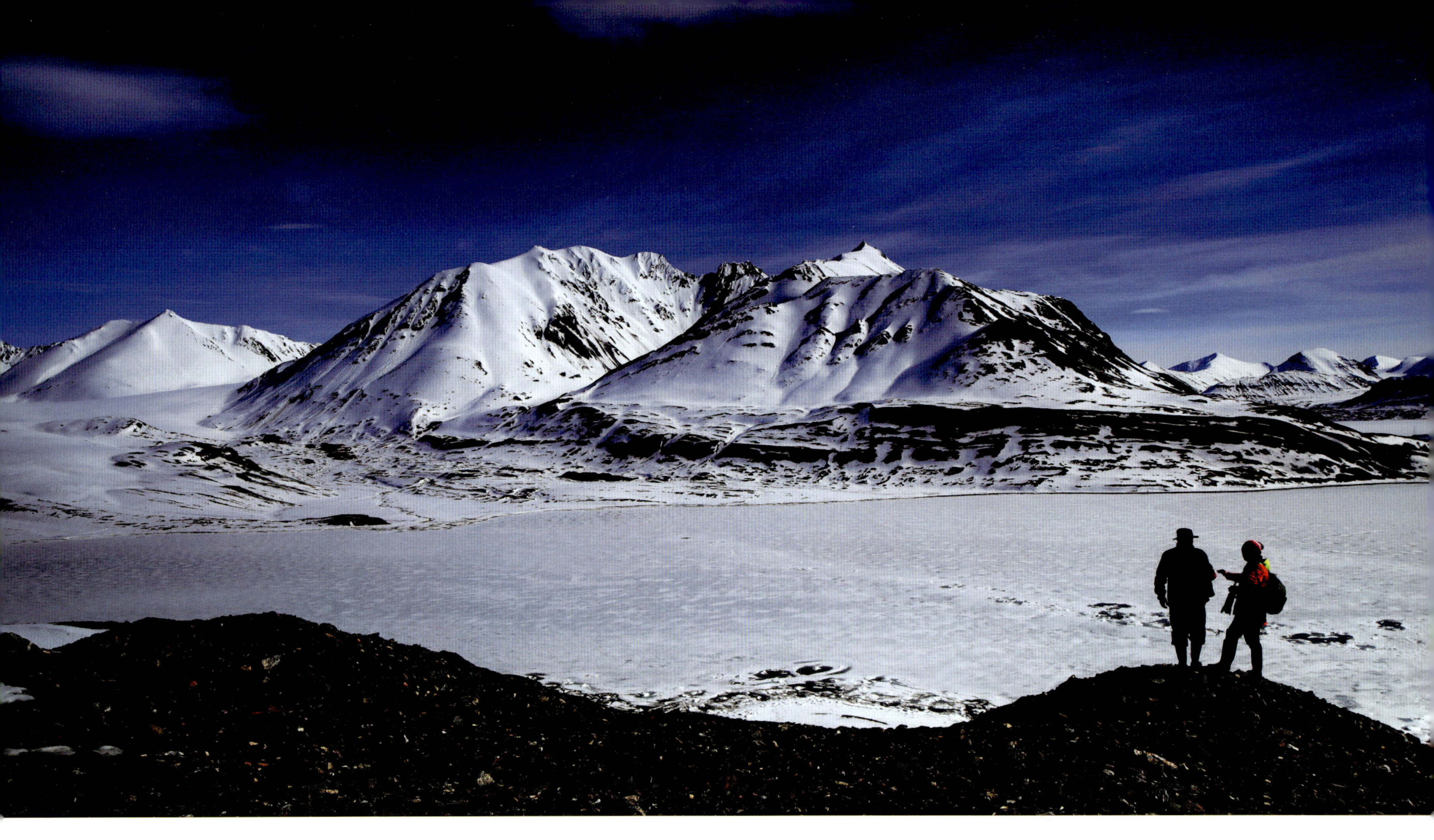

斯瓦爾巴德暢想曲 / 攝影: 趙幹成
Svalbard Rhapsody by Zhao Gancheng

黄土高原雪景 / 攝影: 牟健爲
Loess Plateau Snow Scene by Mou Jianwei

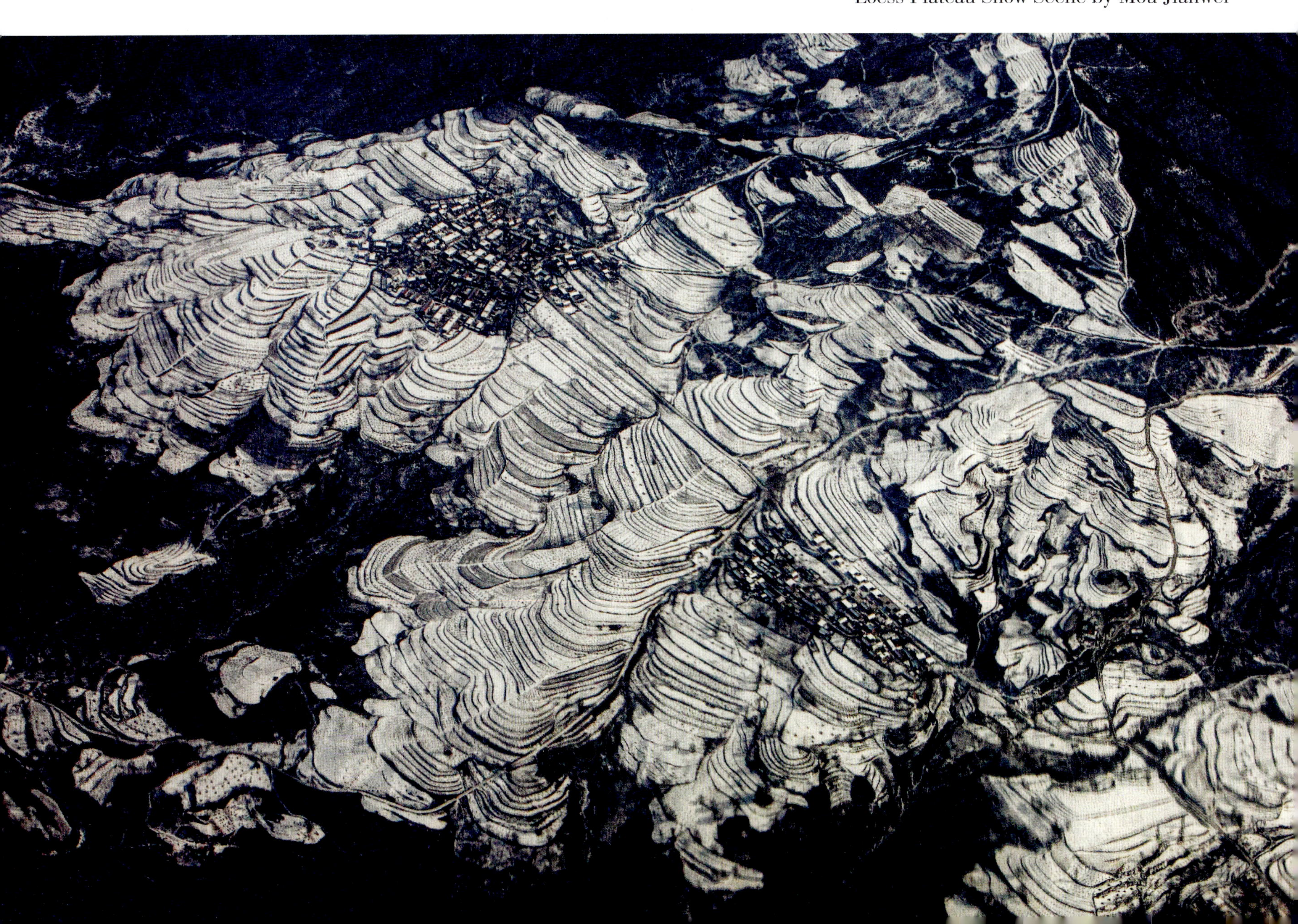

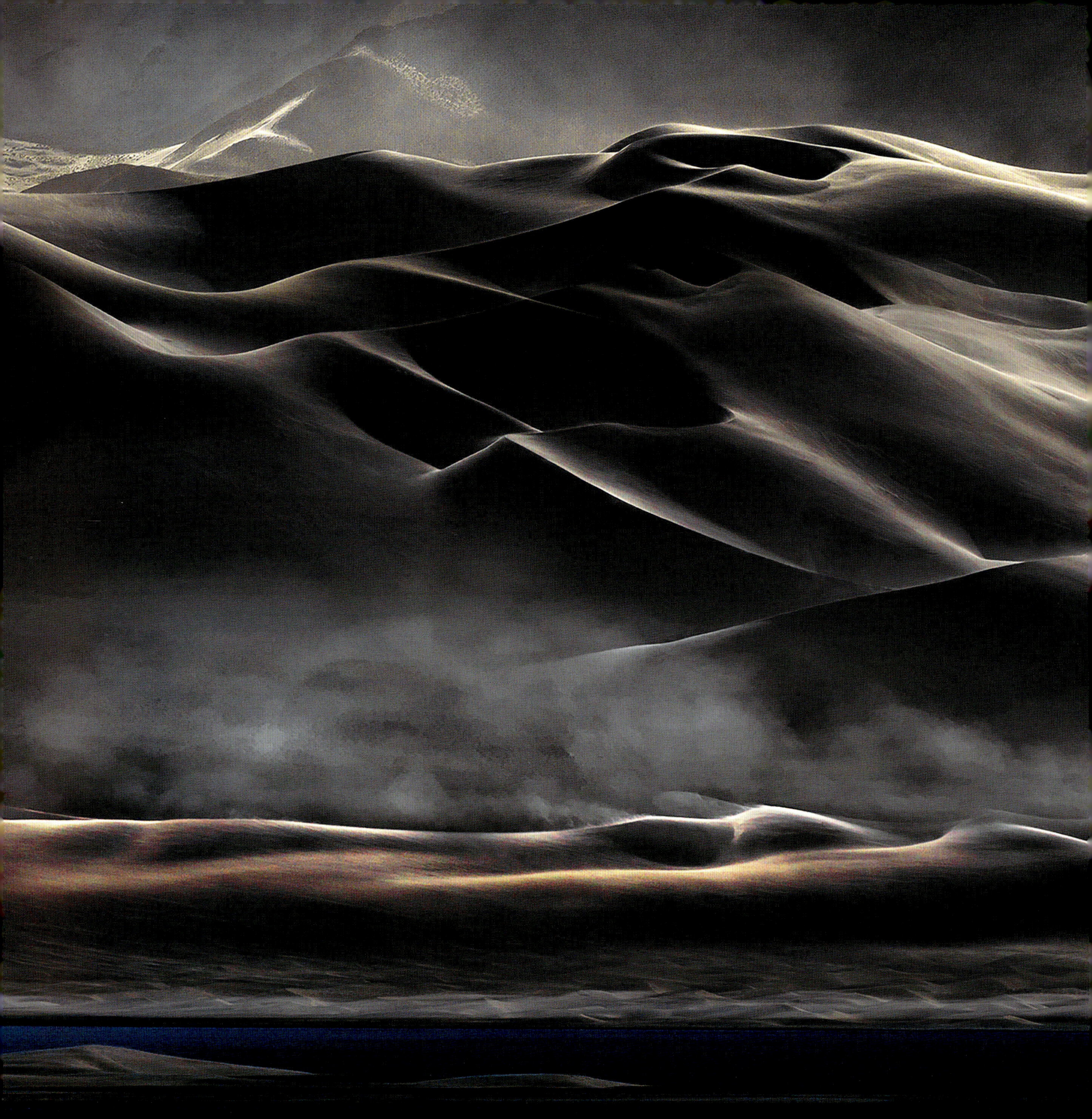

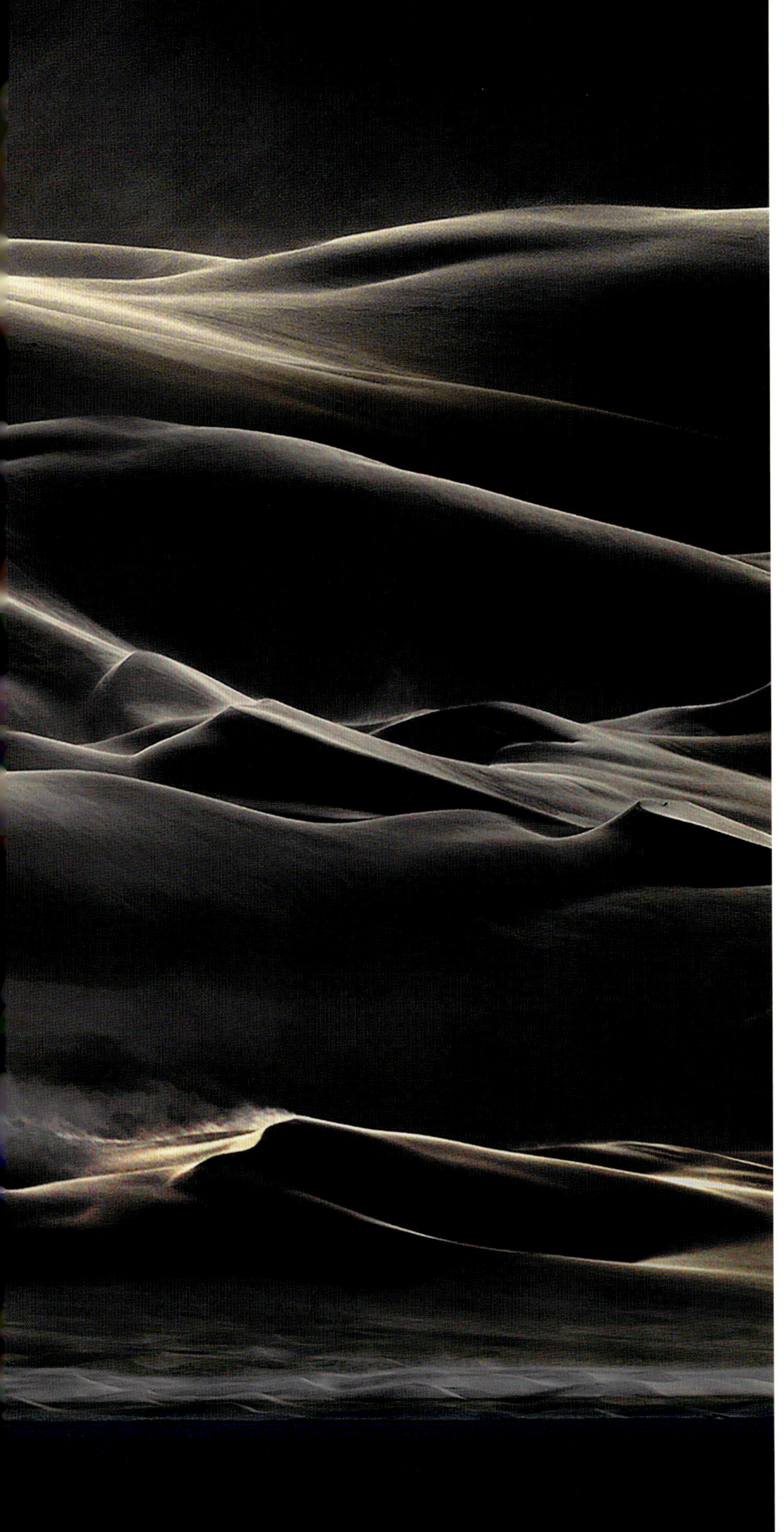

昆侖飛沙 / 攝影: 彭雪平
Flying Sands of Kunlun by Peng Xueping

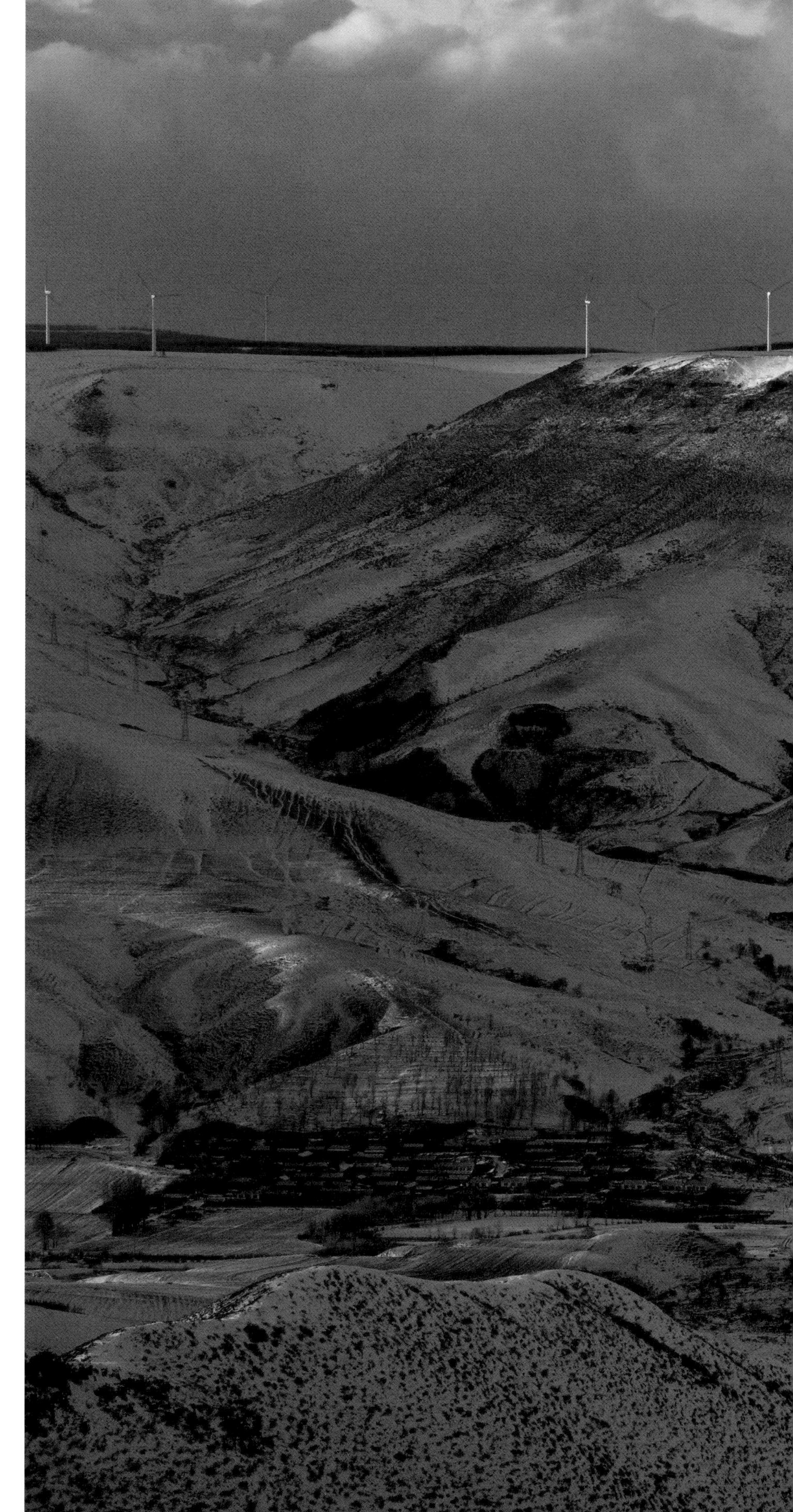

克什克騰風光 / 攝影: 陳秀慶
Keshiketeng Landscape
by Chen Xiuqing

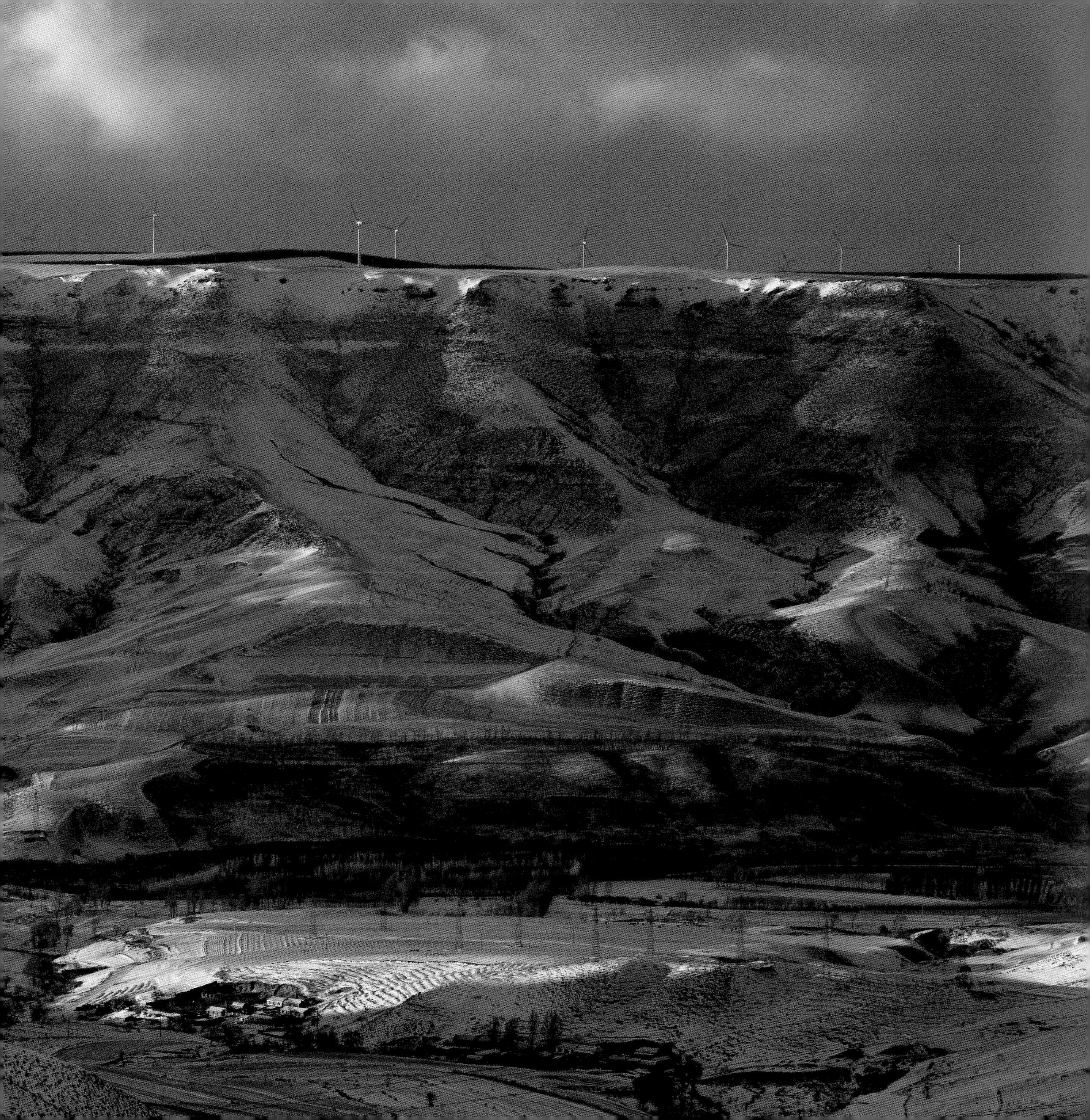

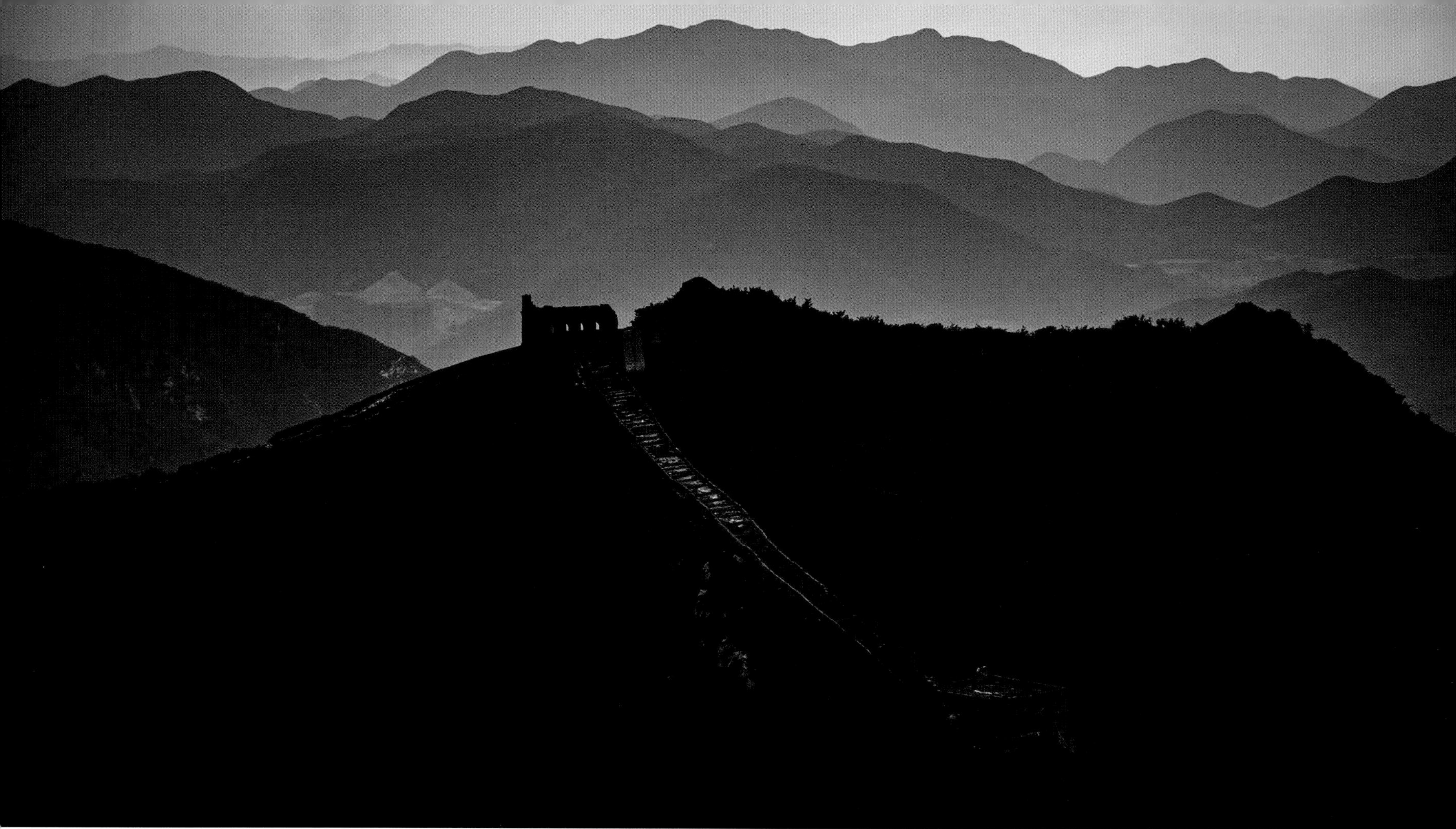

水墨長城 / 攝影：魏德華
Ink Great Wall by Wei Dehua

眺望遠古(西溝長城) / 攝影: 魏德華
Looking at Ancient Times (Xigou Great Wall) by Wei Dehua

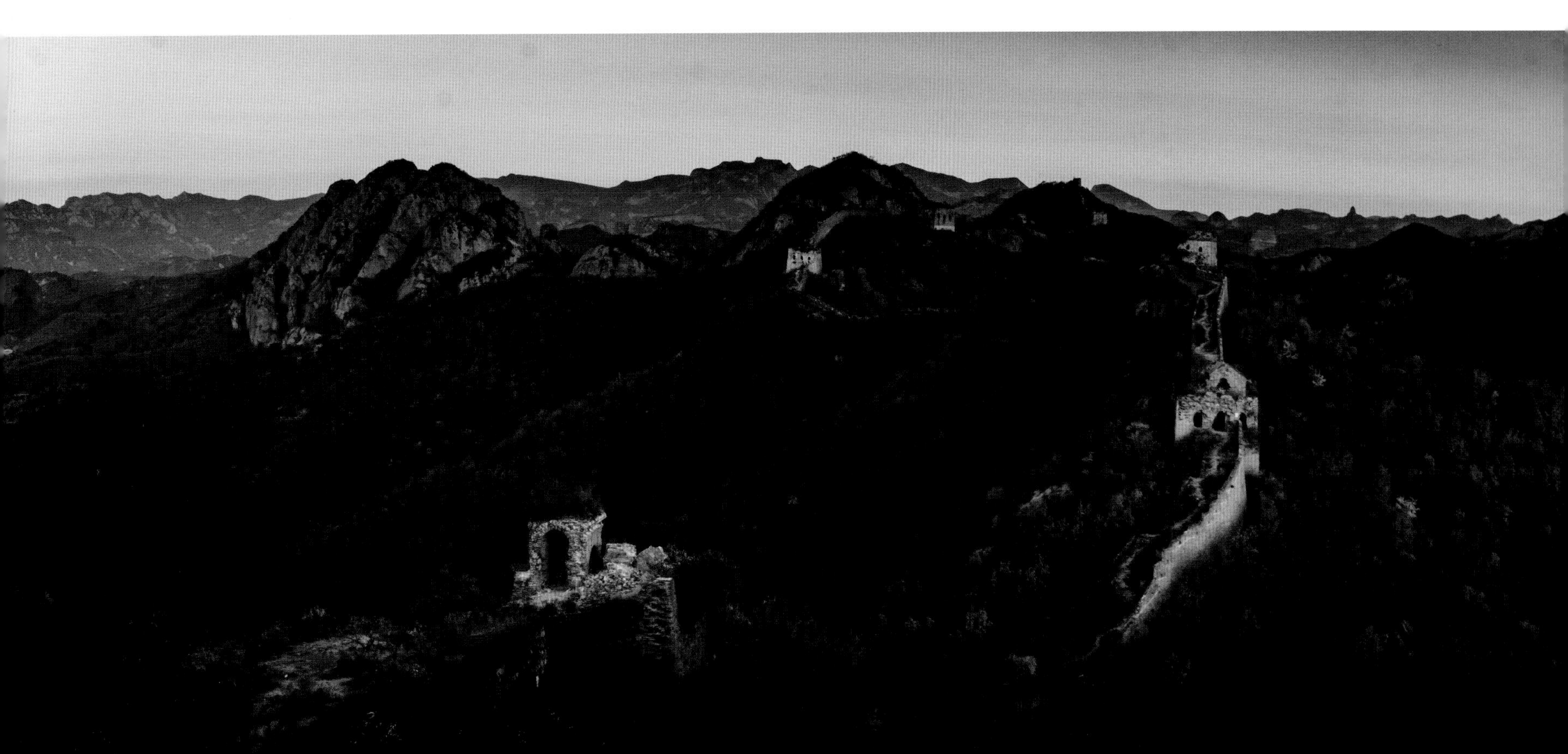

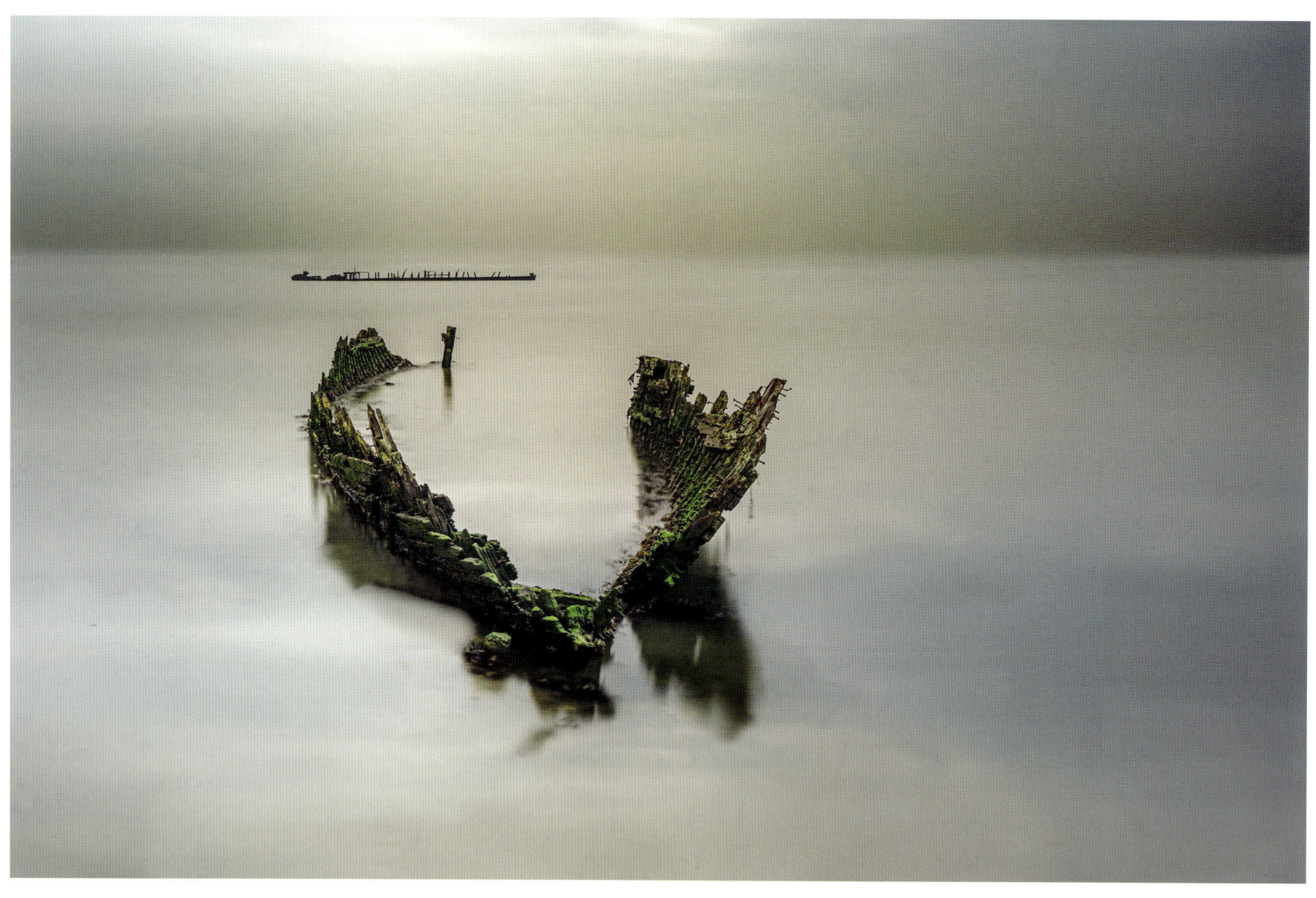

沼澤河口沉船
Swale Estuary Wreck by Julian Rouse LRPS

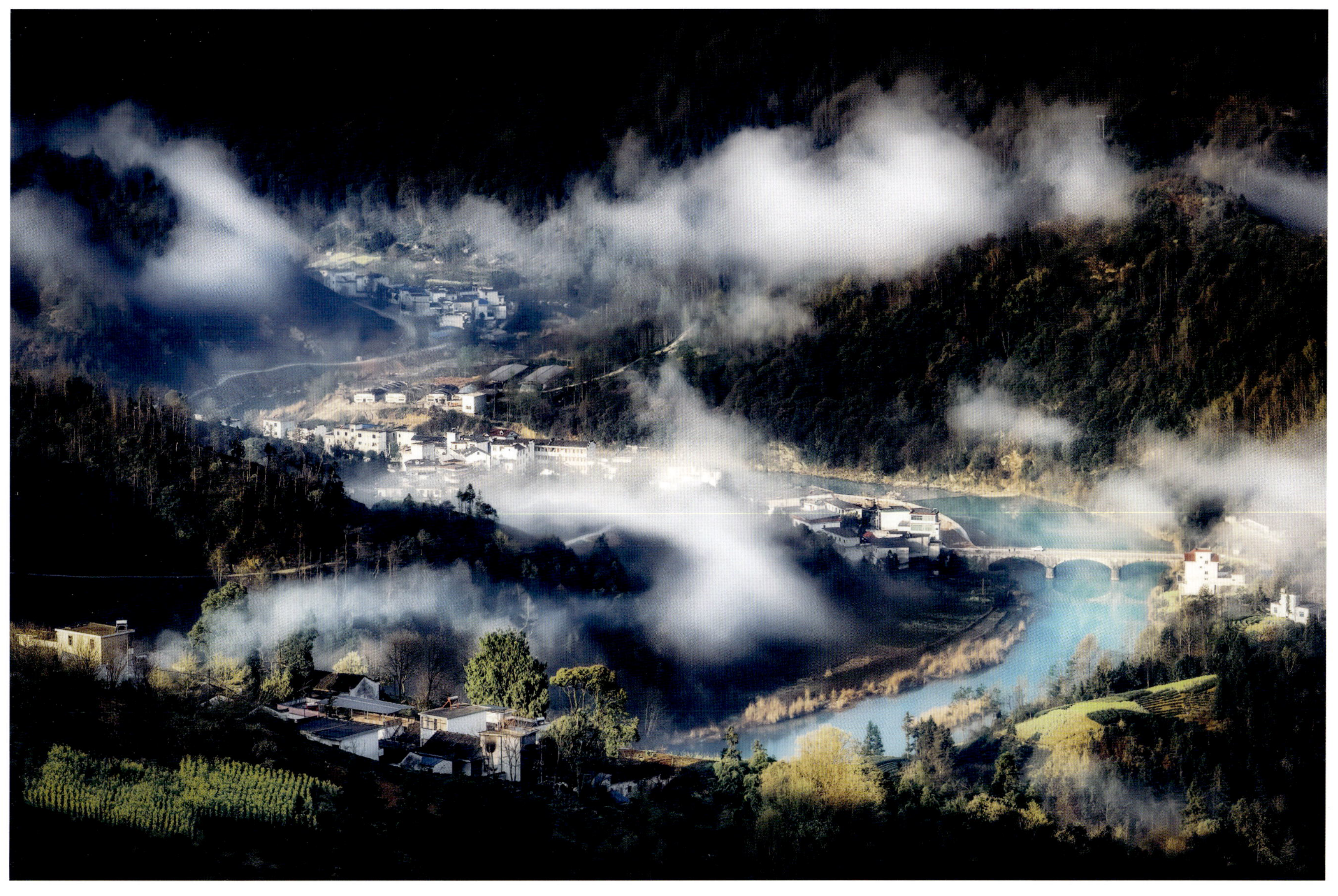

皖南喀納斯 / 攝影: 陸佳敏
Kanas, Southern Anhui by Lu Jiamin

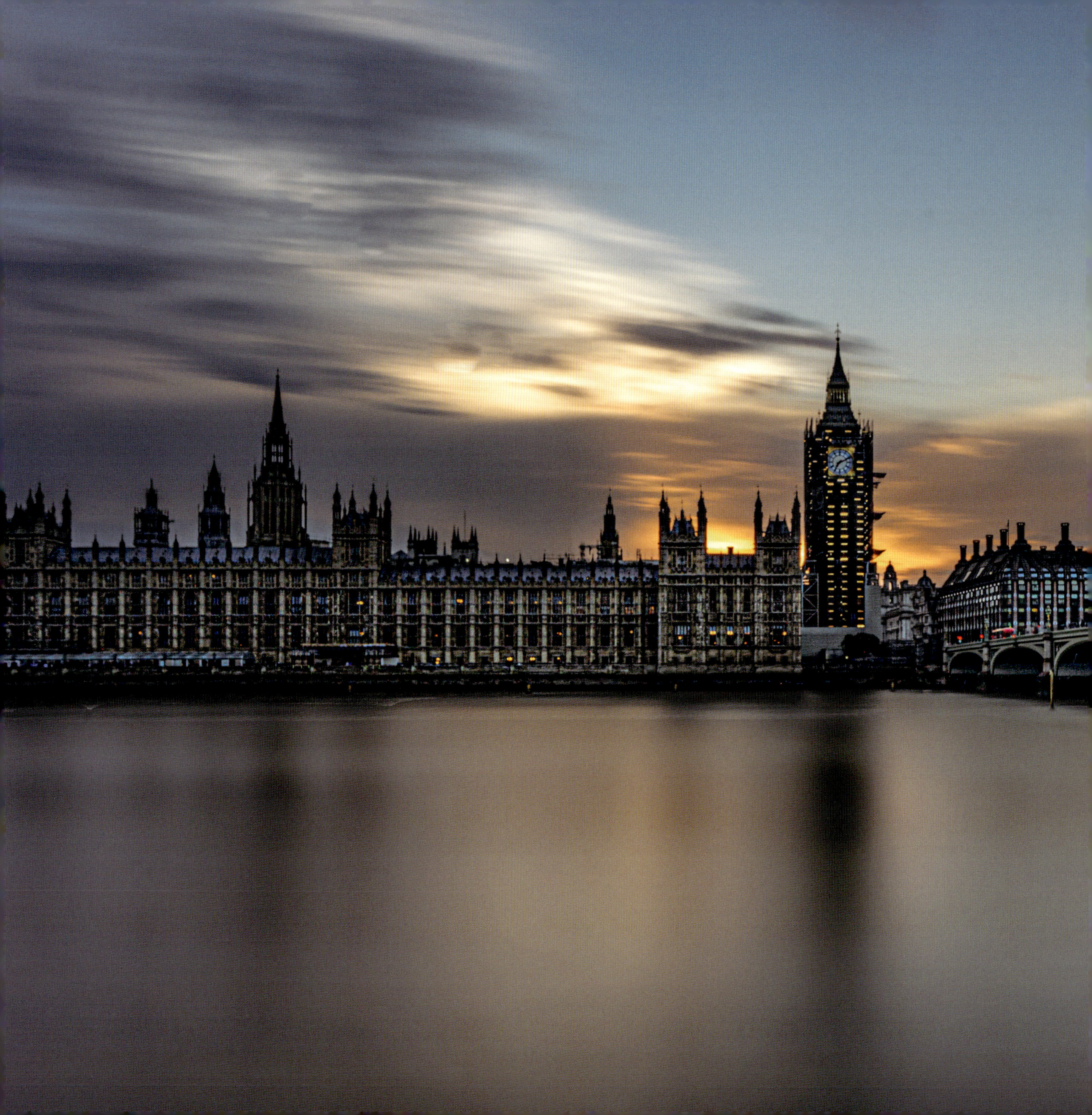

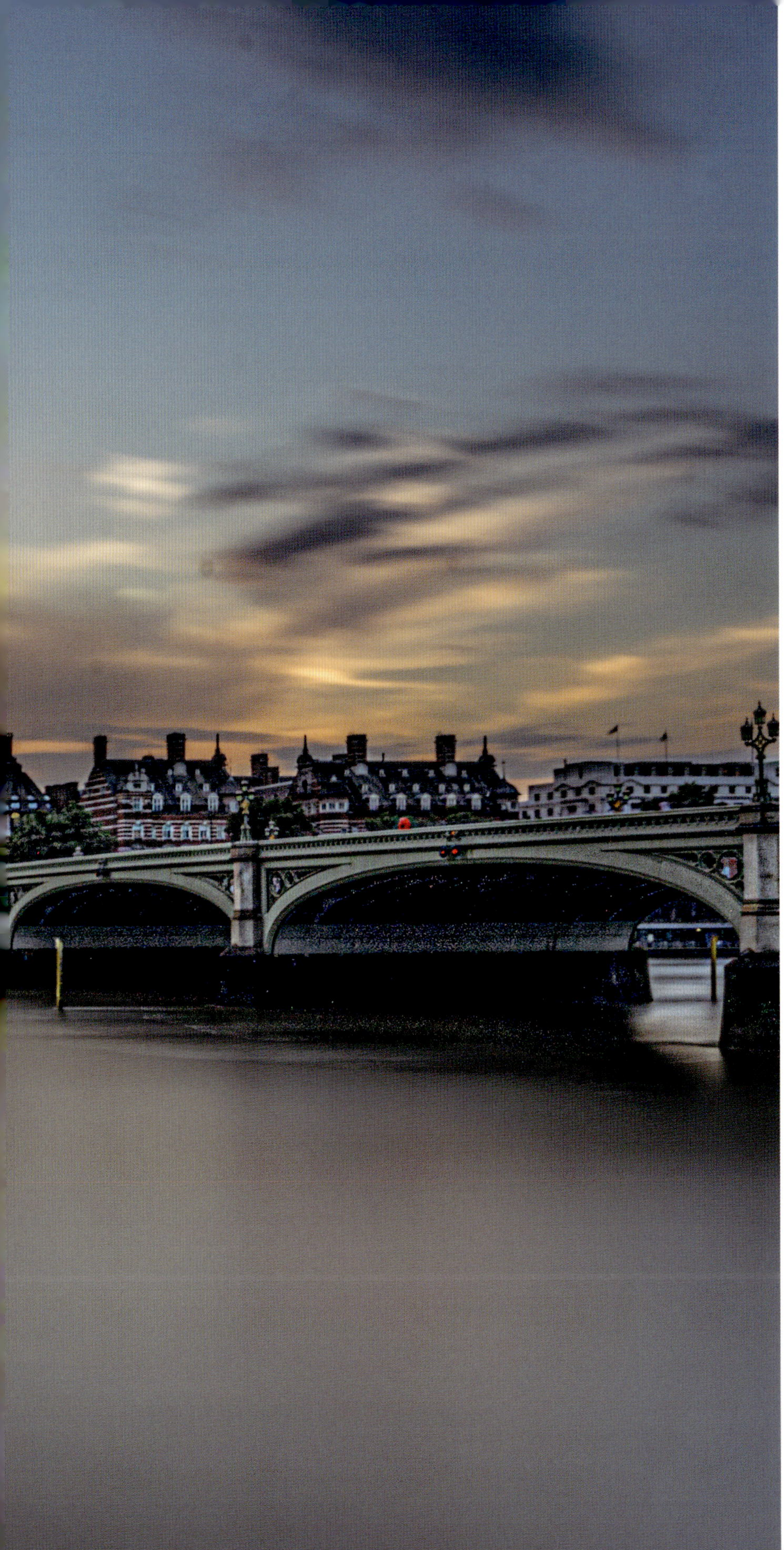

威斯敏斯特
Westminster by Julian Rouse LRPS

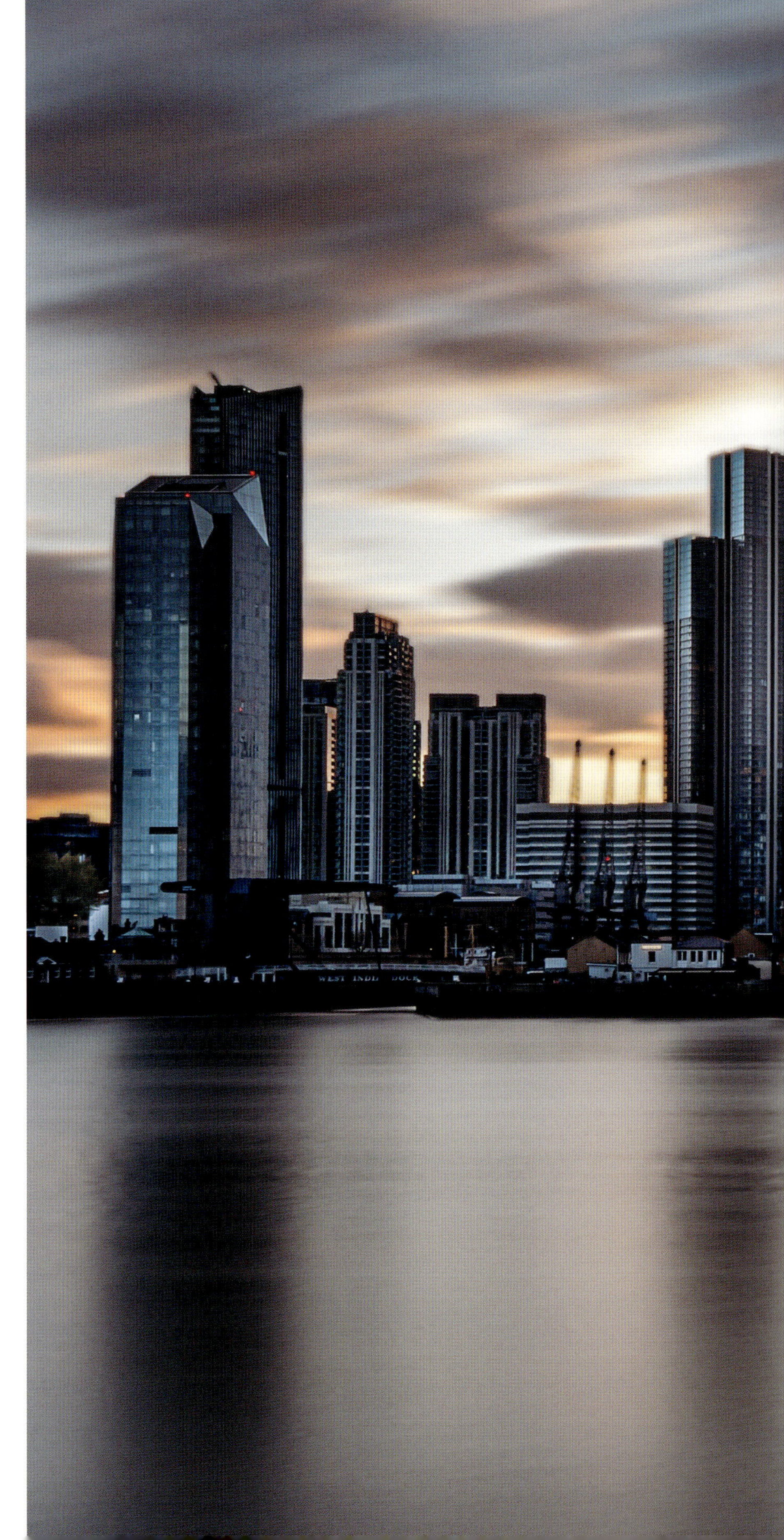

金絲雀碼頭
Canary Wharf by Julian Rouse LRPS

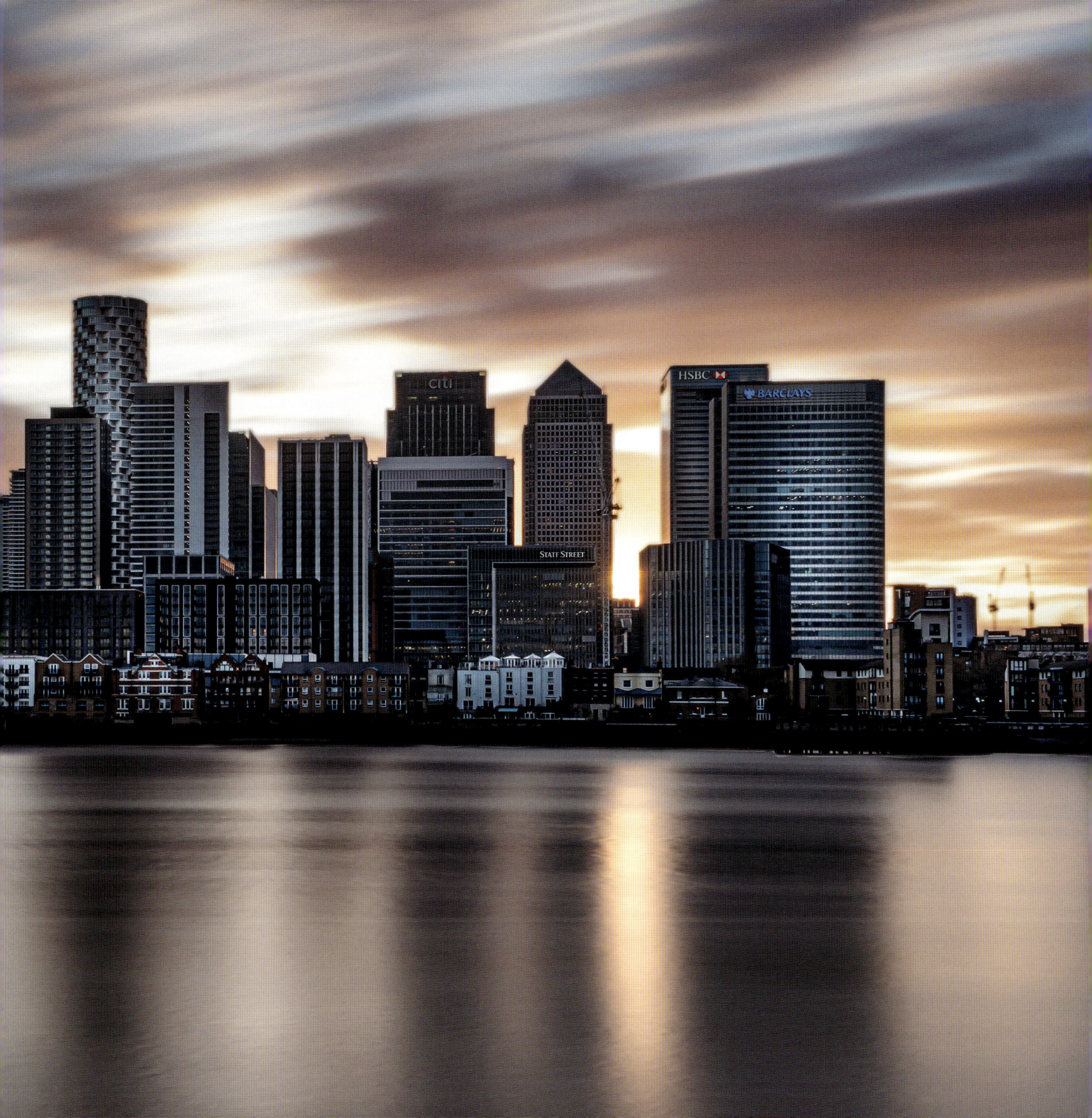
citi
HSBC
BARCLAYS
STATE STREET

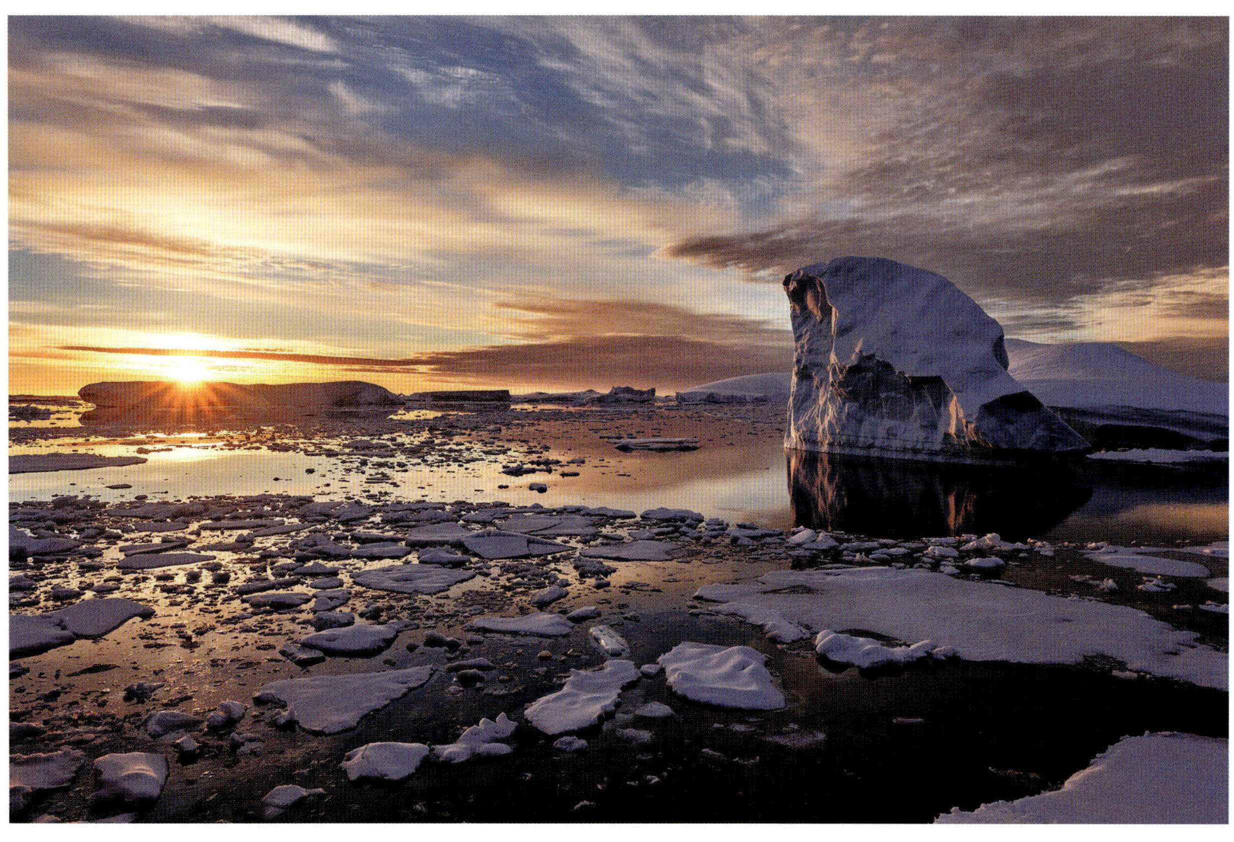

南極洲的夕陽
Antarctic Sunset
by Anthony Macaulay

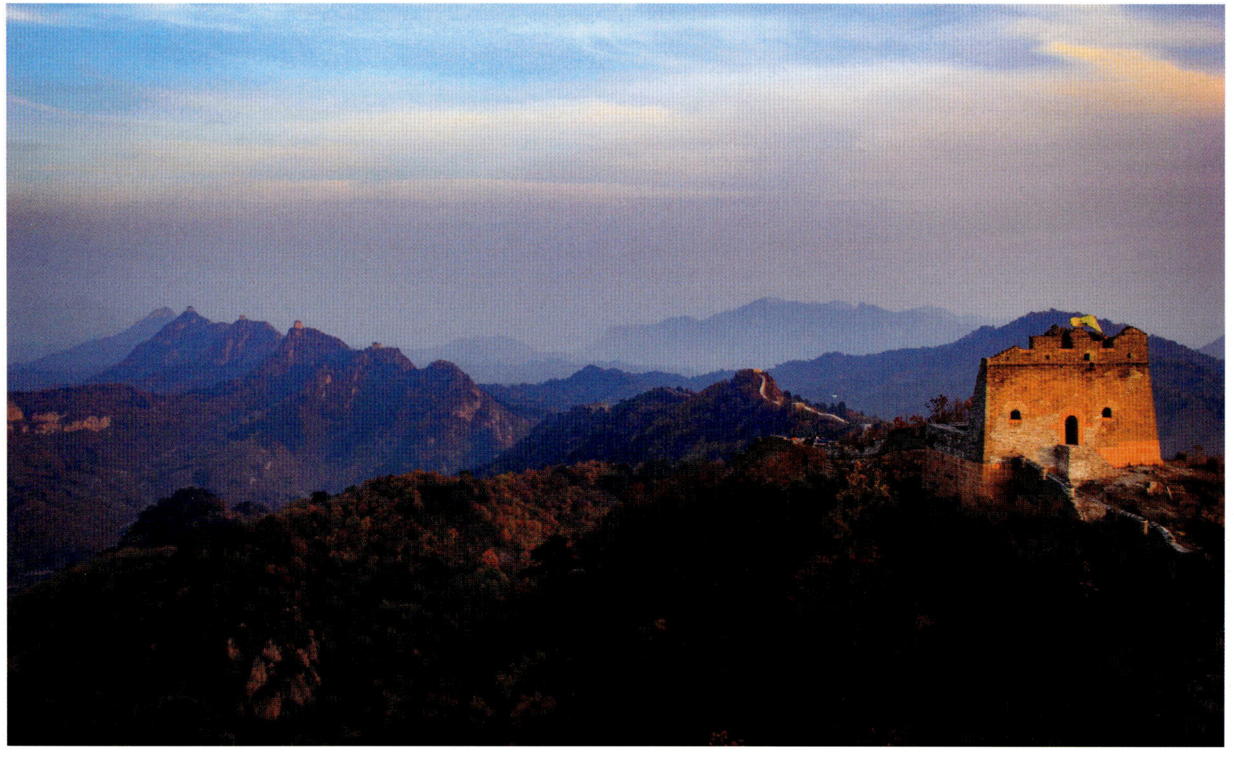

傲立東方 / 攝影: 董廣平
Standing Proudly in the East
by Dong Guangping

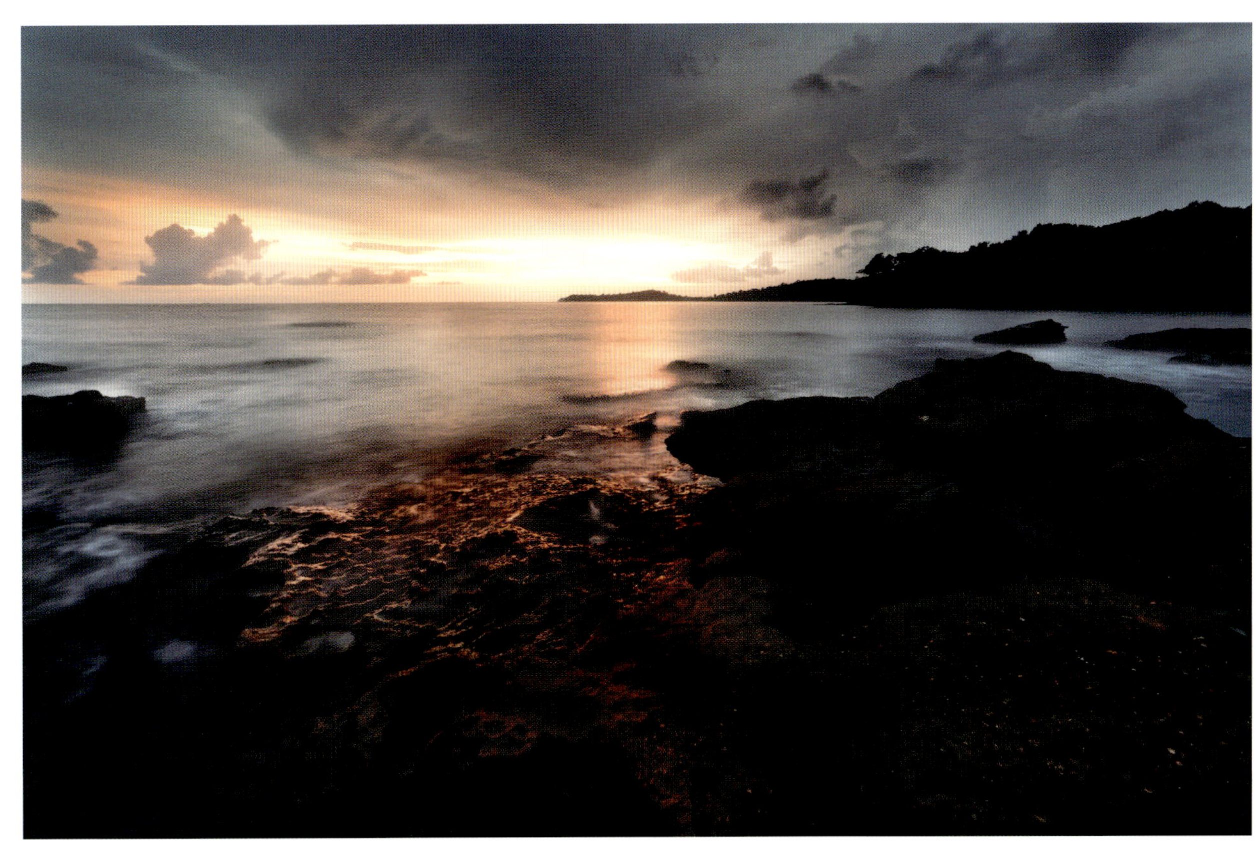

追光 / 攝影: 潘楊
Chasing Light by Pan Yang

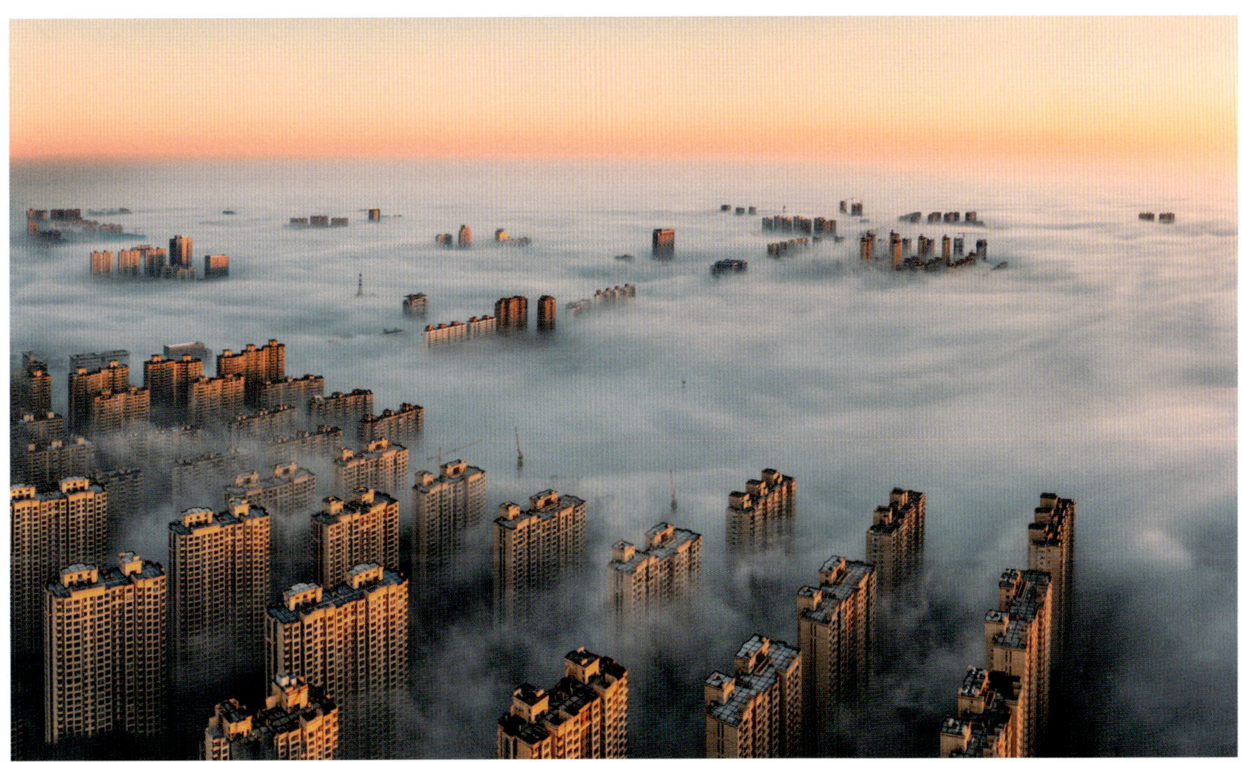

海安, 曉城仙境 / 攝影: 陳月斌
Haian, Dawn City Wonderland
by Chen Yuebin

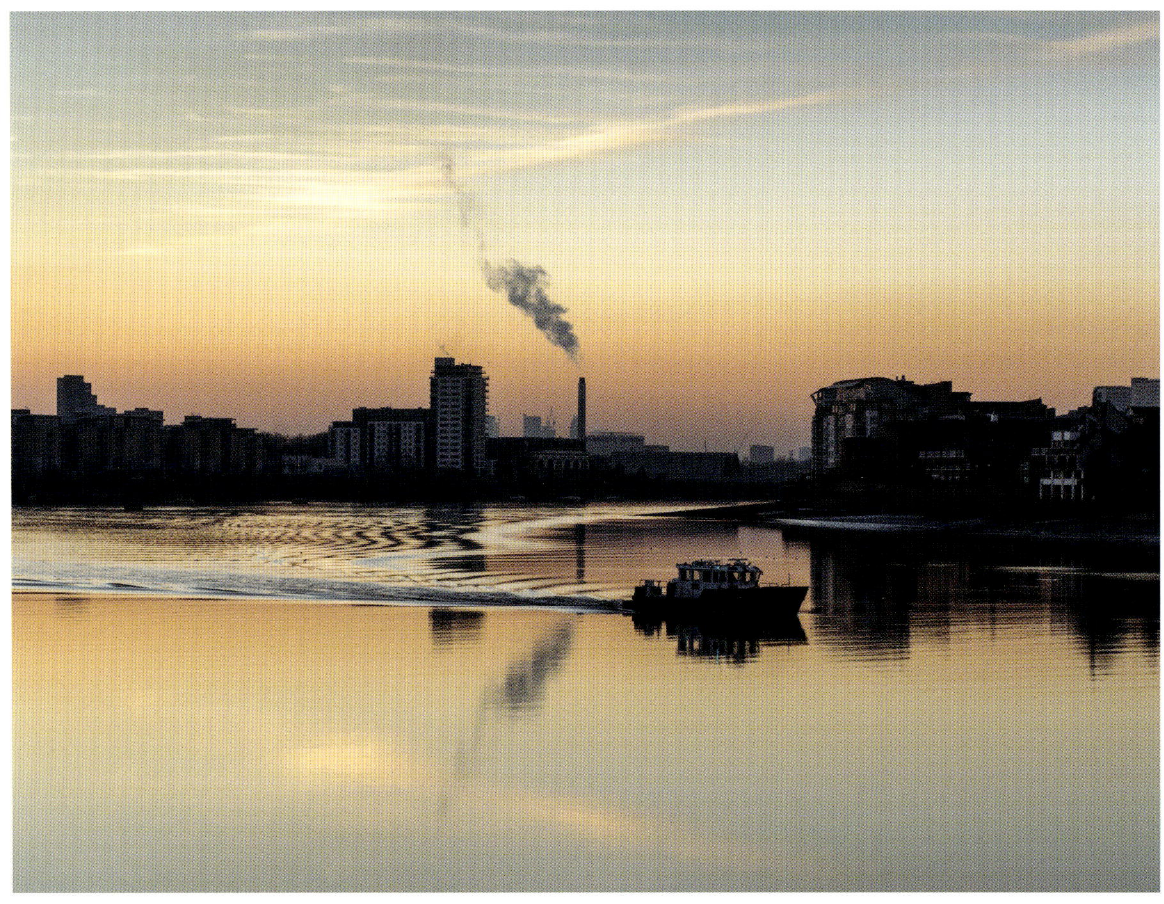

格林威治的泰晤士河上的夜晚
Evening on the Thames at Greenwich
by Kathryn Alkins

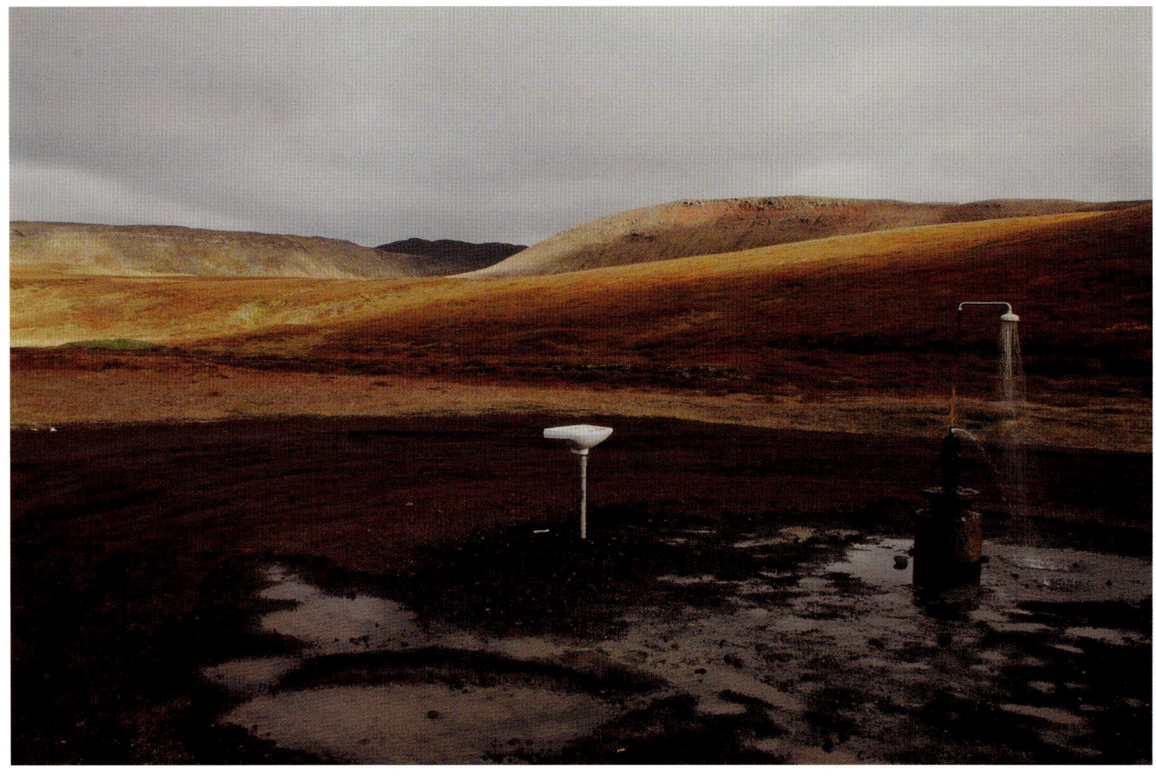

冰島
Iceland by Isky Gordon

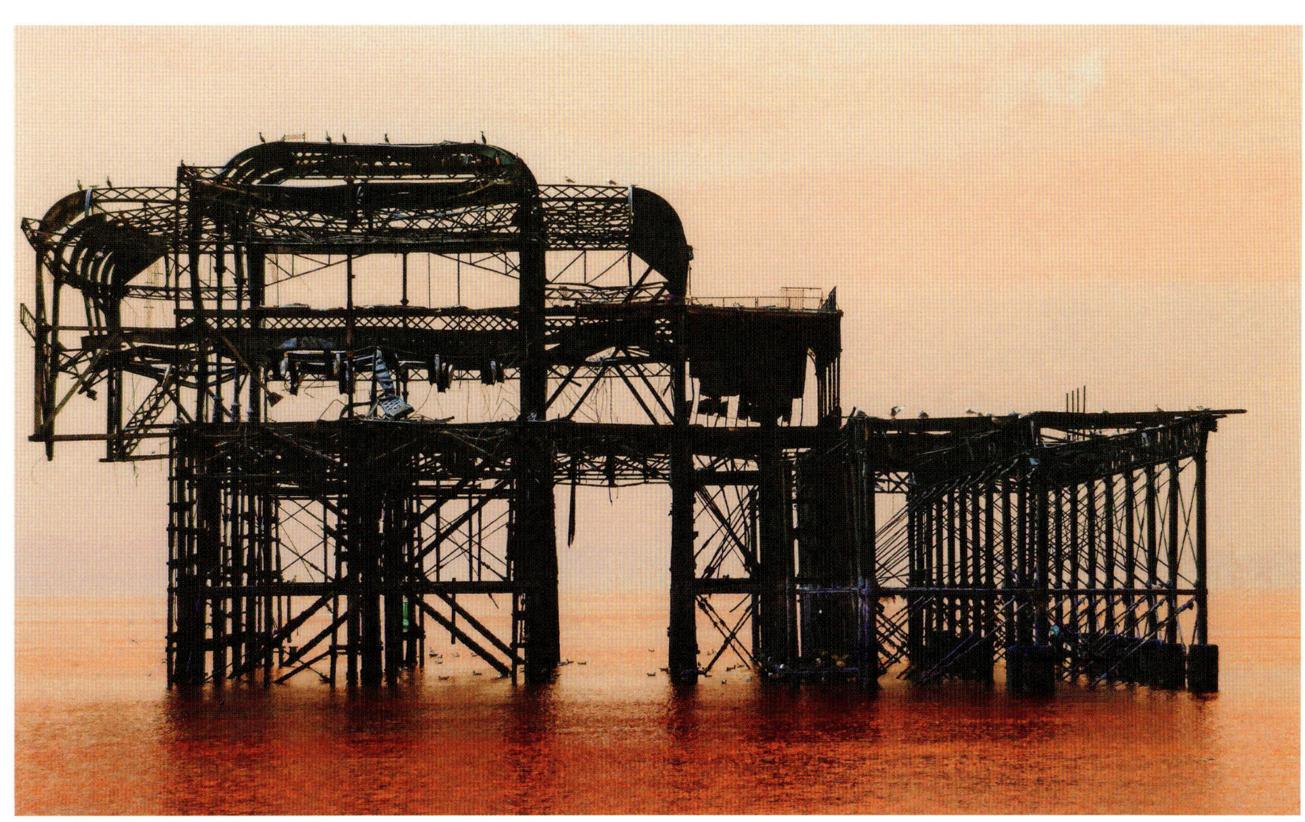

布萊頓西碼頭
West Pier Brighton
by David Lewis ARPS

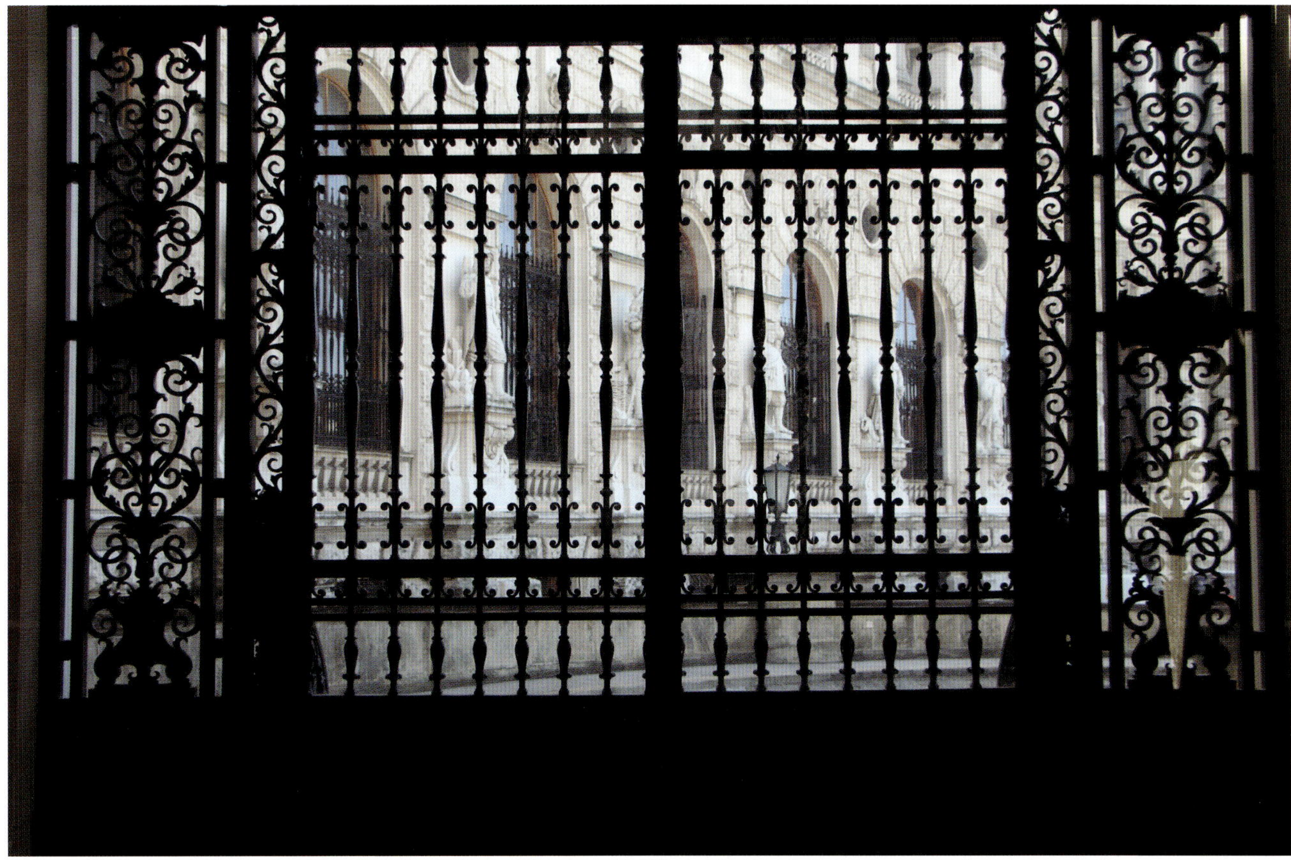

無間 / 攝影: 李志强
Seamless by Li Zhiqiang

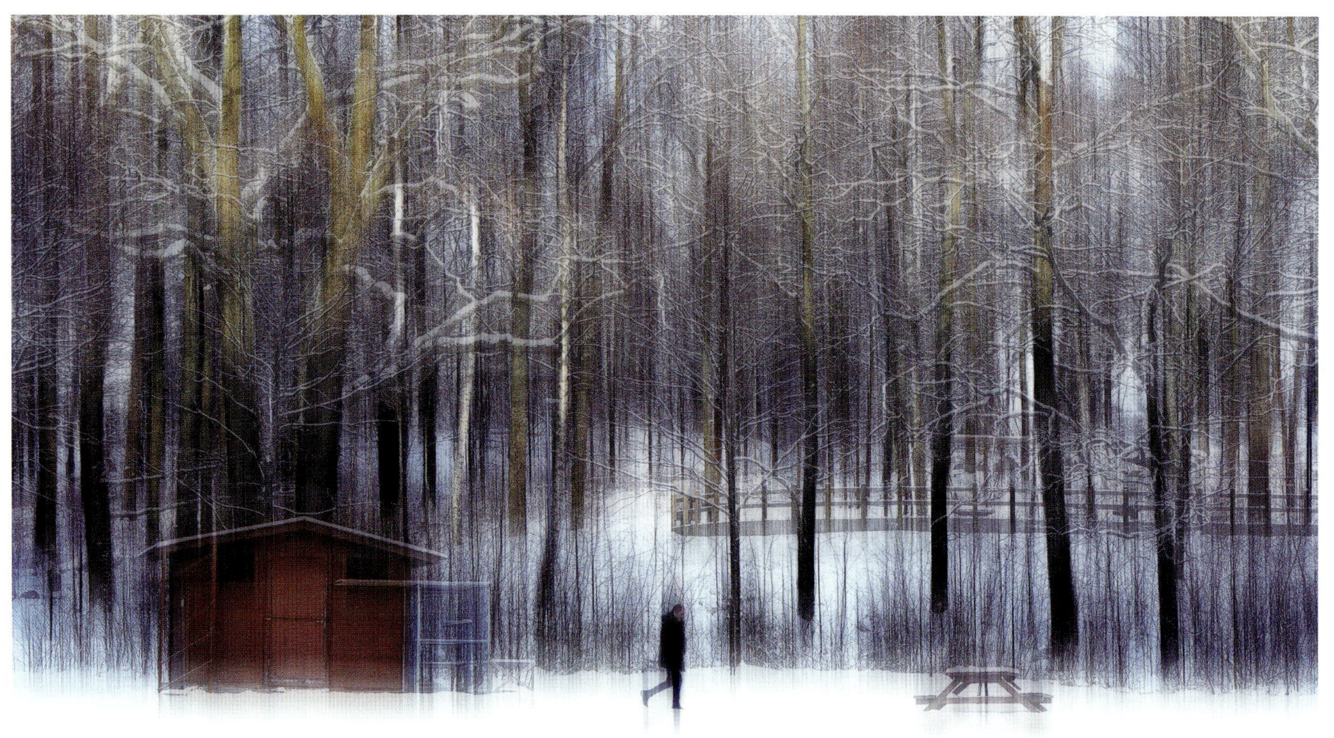

層林盡染 / 攝影: 龐其銘
The Forest is Full of Dye
by Pang Qiming

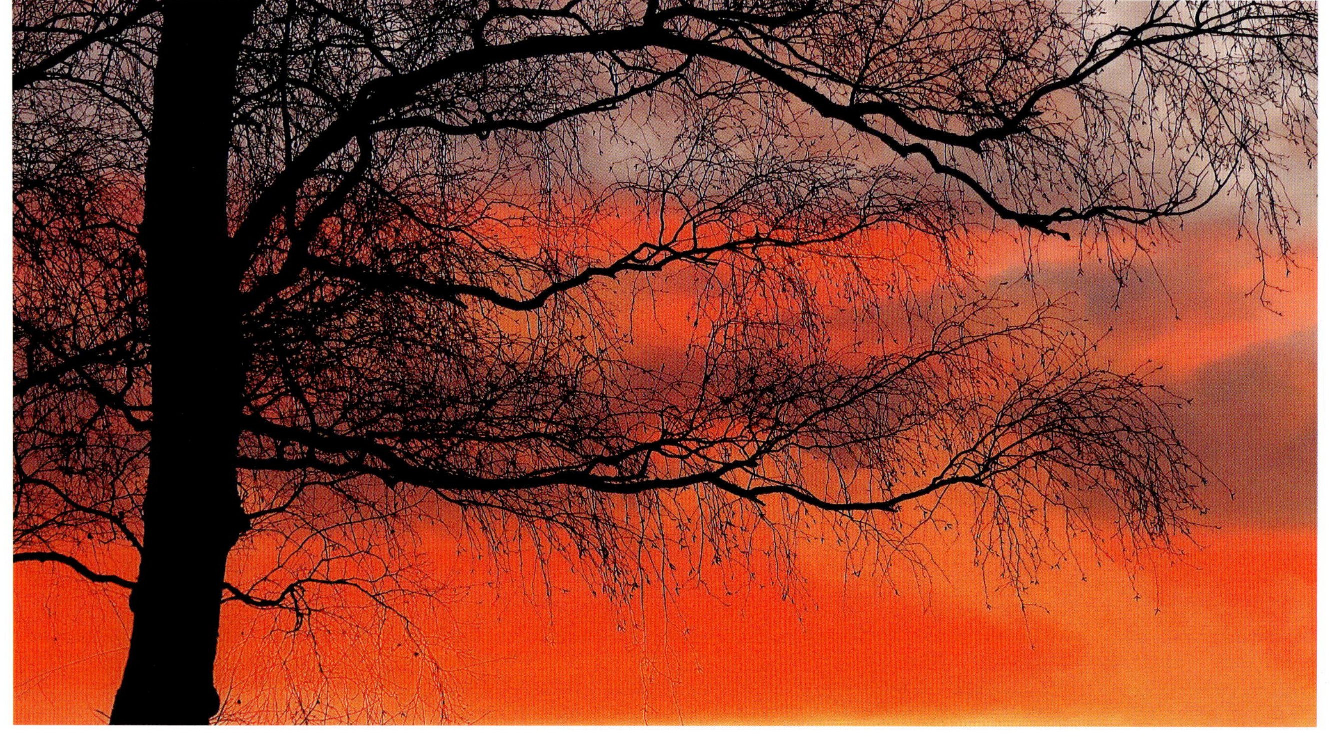

樹後的丹霞 / 攝影: 龐其銘
Red Sunset Behind Trees
by Pang Qiming

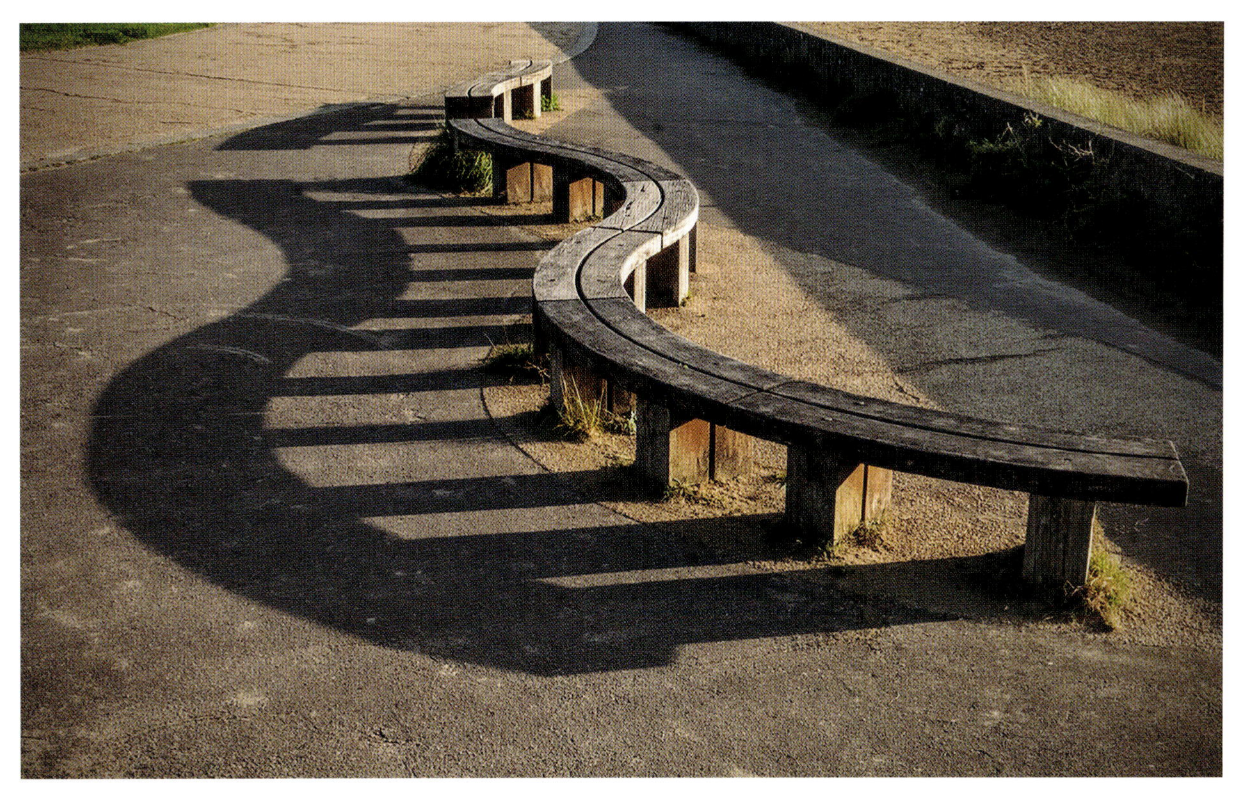

孤獨
Solitude by Girish Gosai ARPS

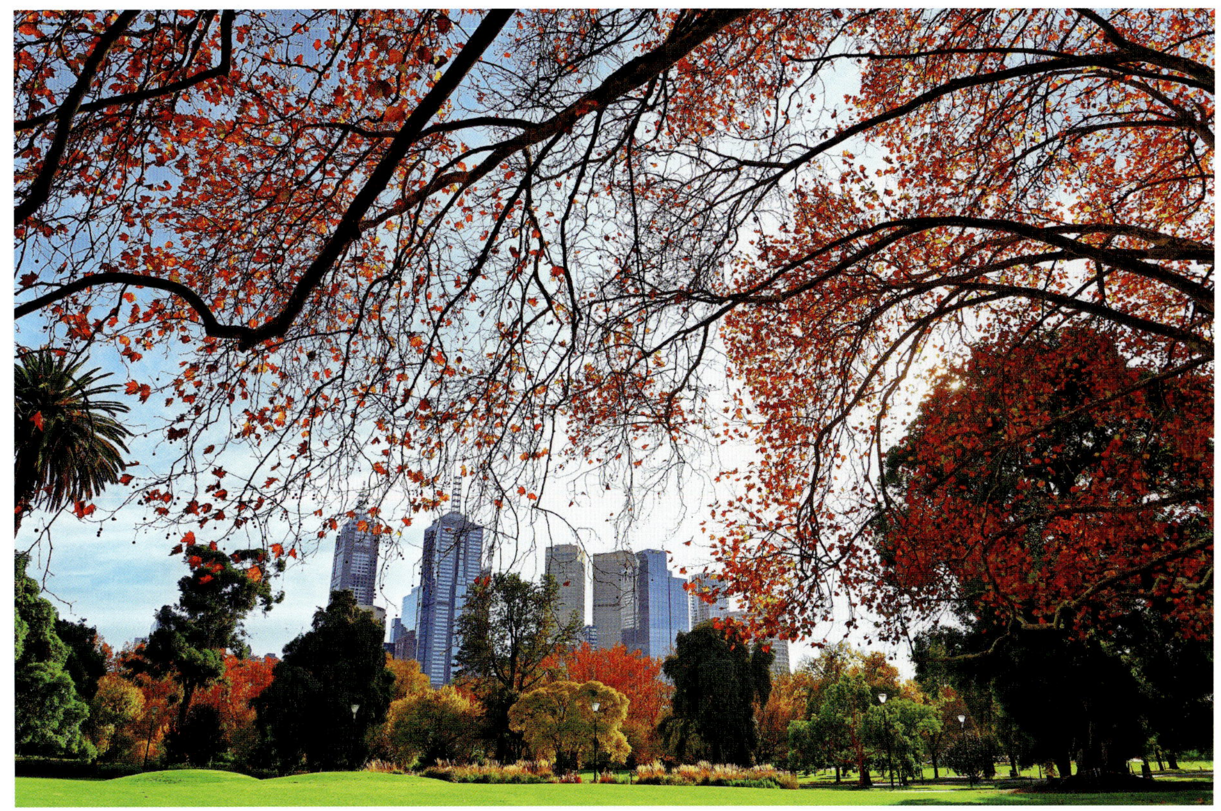

秋 / 攝影: 周兆年
Autumn by Zhou Zhaonian

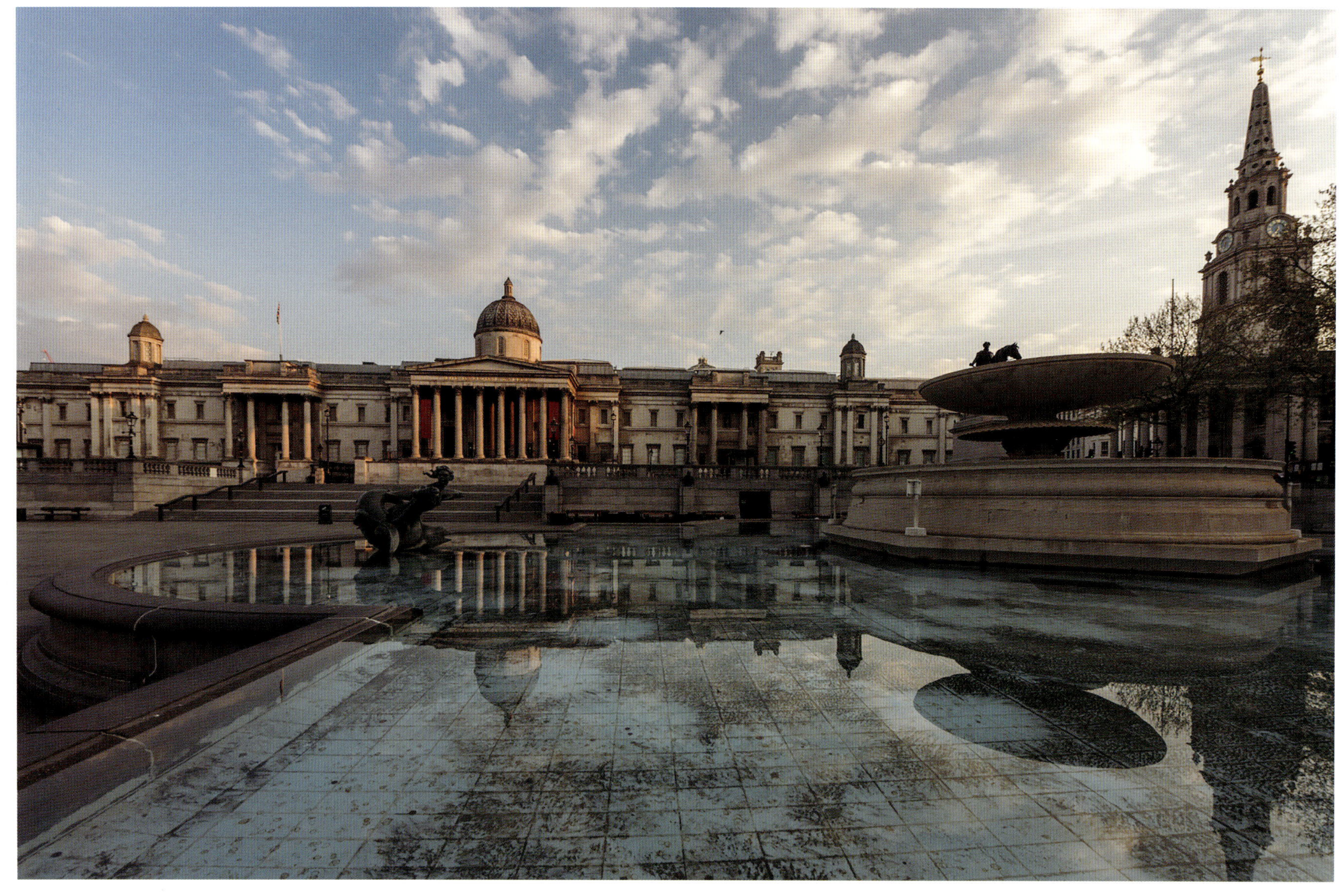

特拉法加廣場噴泉的倒影
Reflections in Trafalgar Square Fountains by Nick Jackson

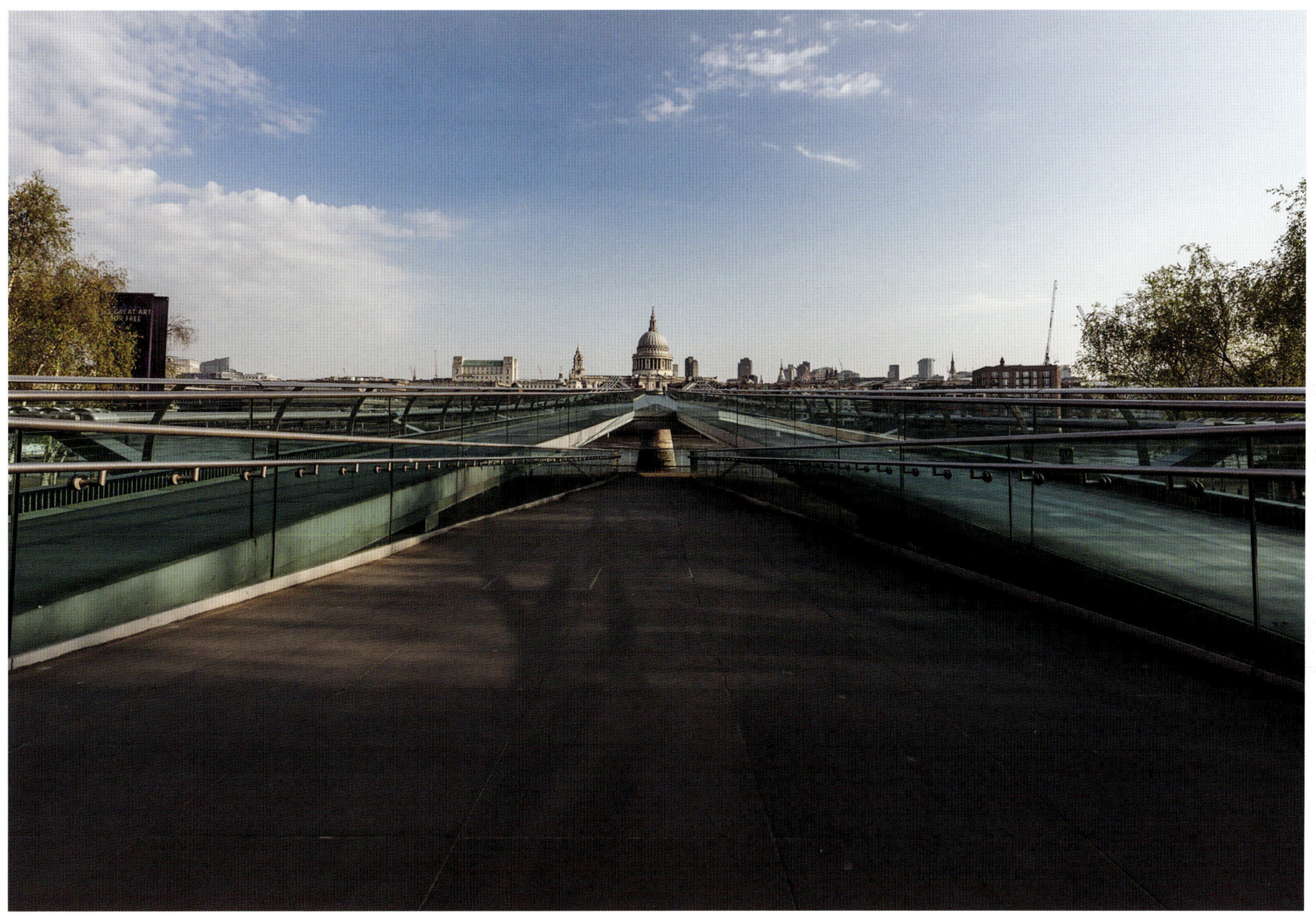

封鎖期間的千禧橋
Millennium Bridge During Lockdown by Nick Jackson

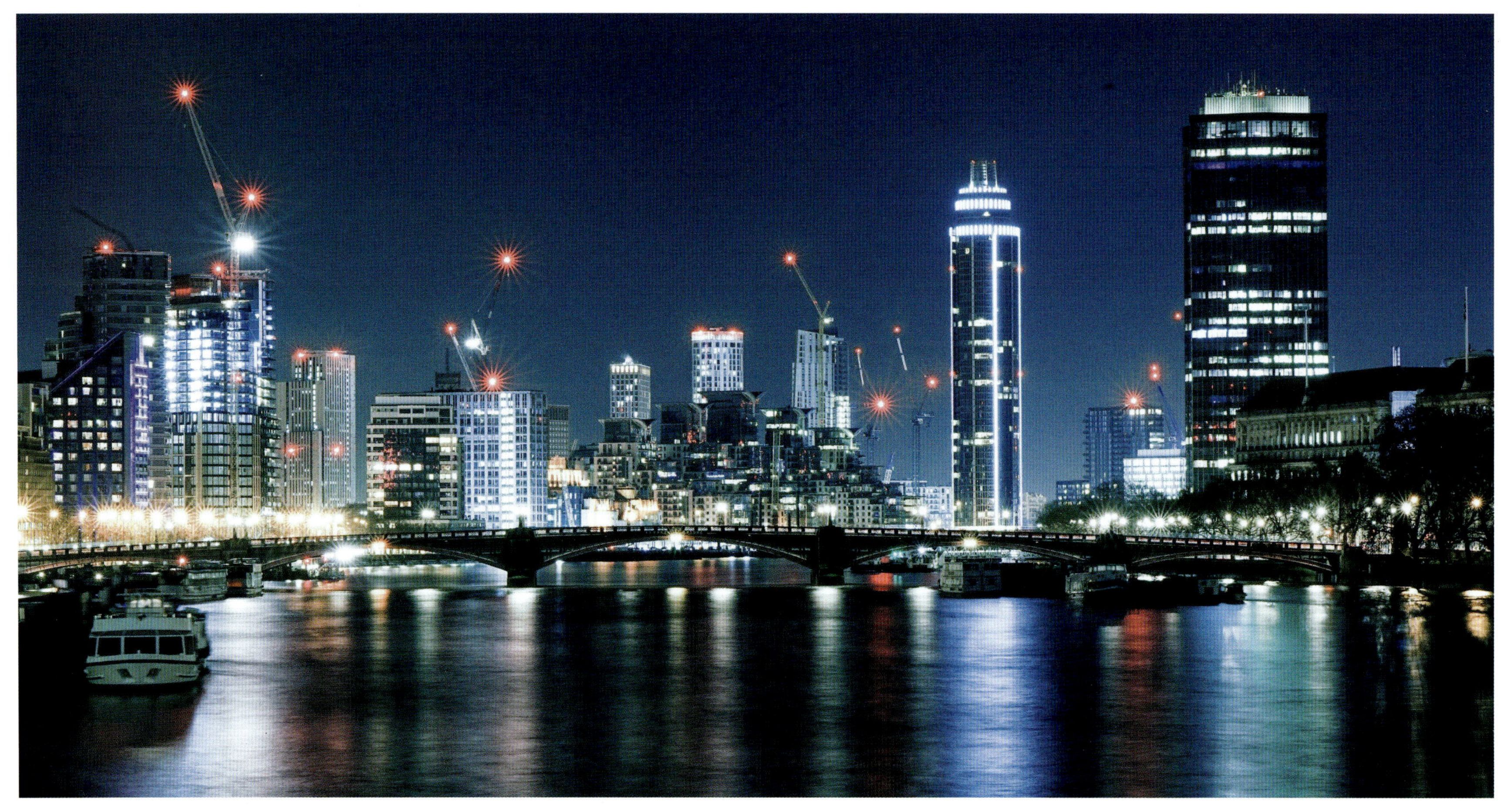

日與夜倫敦 / 攝影: 蔡林宇
Day and Night of London by Cai Linyu

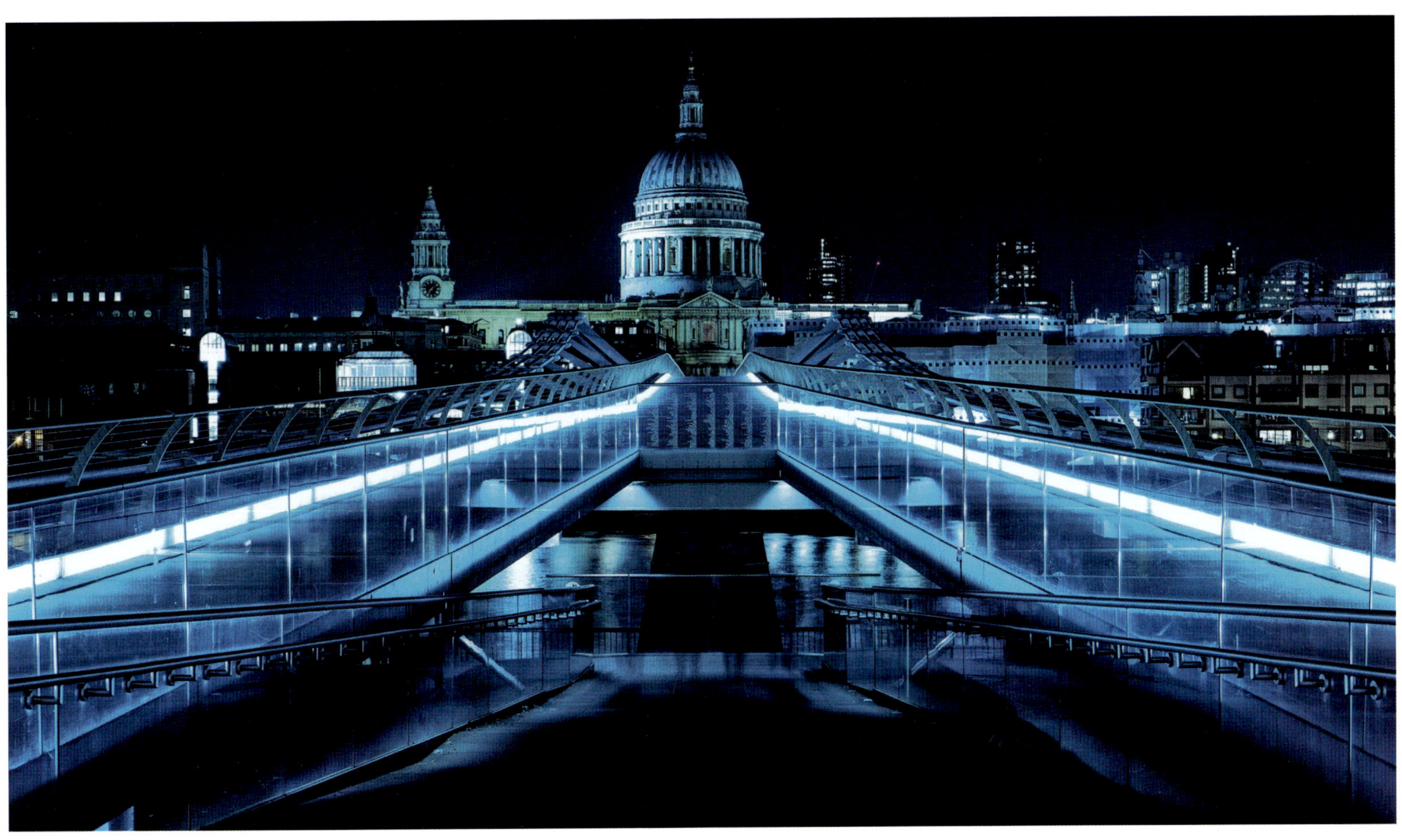

聖保羅
St Pauls by Dan Waller LRPS

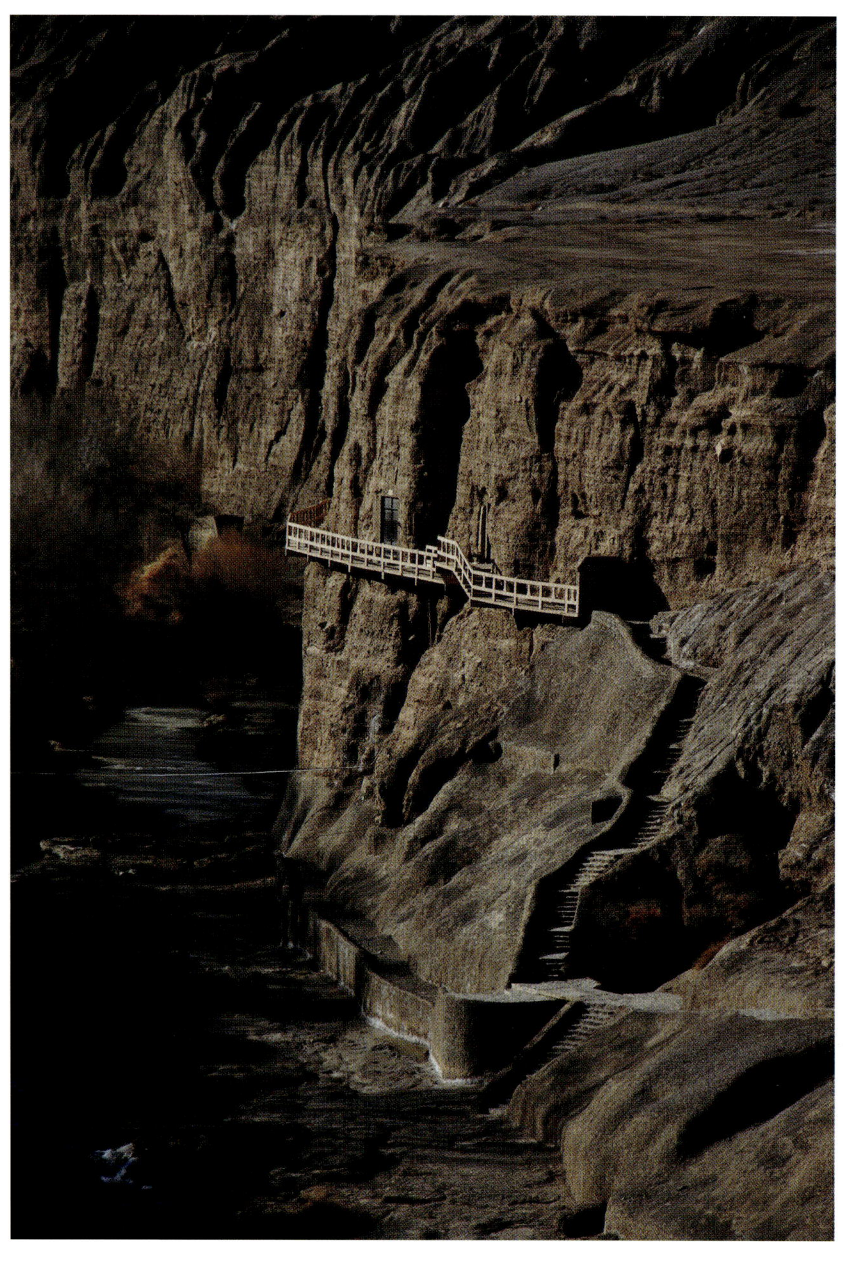

榆林石窟 / 攝影: 吕愛
Yulin Grottoes by Lv Ai

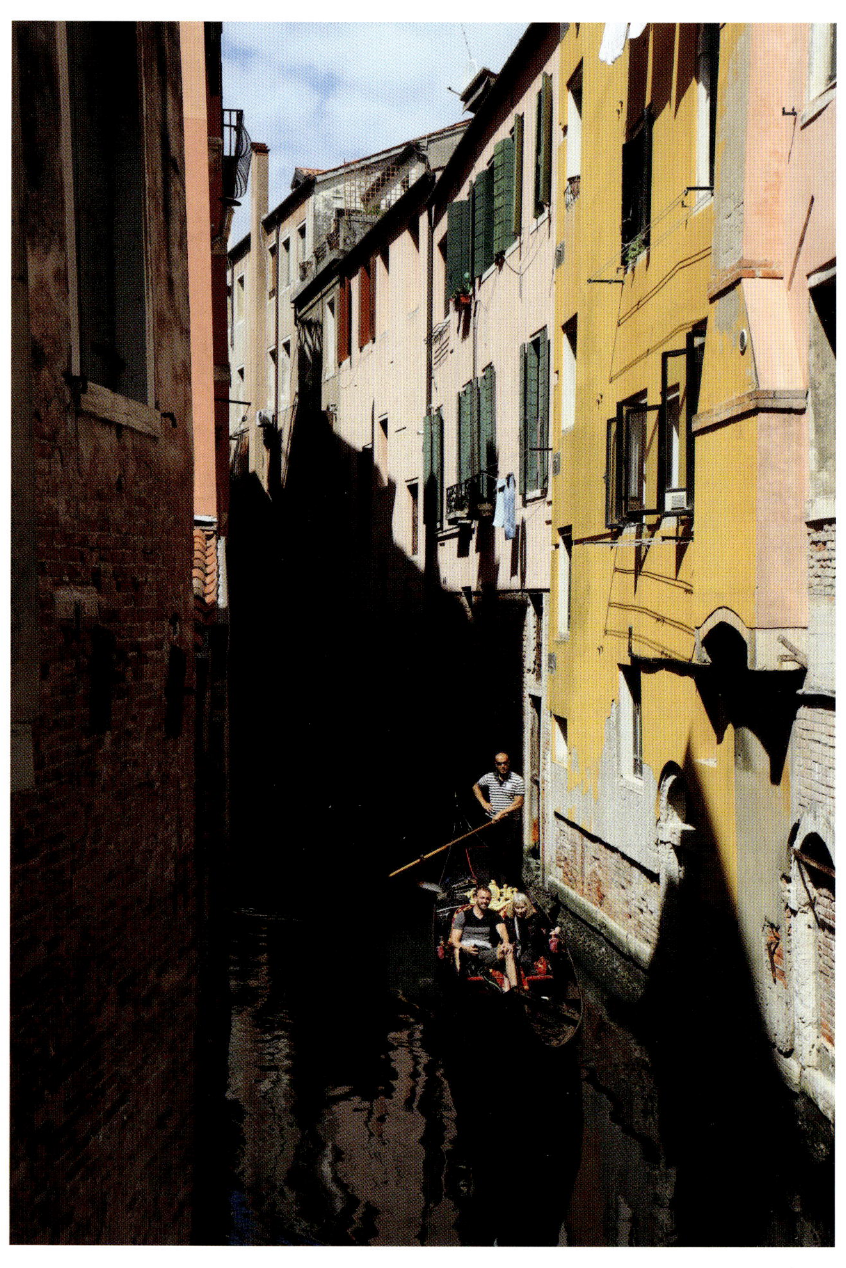

光影 / 攝影: 白丹珩
Light and Shadow by Bai Danheng

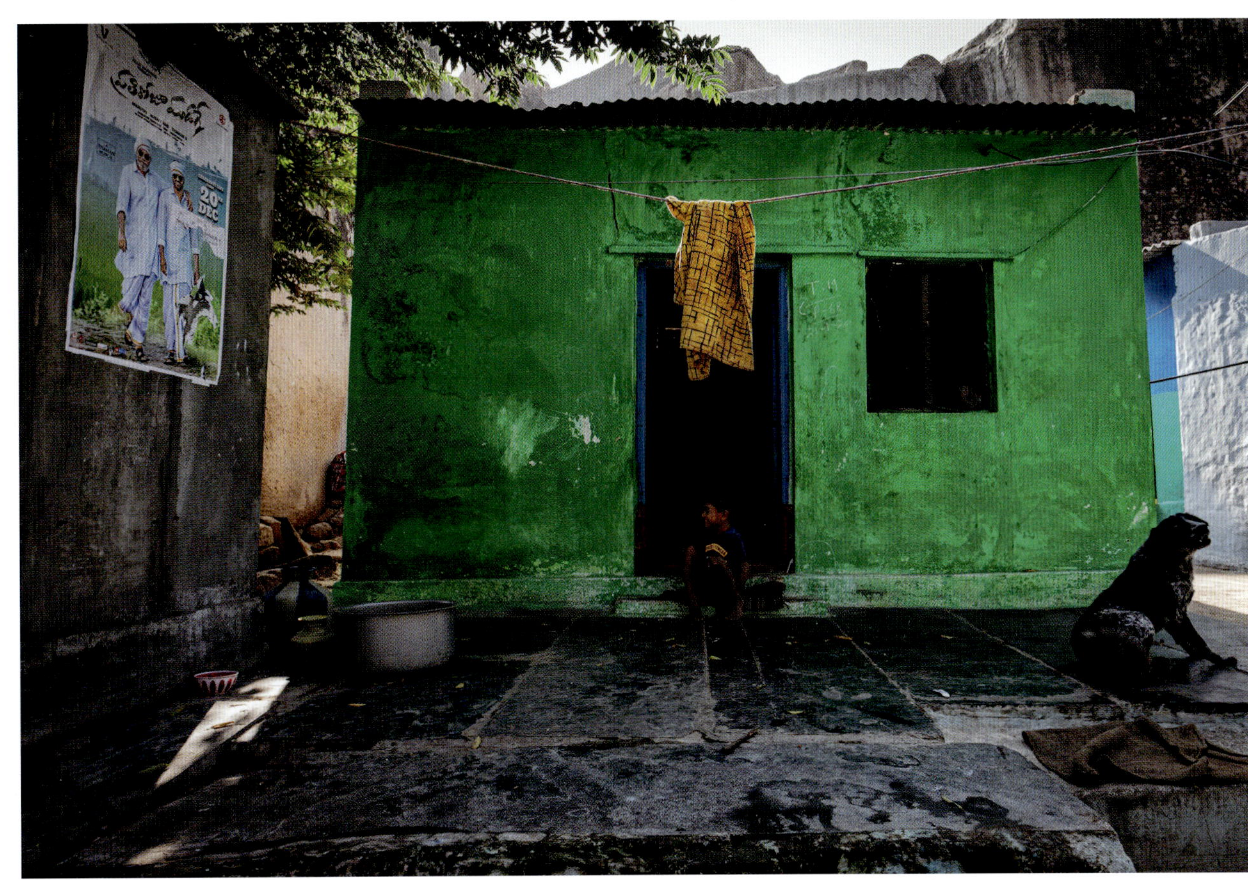

亨比村莊
Village Scene, Hampi
by David Pollard ARPS

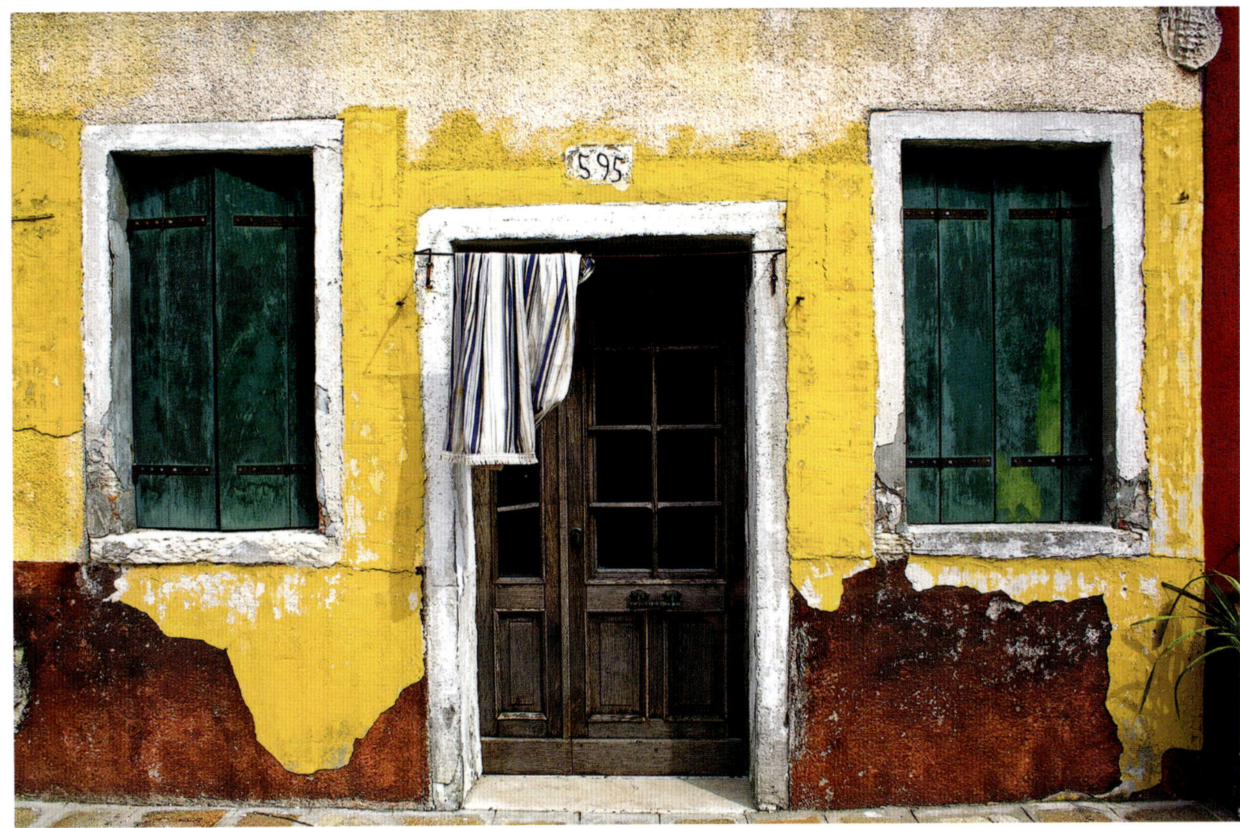

黄房子
Yellow House by John Probert

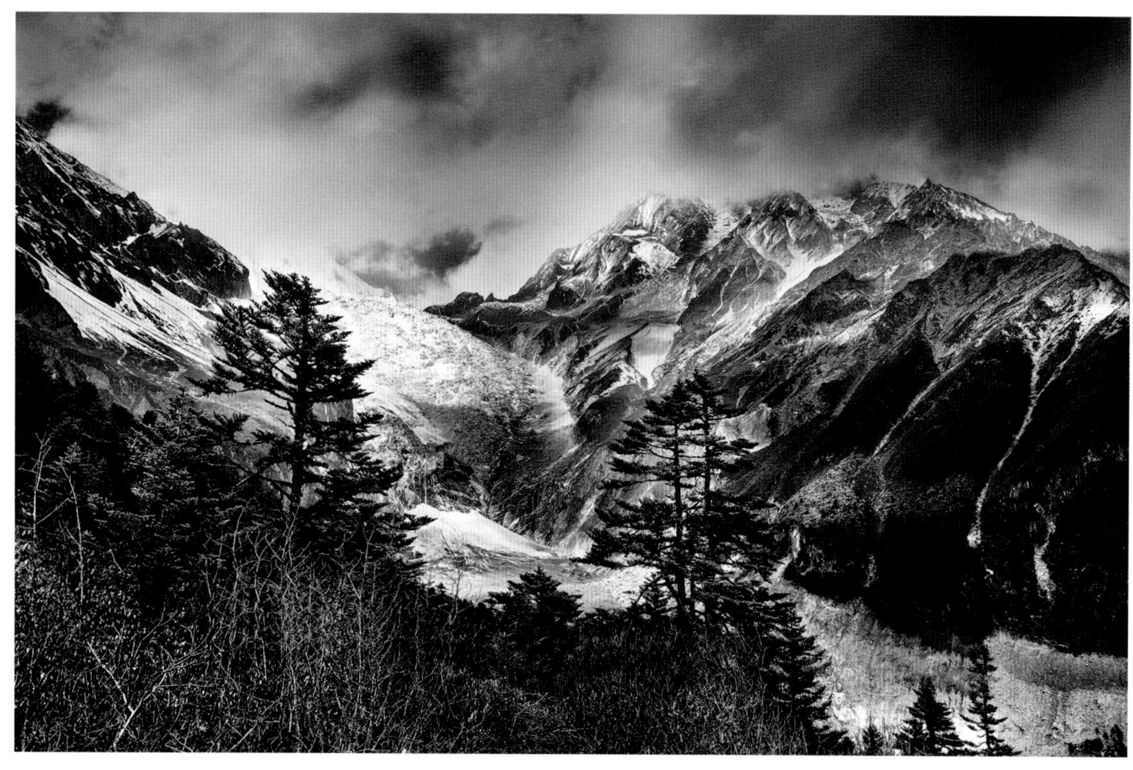

風雲貢嘎山 / 攝影: 周杰祥
Wind and Cloud Gongga Mountain
by Zhou Jiexiang

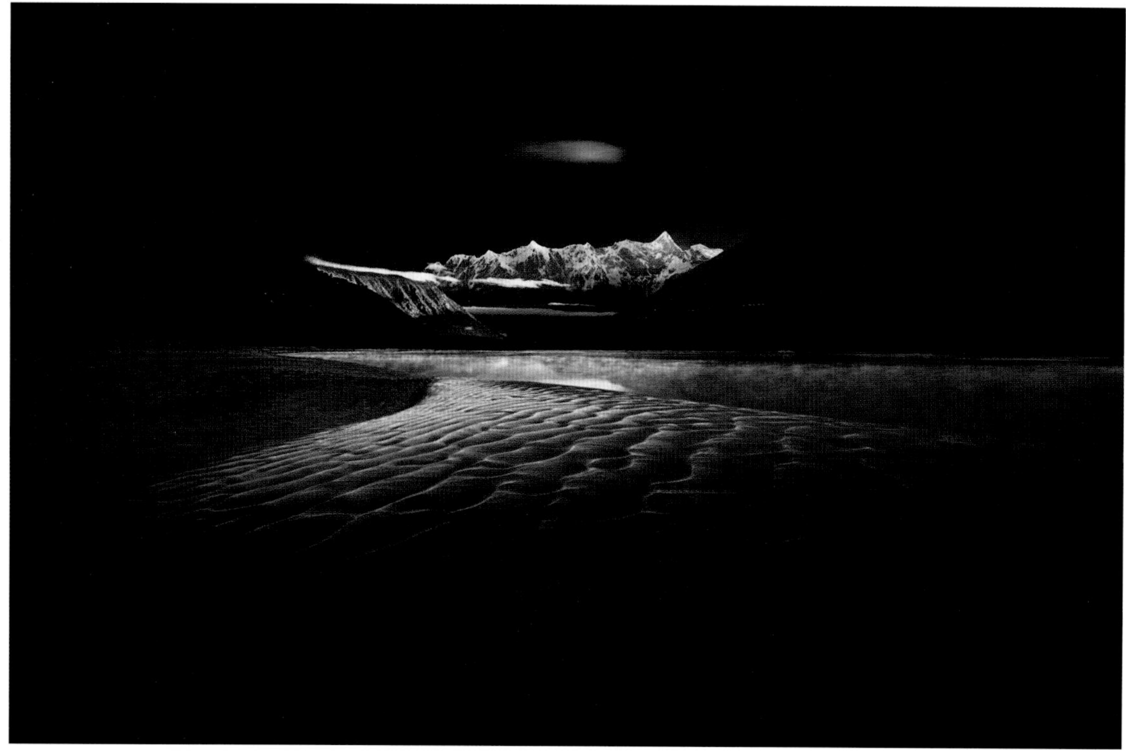

南迦巴瓦峰的印象 / 攝影: 周杰祥
Impression of Namjagbarwa
by Zhou Jiexiang

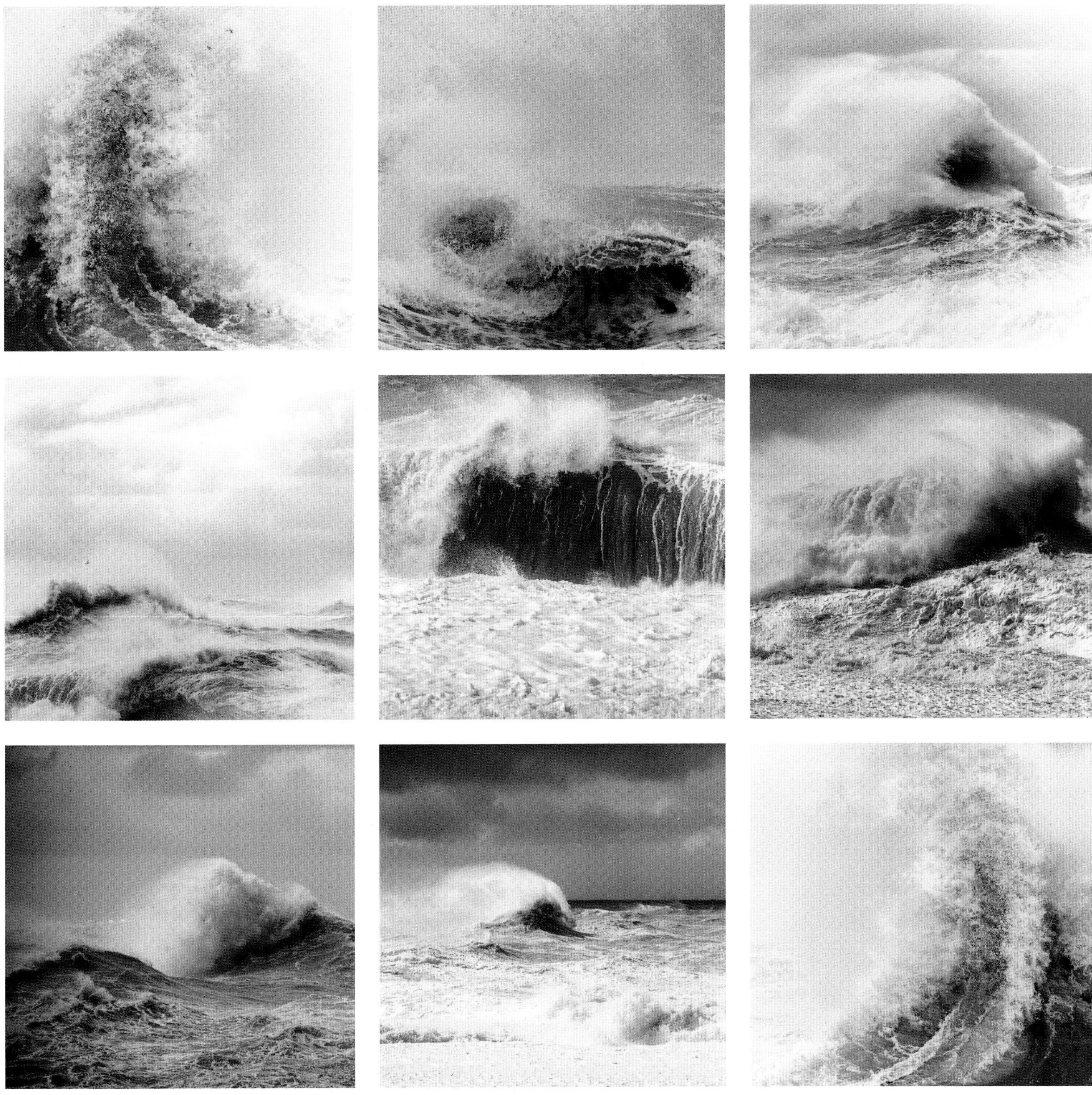

九浪
Nine Waves by Karen Brickley LRPS

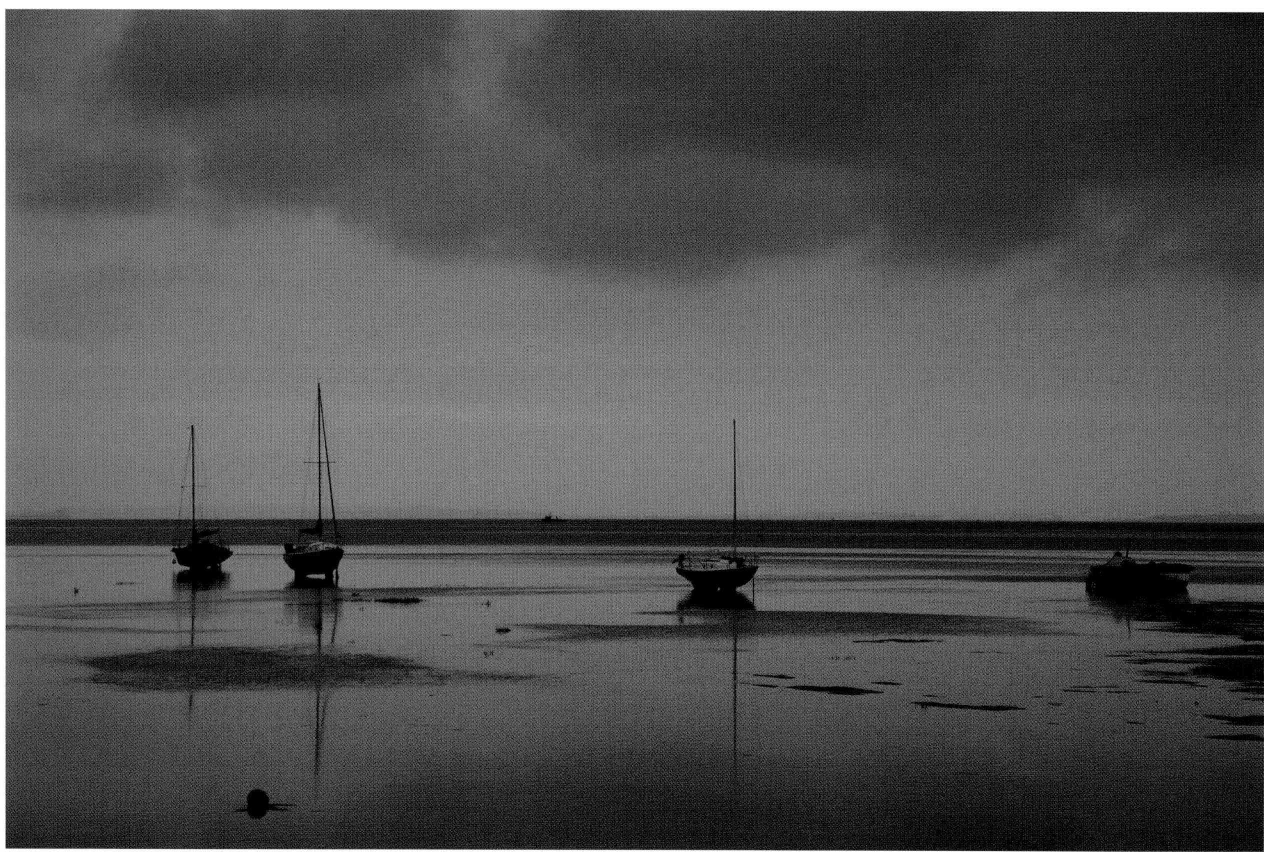

低潮期
Low Tide
by Mike Walker

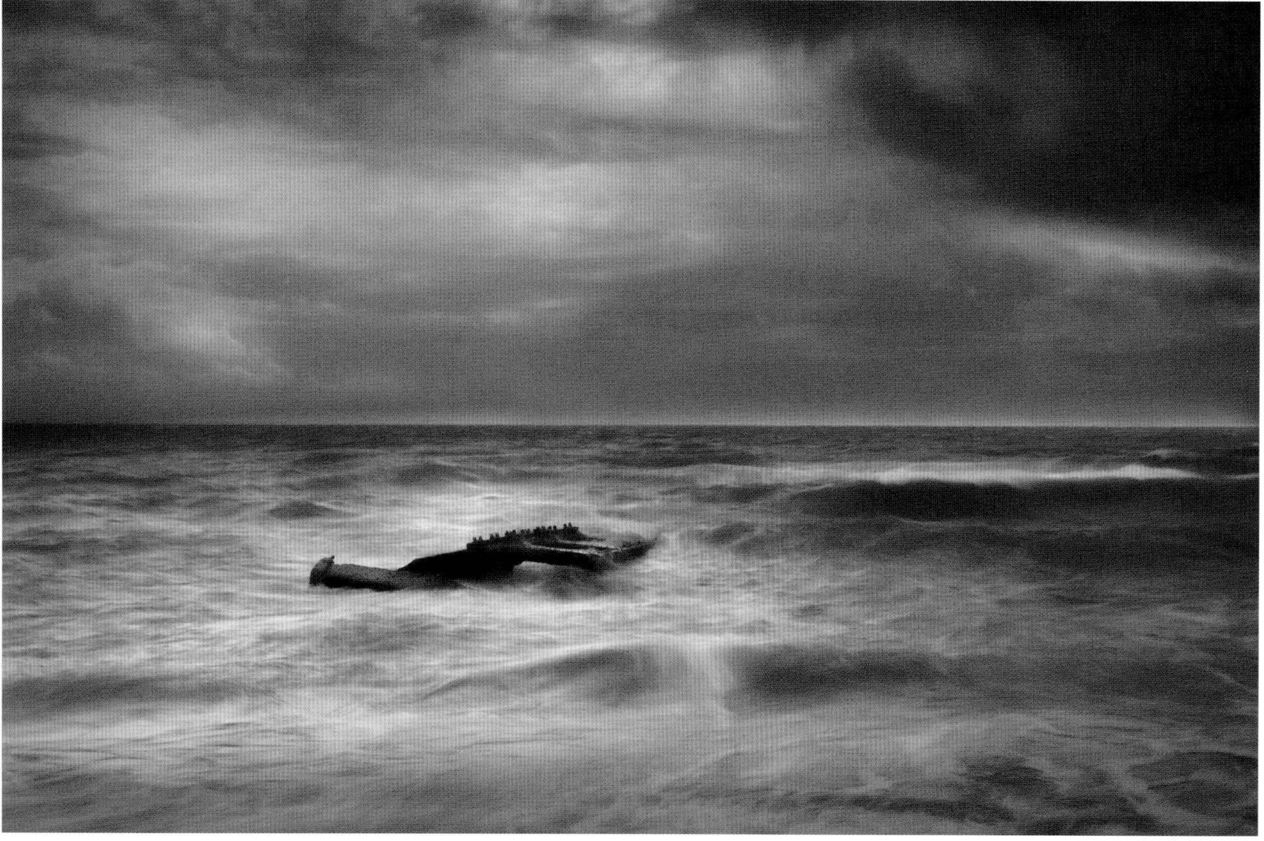

荒野殘骸
Wild Wreck
by Sue Oakford

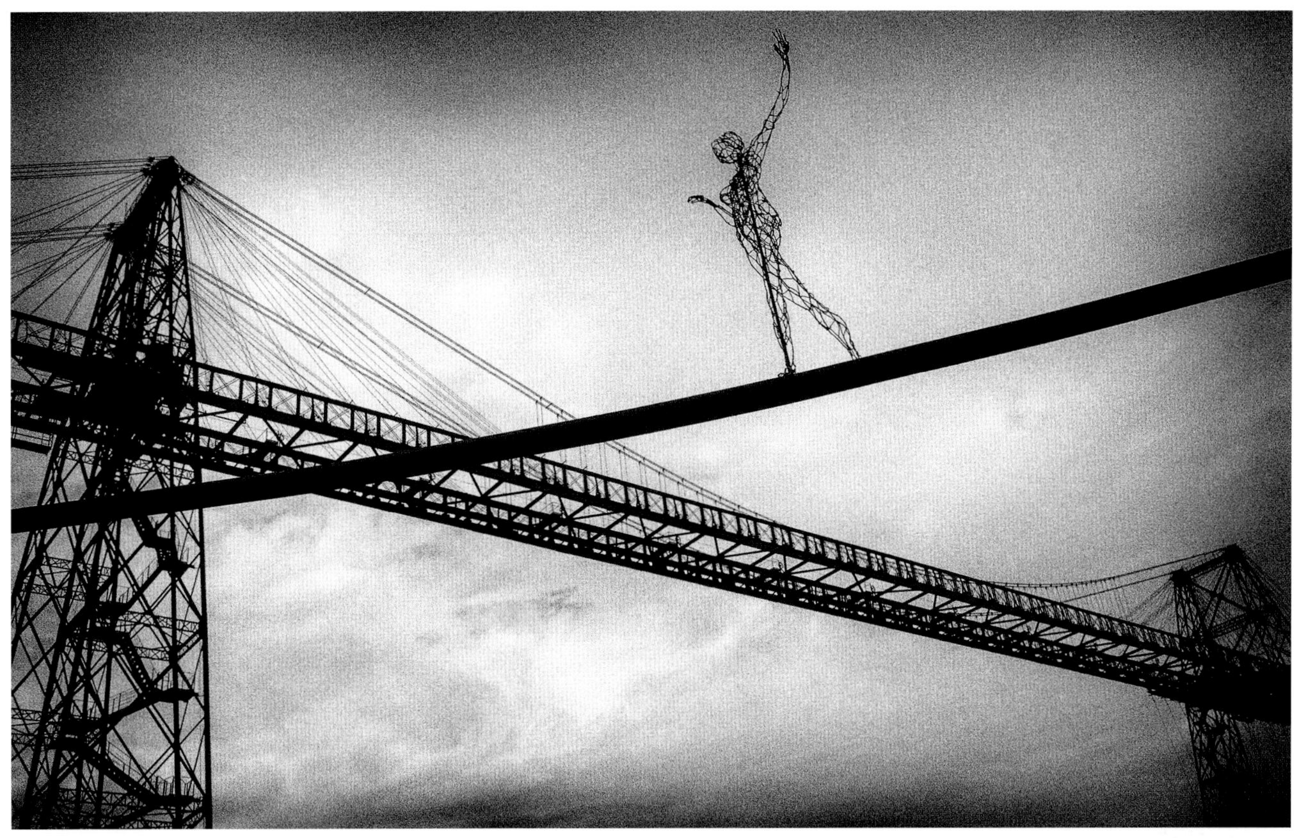

走鋼絲的人
Wire Walker
by Roger Ford FRPS

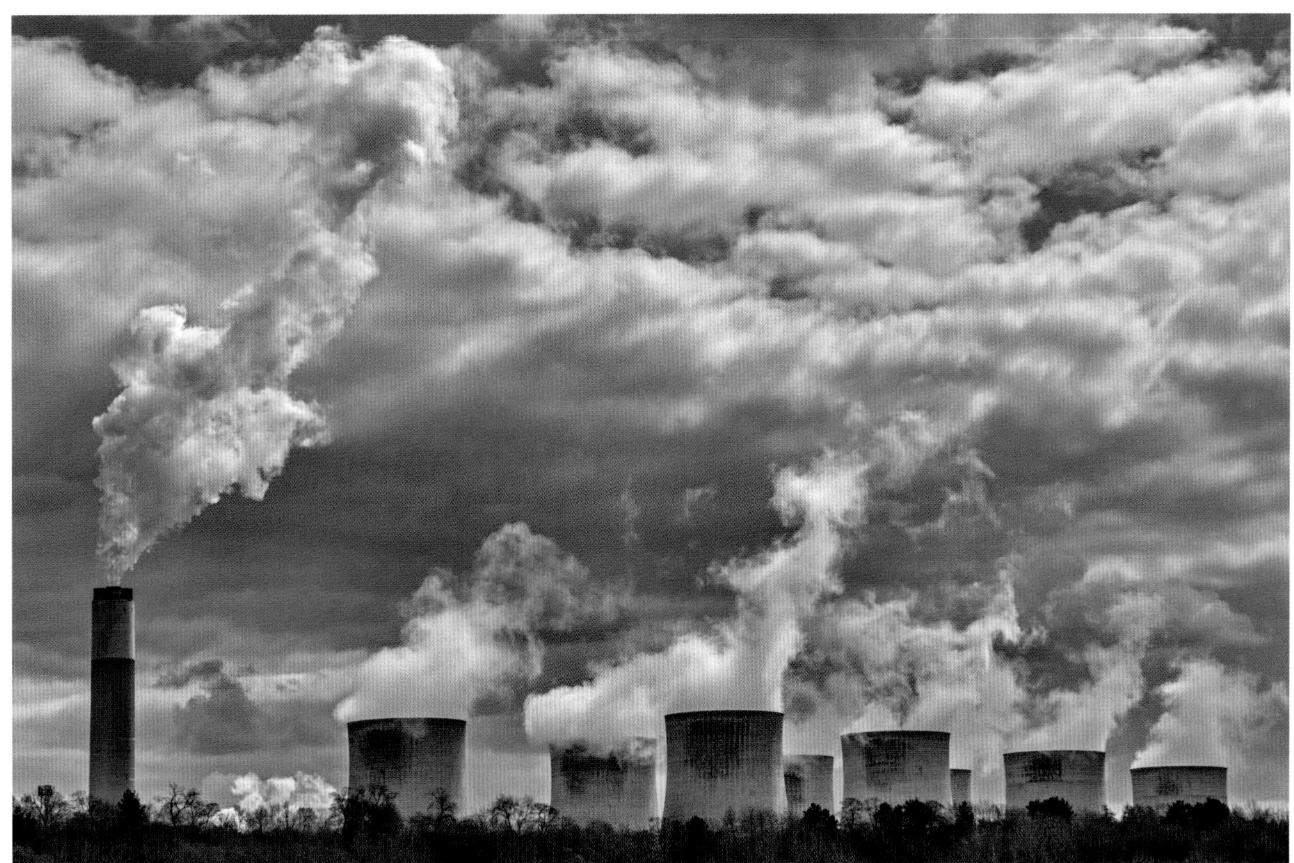

冷却塔和烟囱
Cooling Towers and Chimney
by Dawn Clifford LRPS

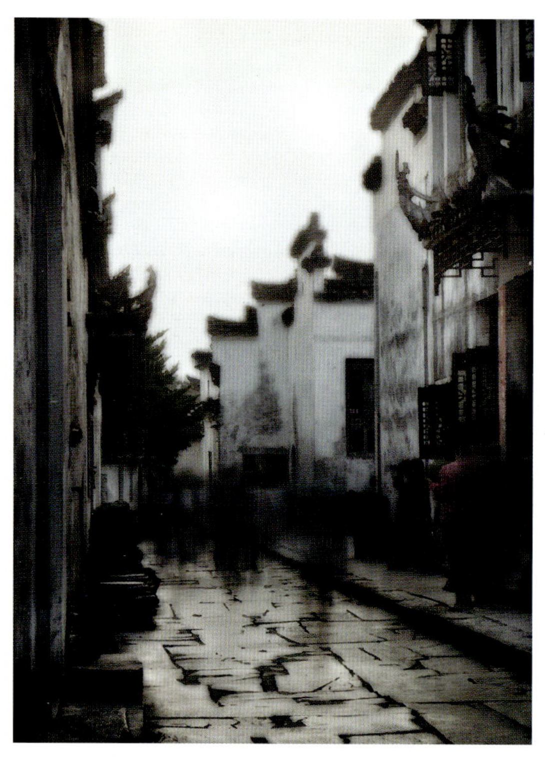

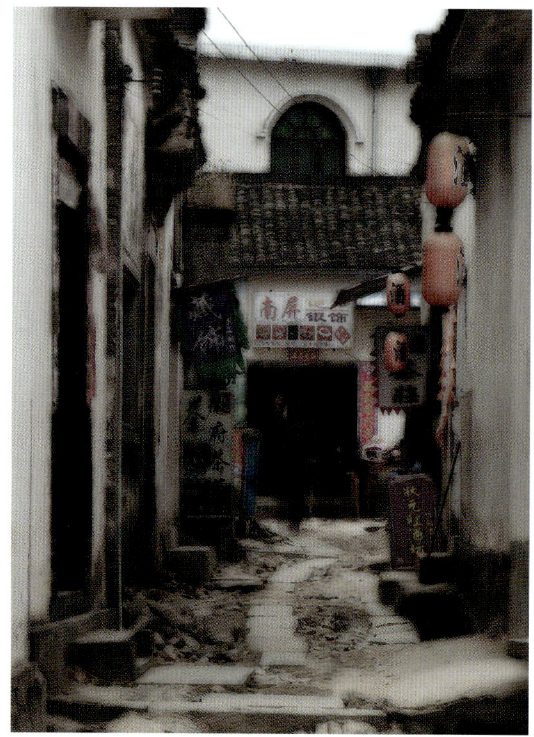

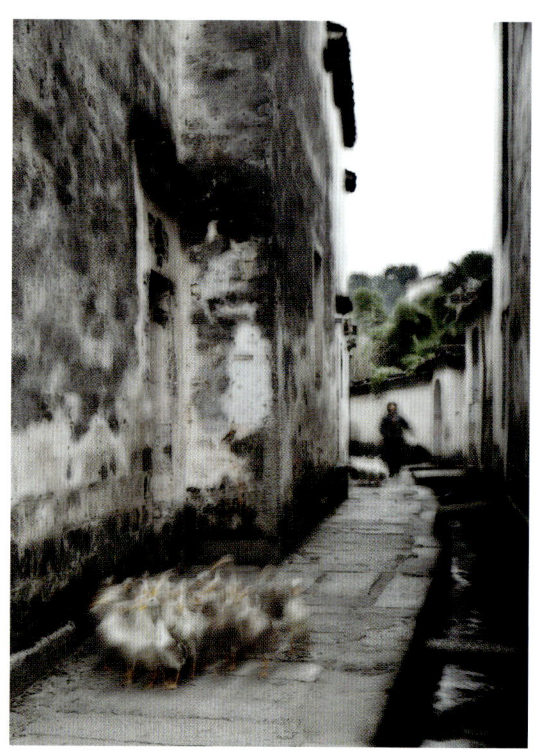

小道 / 攝影: 牟嘉
Trail by Mou Jia

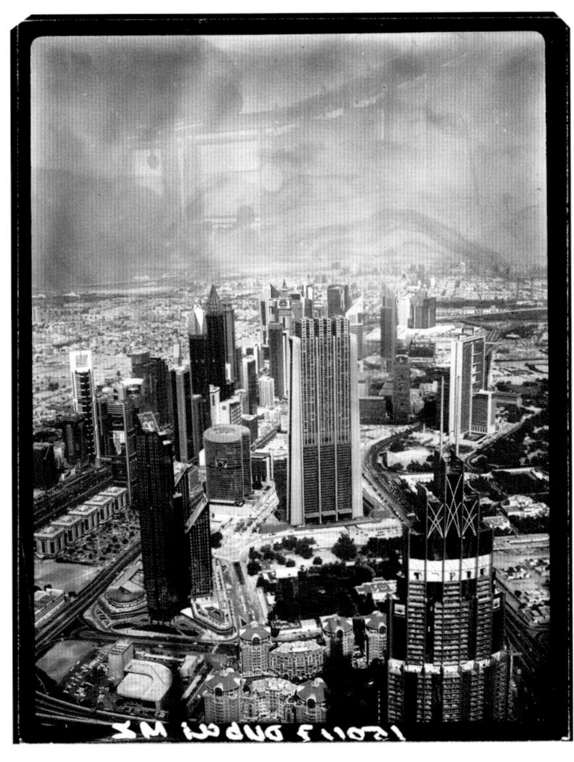

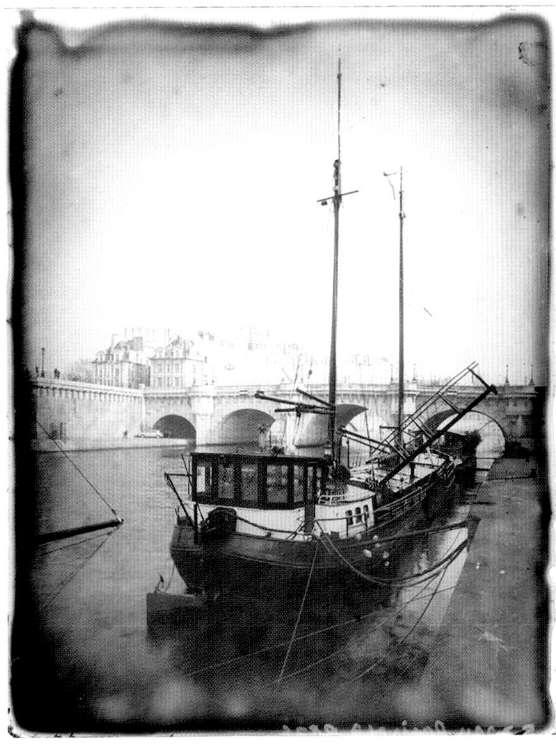

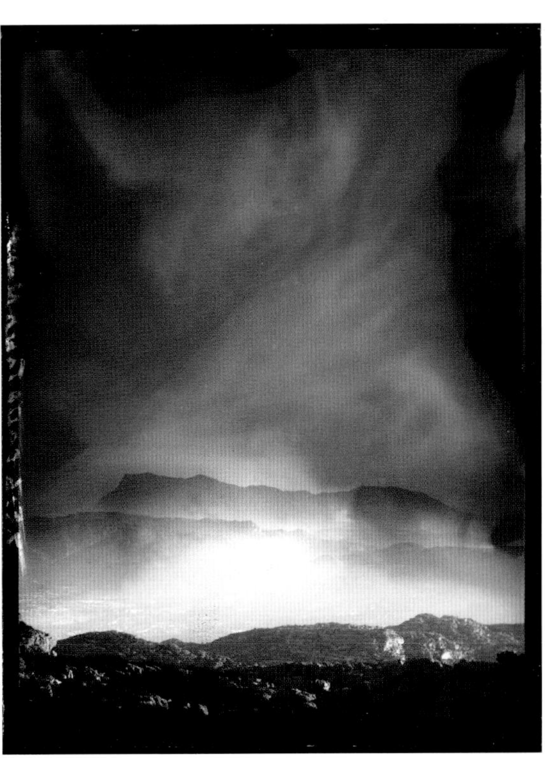

迪拜, 塞納河一角, 南非好望角 (使用玻璃幹版攝制) / 攝影: 章毅
Dubai, A Corner of the Seine, the Cape of Good Hope in South Africa (Daguerreotype)
by Zhang Yi

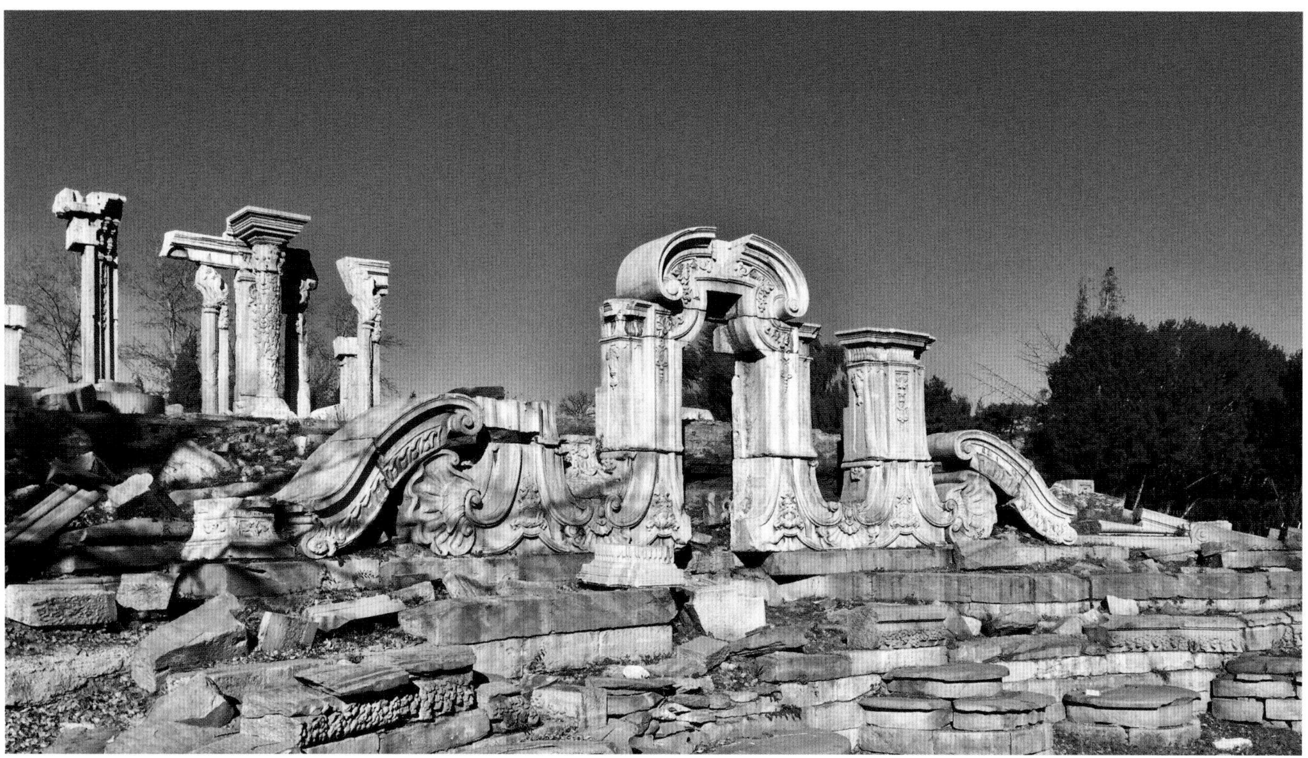

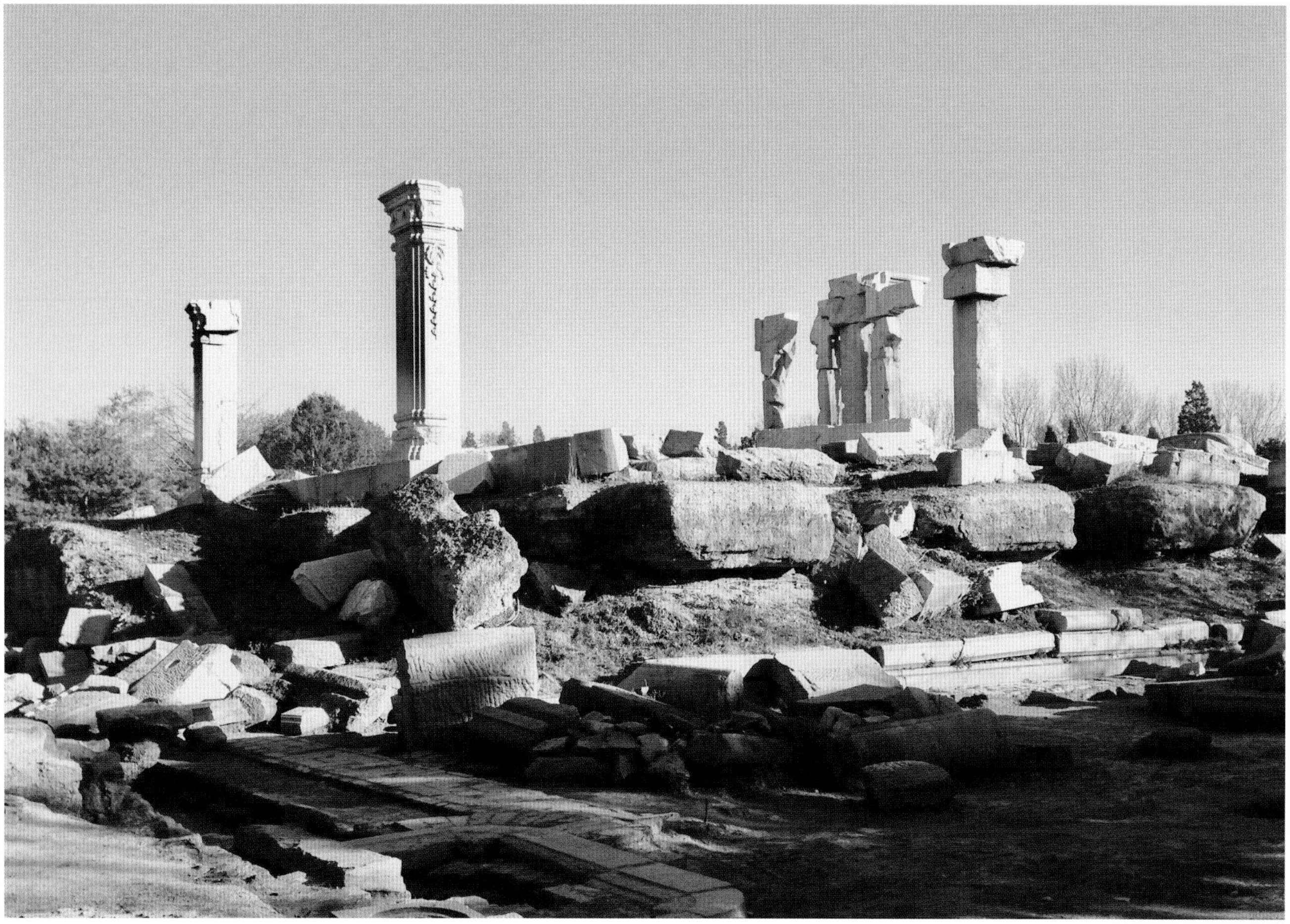

消失的記憶 /
攝影: 劉金城
The Lost Memory
by Liu Jincheng

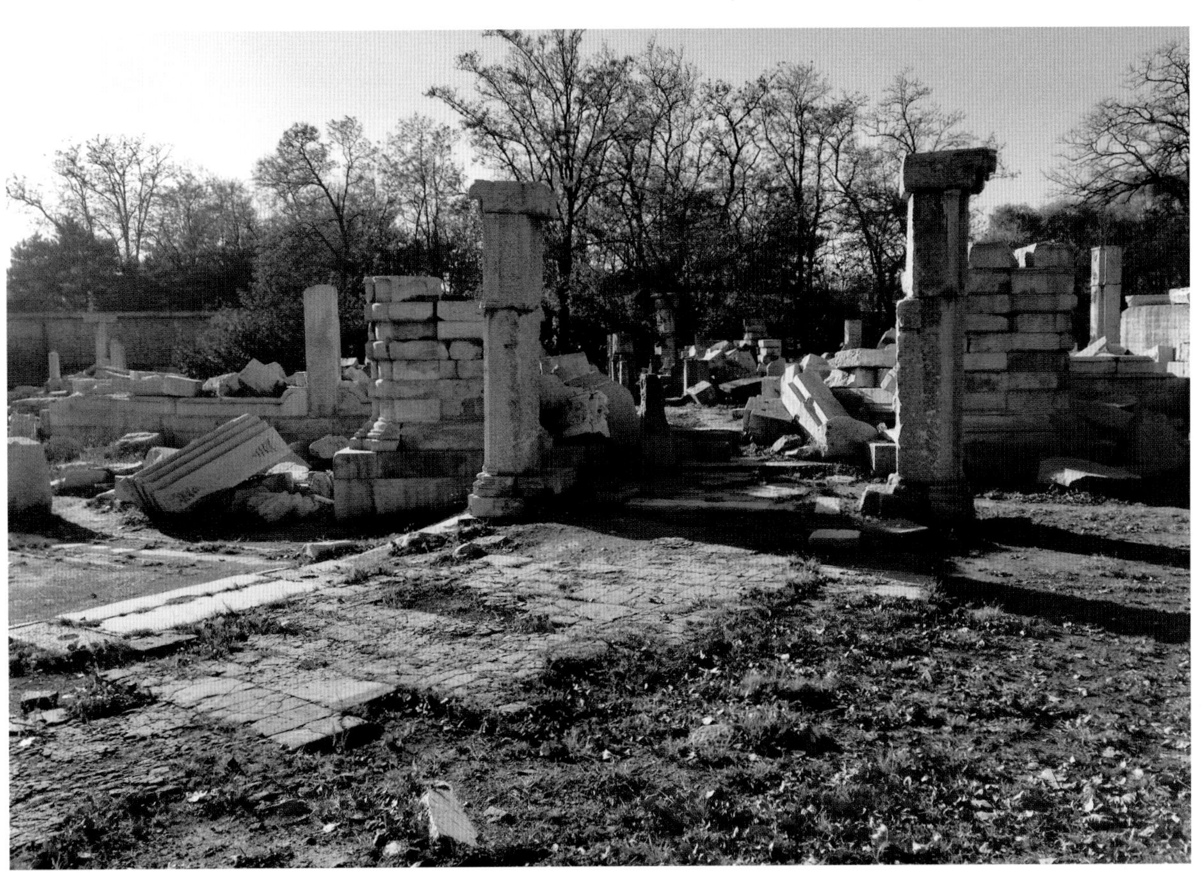

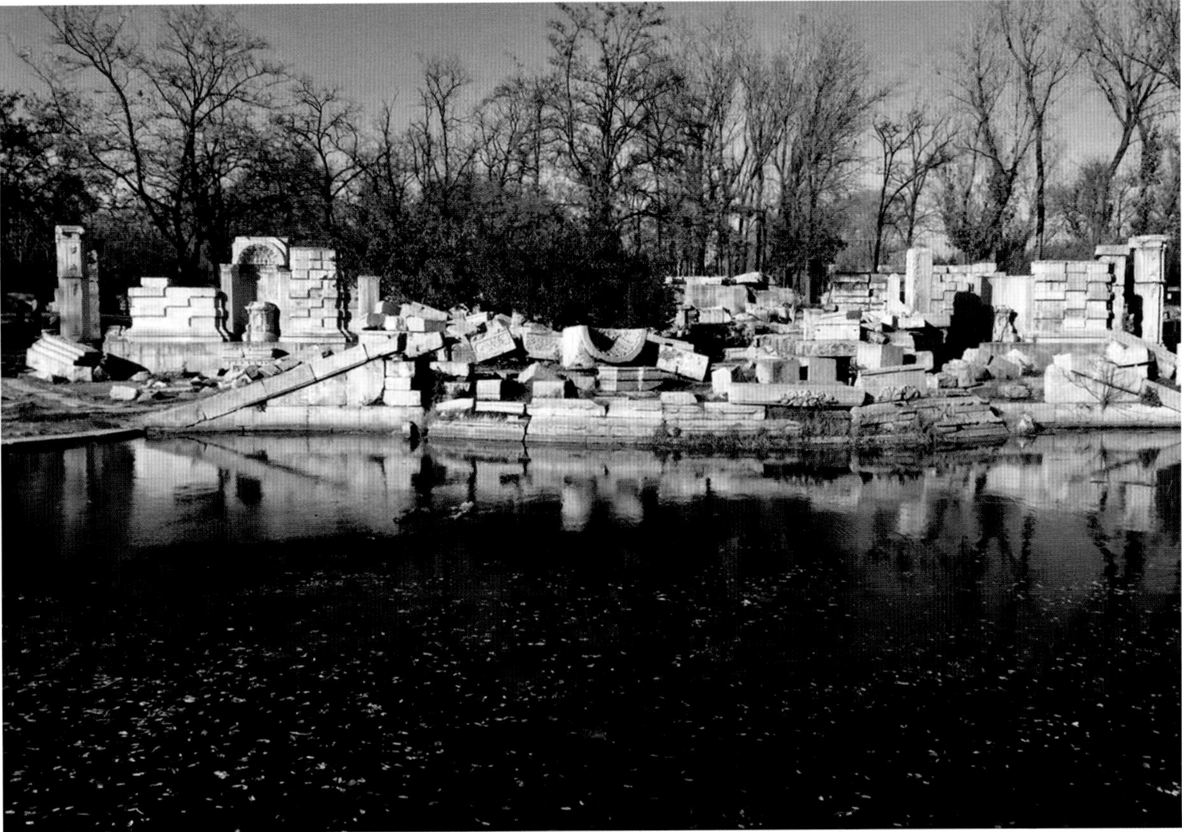

消失的記憶 /
攝影: 劉金城
The Lost Memory
by Liu Jincheng

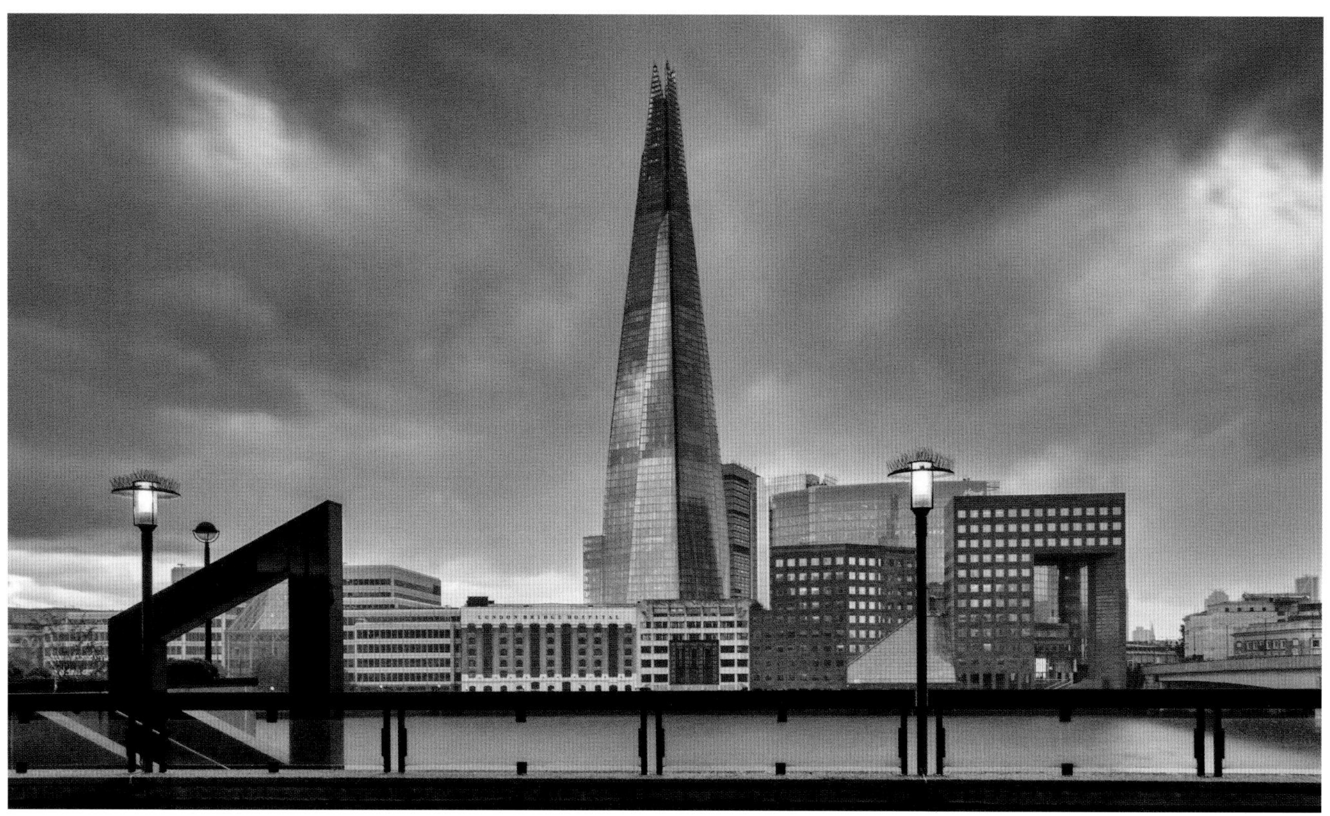

碎片大厦
The Shard
by Philip Brown LRPS

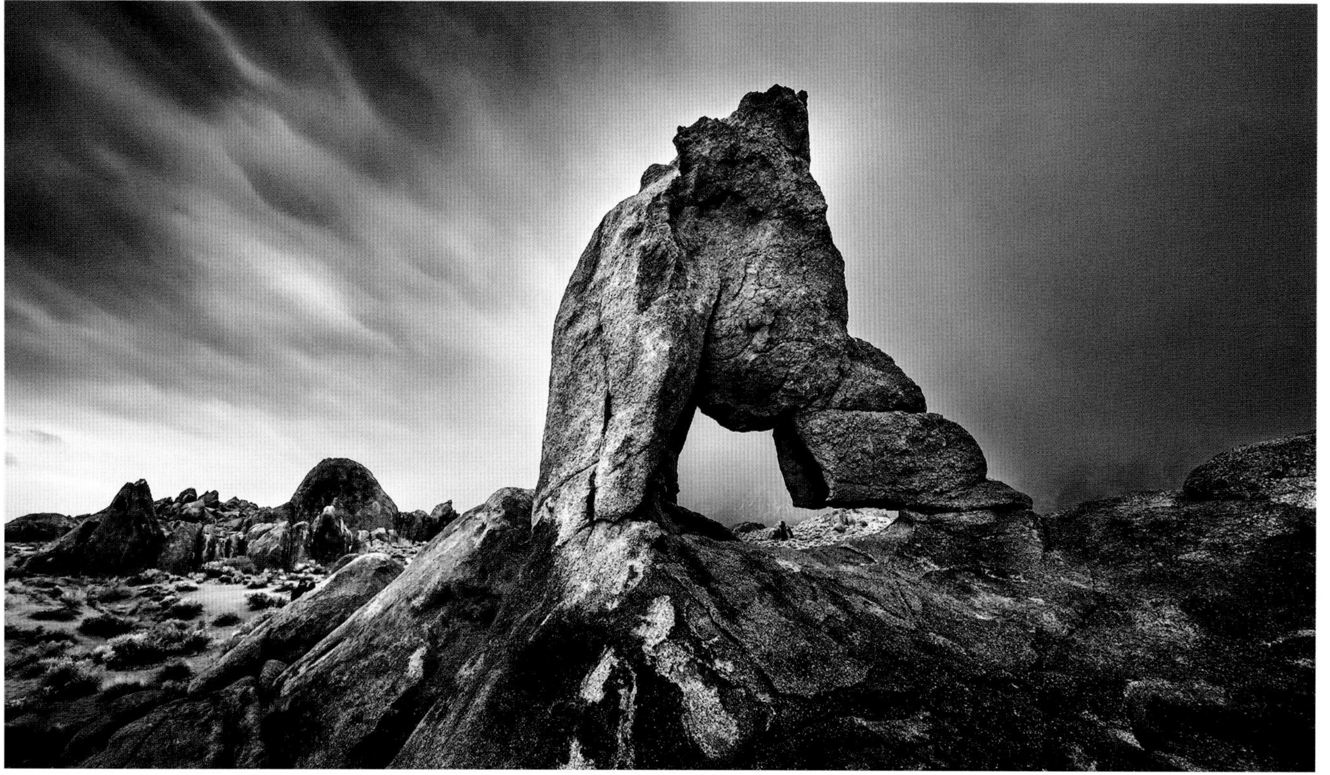

阿拉巴馬山奇石 /
攝影: 黄立亞
Alabama Mountain
Strange Rock
by Huang Liya

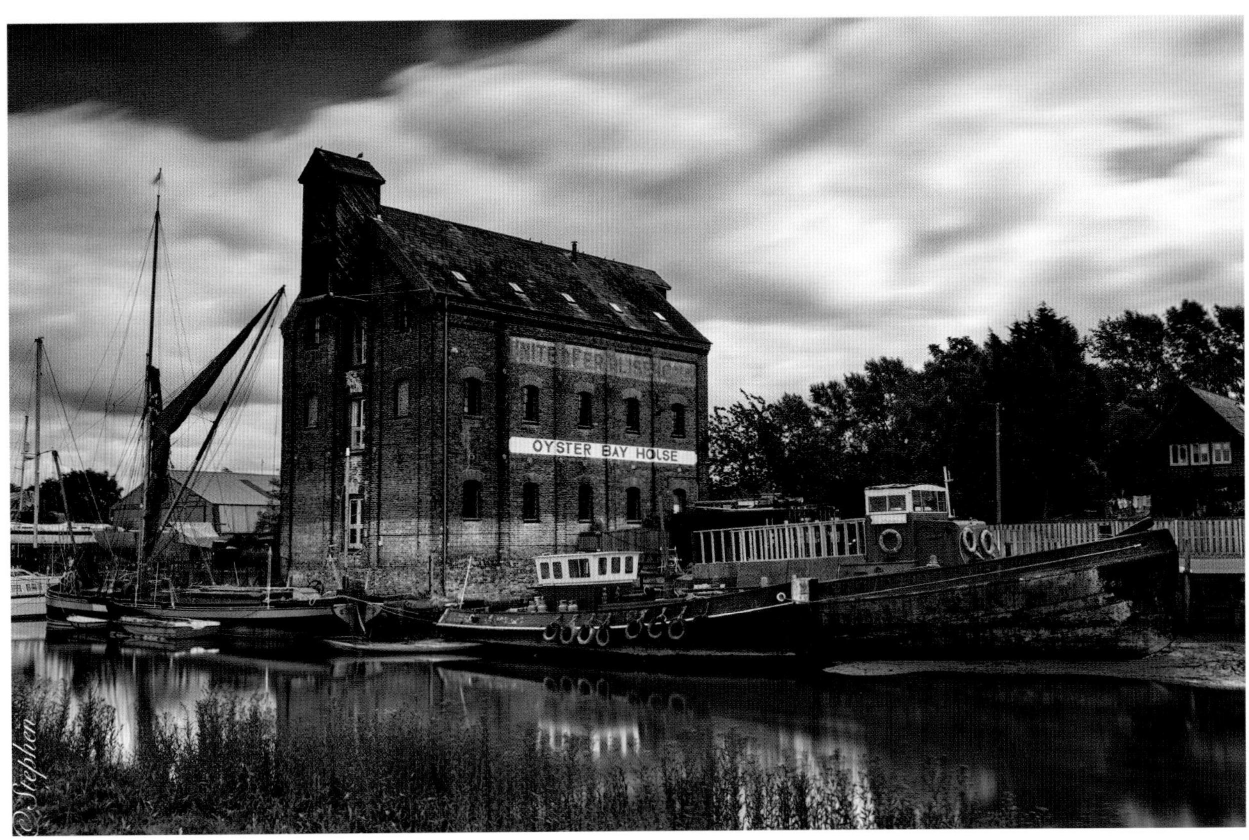

法弗捻姆
Faversham
by Stephen Roberts

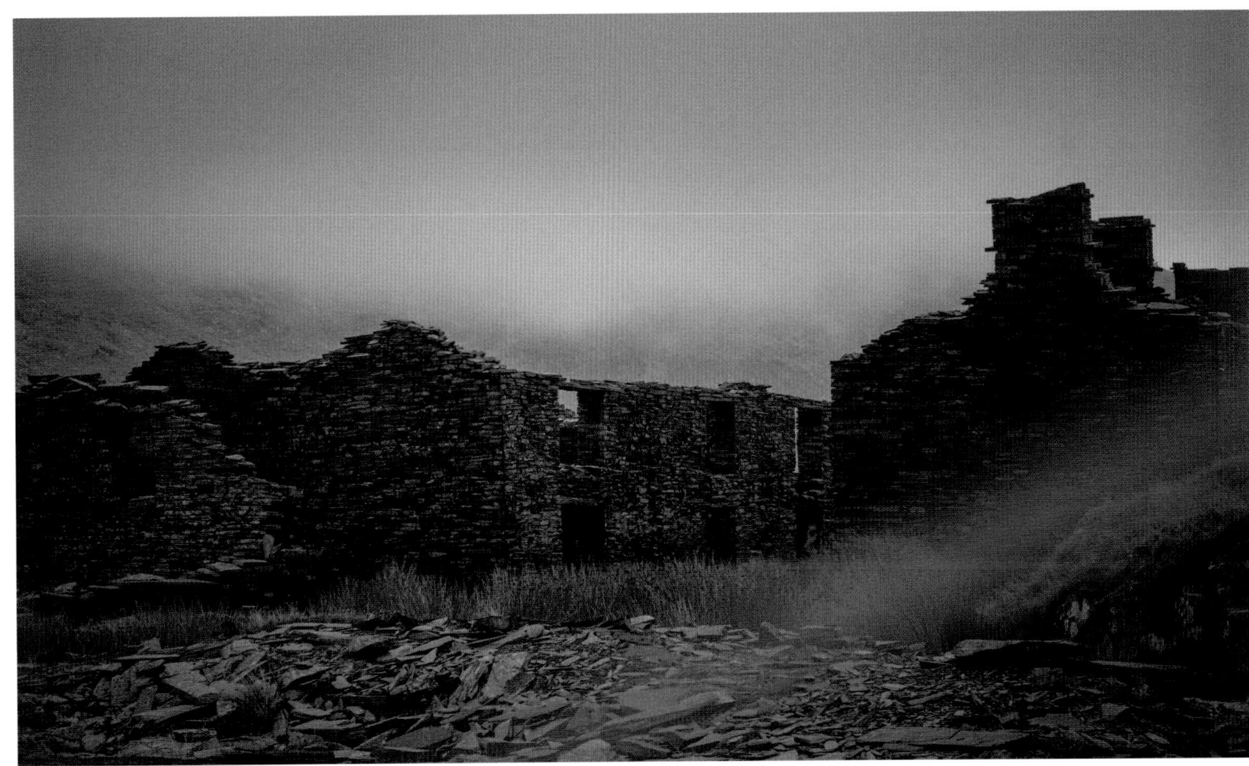

石板礦的霧
Fog at the Slate Mine
by Andy Norman LRPS

WILDLIFE 野生動物

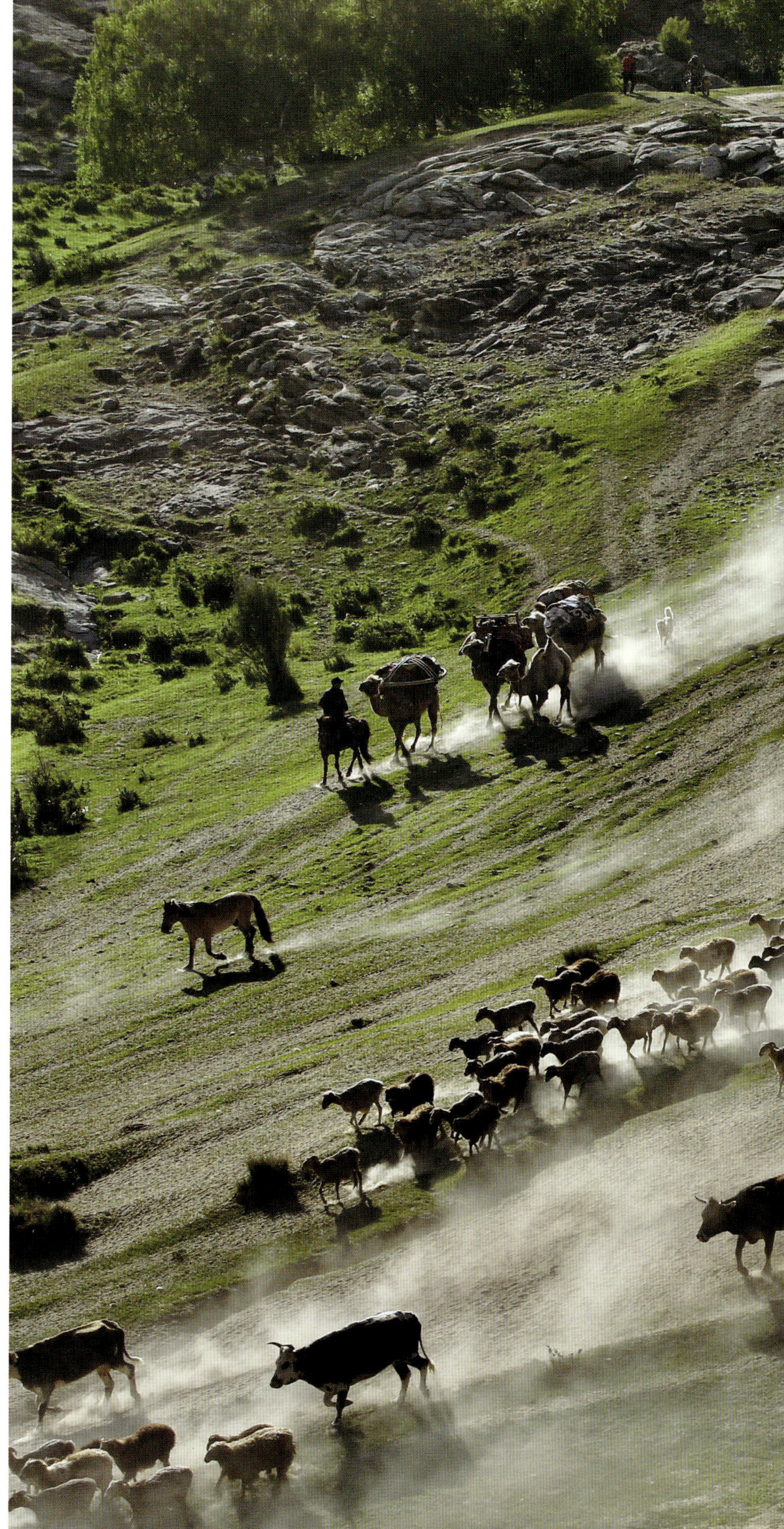

遷徙 / 攝影: 崔明浩
Migration by Cui Minghao

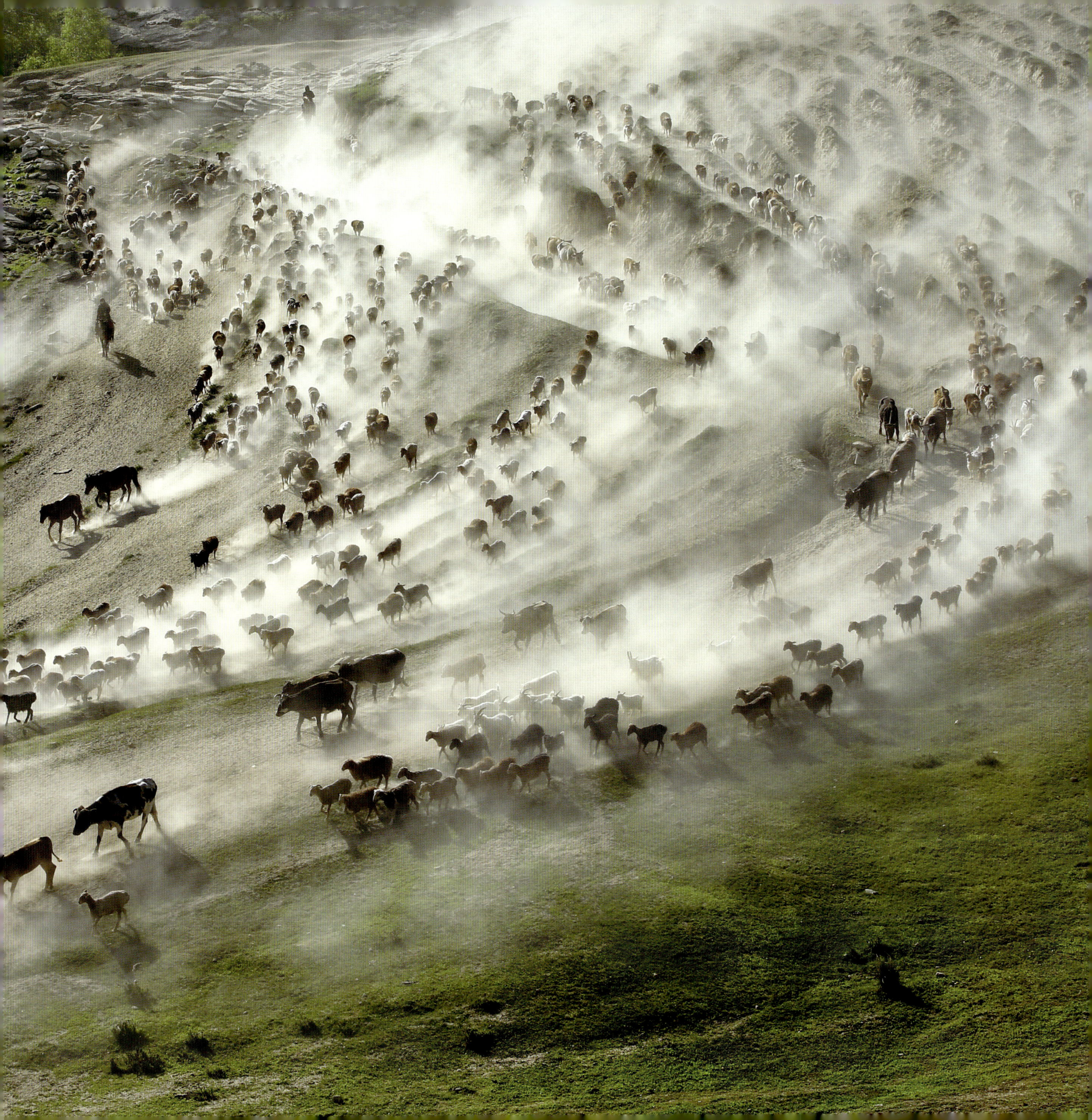

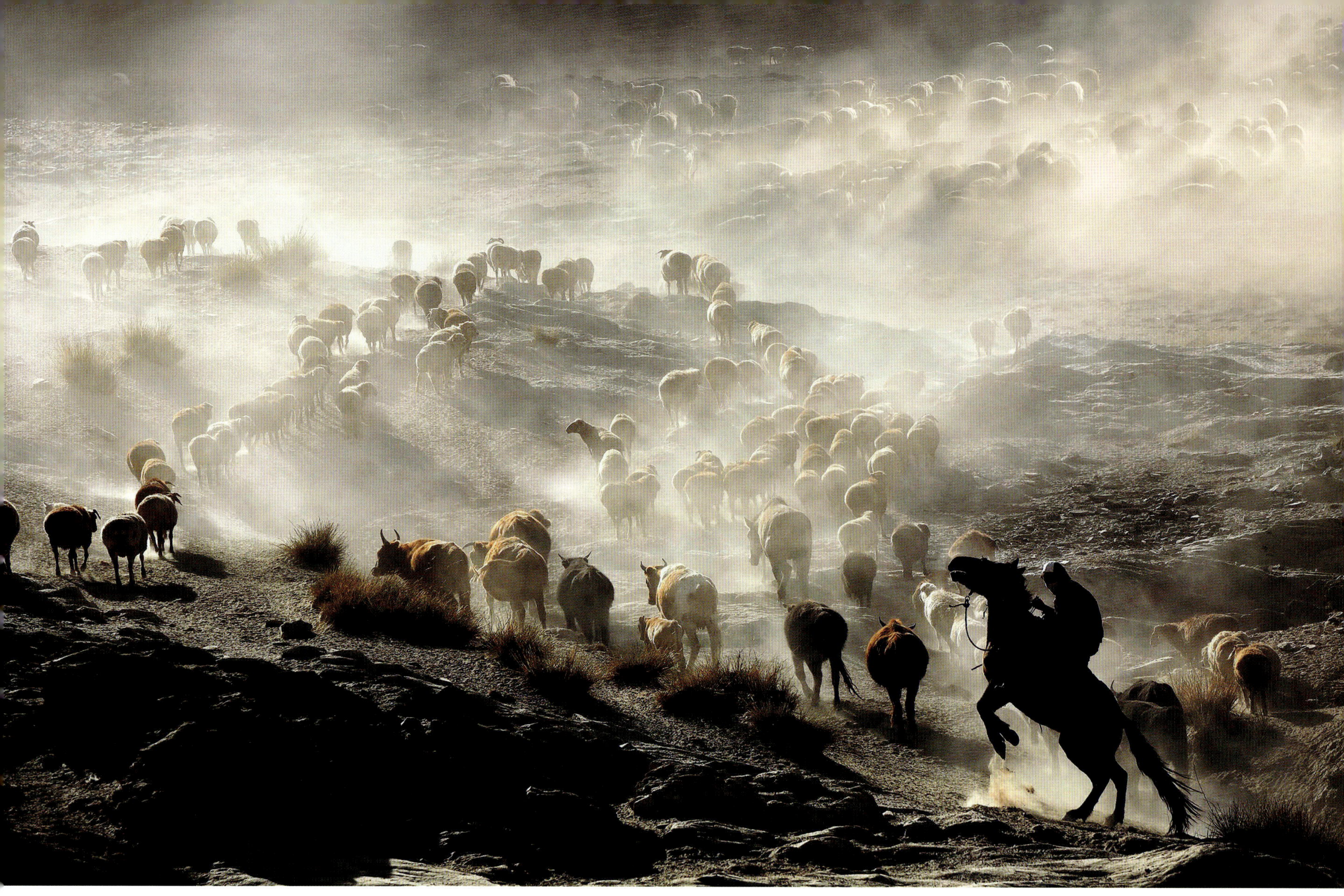

北疆轉場 / 攝影: 黄松辉
North Xinjai Transition by Huang Songhui FRPS

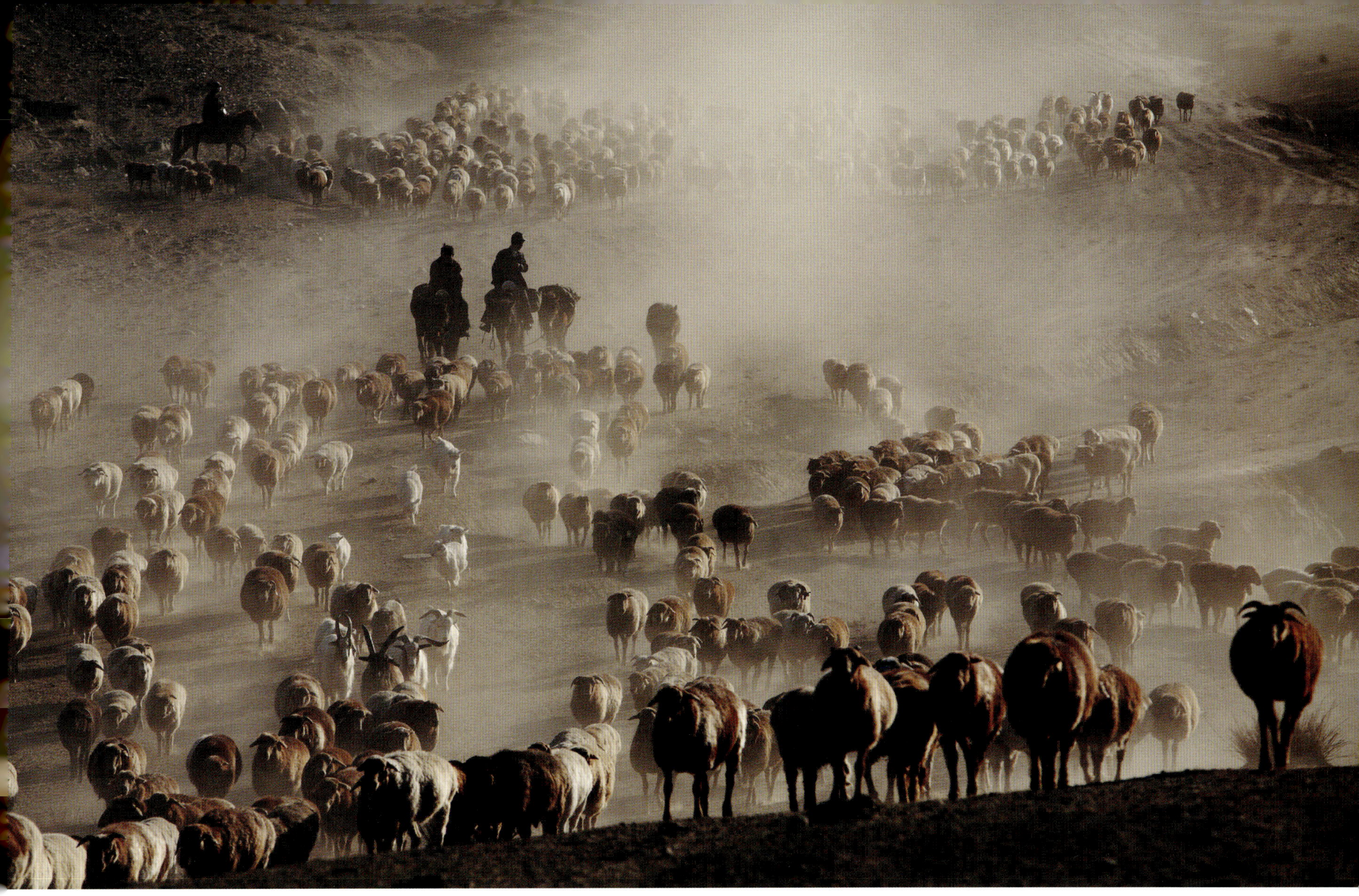

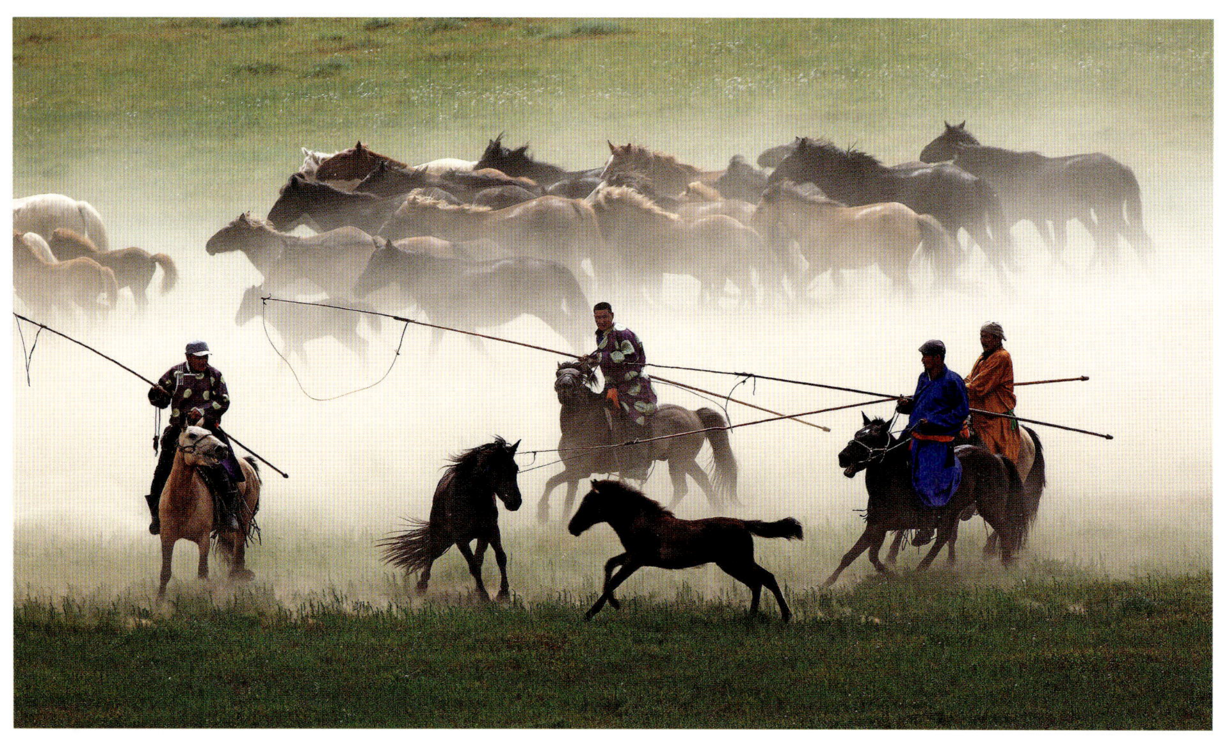

套馬 / 攝影: 黄鬆輝
Horse Roping
by Huang Songhui FRPS

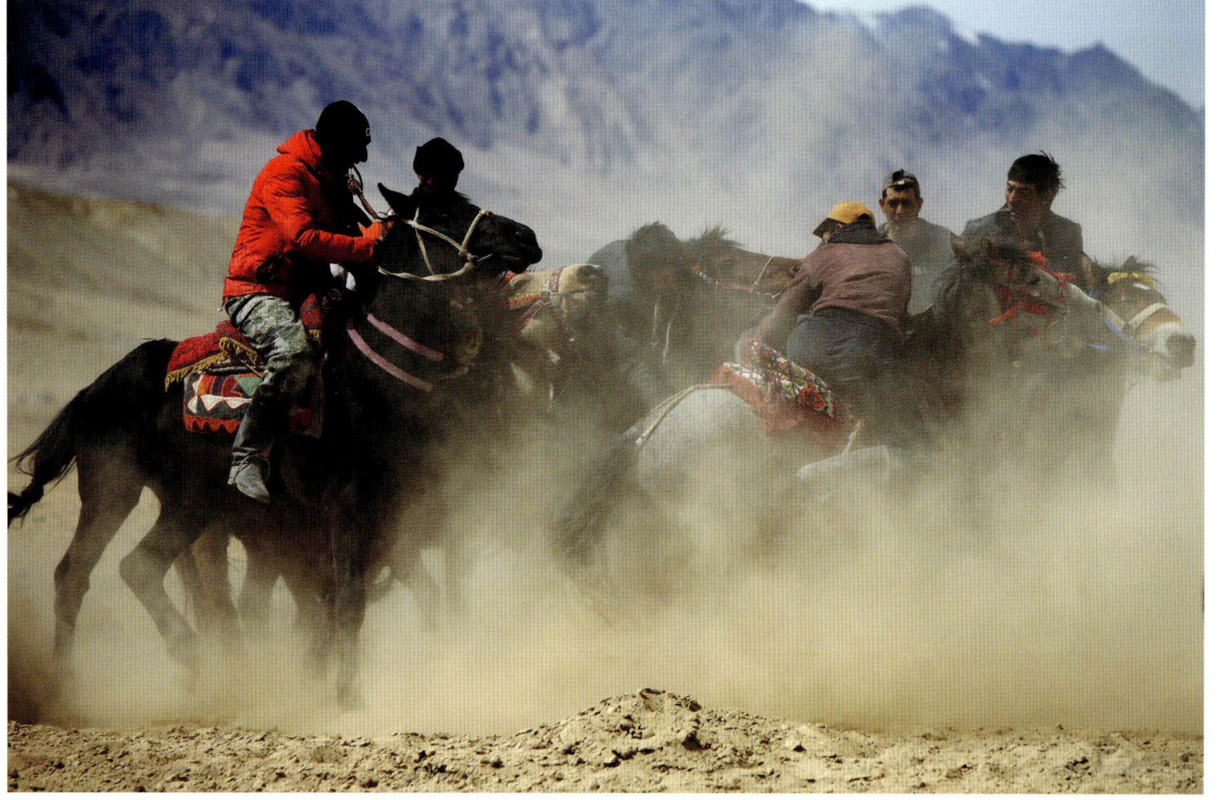

帕米爾的節日 / 攝影: 劉淑琴
Pamir's Festival by Liu Shuqin

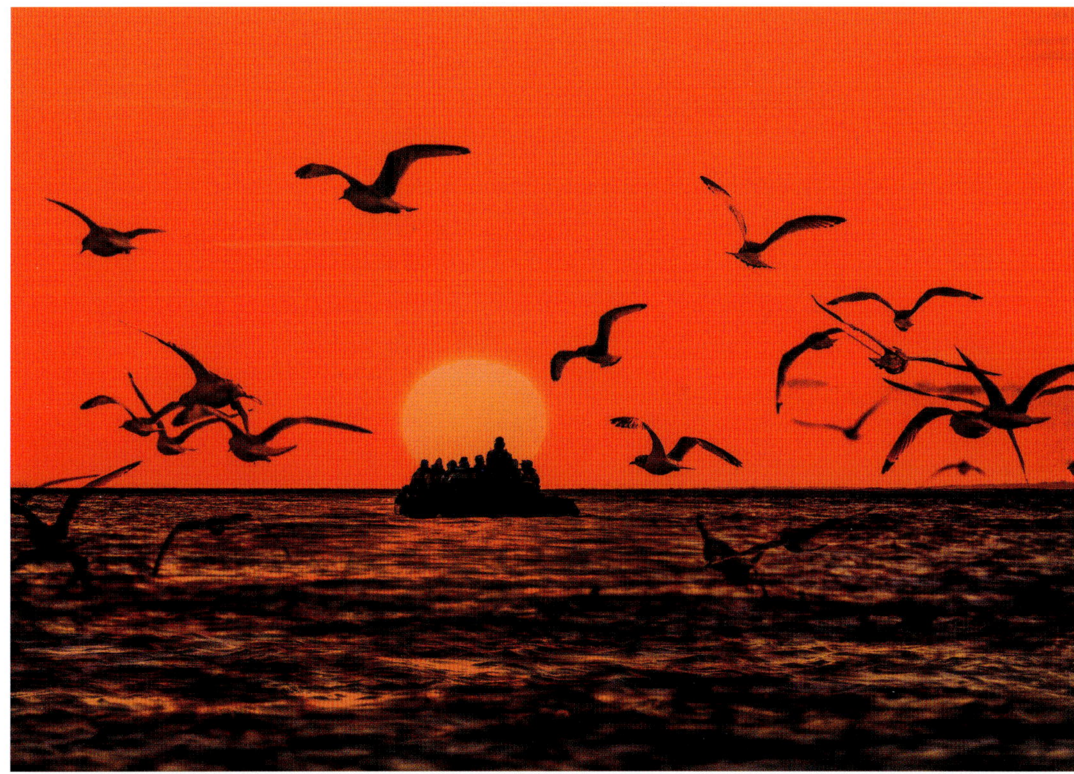

北極西北航道巡游利奧波德王子島海上日出 /
攝影: 劉連存
Arctic Northwest Passage Cruise Prince Leopold Island Sunrise at Sea by Liu Liancun

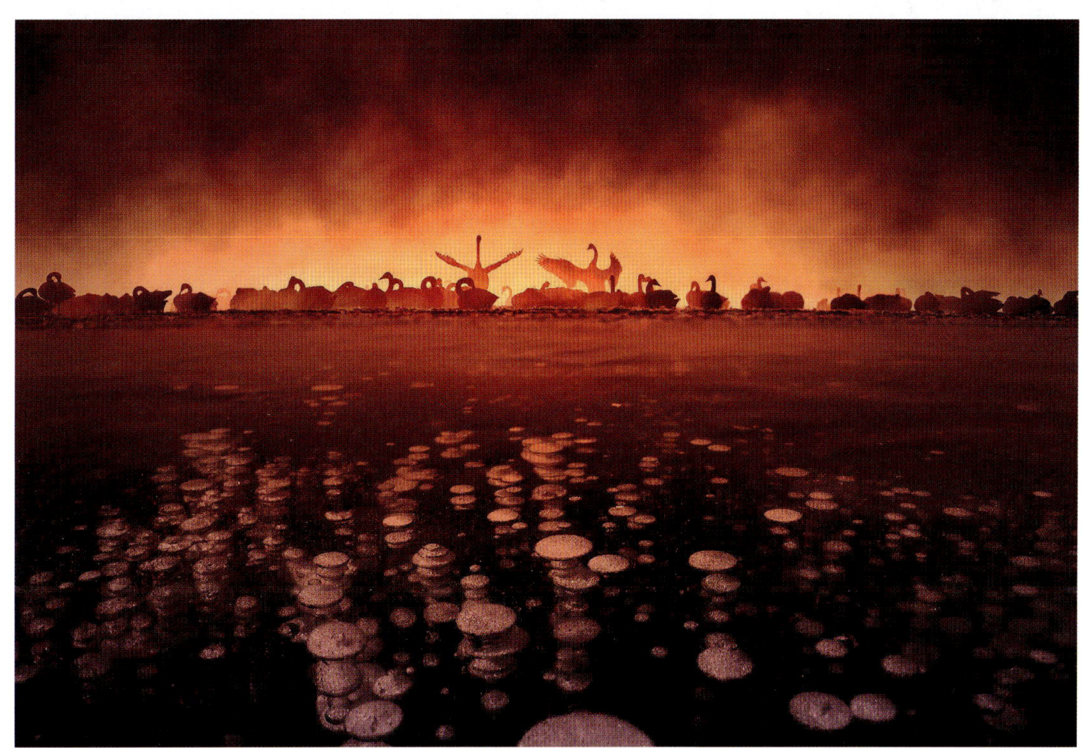

冬日天鵝湖 / 攝影: 張蔭鰲
Winter Swan Lake by Zhang Yinao

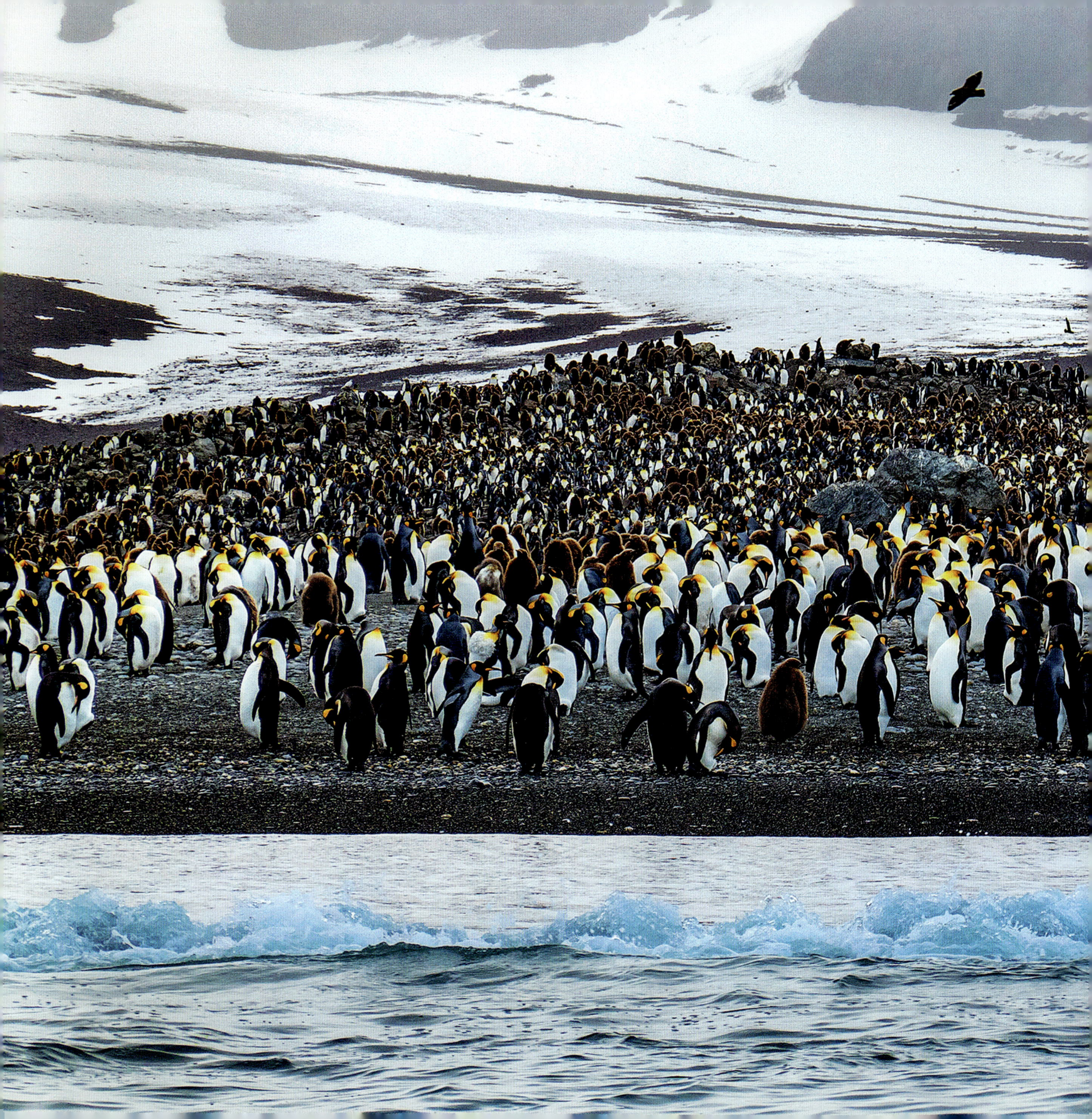

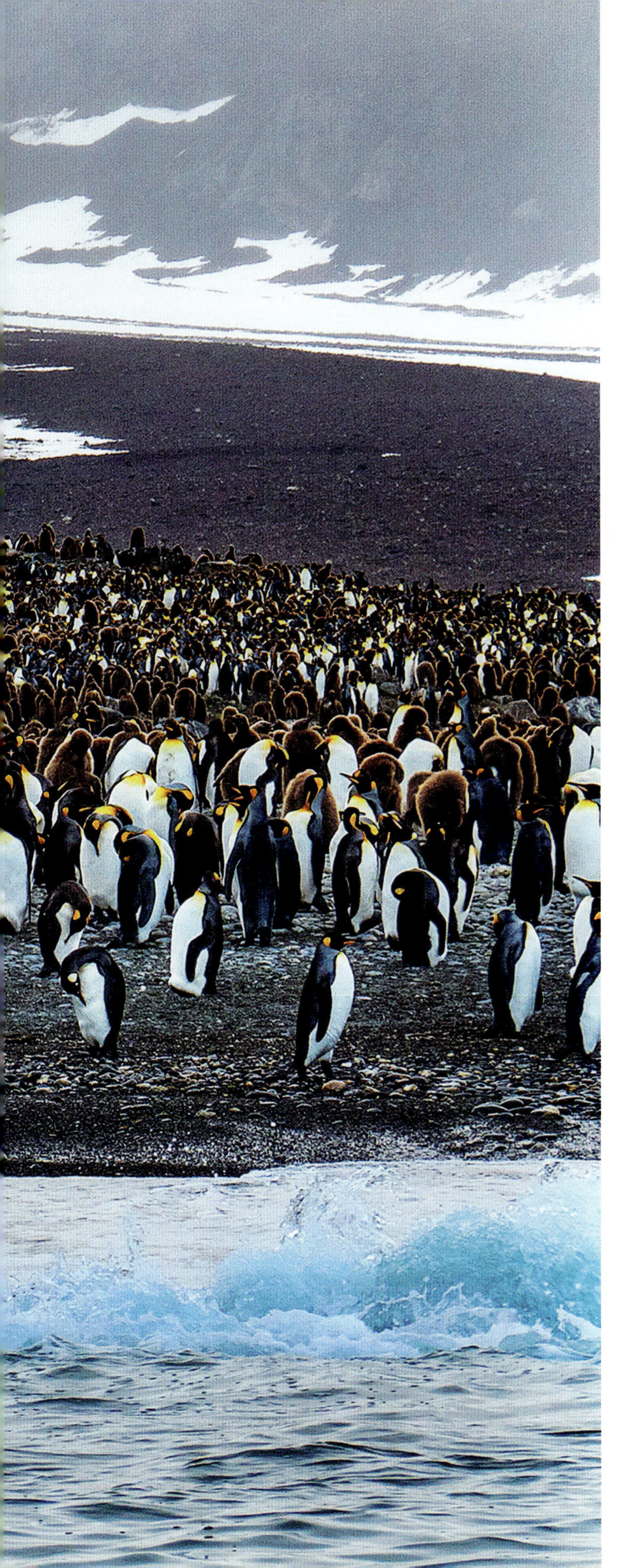

數以萬計的王企鵝聚集在艾瑟胡爾灣 / 攝影：劉連存
Tens of Thousands of King Penguins Gathering in Elsehur Bay
by Liu Liancun

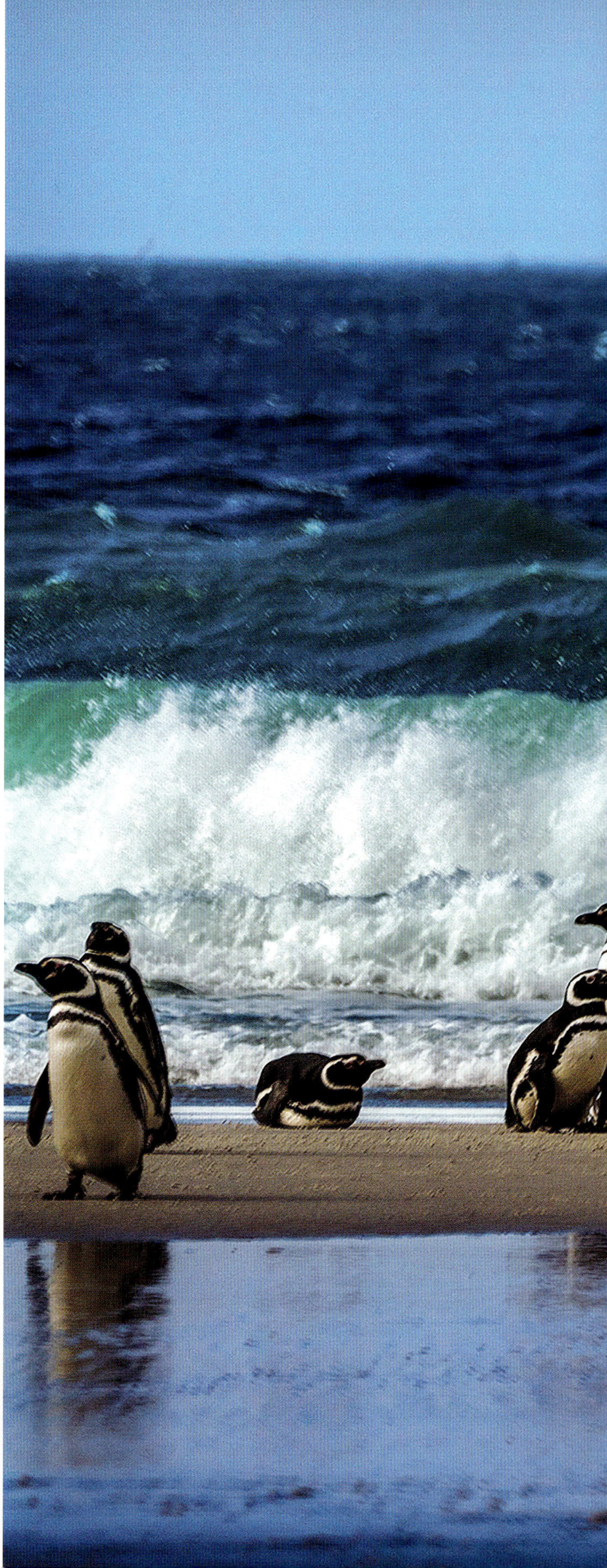

南極桑德斯島海邊嬉戲的企鵝 / 攝影: 劉連存
Penguins Frolicking on the Beach of Saunders Island, Antarctica
by Liu Liancun

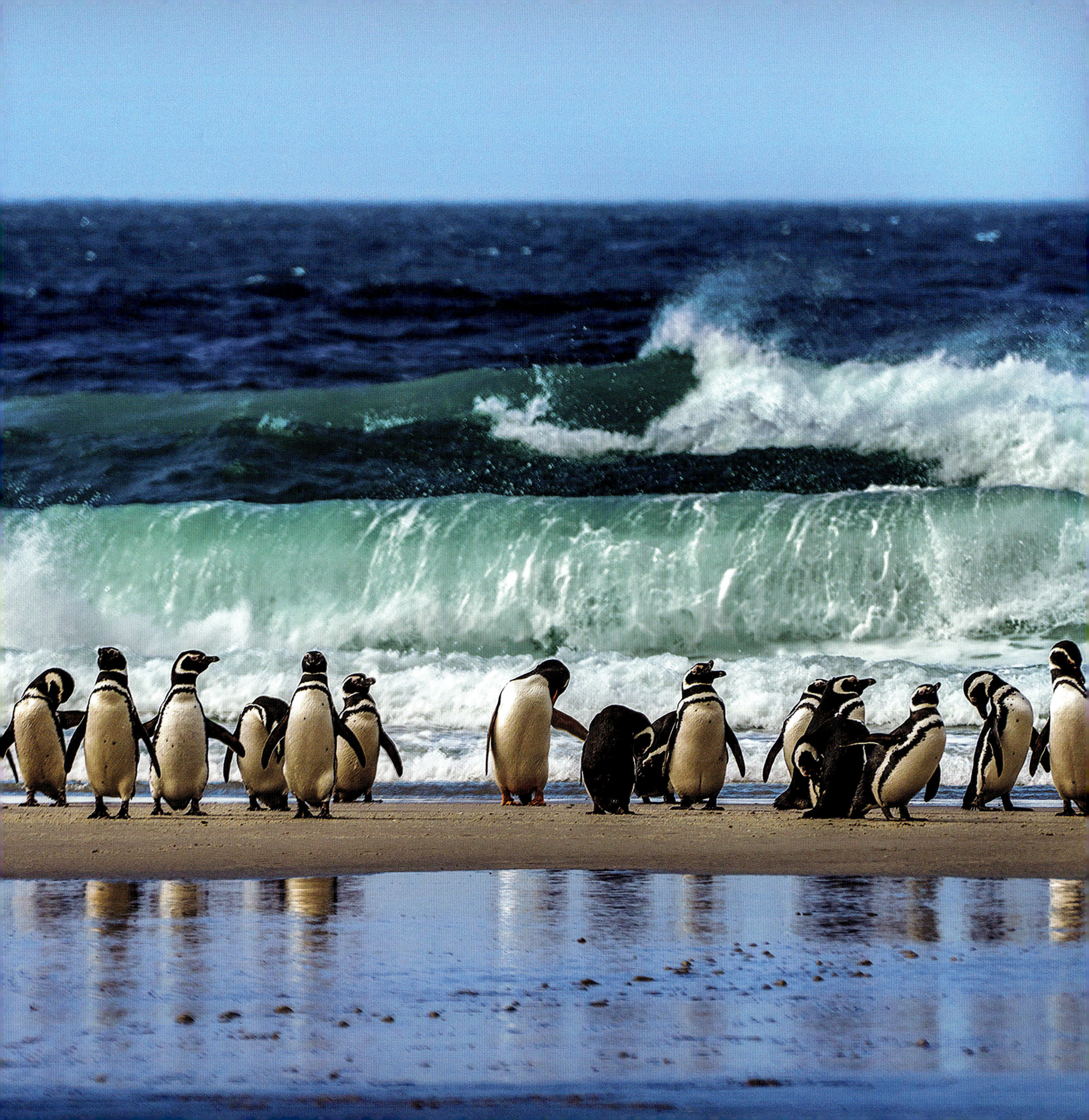

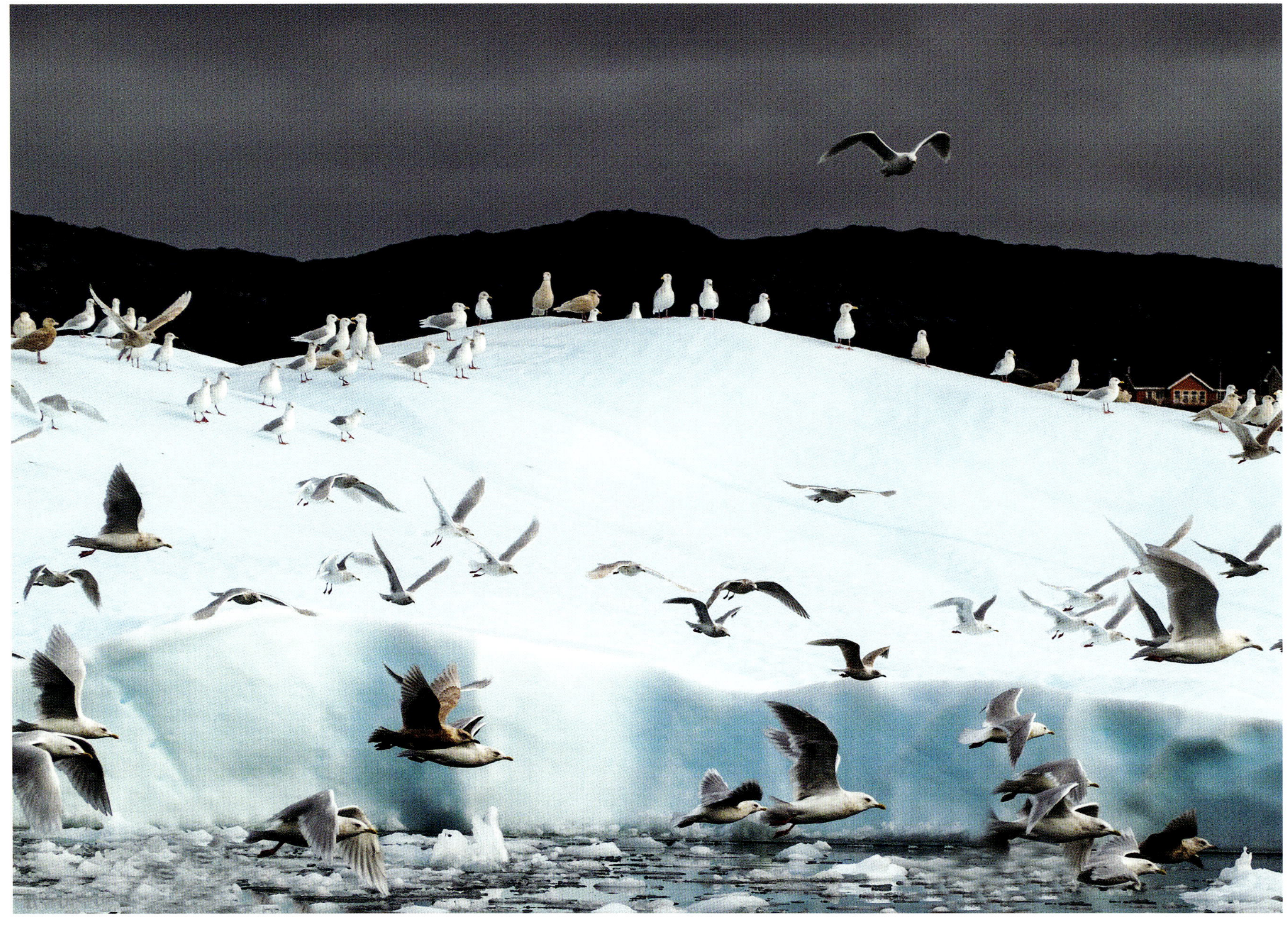

北極西北航道上的北極鷗 / 攝影: 劉連存
Arctic Gulls on the Northwest Passage of the Arctic
by Liu Liancun

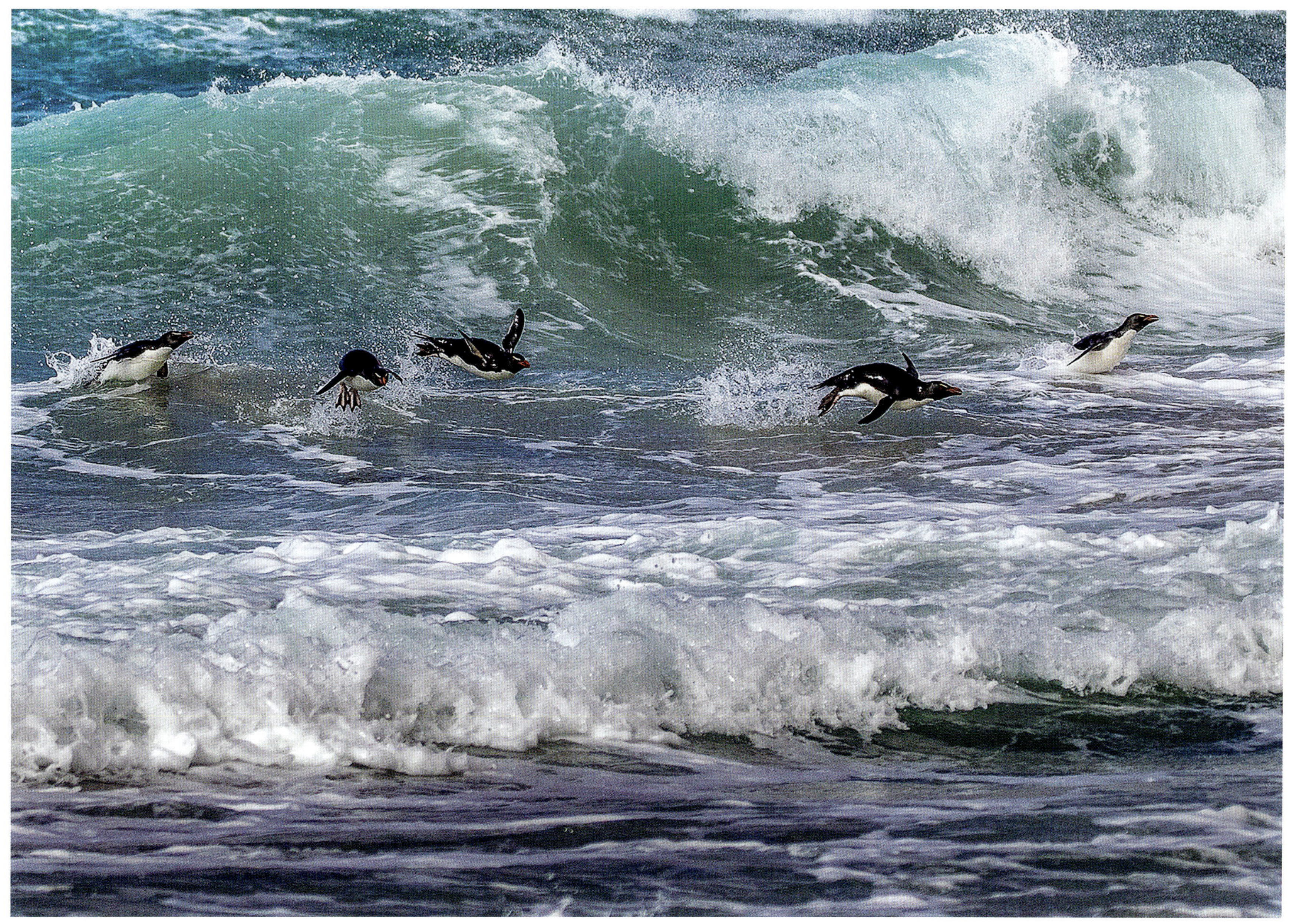

南極桑德斯島海邊衝浪的企鵝 / 攝影: 劉連存
Penguins Surfing on the Beach at Saunders Island, Antarctica
by Liu Liancun

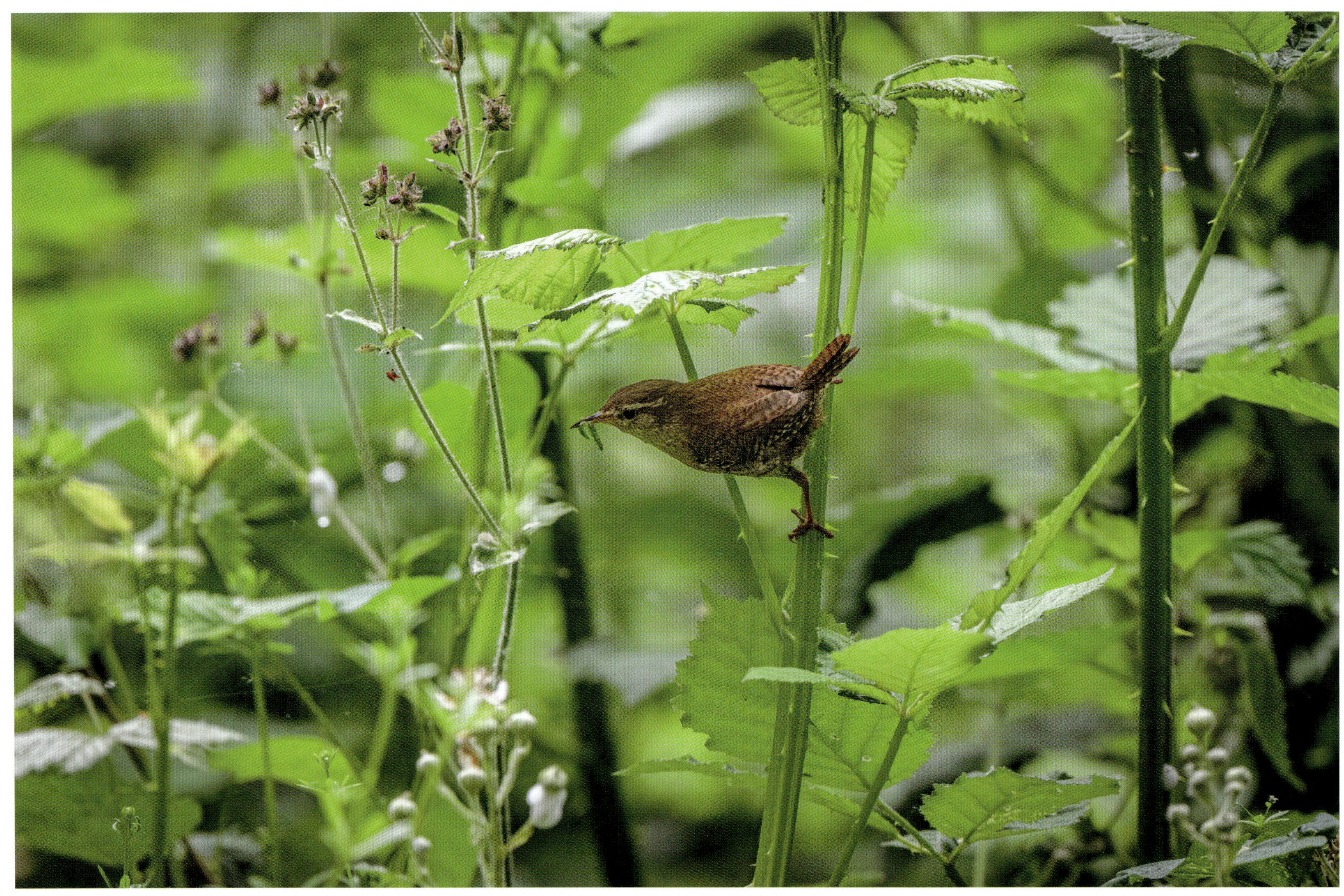

捕食
Prey by Jennette Russell LRPS

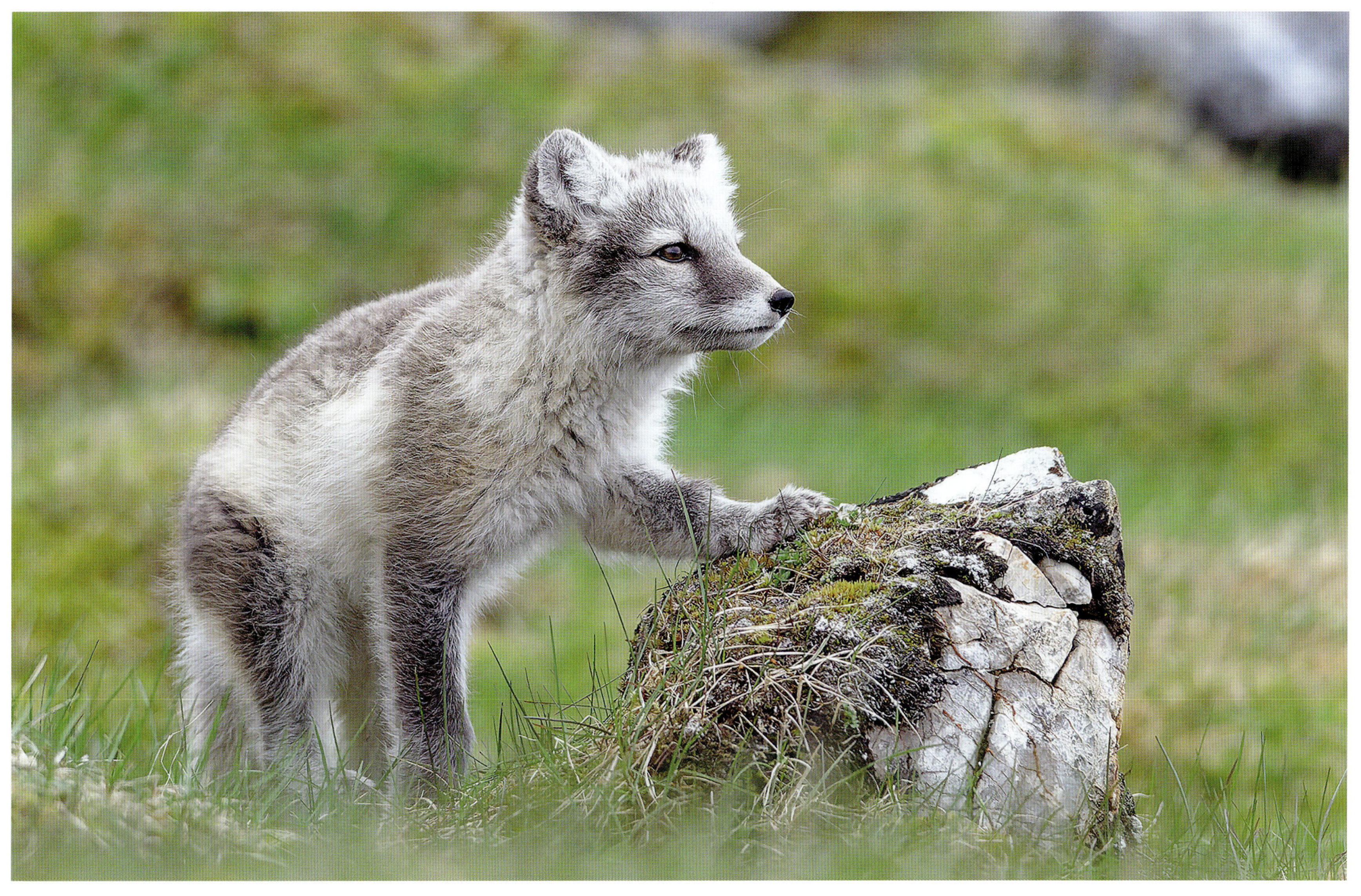

北極狐
Arctic Fox by Anthony Macaulay

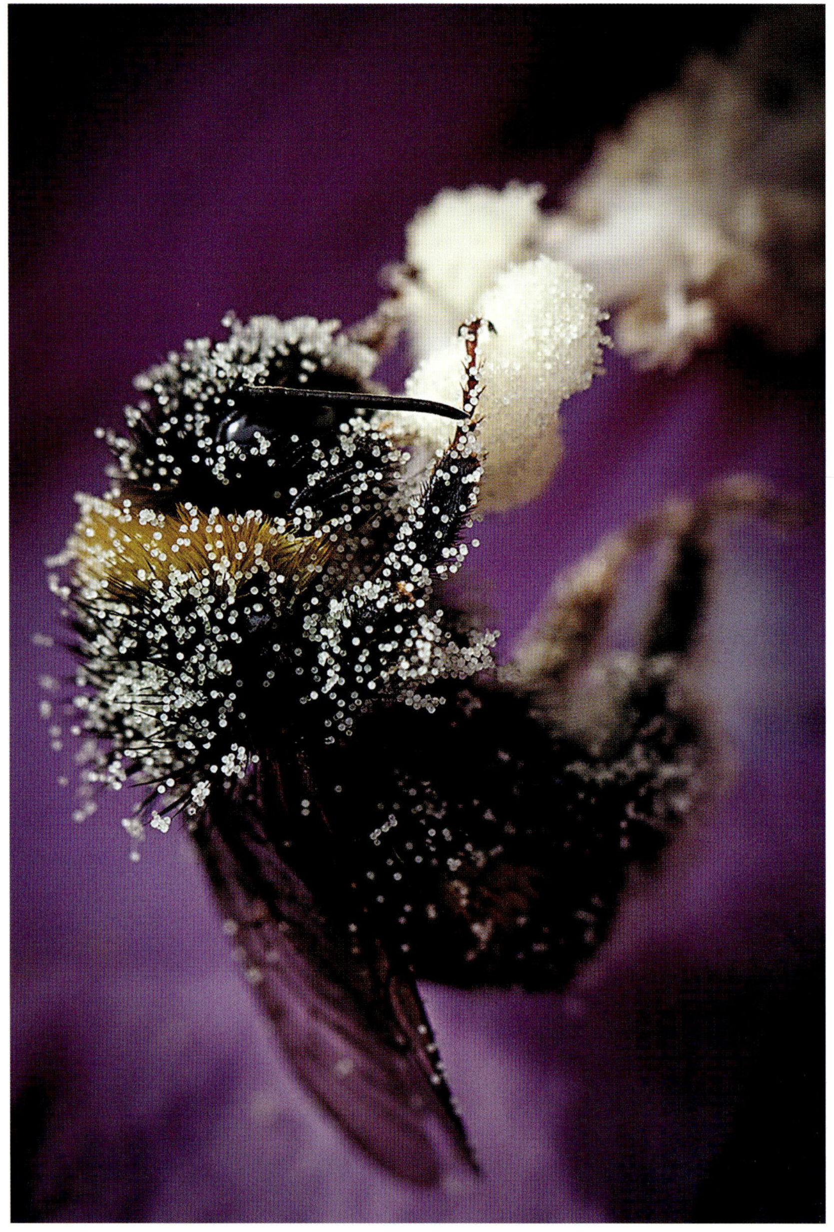

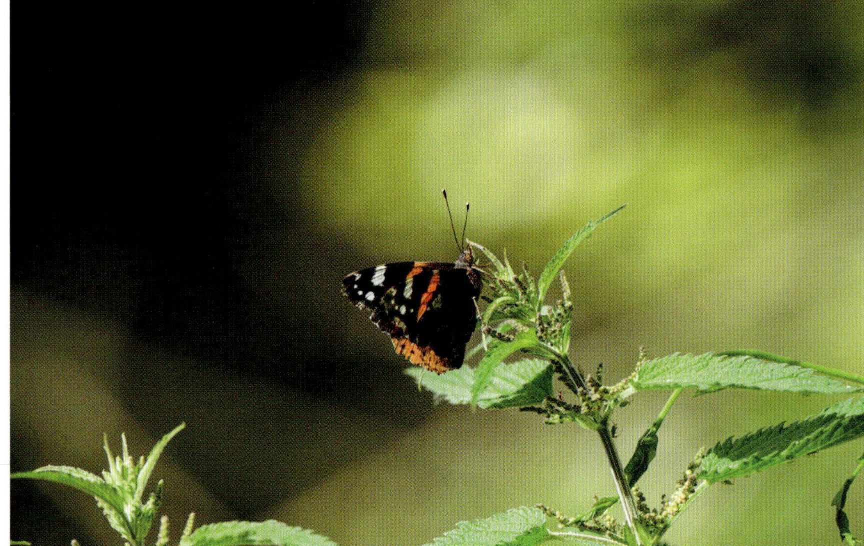

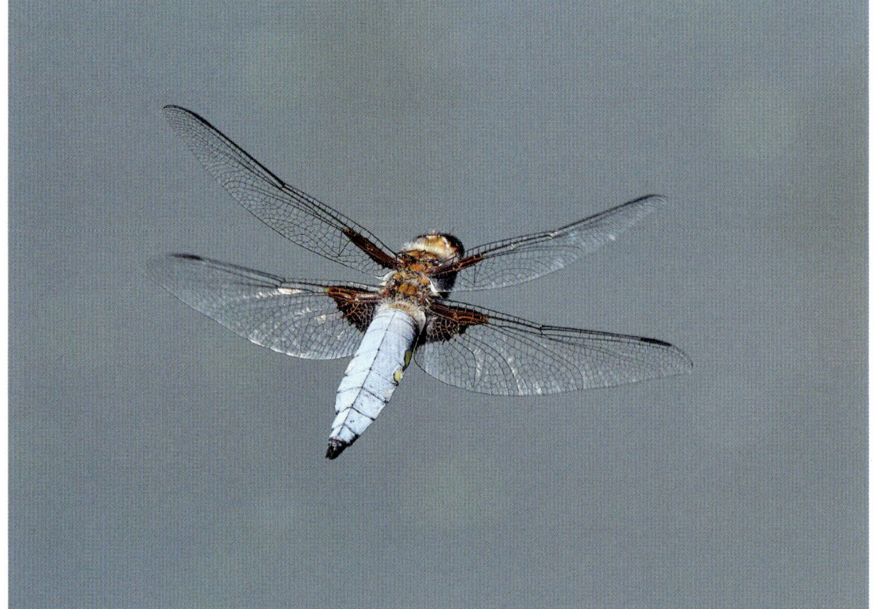

蜜蜂
Bee by Lia Cumming

蝴蝶
Butterfly
by Jennette Russell LRPS

蜻蜓
Dragonfly
by Clive Wade LRPS

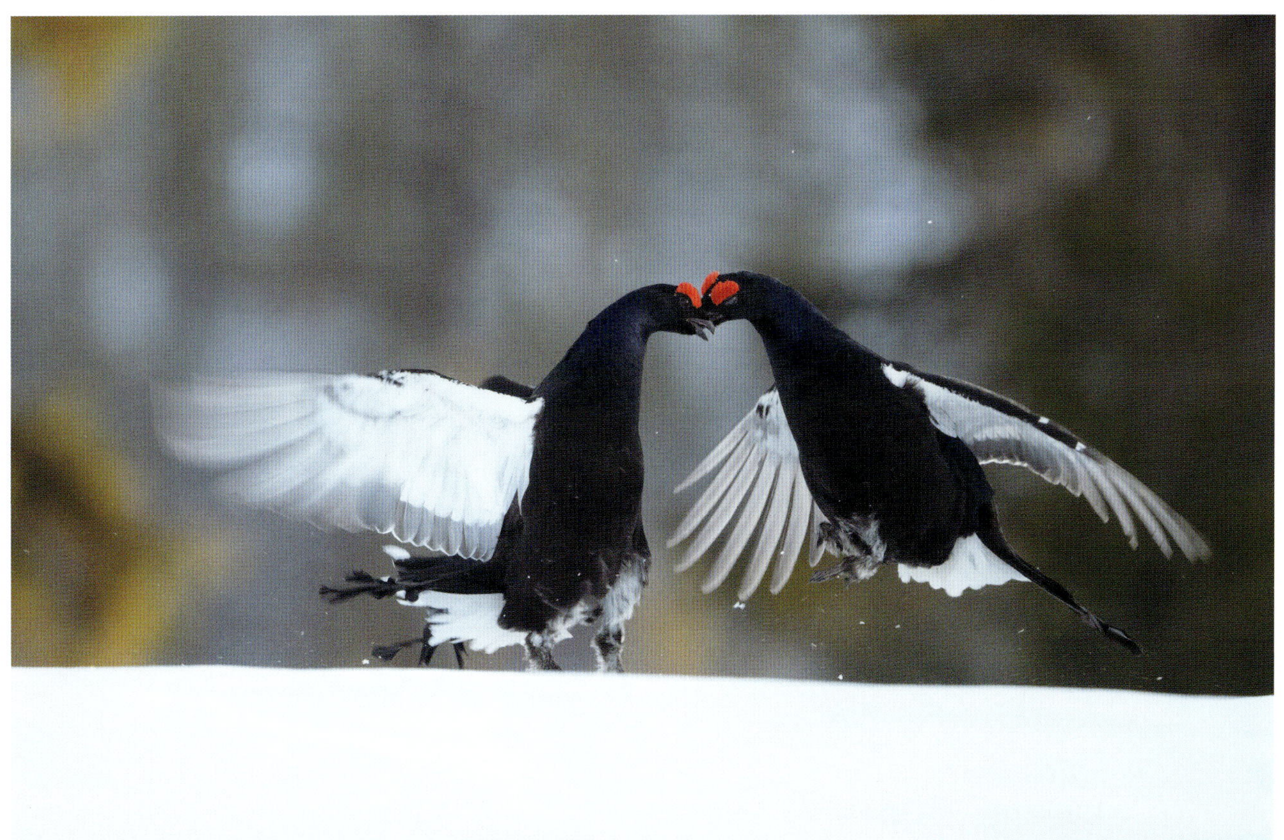

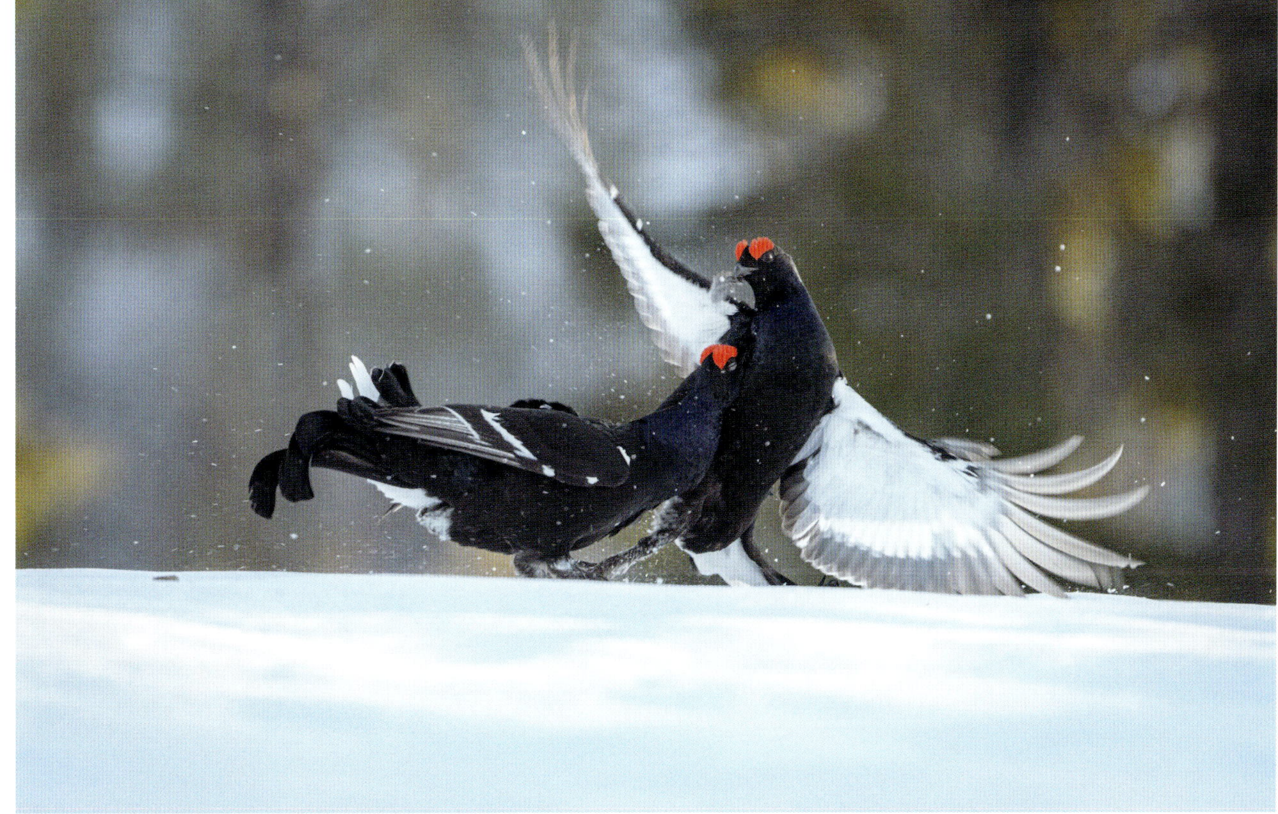

芬蘭的春天-黑鬆鷄
Finland in Spring-Black Grouse Lekking
by Jennette Russell LRPS

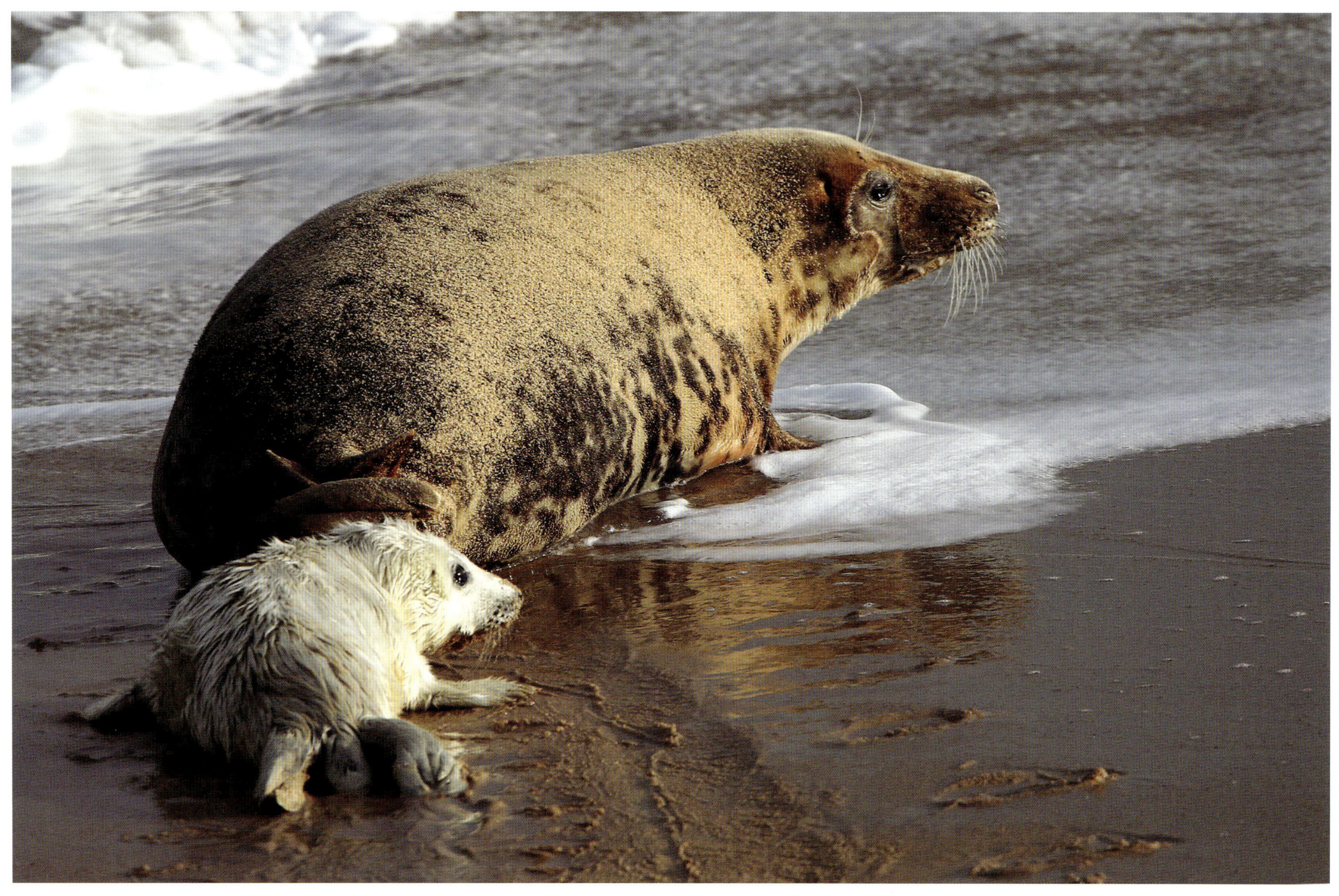

準備上游泳課
Going for a Swimming Lesson by Pat Simmons LRPS

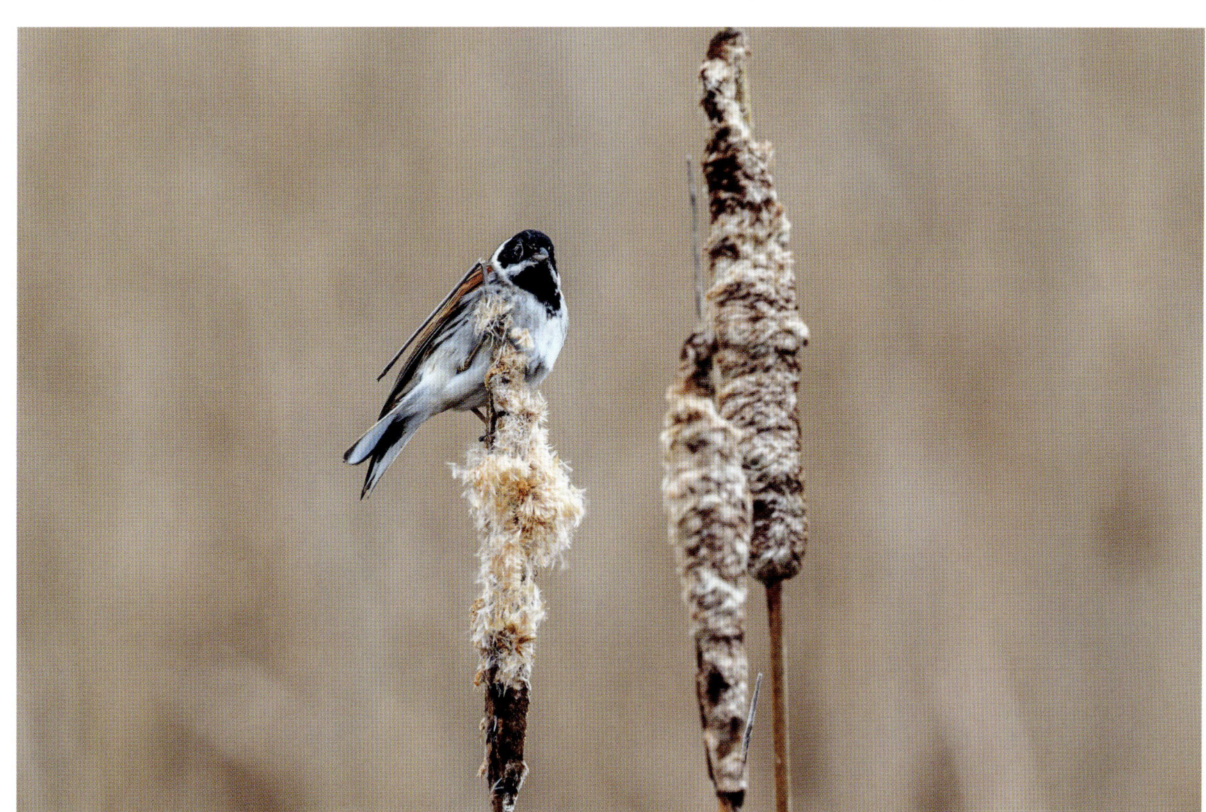

薩默塞特
Somerset
by Jennette Russell LRPS

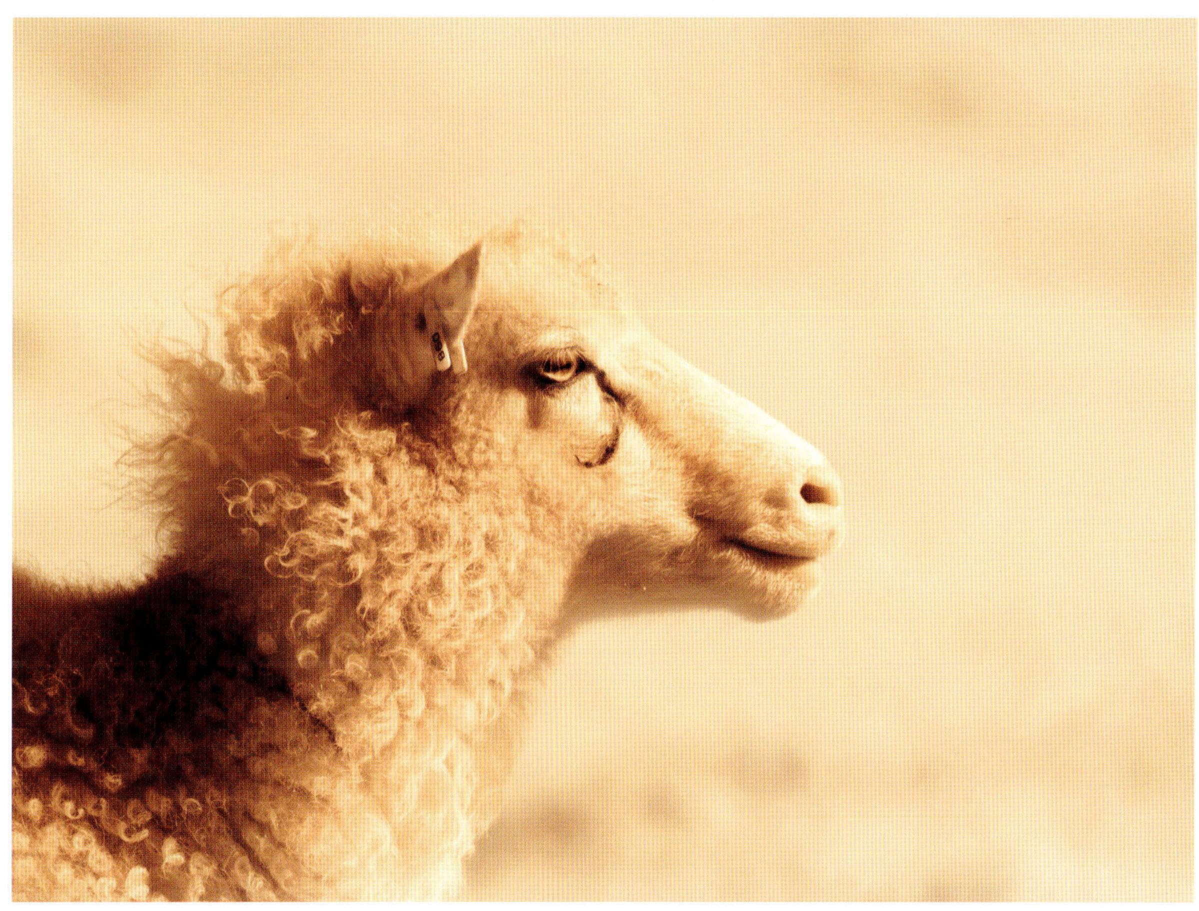

法羅群島的綿羊
Faroese Sheep
by Esther Serrano

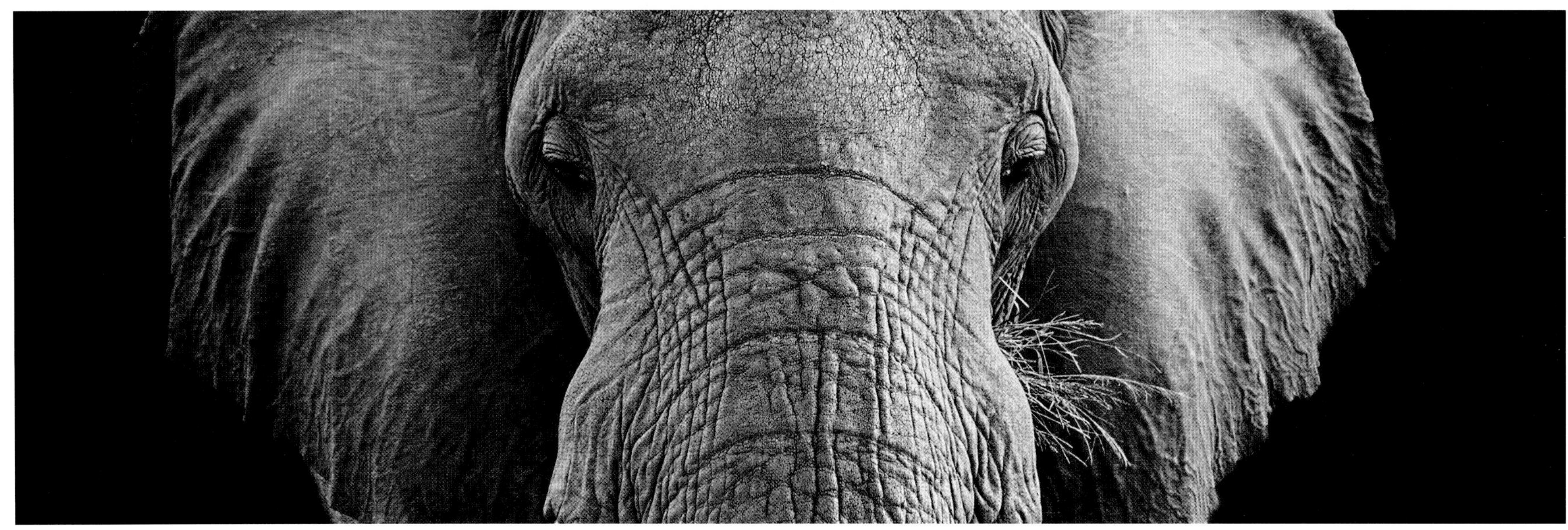

大象
Elephant by Fred Barringrton FRPS, AFIAP

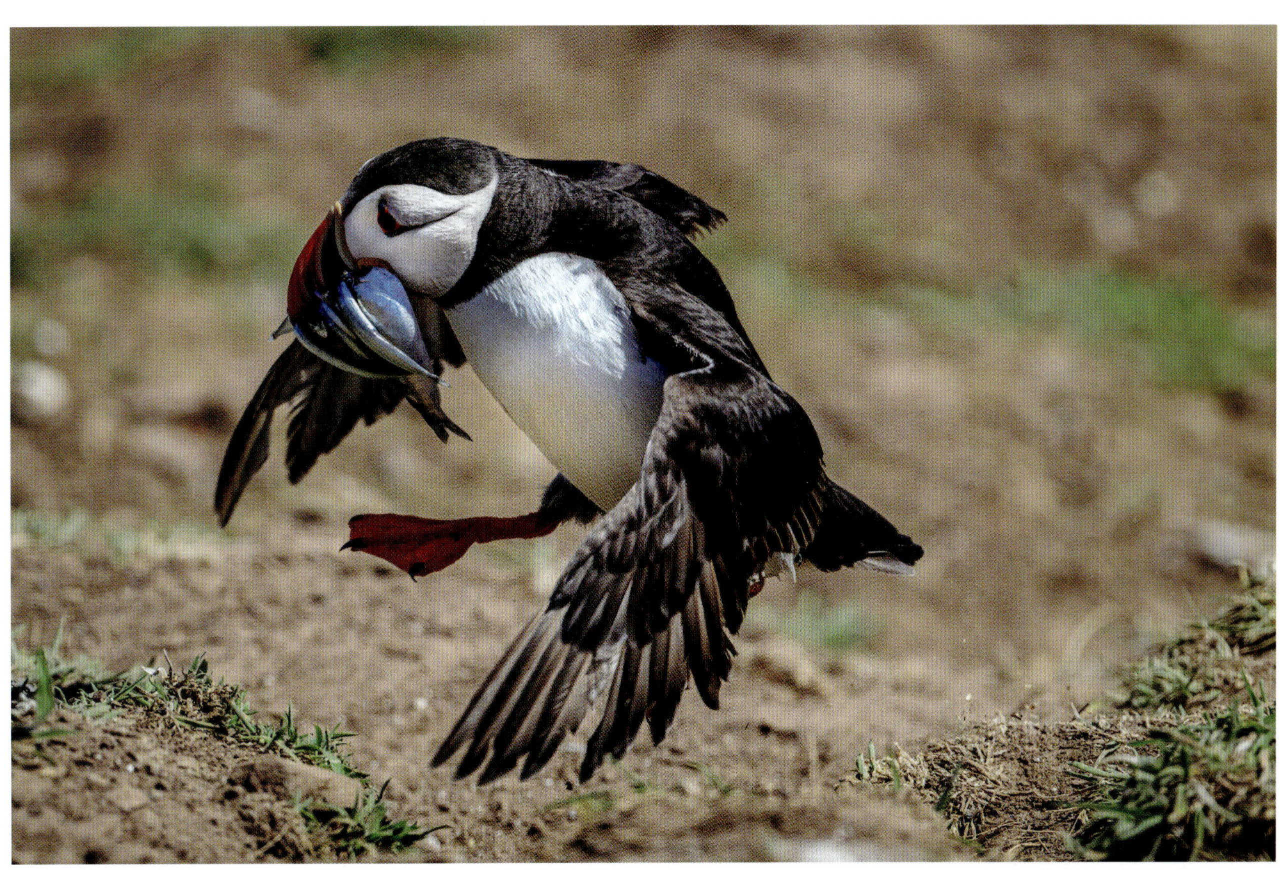

彭布羅克郡斯科默
Pembrokeshire Skomer
by Jennette Russell LRPS

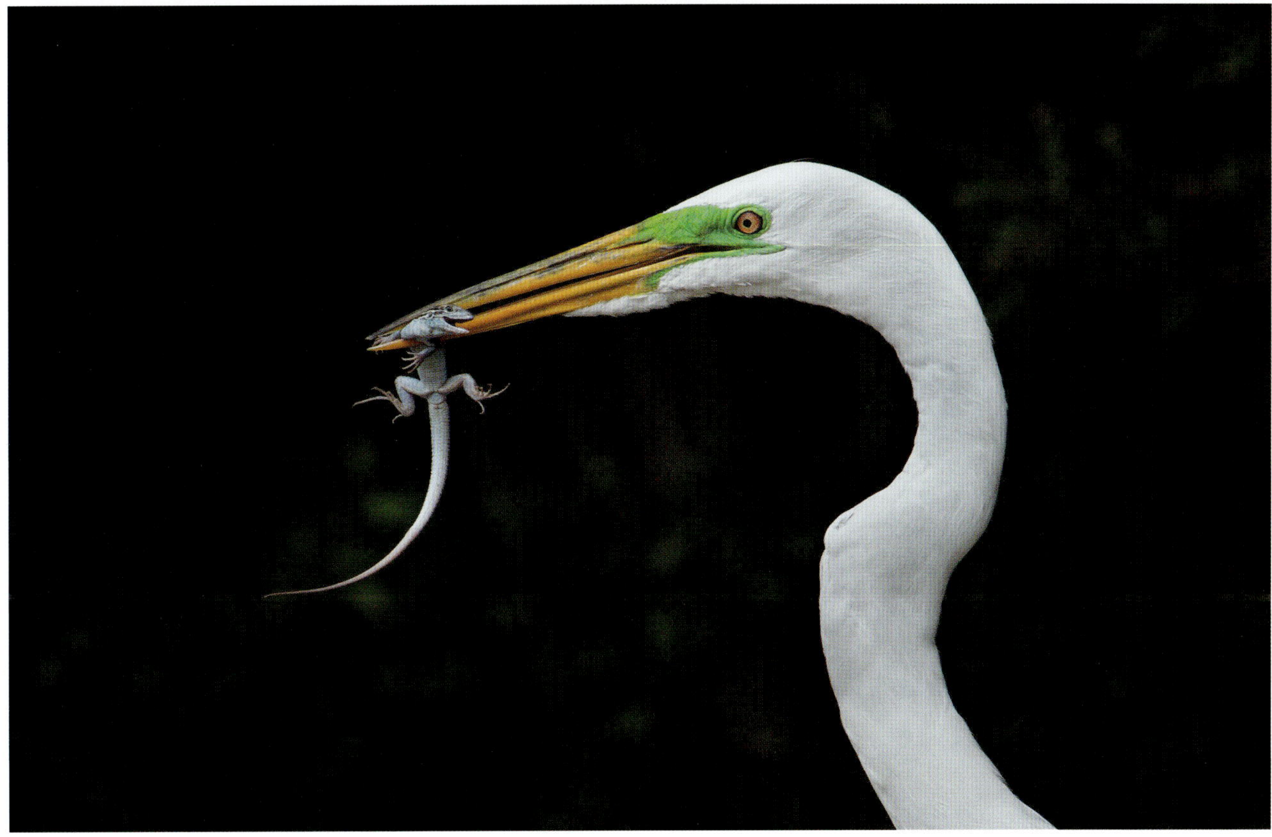

蜥蜴午餐
Lizard for Lunch
by Patrick Hudgell ARPS

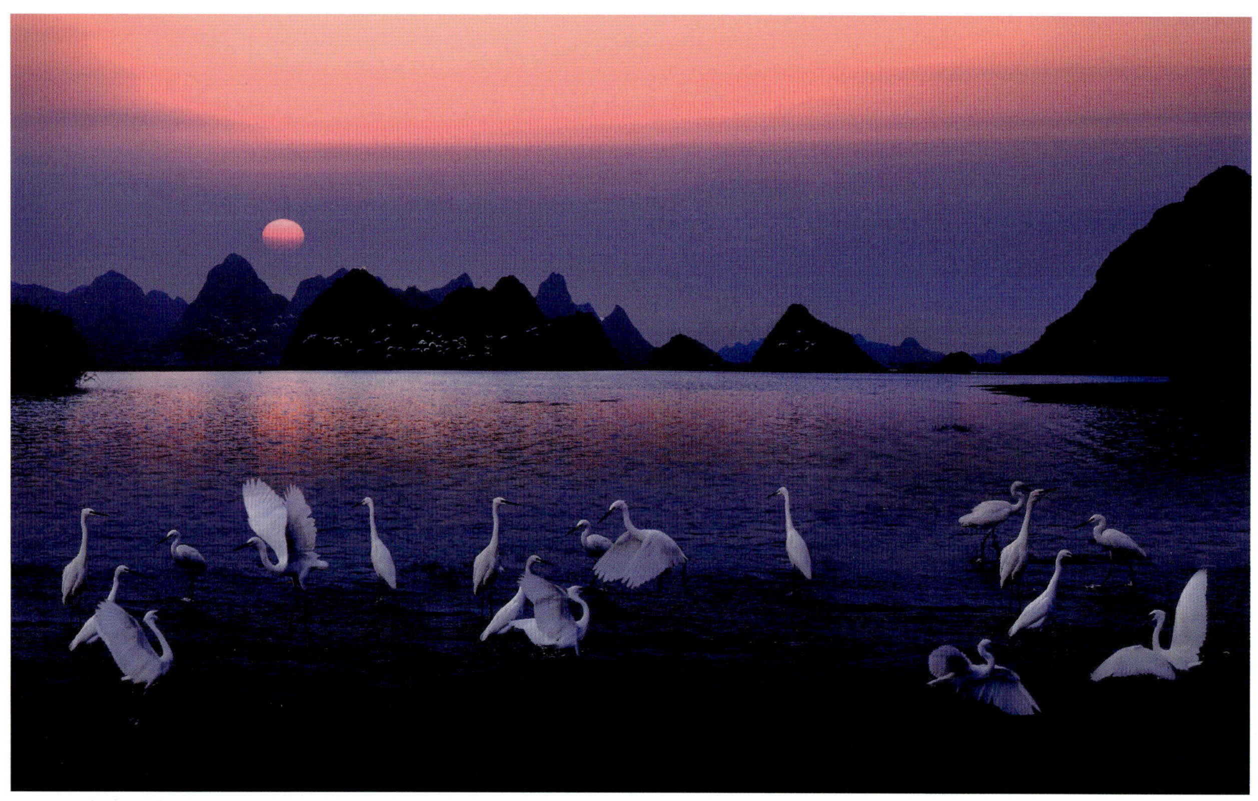

家園普者黑 / 攝影: 彭雪平
Homeland Puzhehei
by Peng Xueping

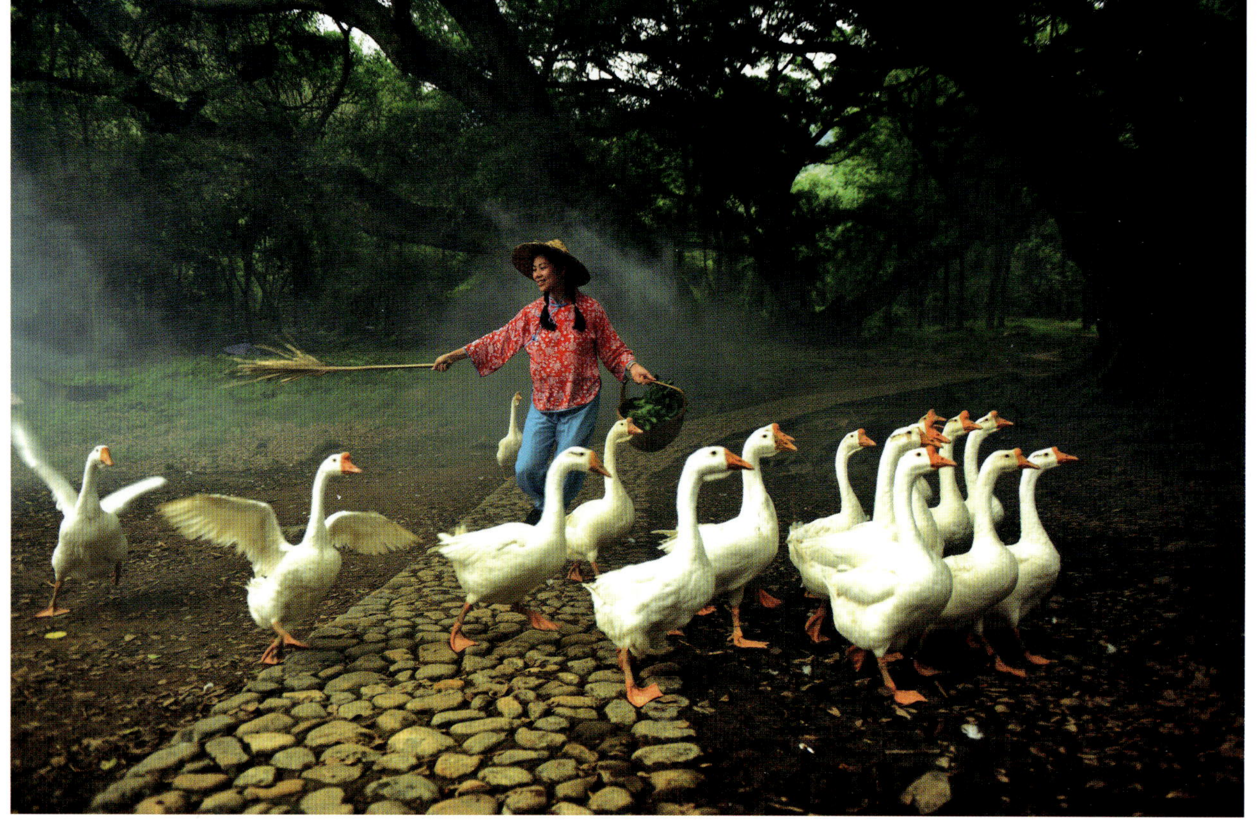

牧鵝女 / 攝影: 孫燕
The Gooseherd Girl
by Sun Yan

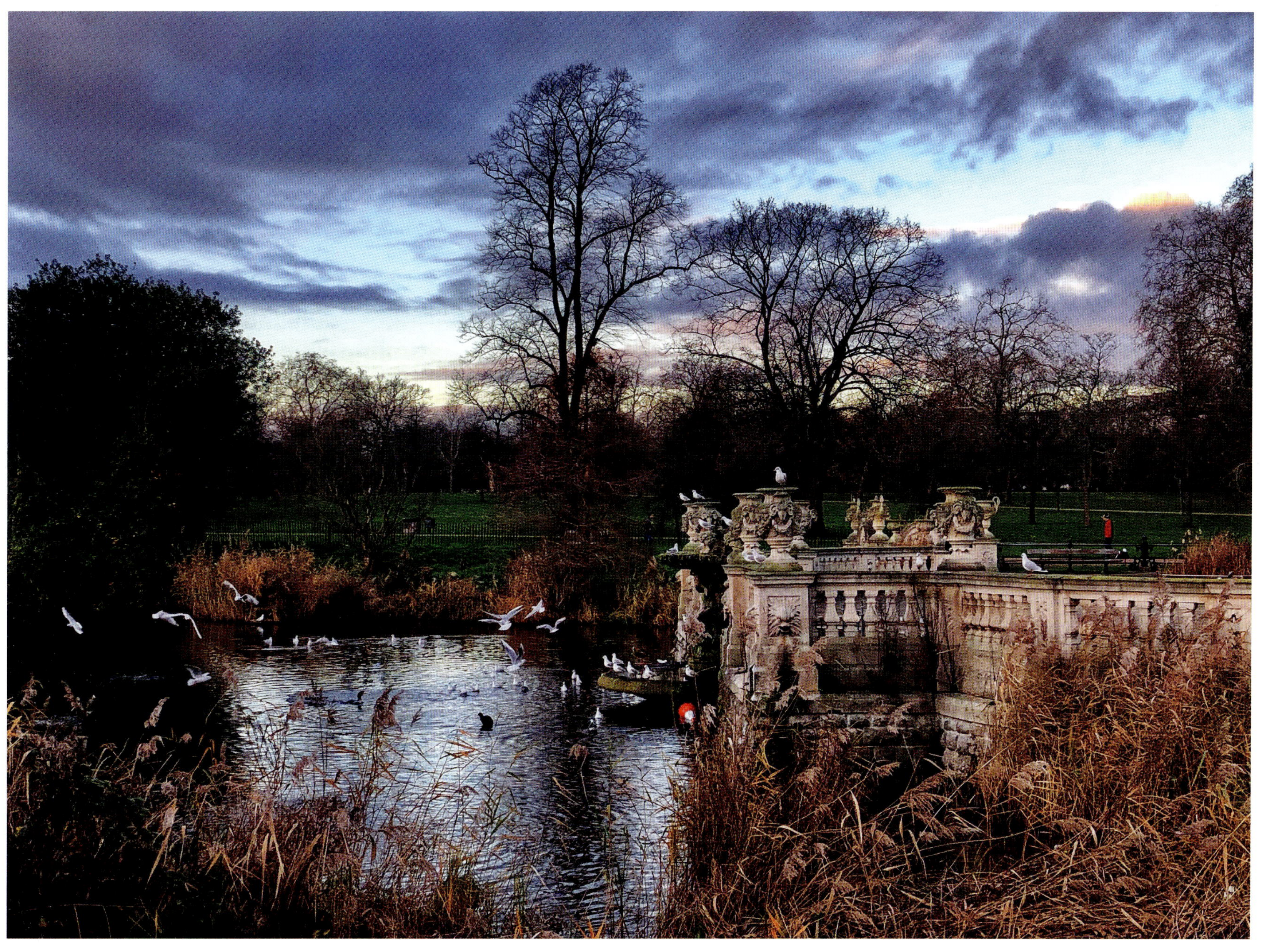

爺爺的花園 / 攝影: 秦蕾
Grandpa's Garden by Qin Lei

DOCUMENTARY 紀實

西班牙隆達，鬥牛場馬車秀
Carriage Show, Bullring, Ronda, Spain
by David Hicks

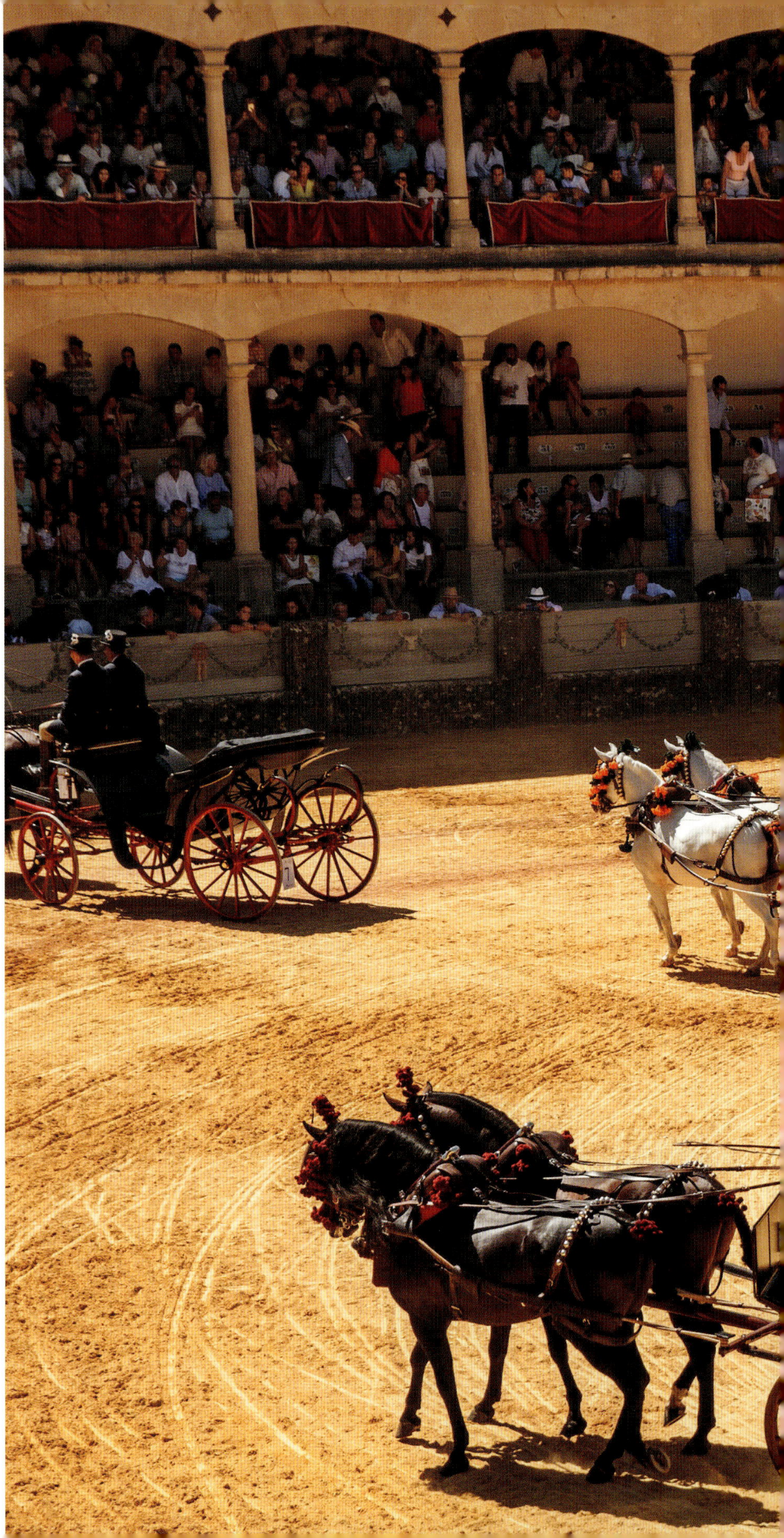

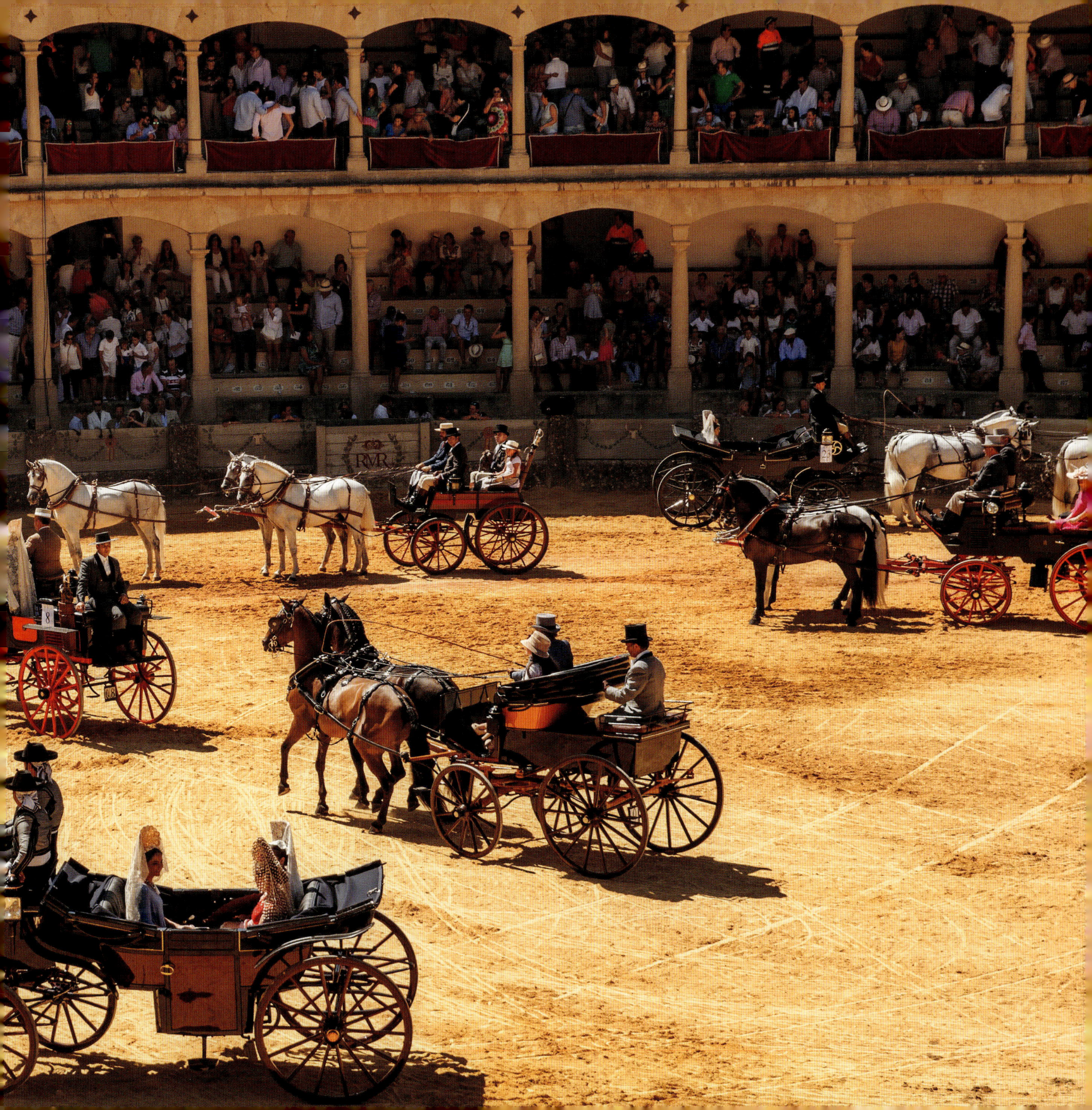
RVR

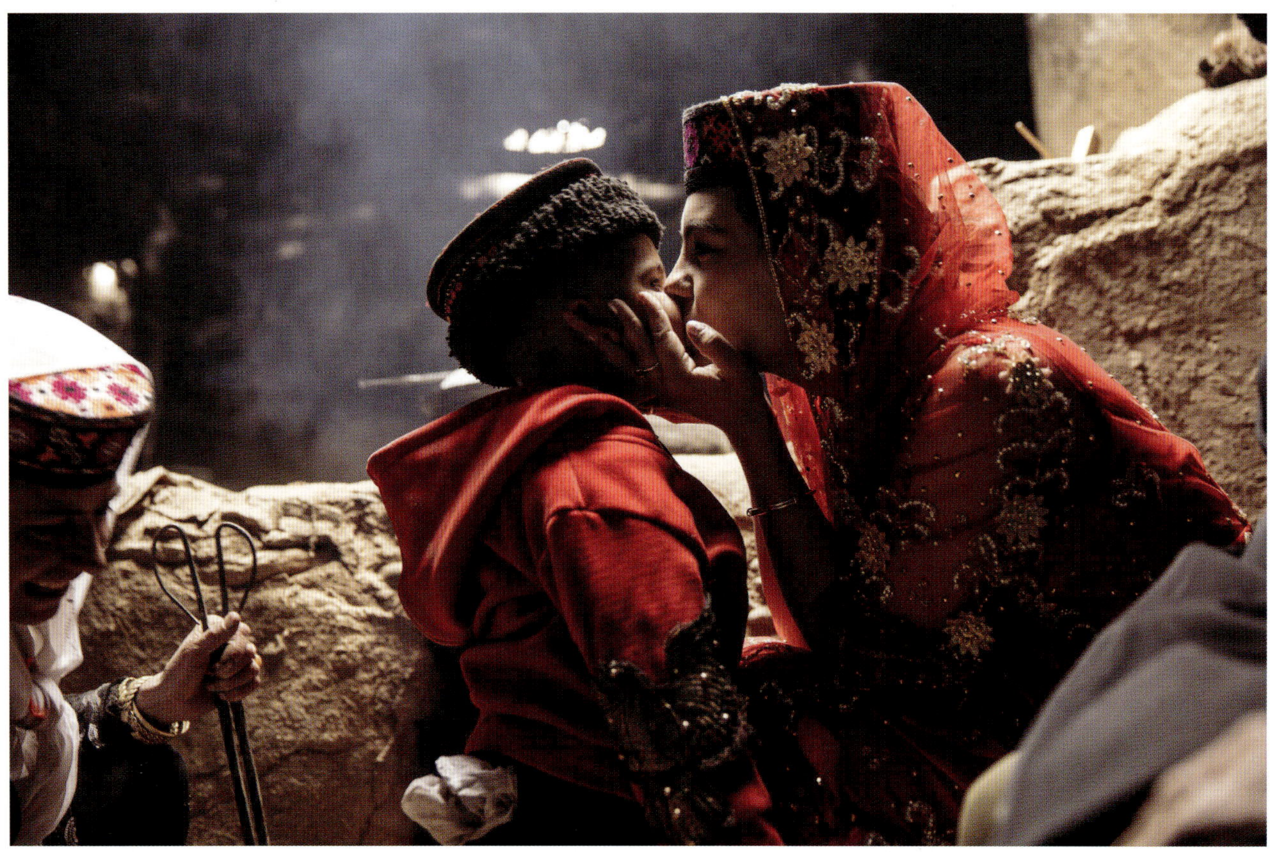

媽媽的吻 / 攝影: 趙幹成
Mother's Kiss
by Zhao Gancheng

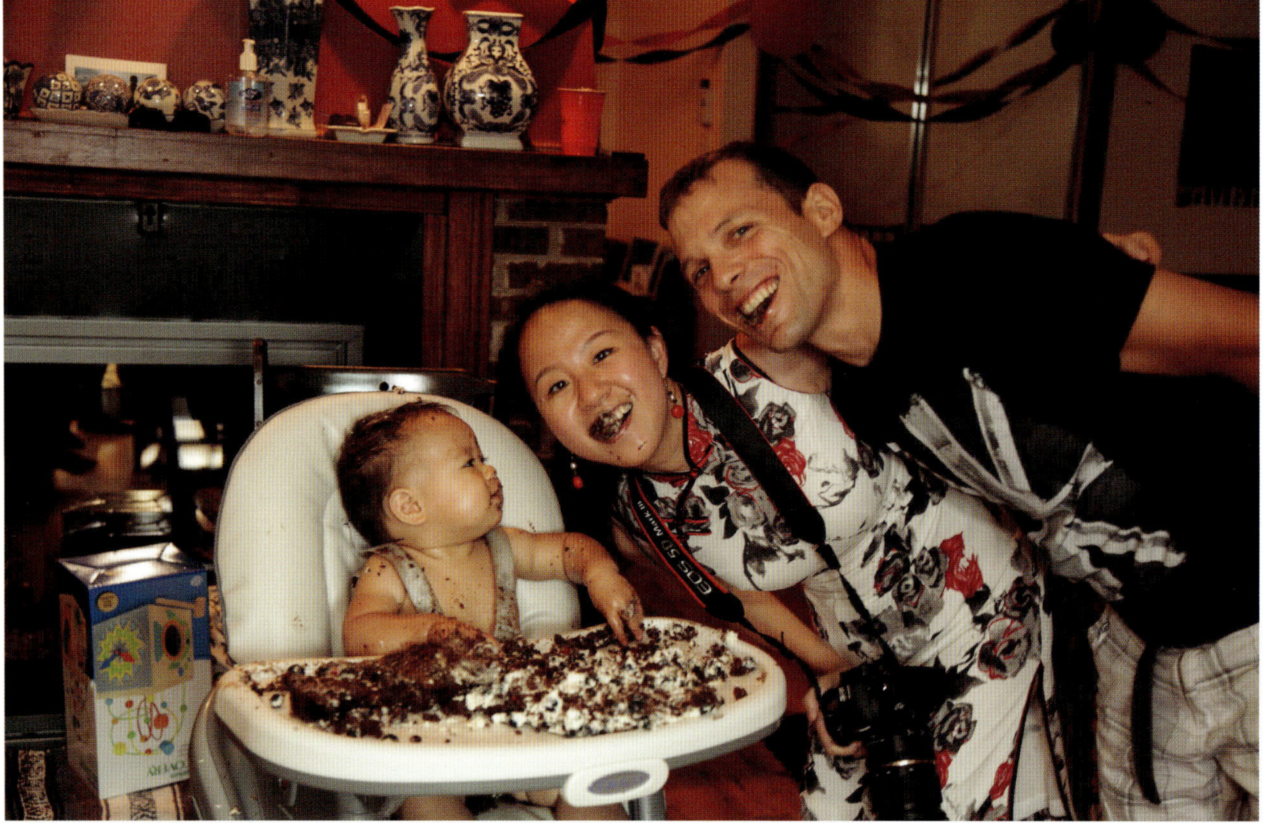

若初的周歲生日 /
攝影: 余鵬
Ruo Chu's Birthday
by Yu Peng

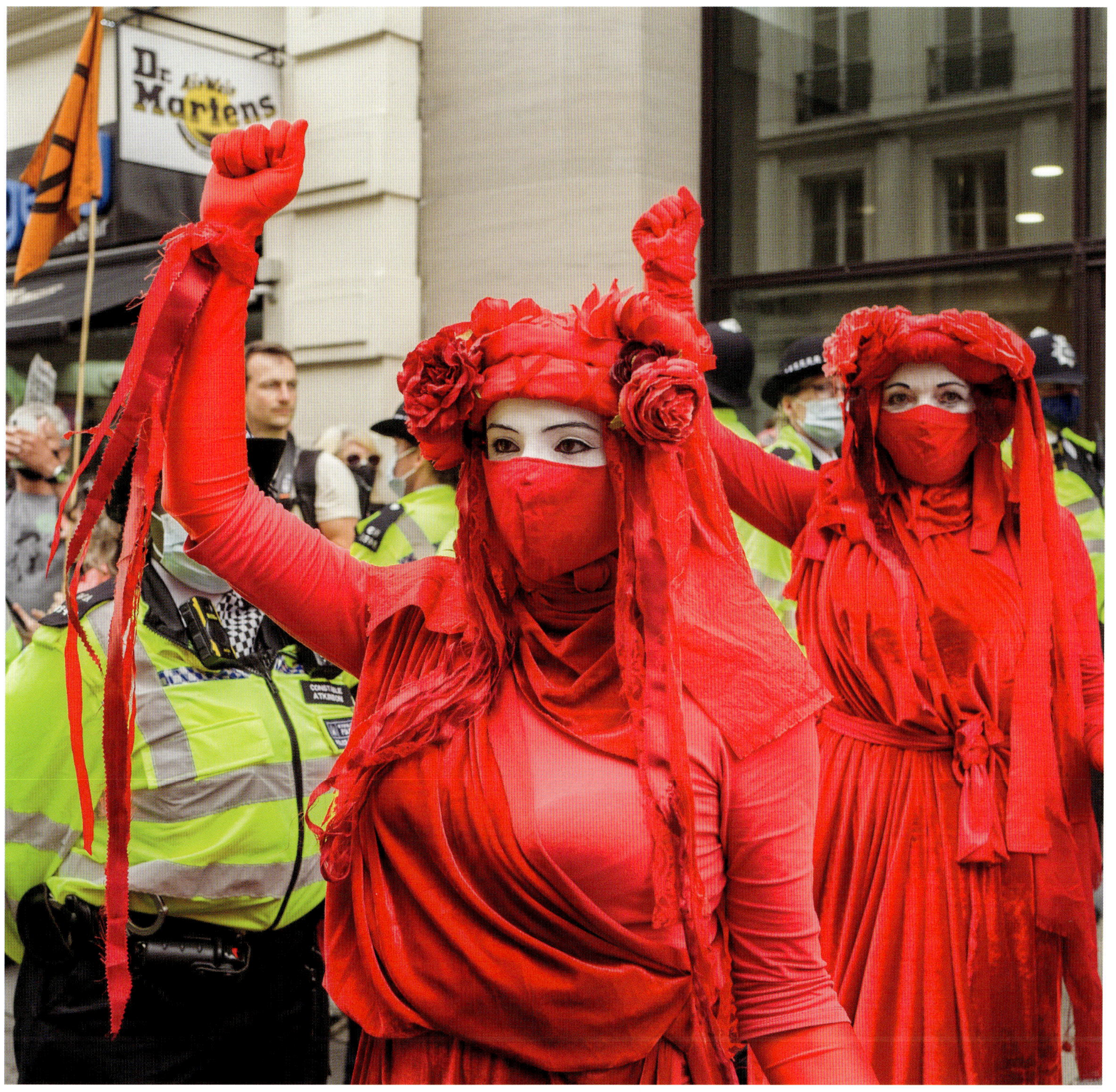

紅色隊伍出發
Red Brigade Departing by Mary Thompson

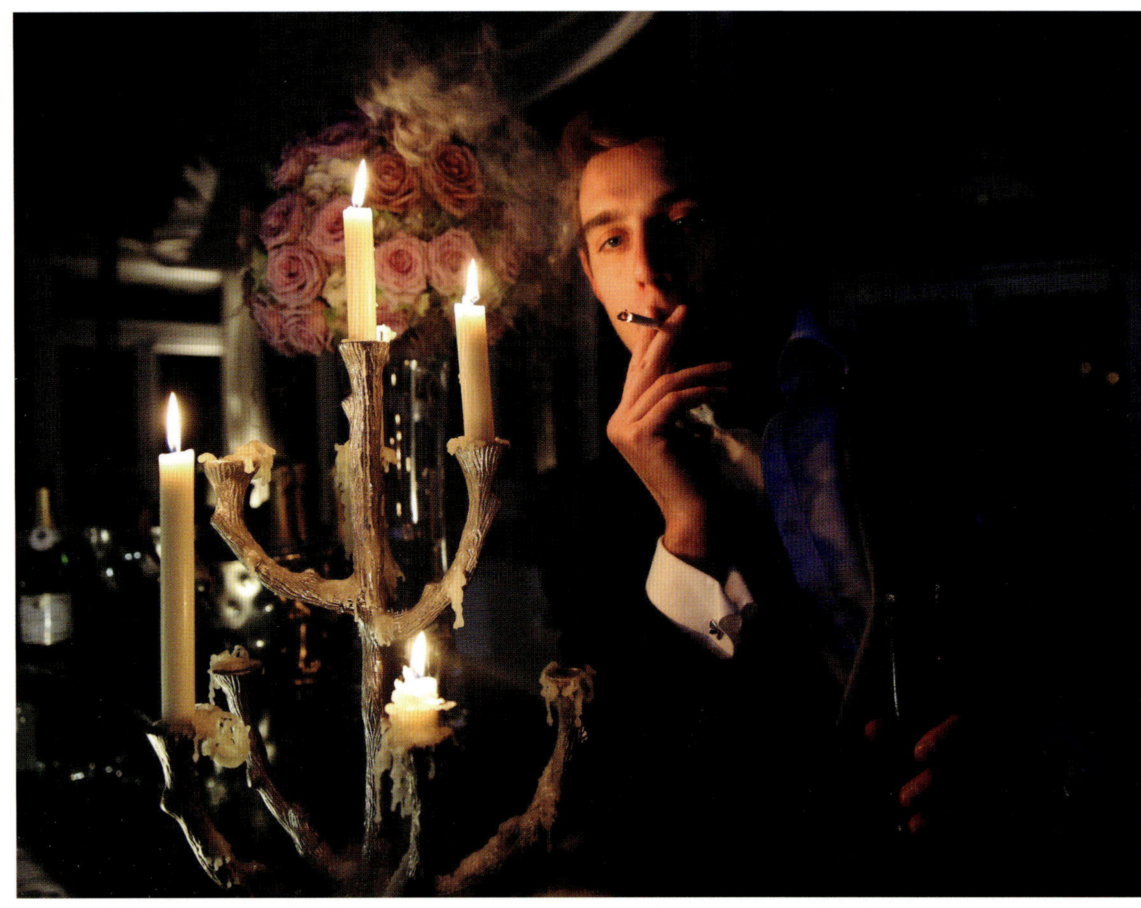

燭光晚餐和雪茄愛好者
Candlabra and Cigar Smoker
by Chris Dawes

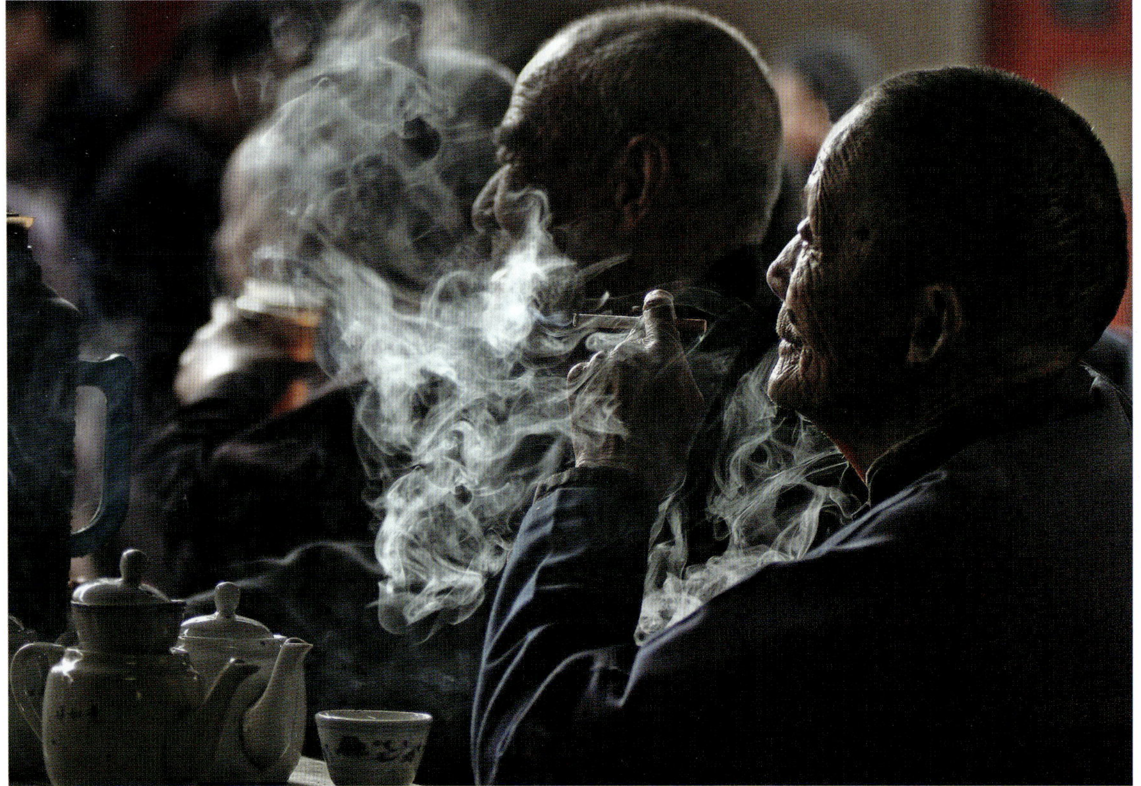

茶館印象 / 攝影: 方旭升
Teahouse Impressions
by Fang Xusheng

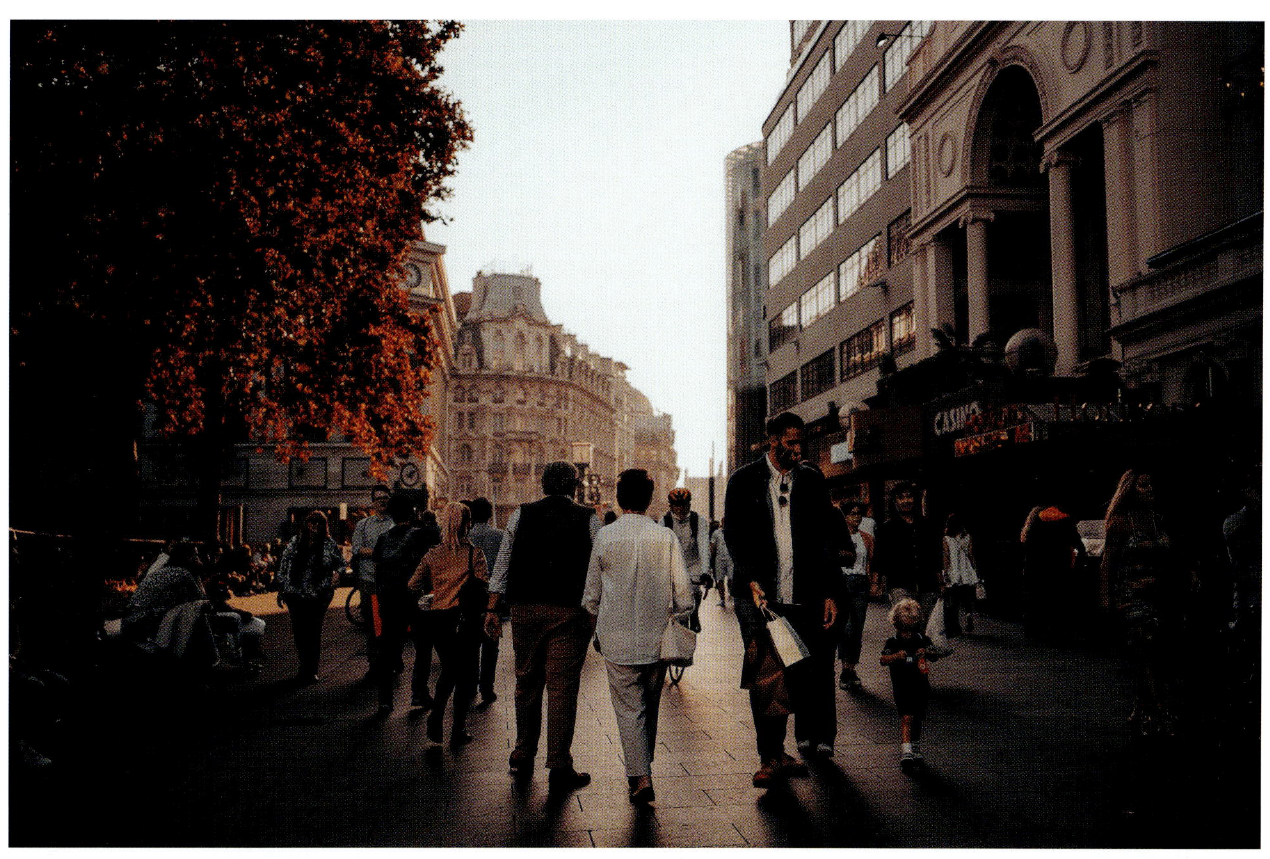

城市掠影 / 攝影: 農賀迪
City Snapshot by Nong Hedi

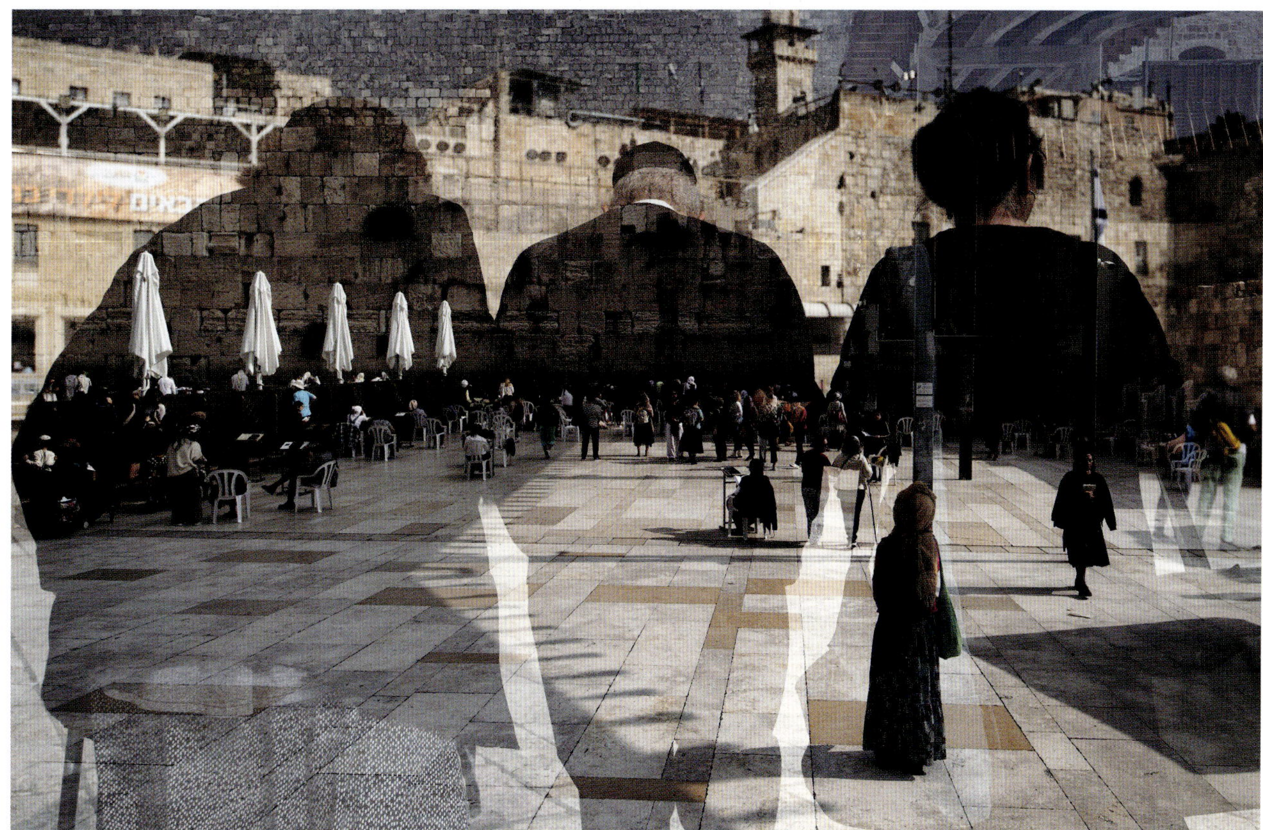

哭墻 / 攝影: 湯慧同
Wailing Wall by Tang Huitong

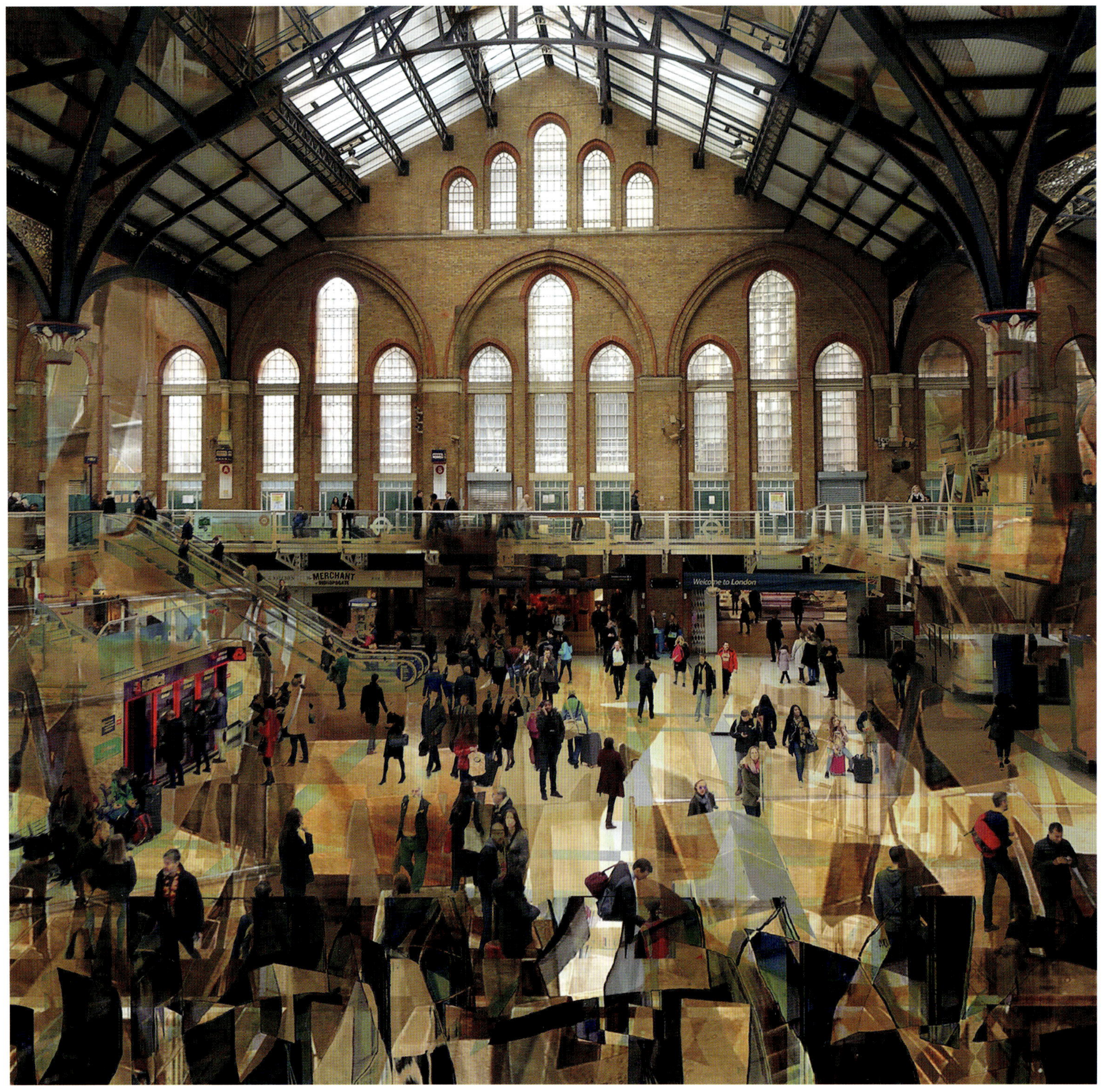

利物浦街的高峰期
Rush Hour at Liverpool Street by John Foster ARPS

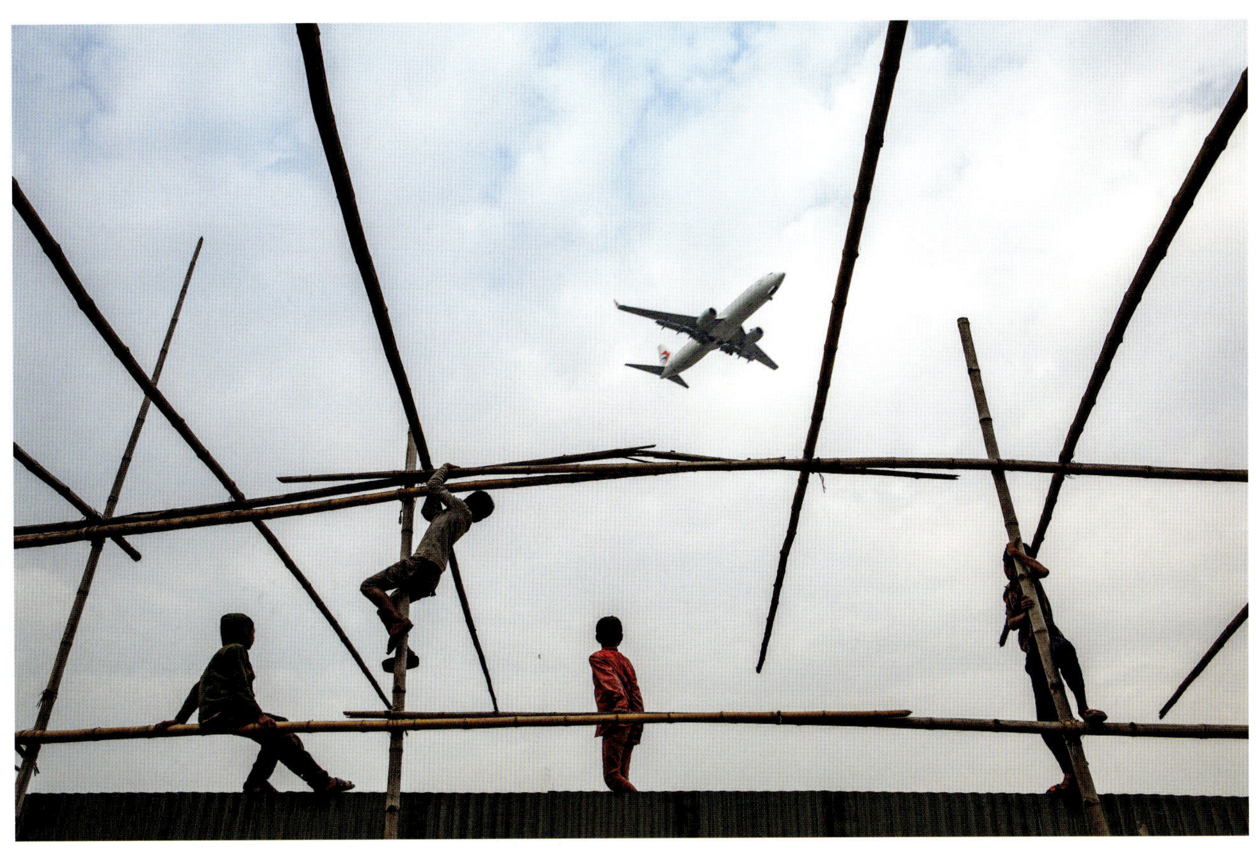

貧民窟 / 攝影: 範軍
Slums by Fan Jun

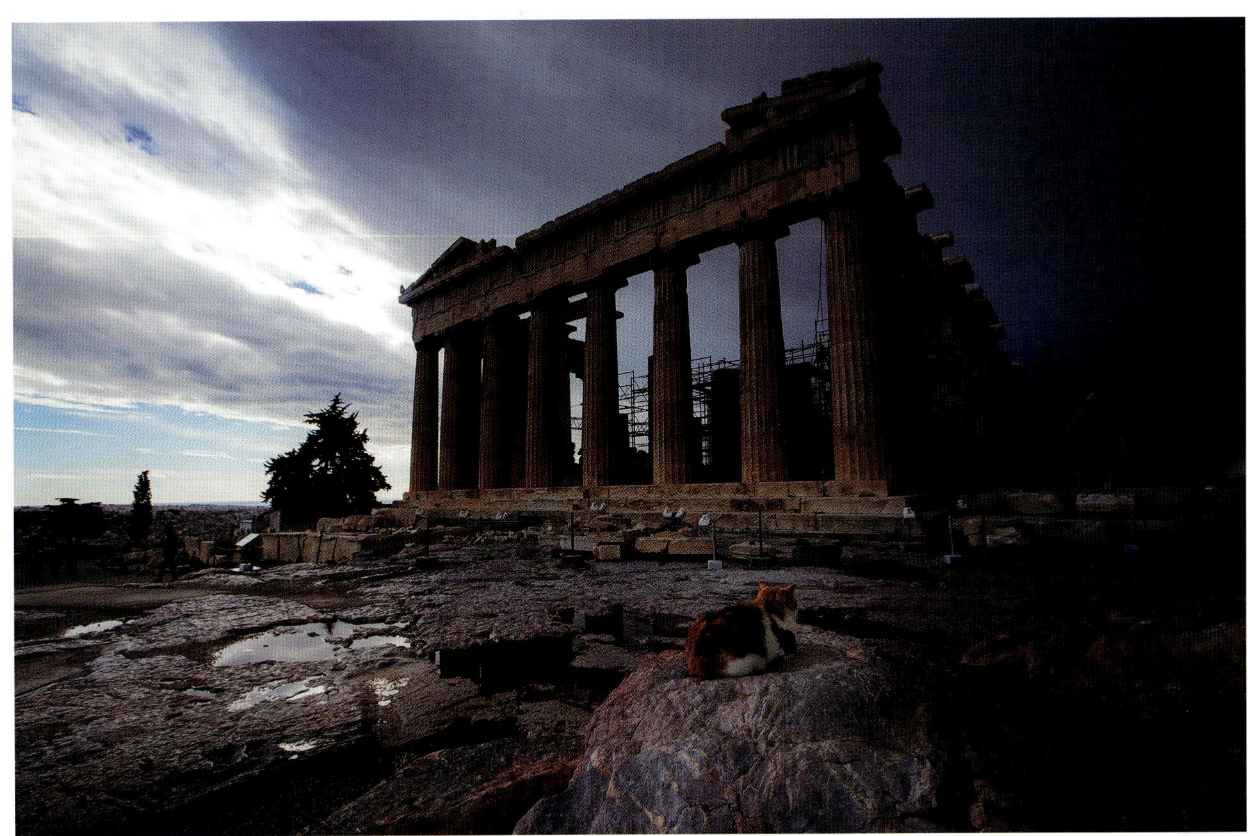

守望雅典 / 攝影: 凌伯勛
Guard Athensa by Ling Boxun

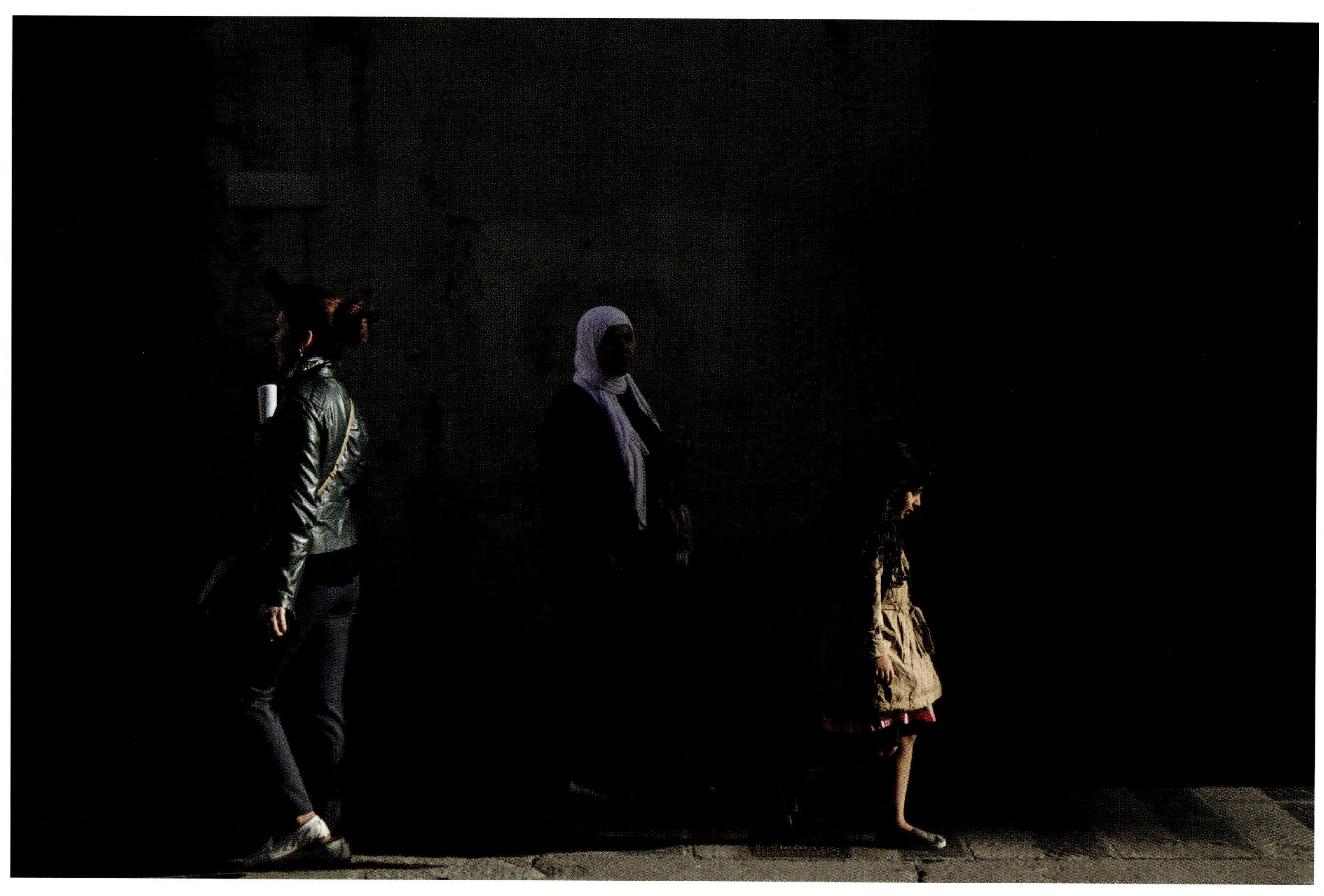

意大利佛羅倫薩街頭 / 攝影: 李培寧
Streets of Florence Italy by Li Peining

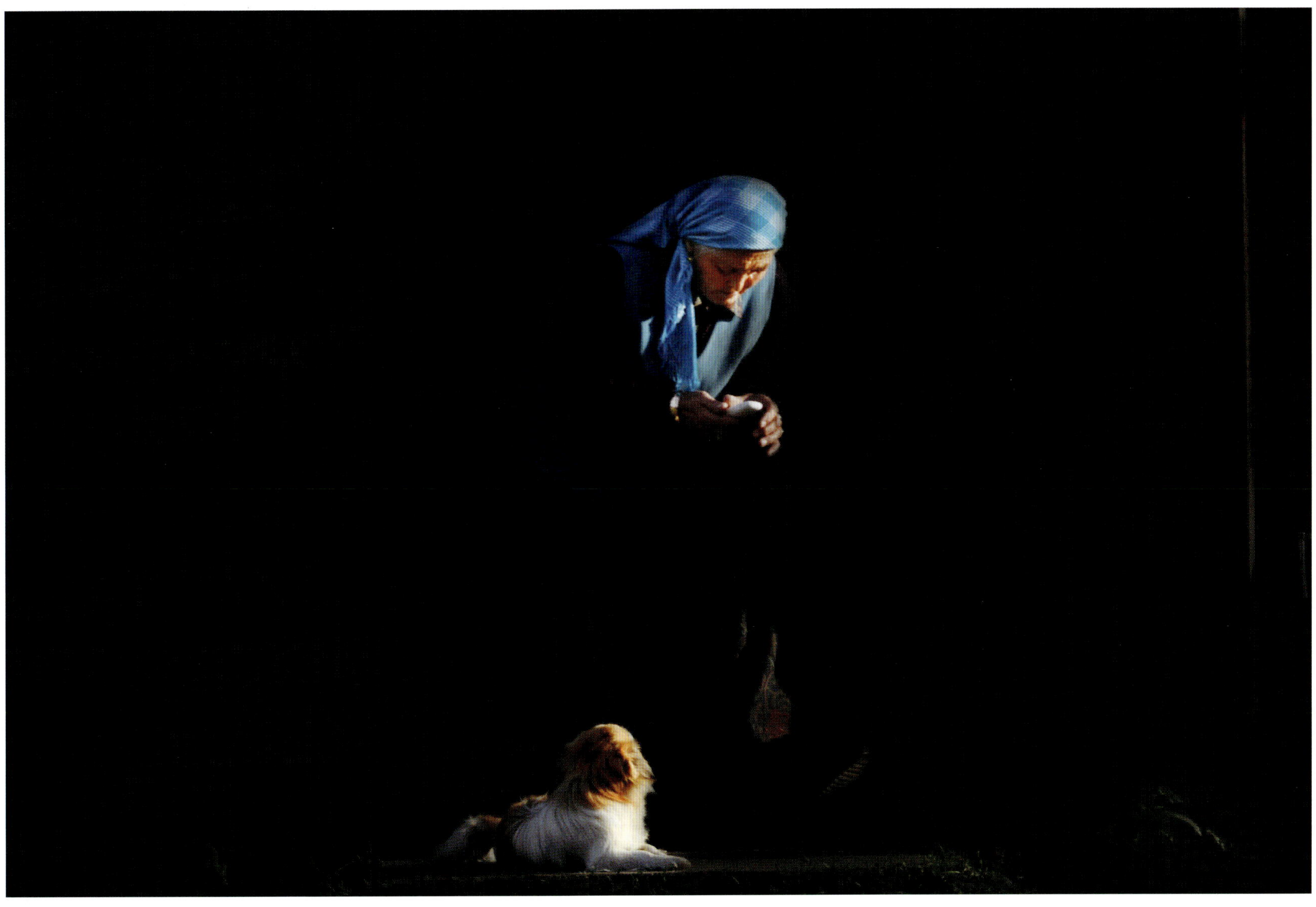

盼望 / 摄影: 崔明浩
Longing for by Cui Minghao

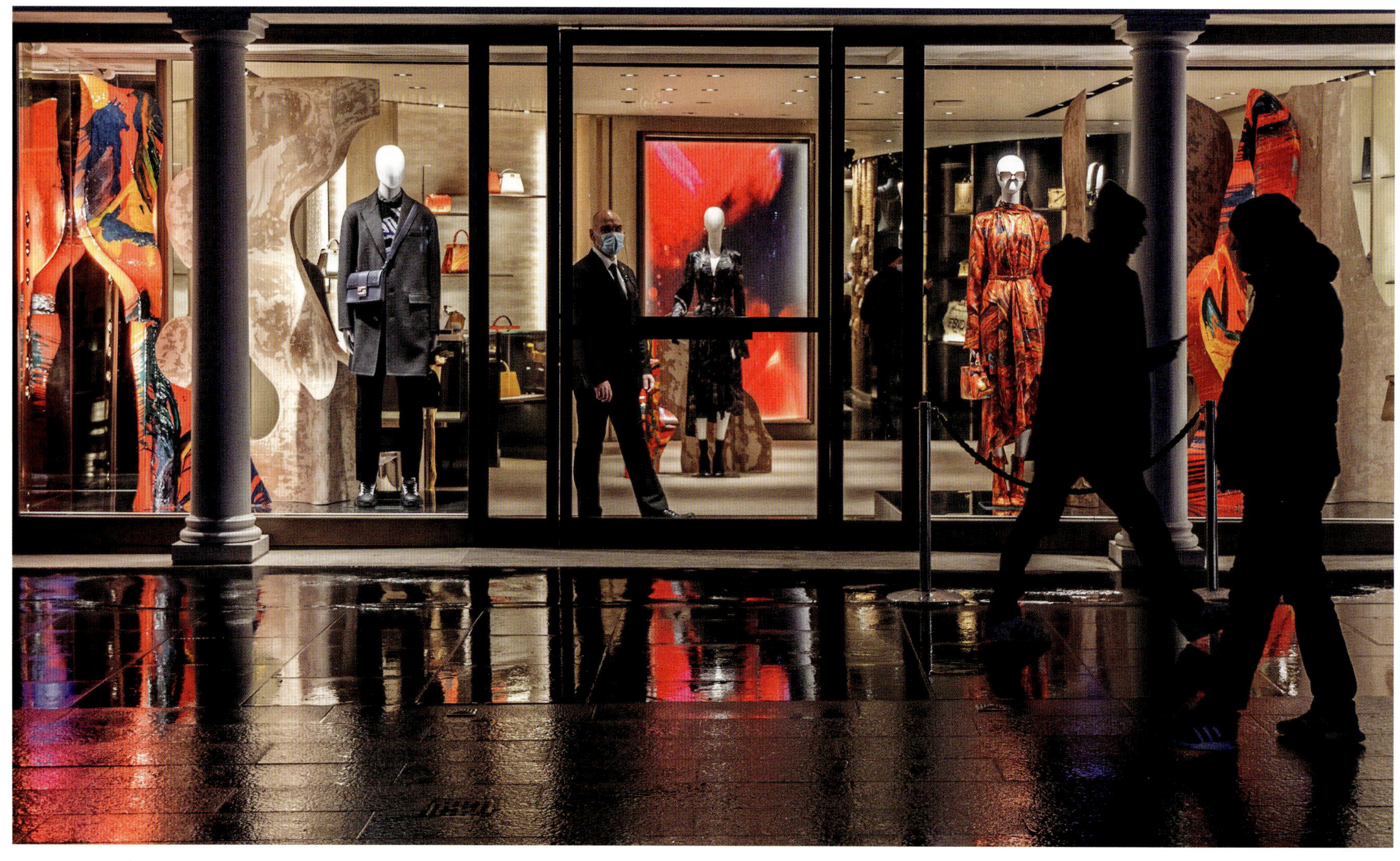

新邦德街的雨夜
Rainy Evening in New Bond Street
by Judy Hicks LRPS

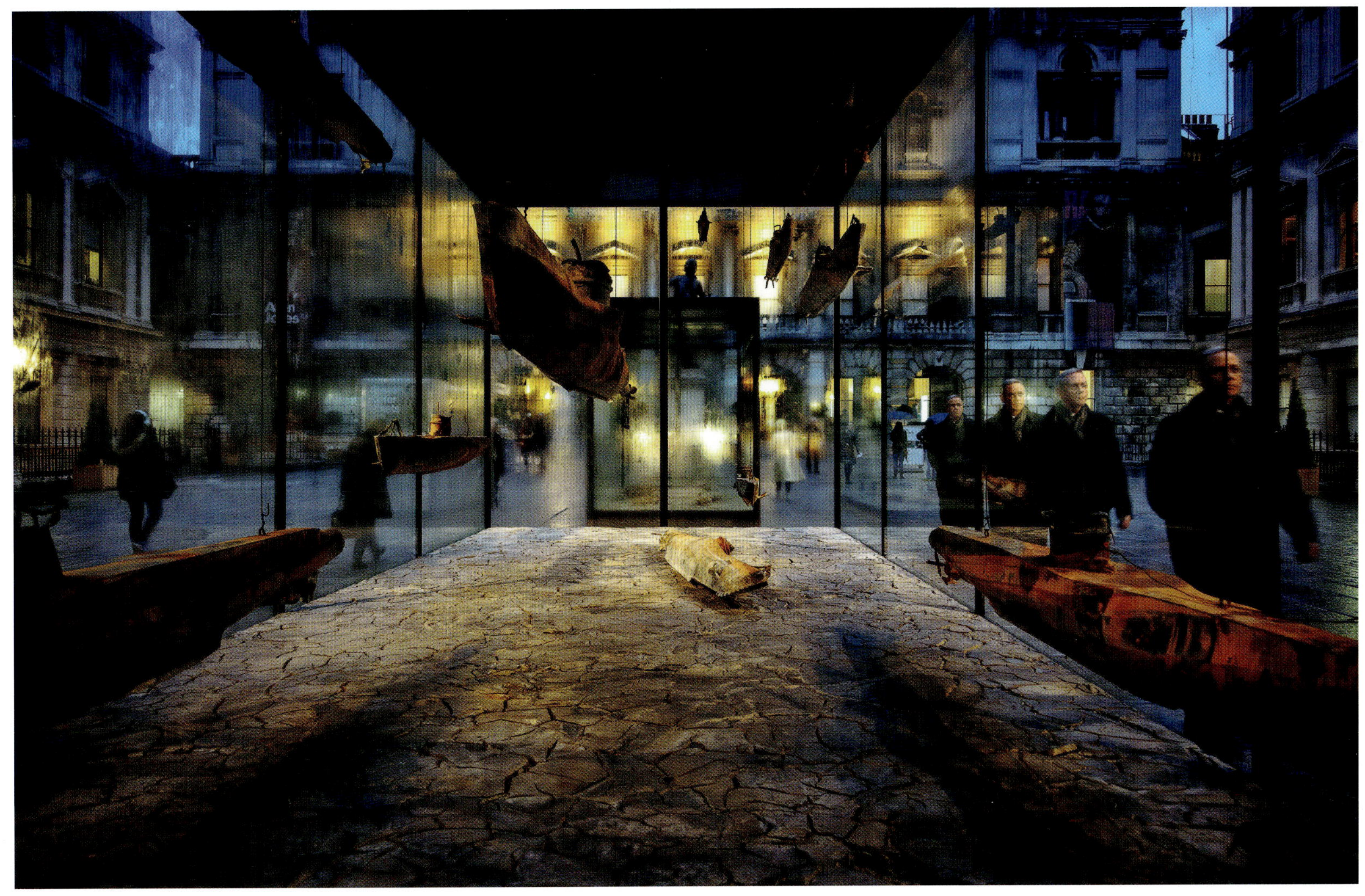

對于安塞姆・基弗來說，戰爭還沒有結束
For Anselm Kiefer the War is not Over Yet
by Mike Woodman

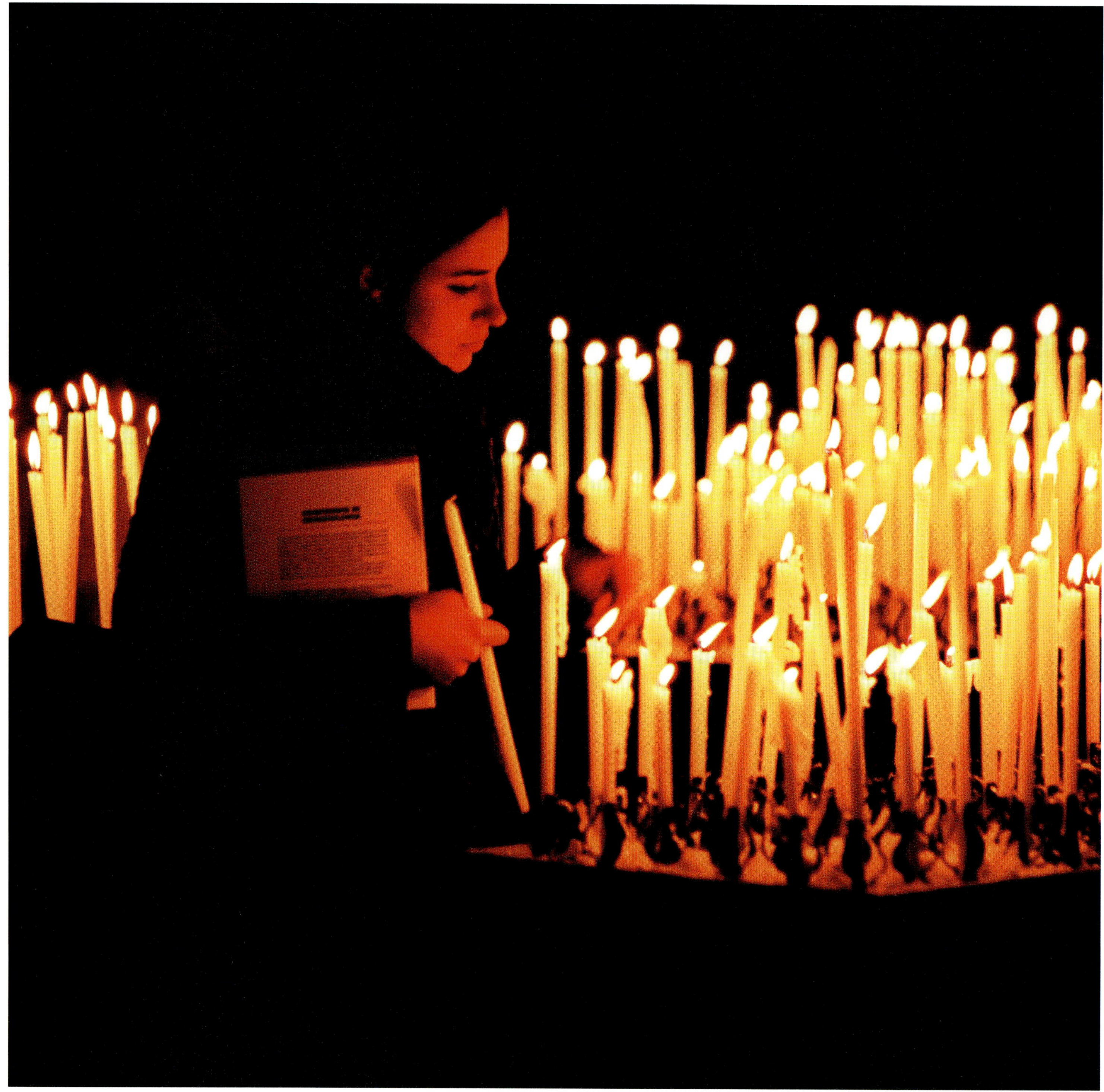

虔誠 / 攝影: 鄭啓東
Pious by Zheng Qidong

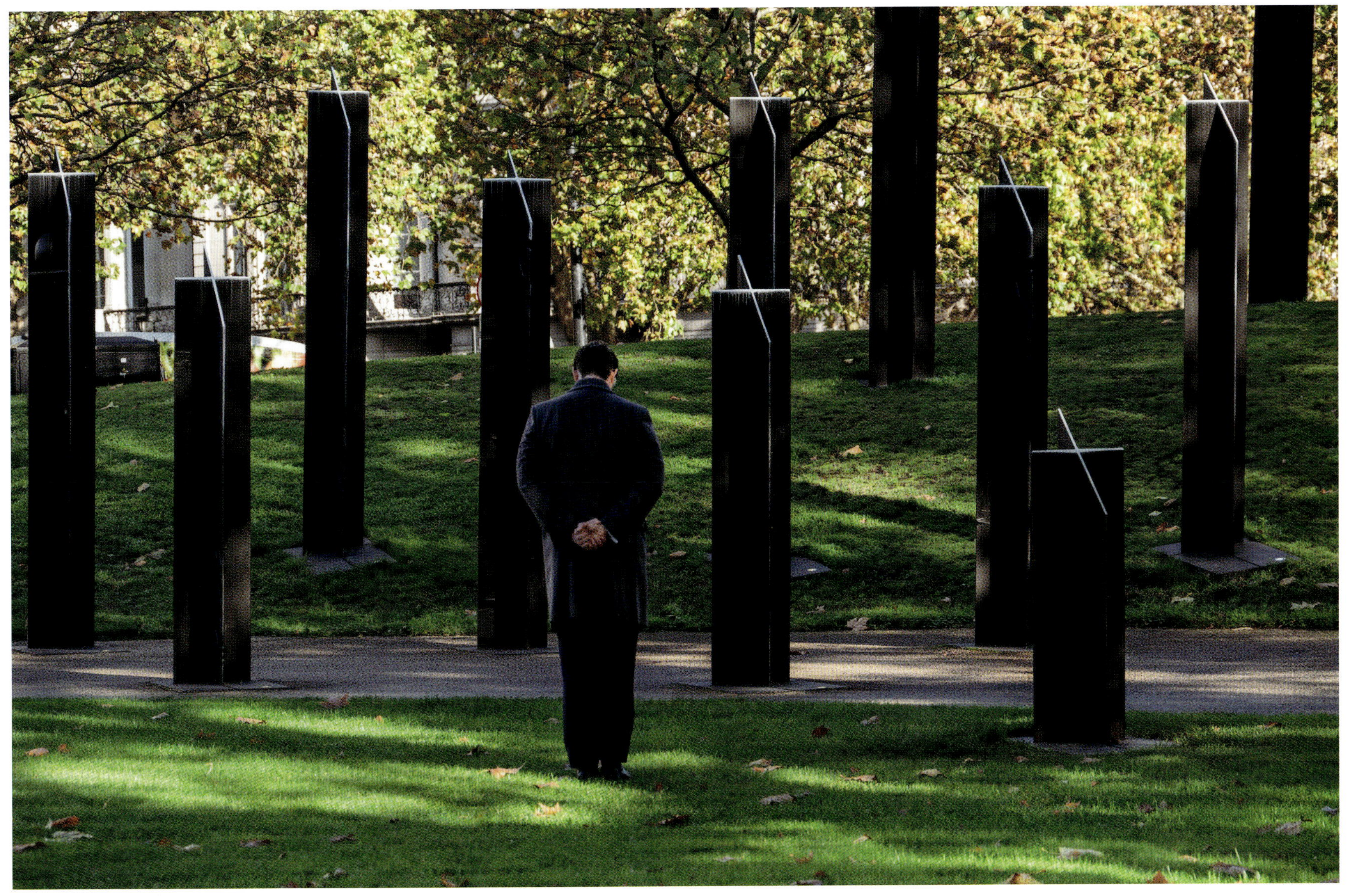

個人紀念
Personal Remembrance by David Hicks

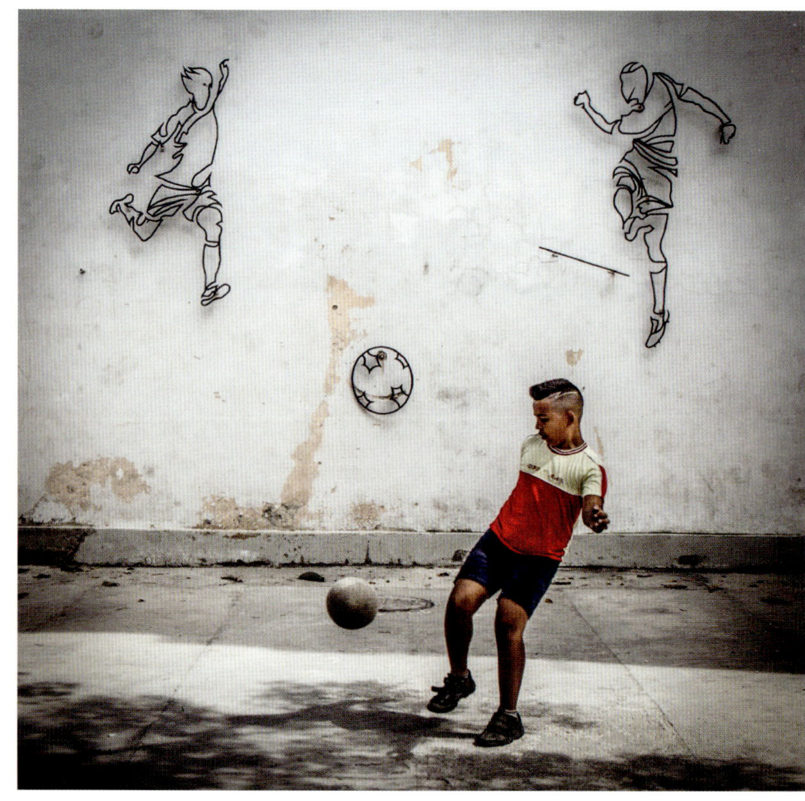

古巴接受
Cuba Accepted
by Lynda Morris LRPS

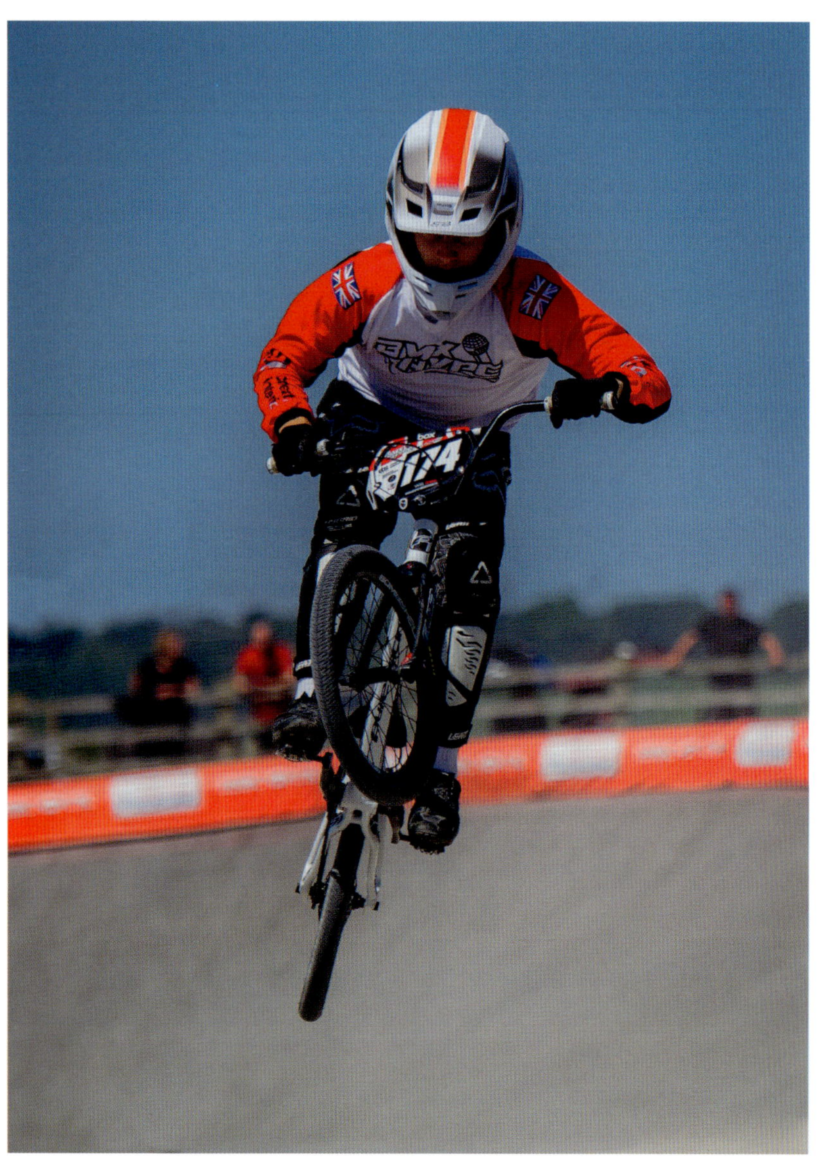

騎士
BMX Rider
by Graham Lingham LRPS

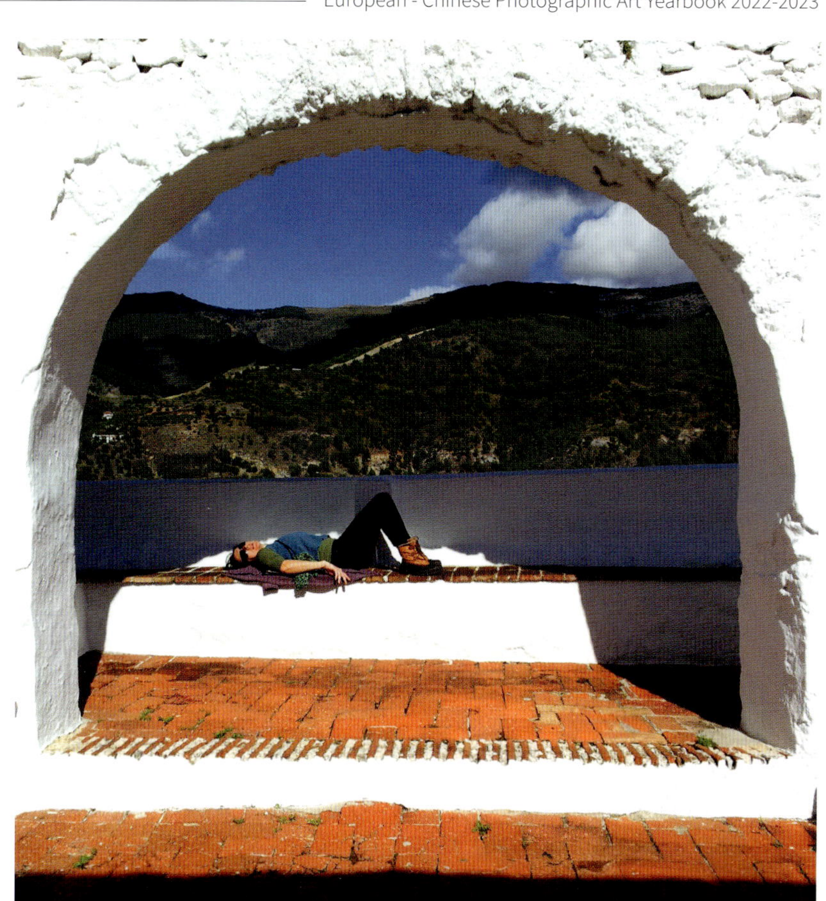

西班牙卡尼利亞斯
Canillas, Spain by Nahem Shoa

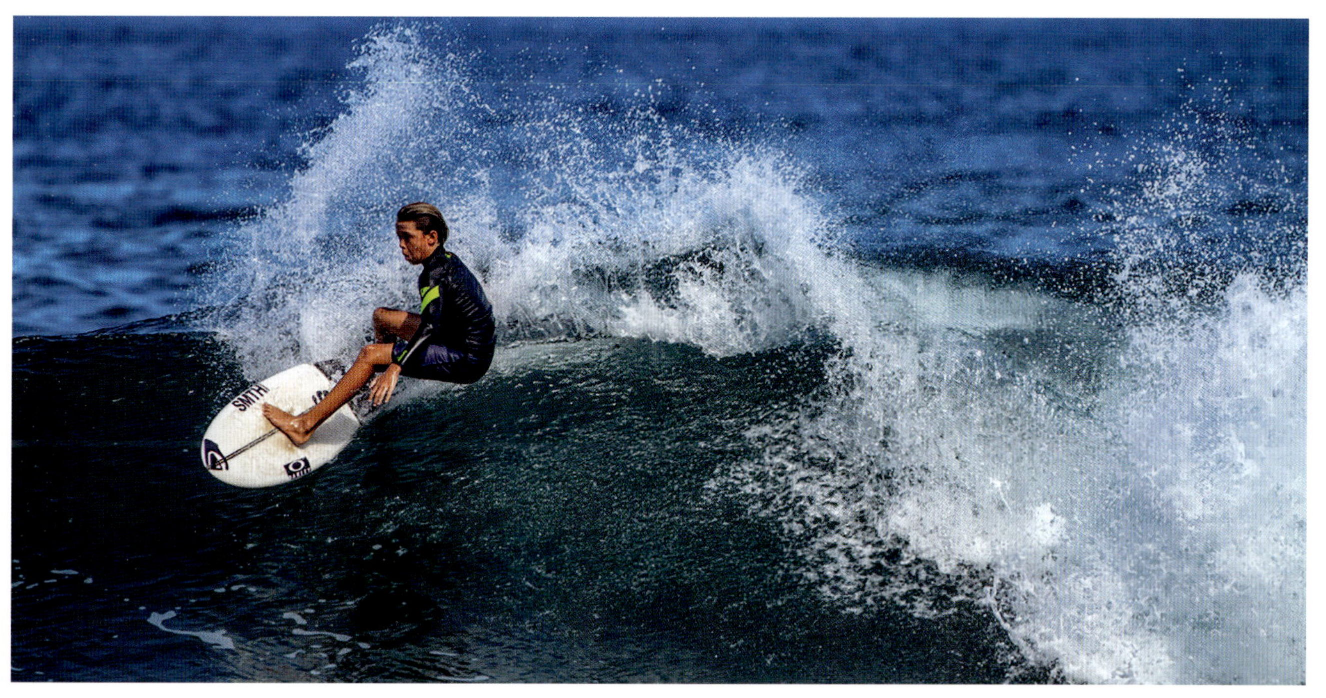

勇士 / 攝影: 王朝盛
Warrior by Wang Zhaosheng

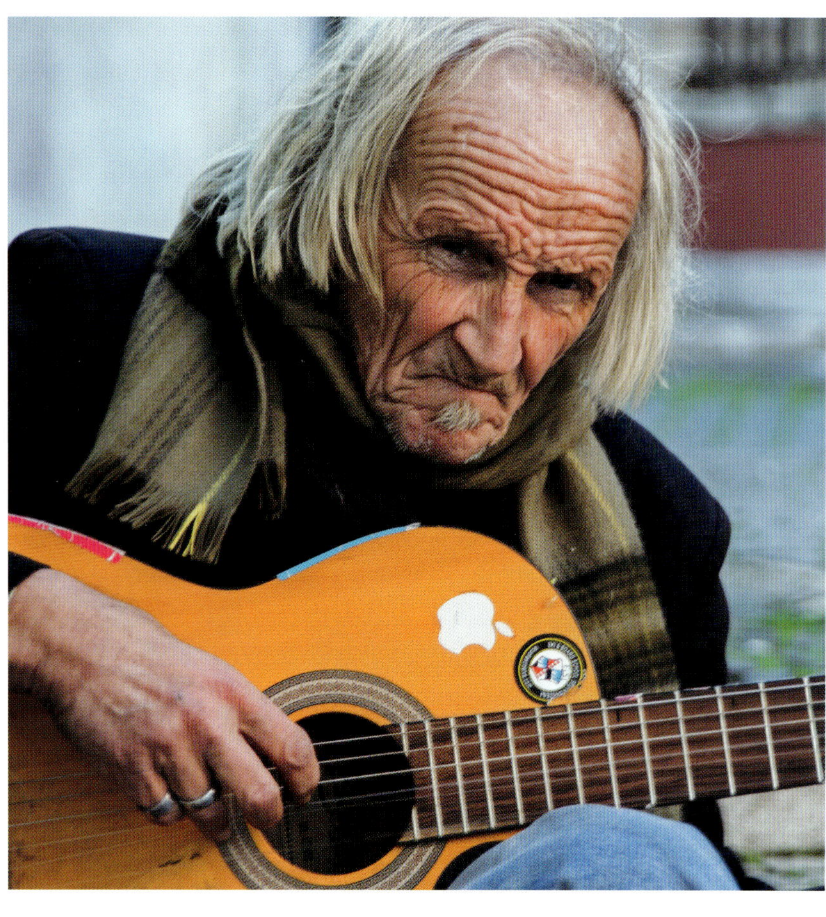

裏斯本街頭藝人
Lisbon Busker by Richard Davison LRPS

男人和他的狗
Man and His Dog
by Jay Charnock FRPS

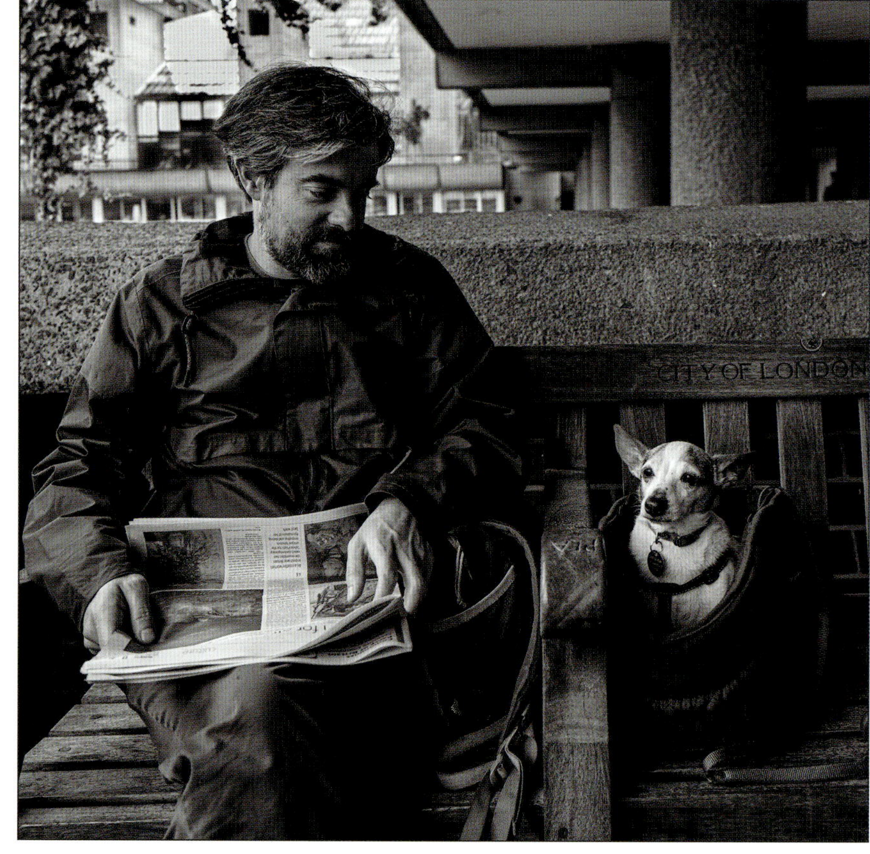

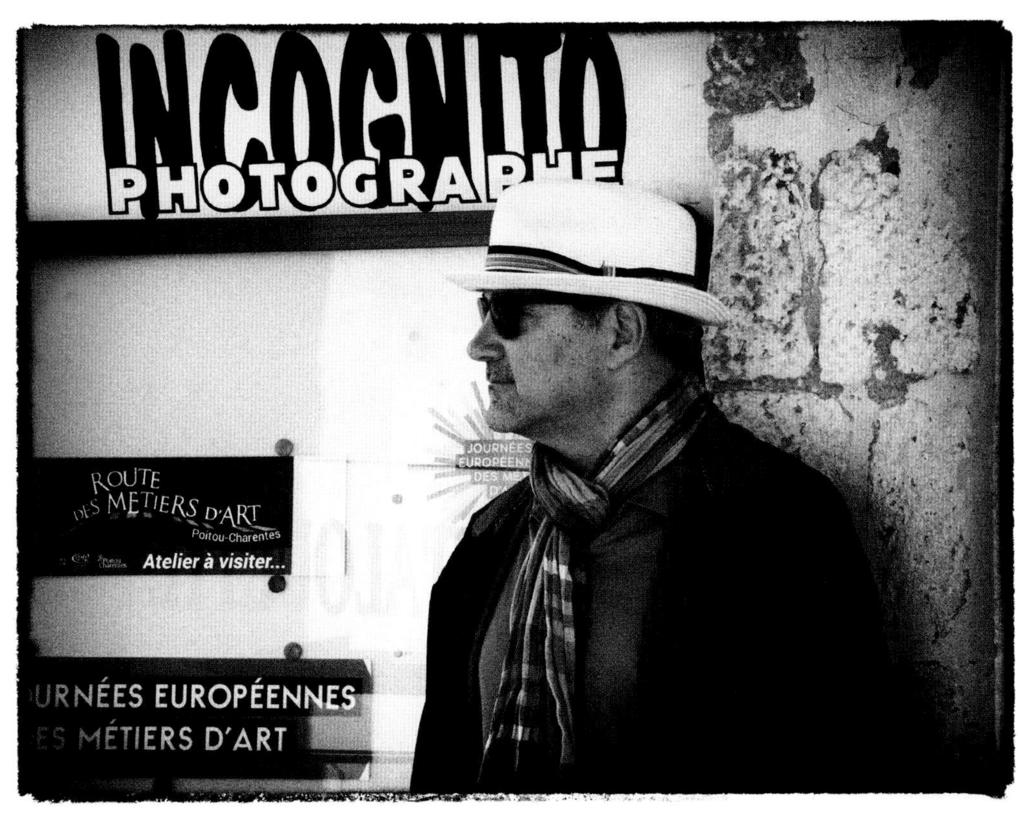

隱姓埋名
Incognito by Angela Ford ARPS

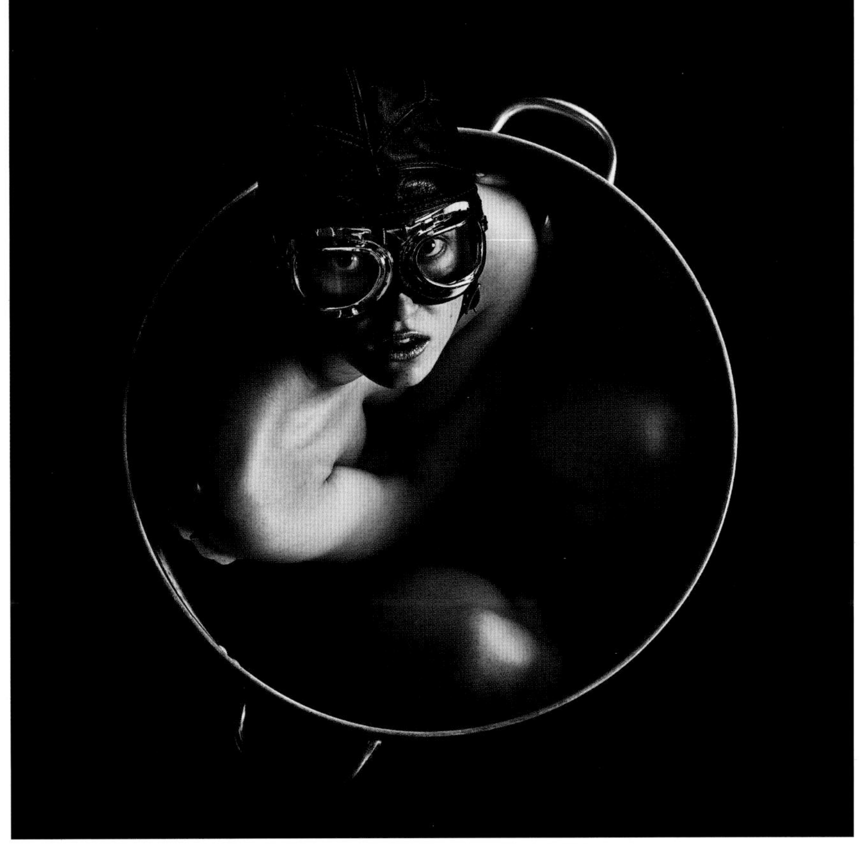

盆栽
Potted by Mike Woodman

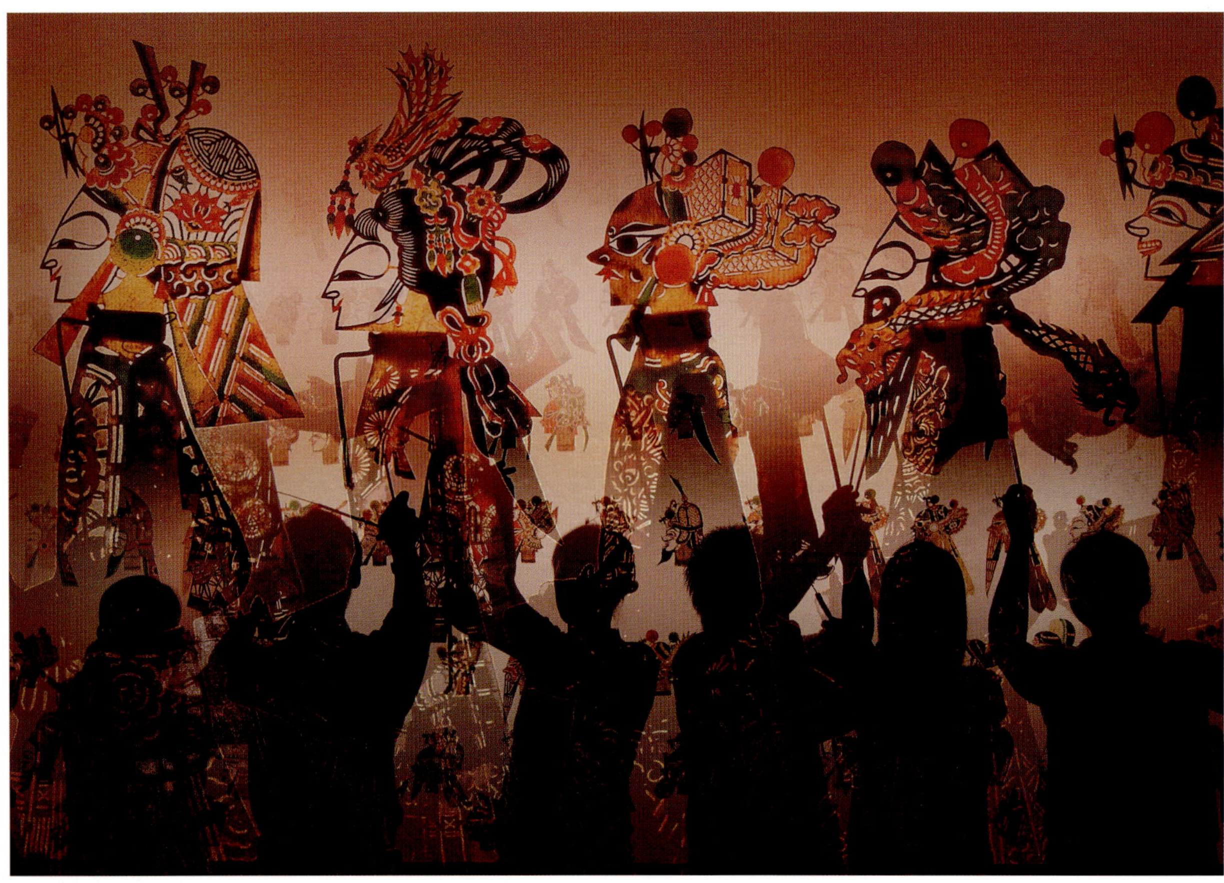

中國皮影 / 攝影: 成貴民
Chinese Leather Shadow
by Cheng Guimin

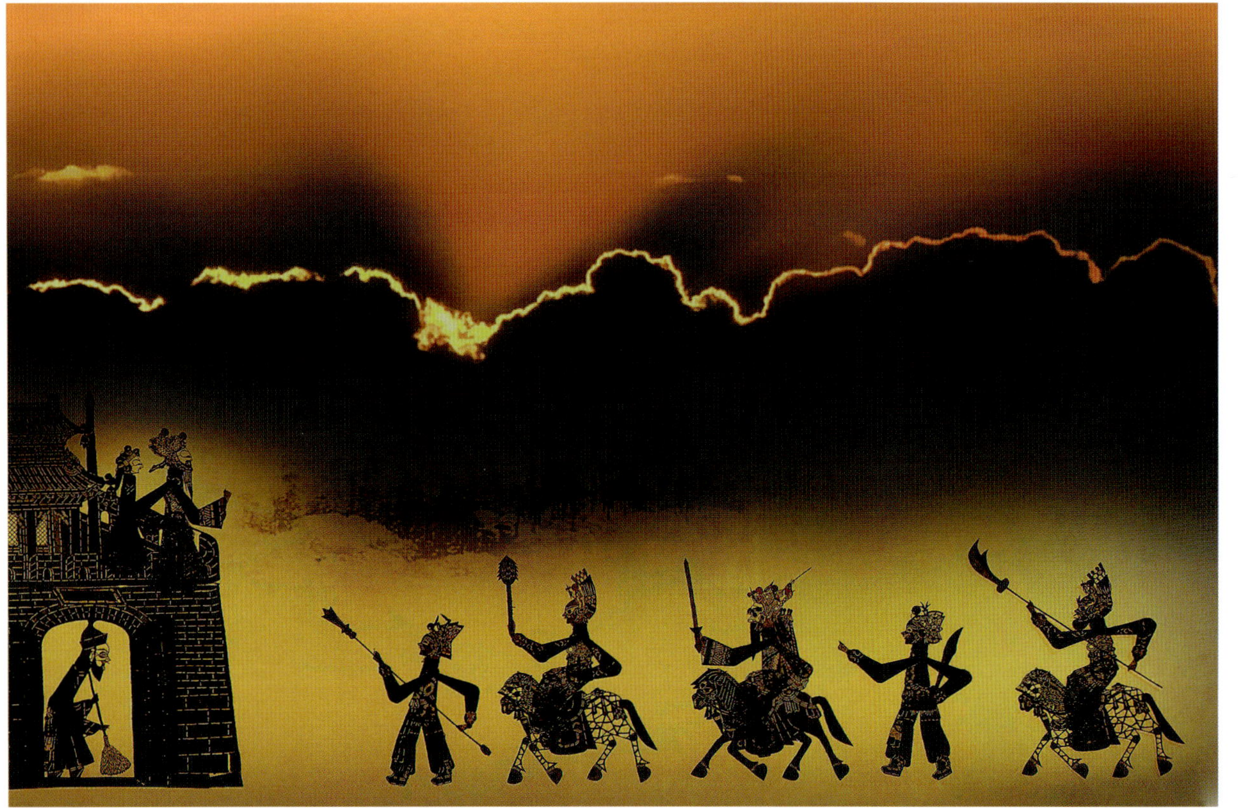

中國皮影 / 攝影: 檀淑貴
Chinese Leather Shadow
by Tan Shugui

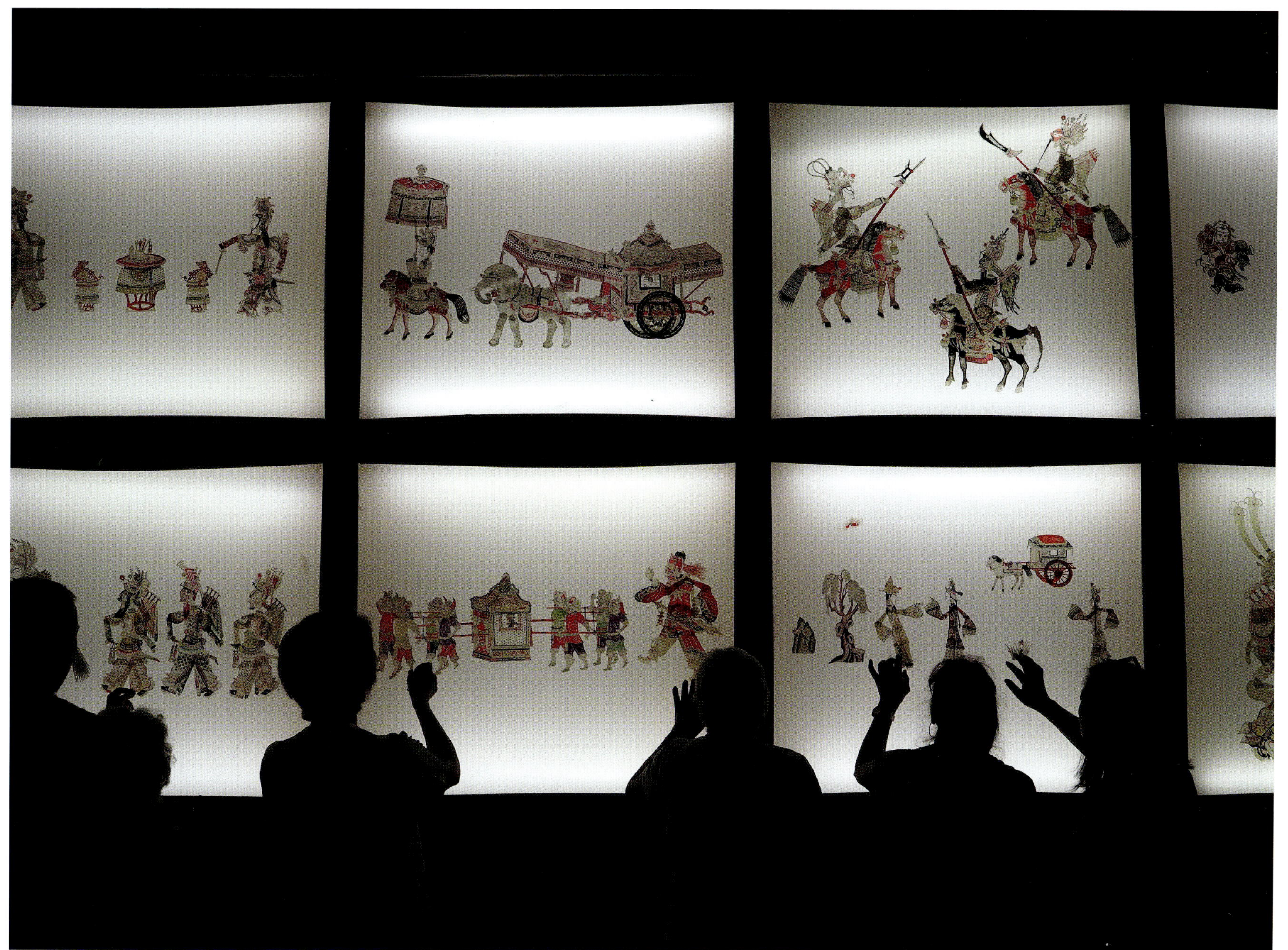

中國皮影
Chinese Leather Shadow by Mike Longhurst FRPS

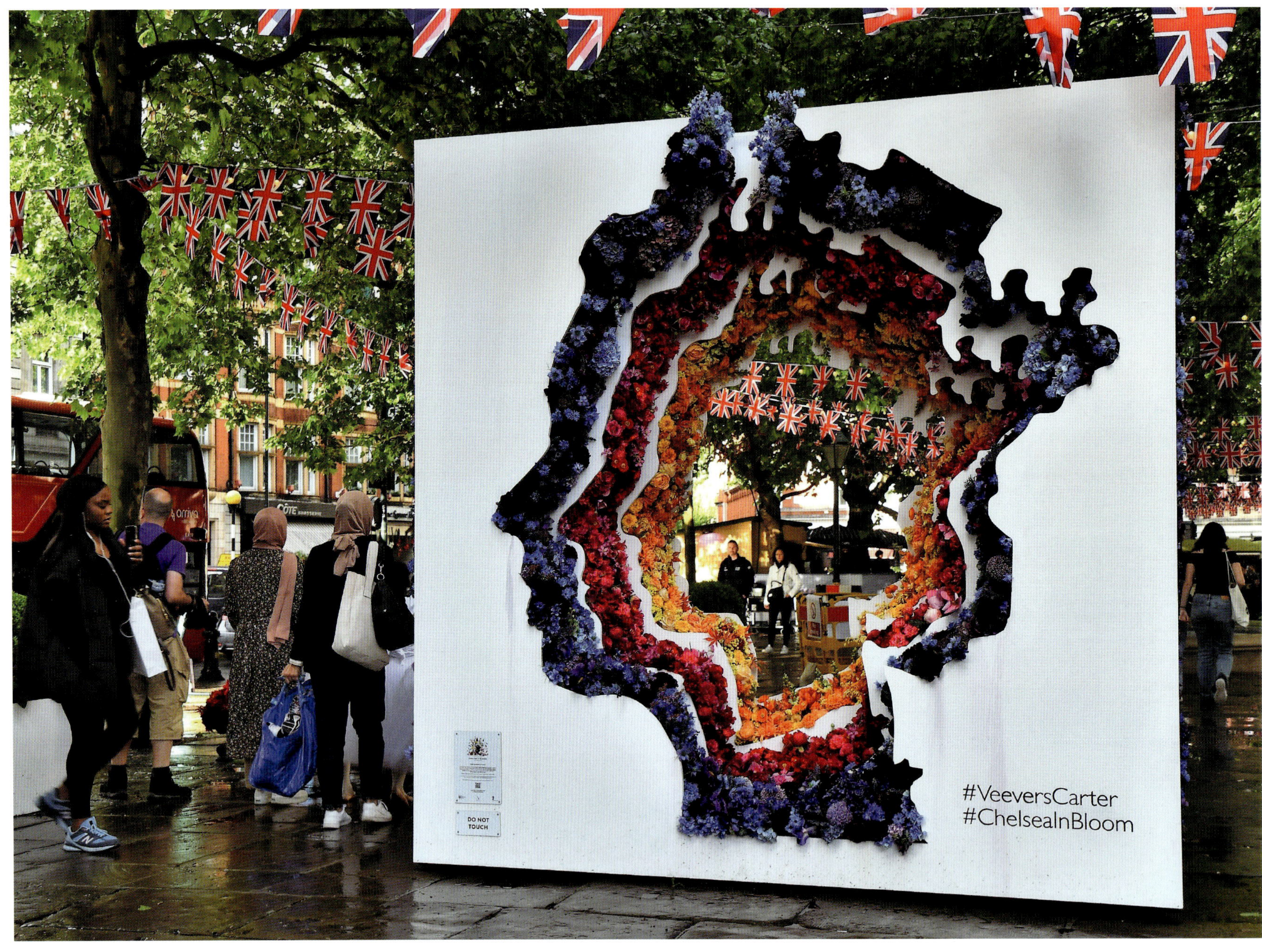

切爾西斯隆廣場鮮花綻放剪影
Chelsea Sloane Square Flowers in Bloom
by Judy Hicks LRPS

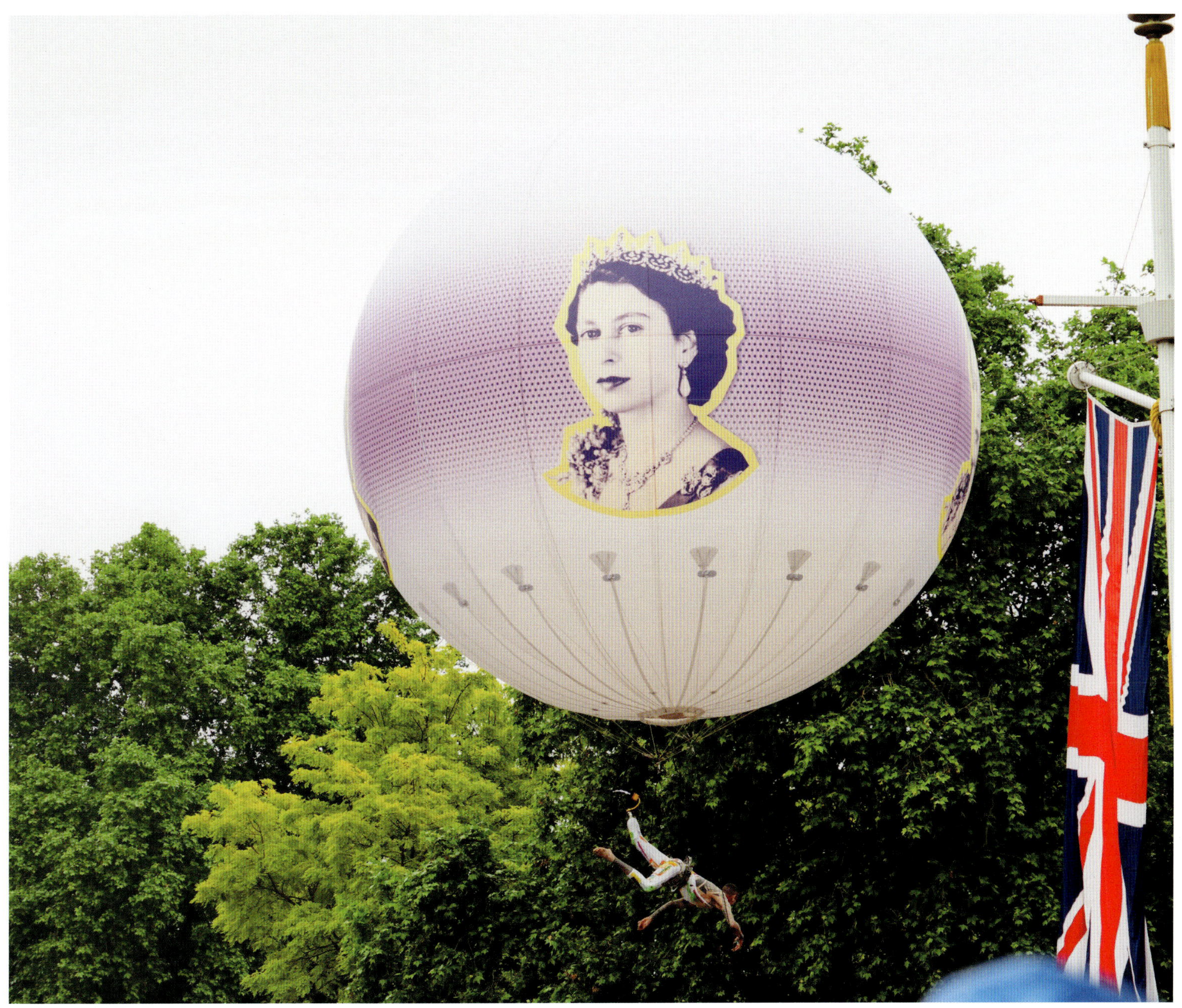

雜技演員與女皇氣球
Queens Balloon Acrobat by Suzanna Mu

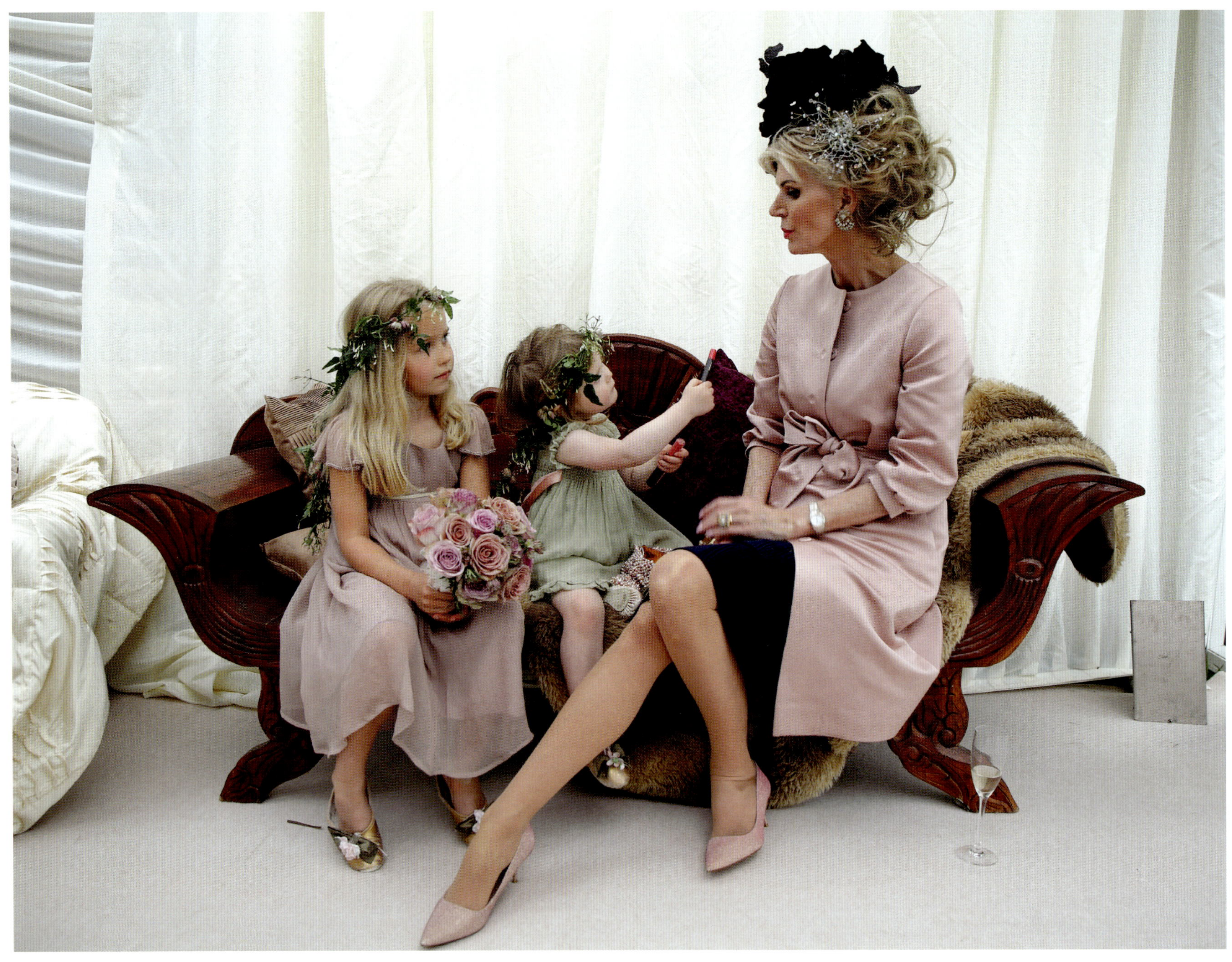

W夫人和伴娘們
Mrs.W and Bridesmaids by Chris Dawes

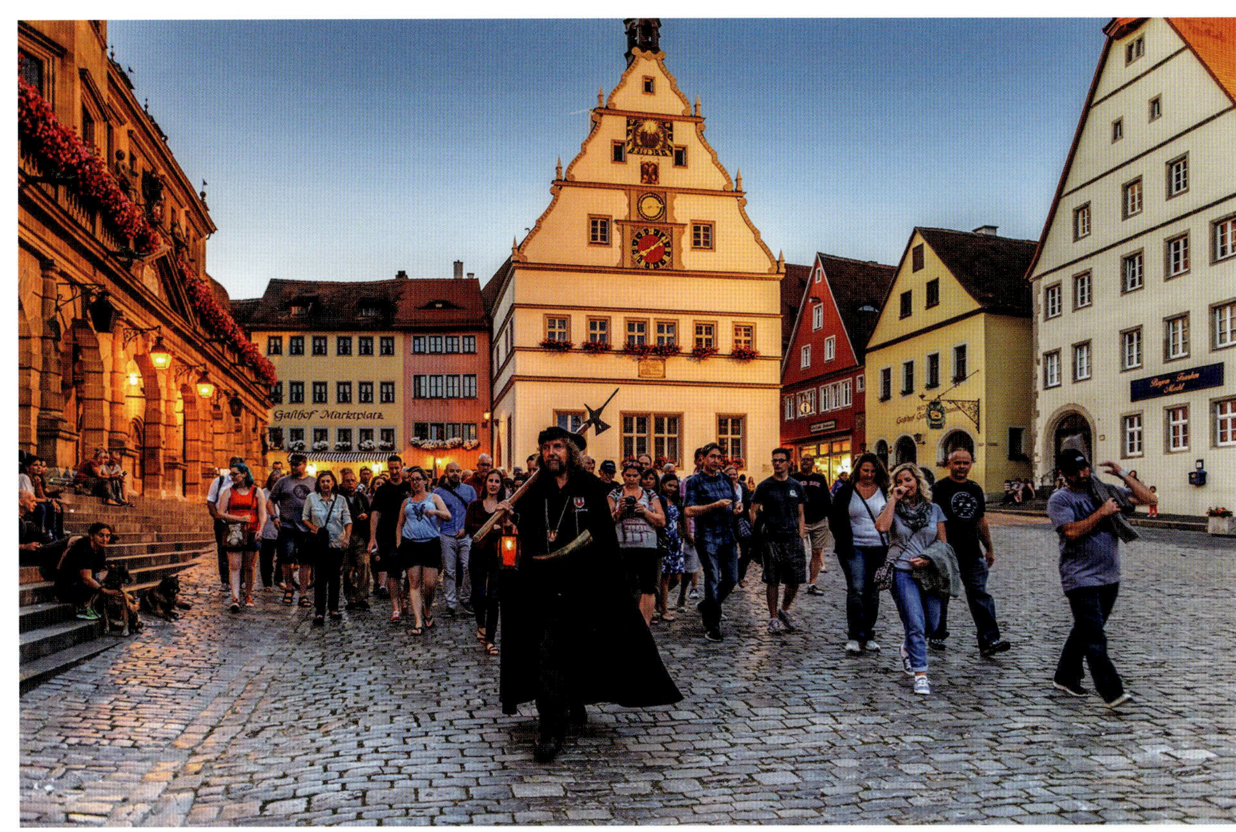

夜游羅滕堡 / 攝影: 魏建棟
Night Tour of Rothenburg
by Wei Jiandong

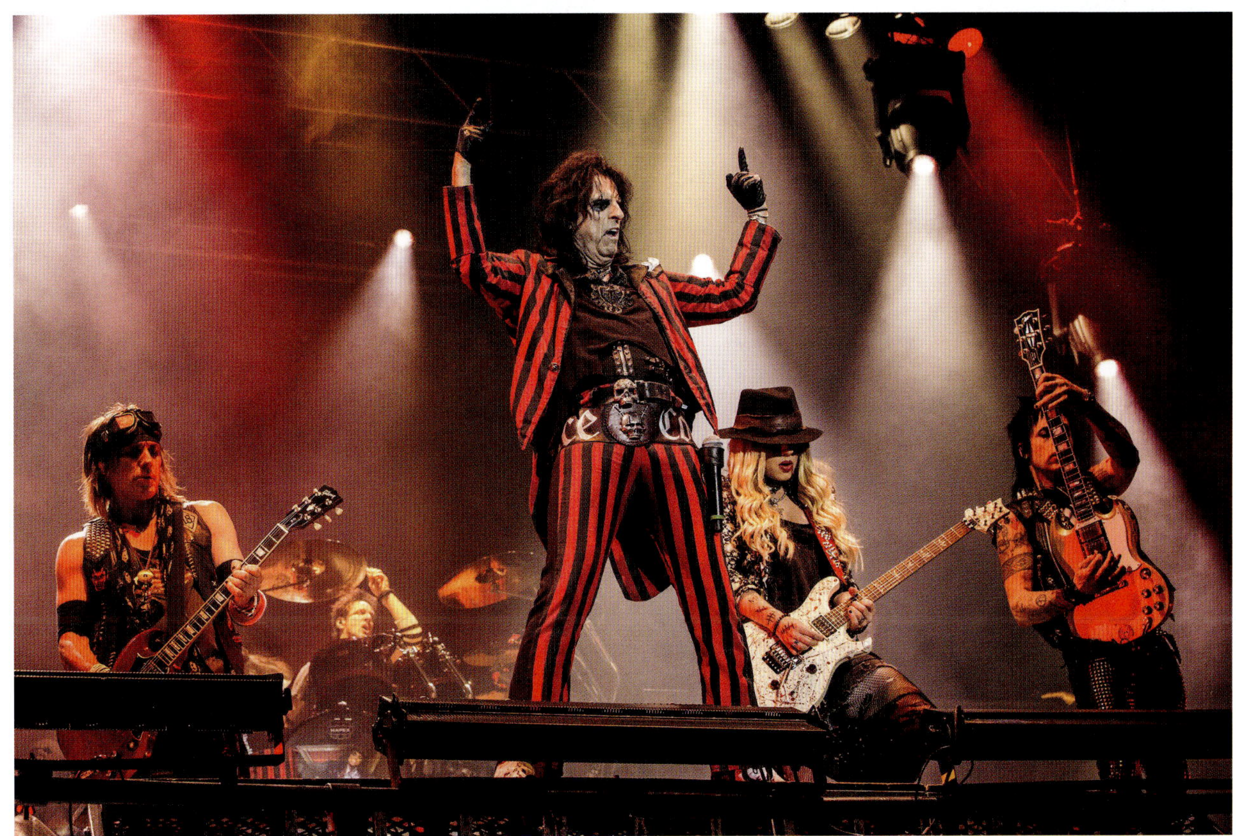

愛麗絲庫珀樂隊在Cropredy演出
Alice Cooper Band at Cropredy
by Colin Clarke ARPS

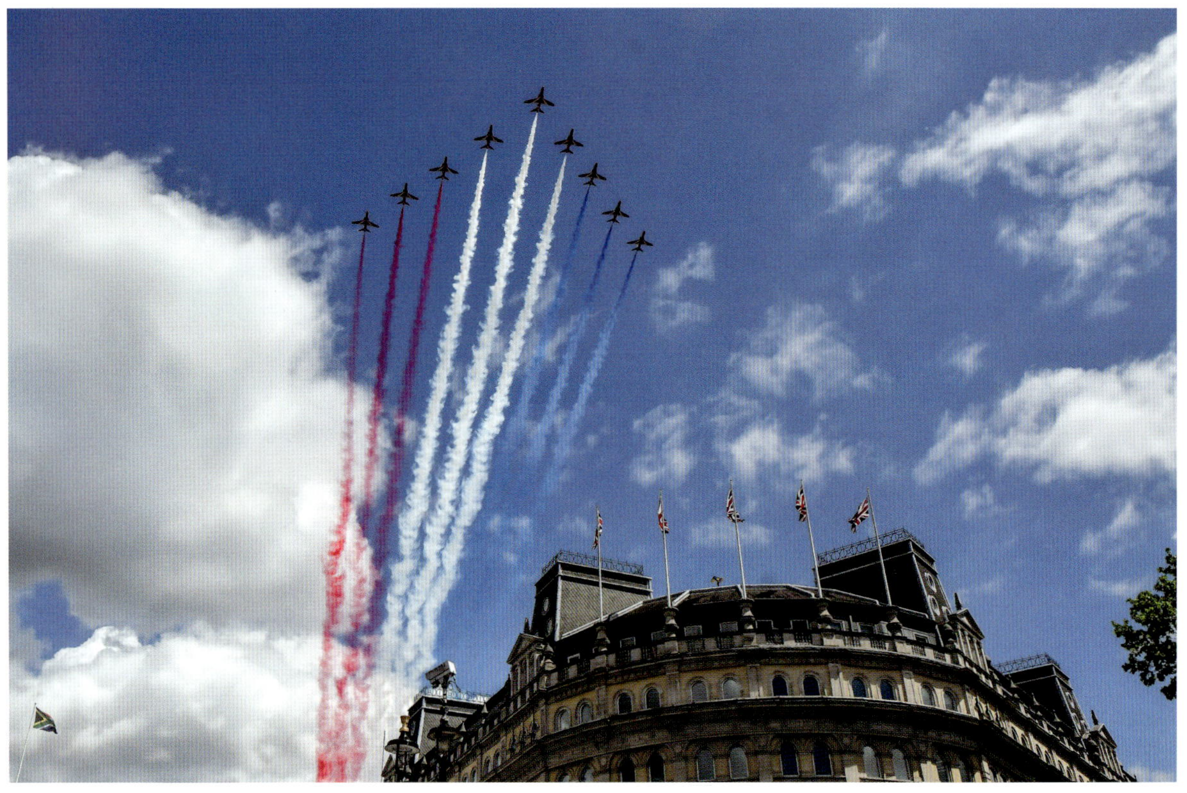

紅箭飛行隊飛躍表演 /
攝影: 李世惠
Queen's Birthday Red Arrows Flypast
by See Li

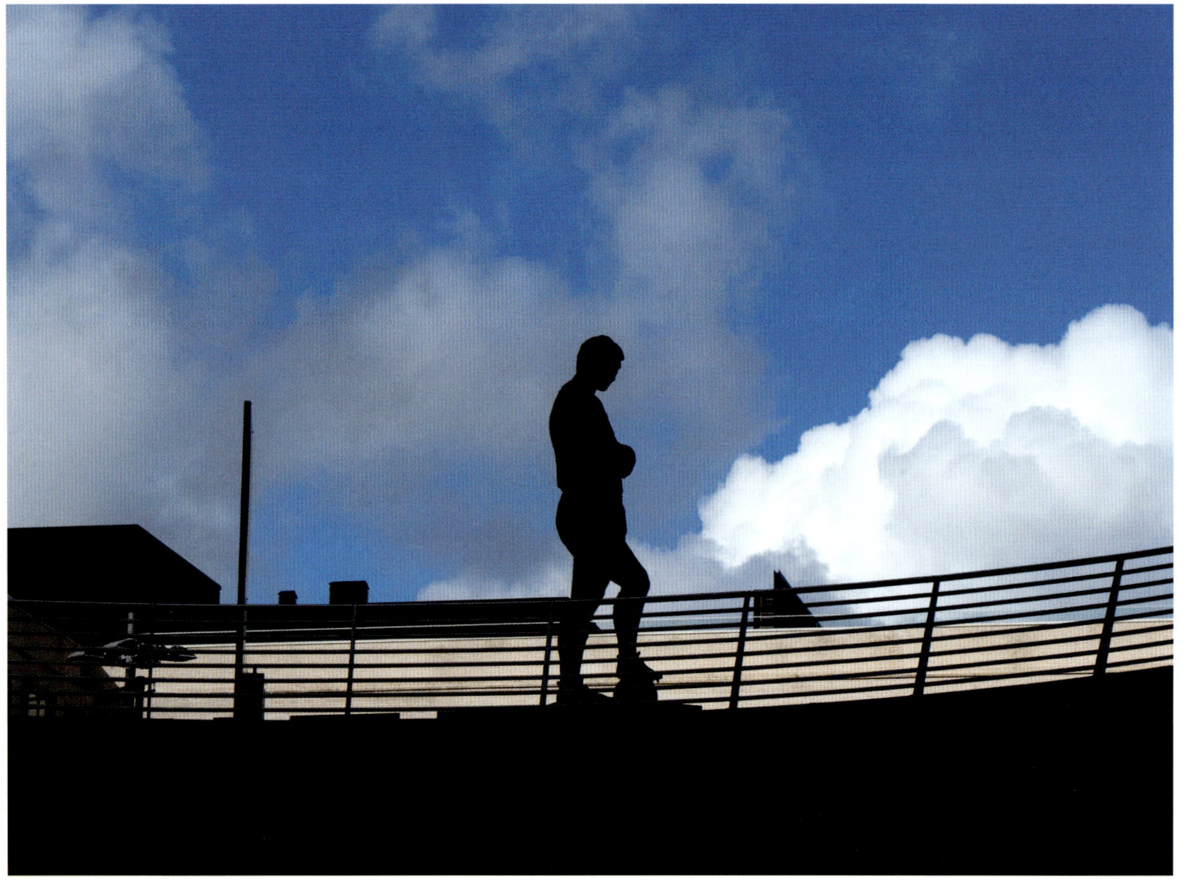

Bobby Moore在溫布利球場
Bobby Moore at Wembley Stadium
by Santosh Puthran

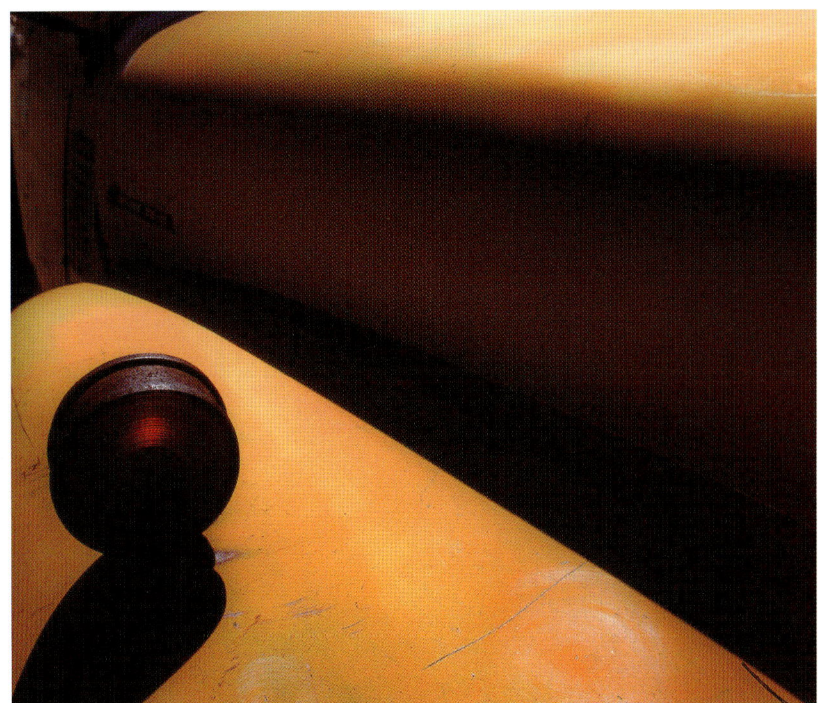

芥末、鐵銹和影子
Mustard, Rust and Shadow
by Quentin Ball ARPS

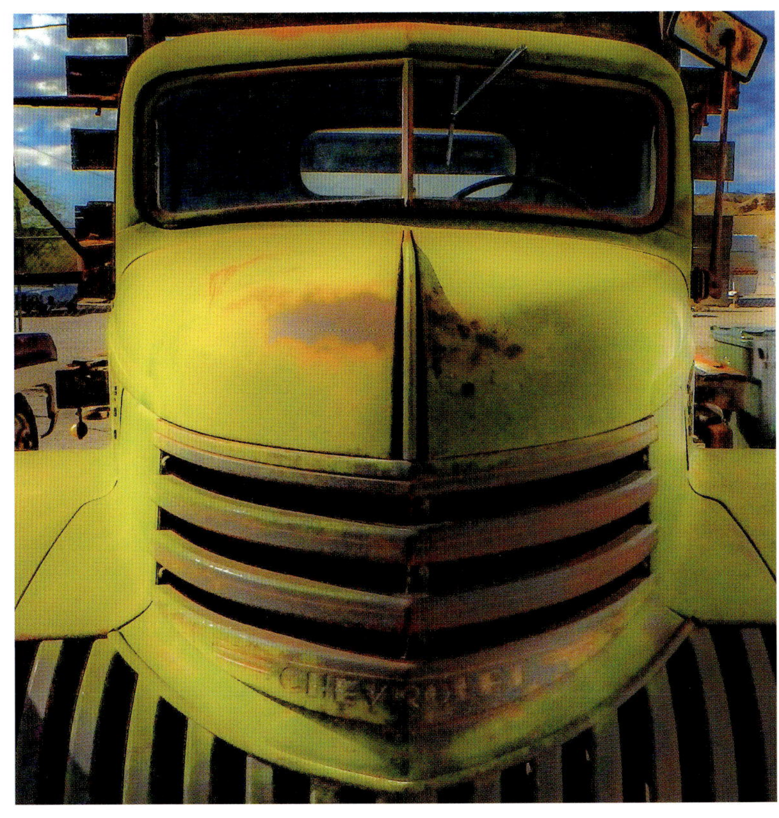

石灰卡車
Lime Truck
by Quentin Ball ARPS

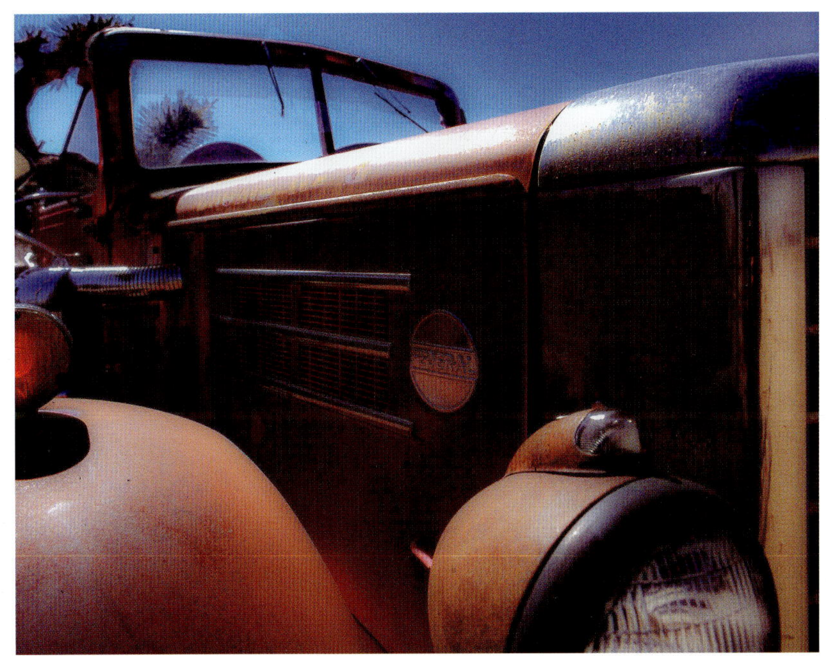

消防車黄金點
Fire Truck, Gold Point
by Quentin Ball ARPS

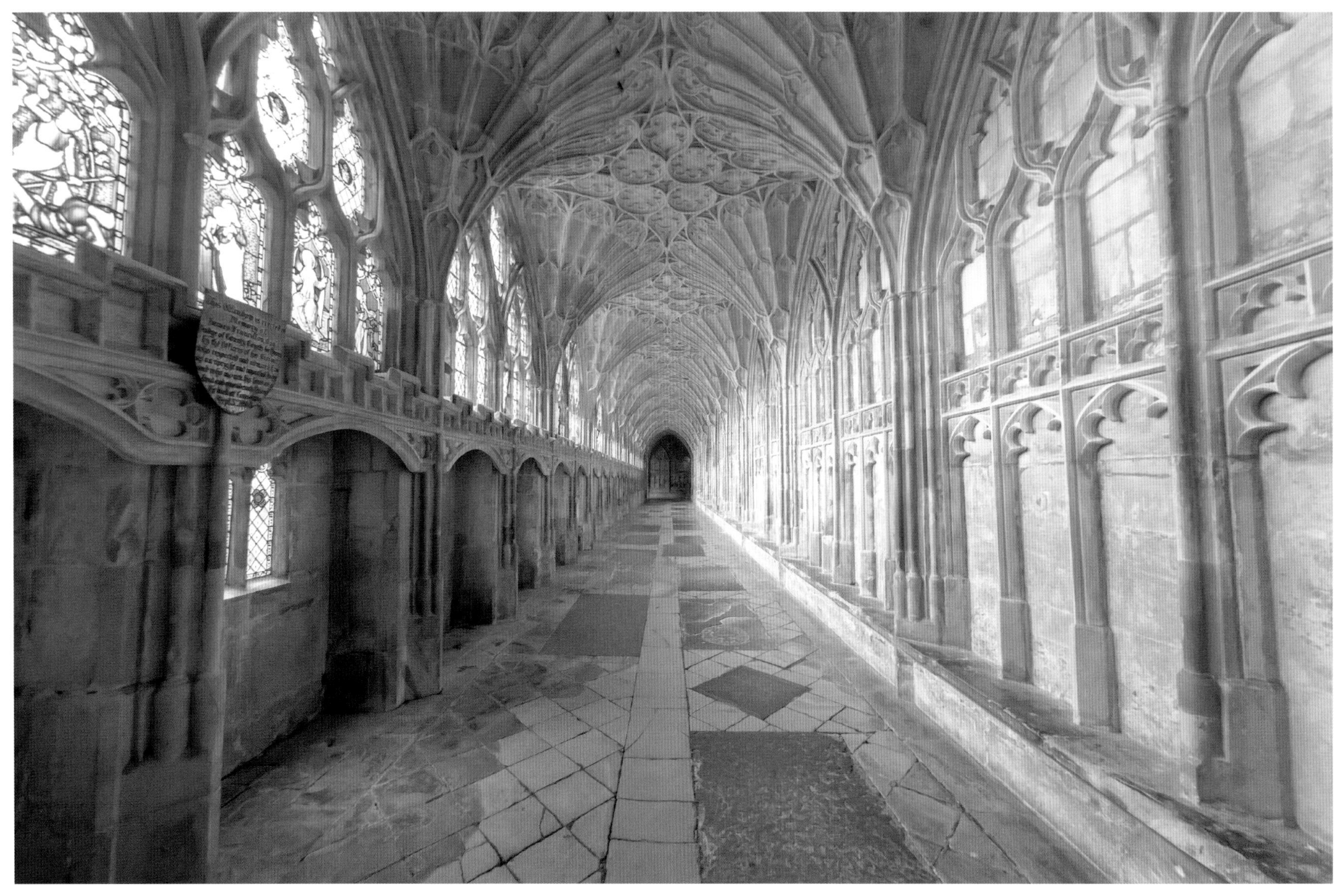

格洛斯特大教堂 / 攝影: 王朝
Gloucester Cathedral by Wang Chao

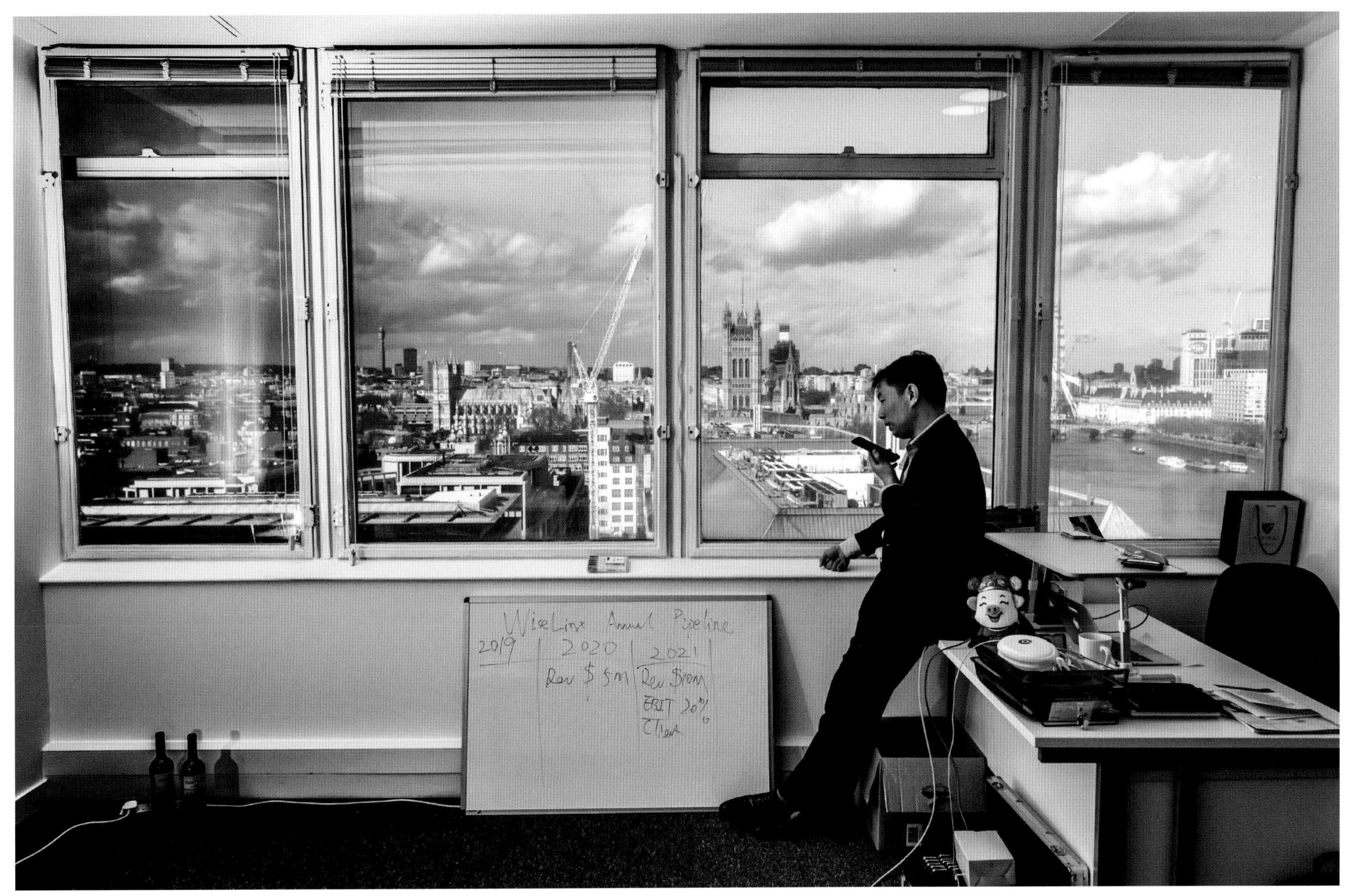

倫敦辦公室 / 攝影: 于陶钧
London Office by Yu Taojun

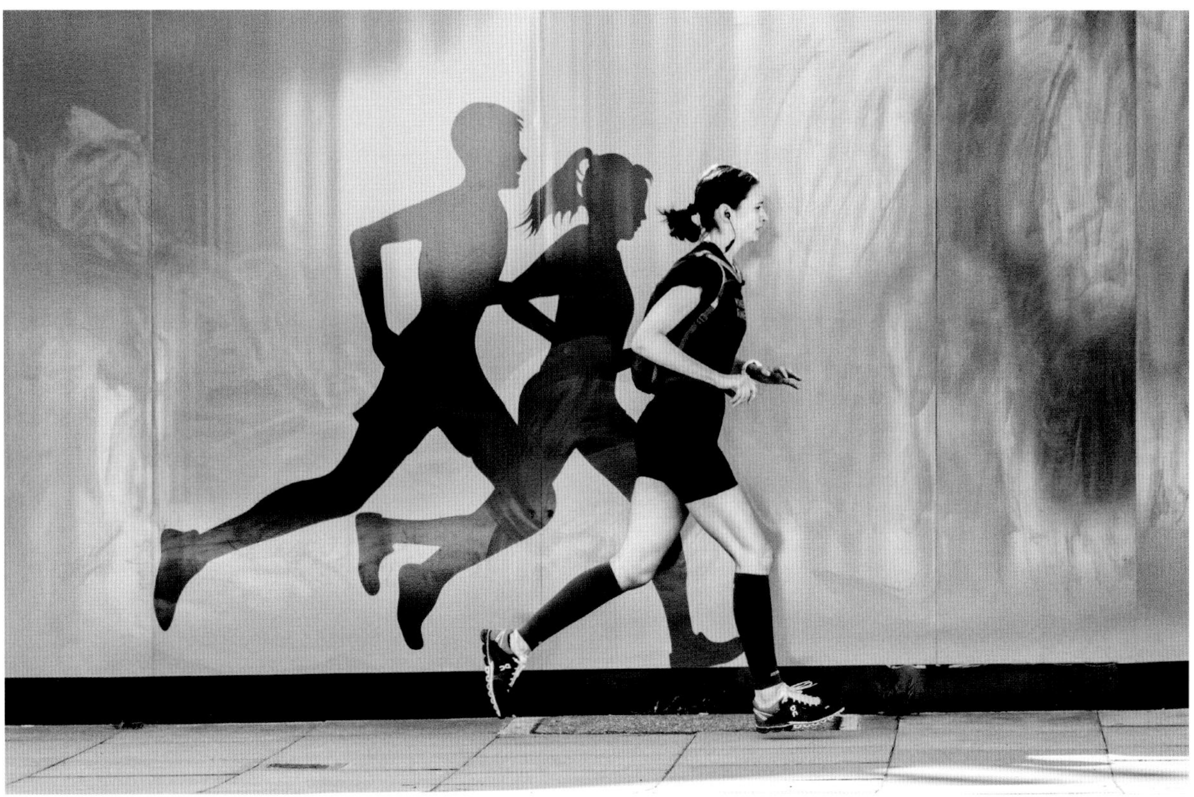

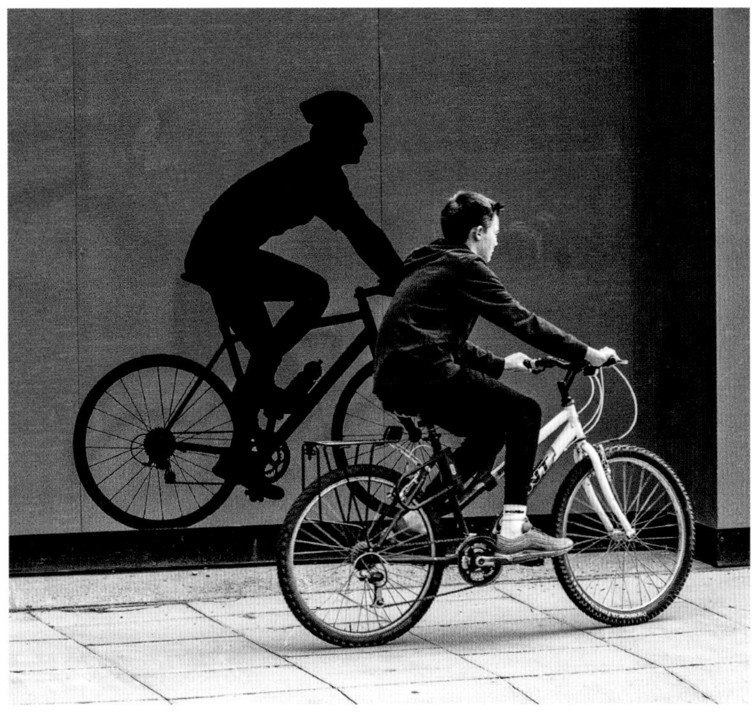

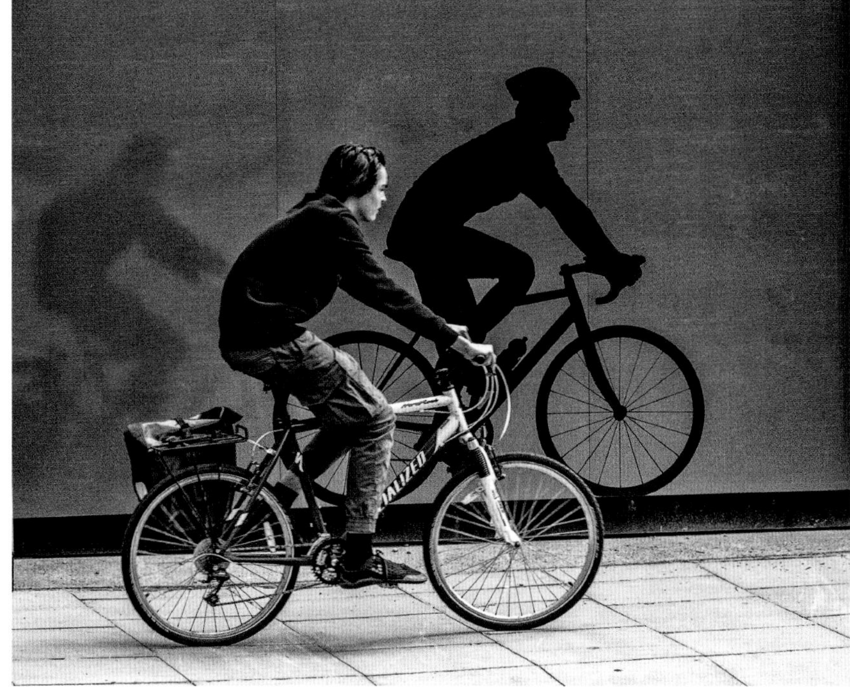

陰影 Shadows
by Andrew Gasson ARPS

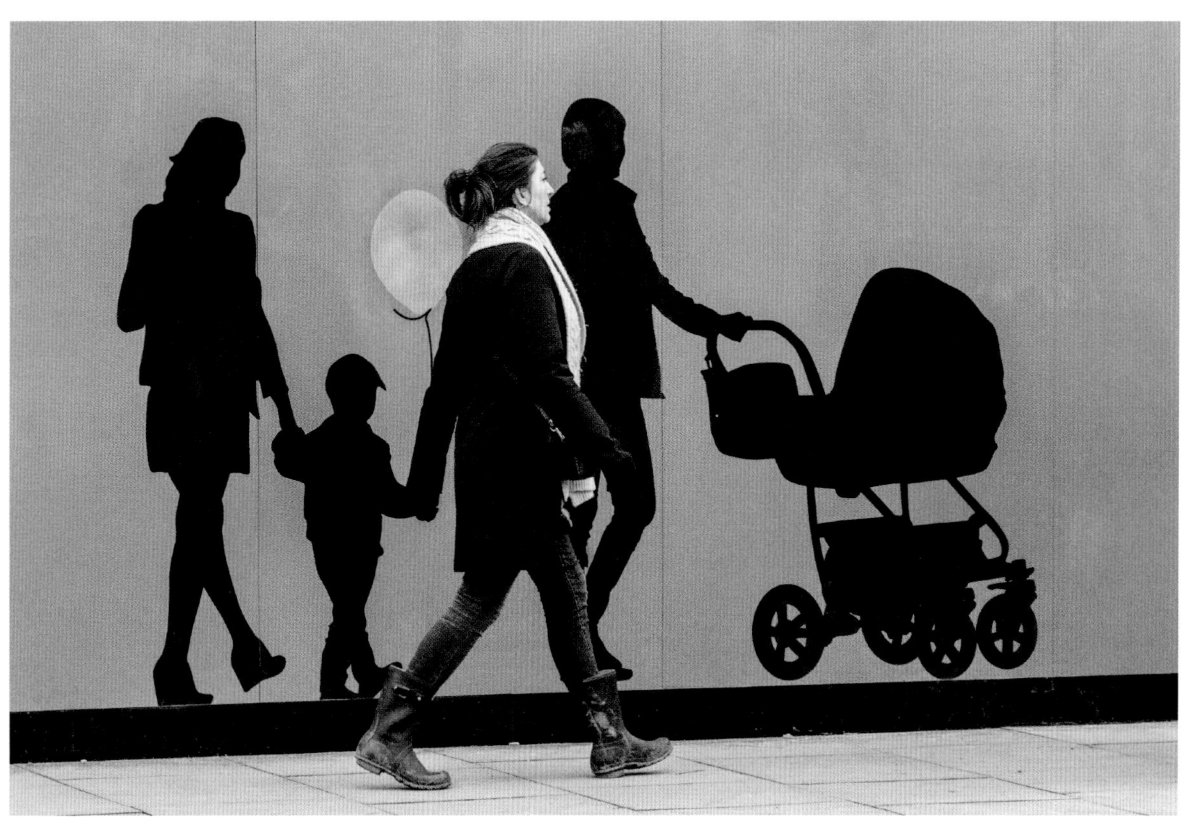

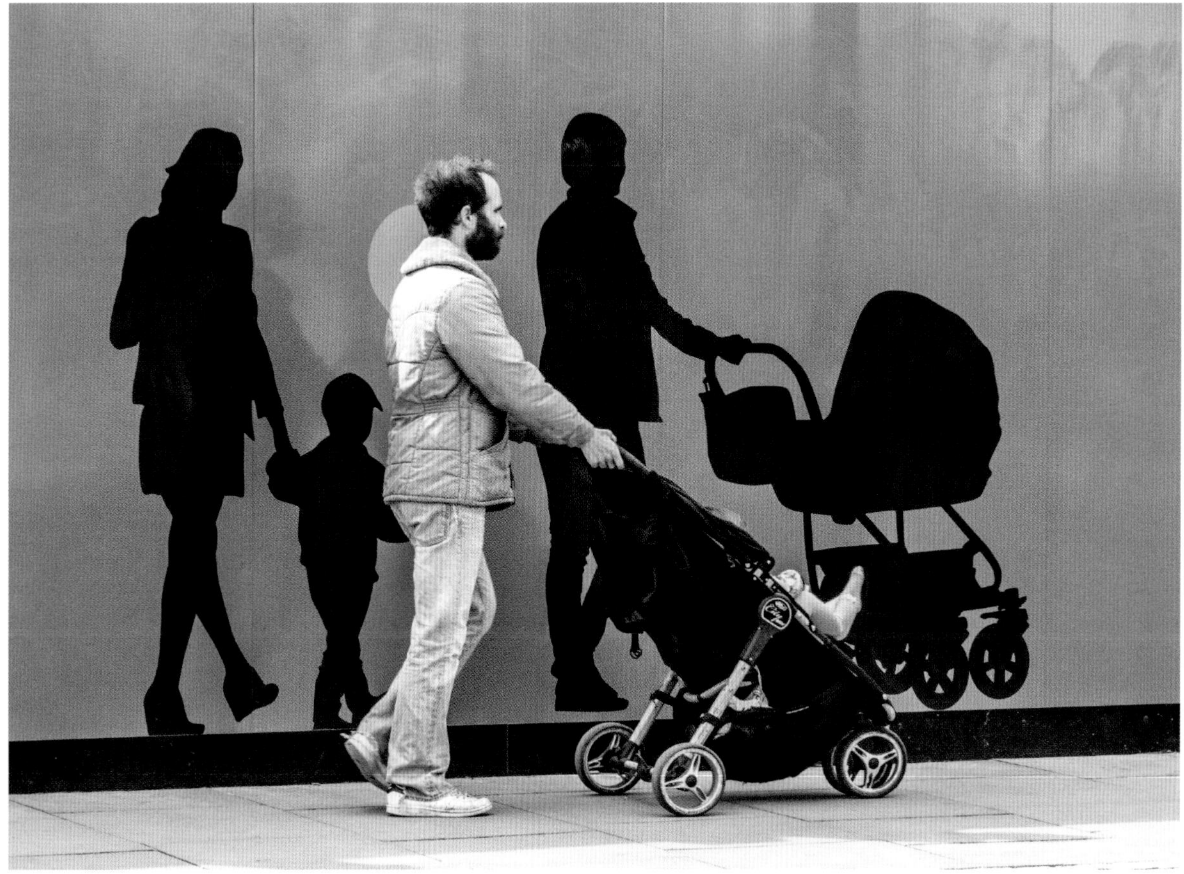

手牵手 Hand in Hand
by Andrew Gasson ARPS

PORTRAITS 肖像

眼見爲實
The Eyes Have It by Dennis Durack

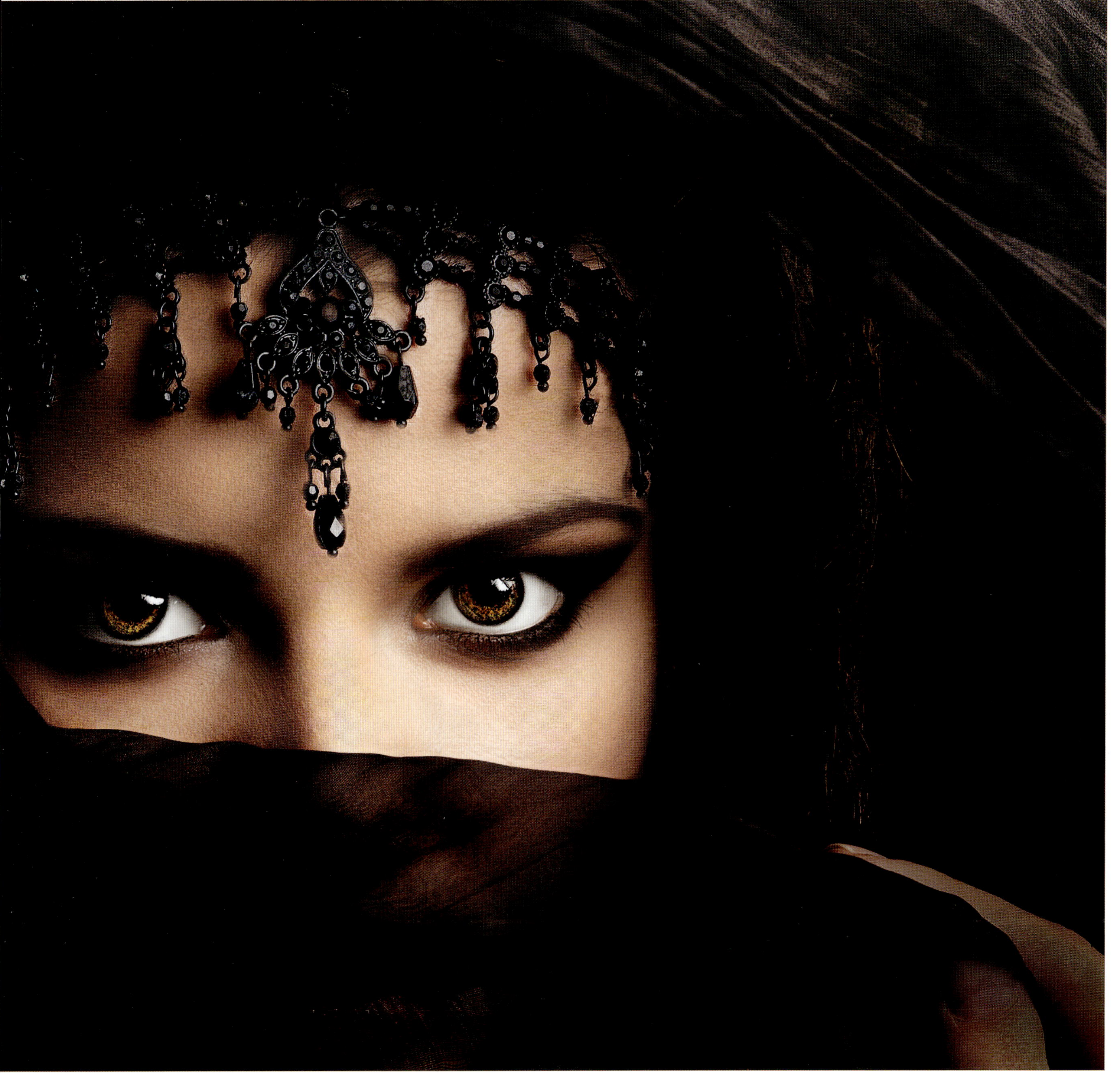

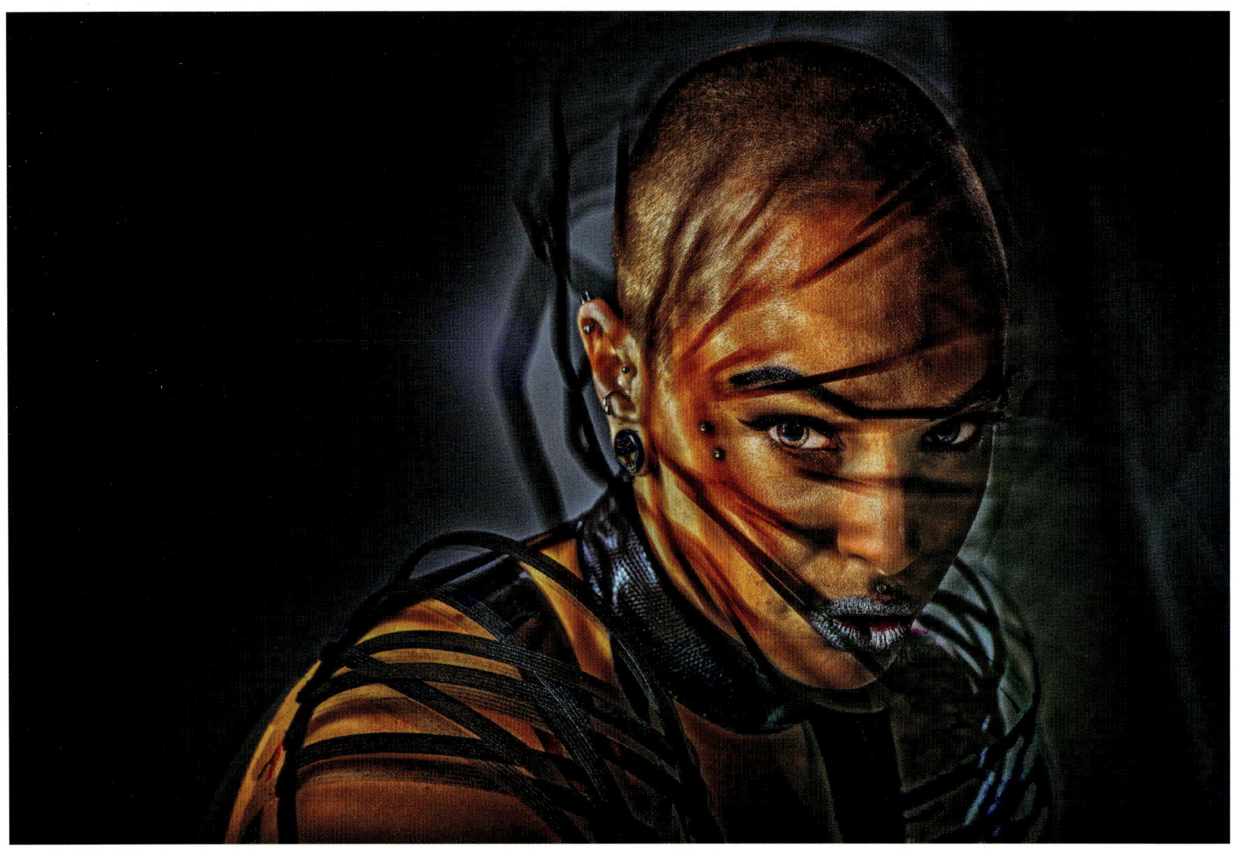

腦波
Brainwave
by Mike Woodman

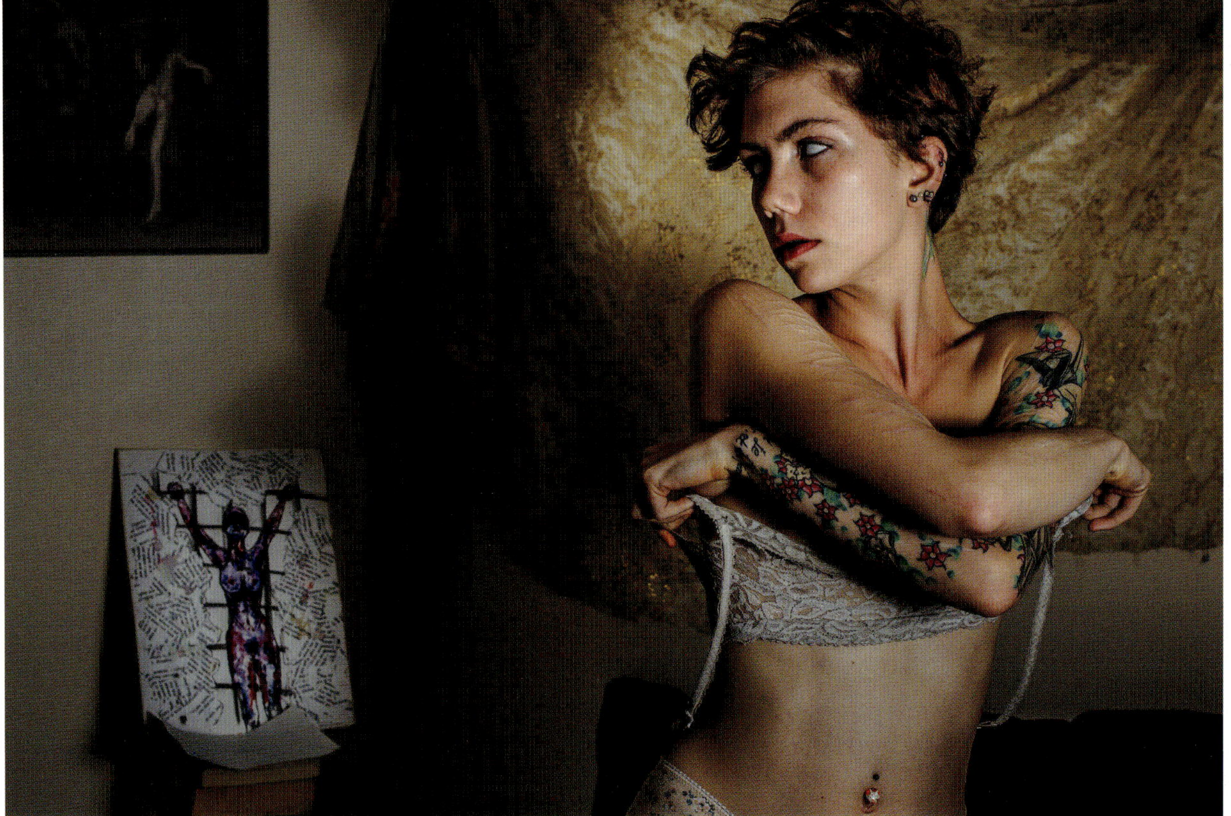

身體形象
Body Image
by Mike Woodman

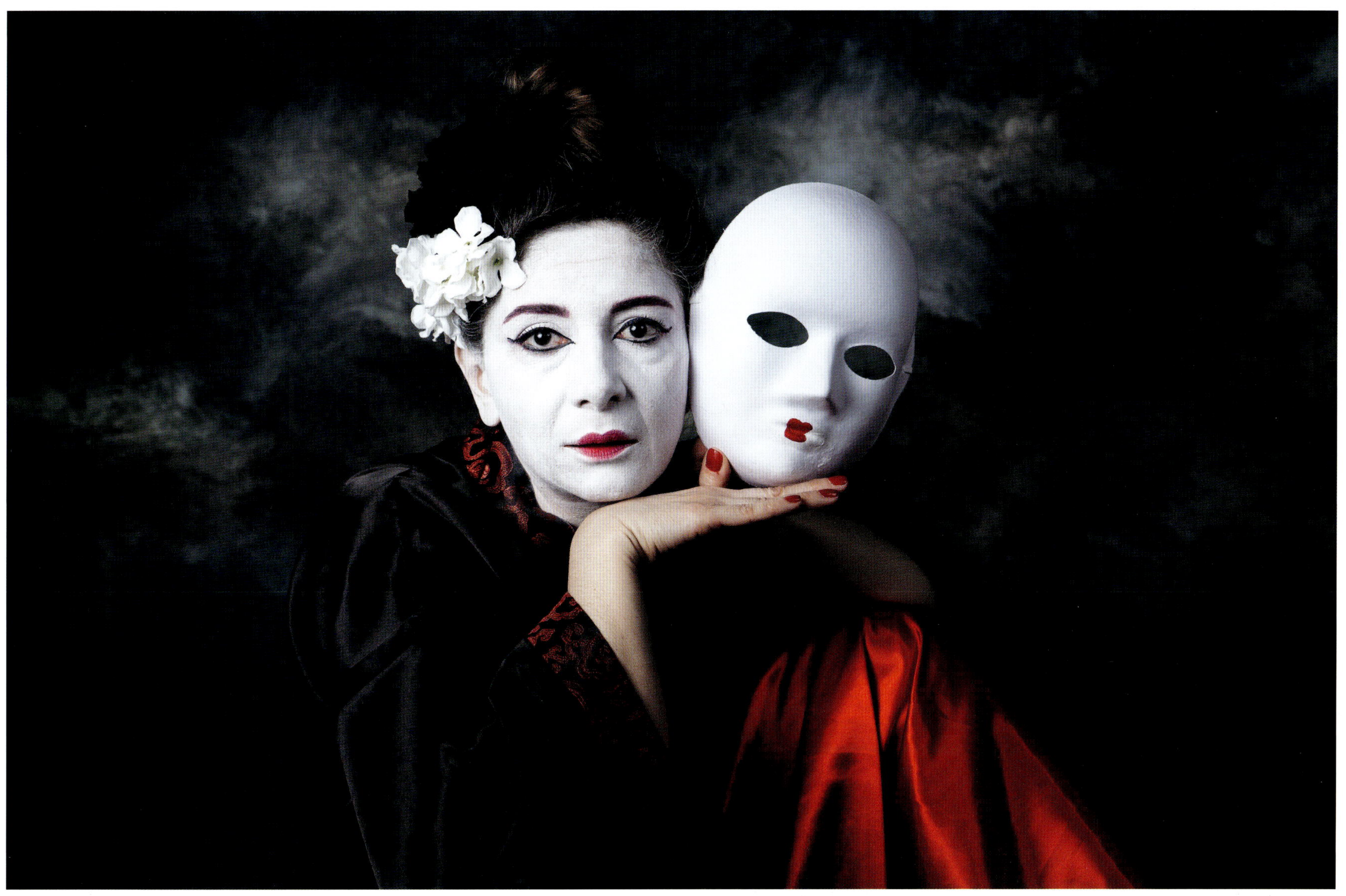

藝妓的兩張面孔
Two Faces of a Geisha by Aidan Huxford

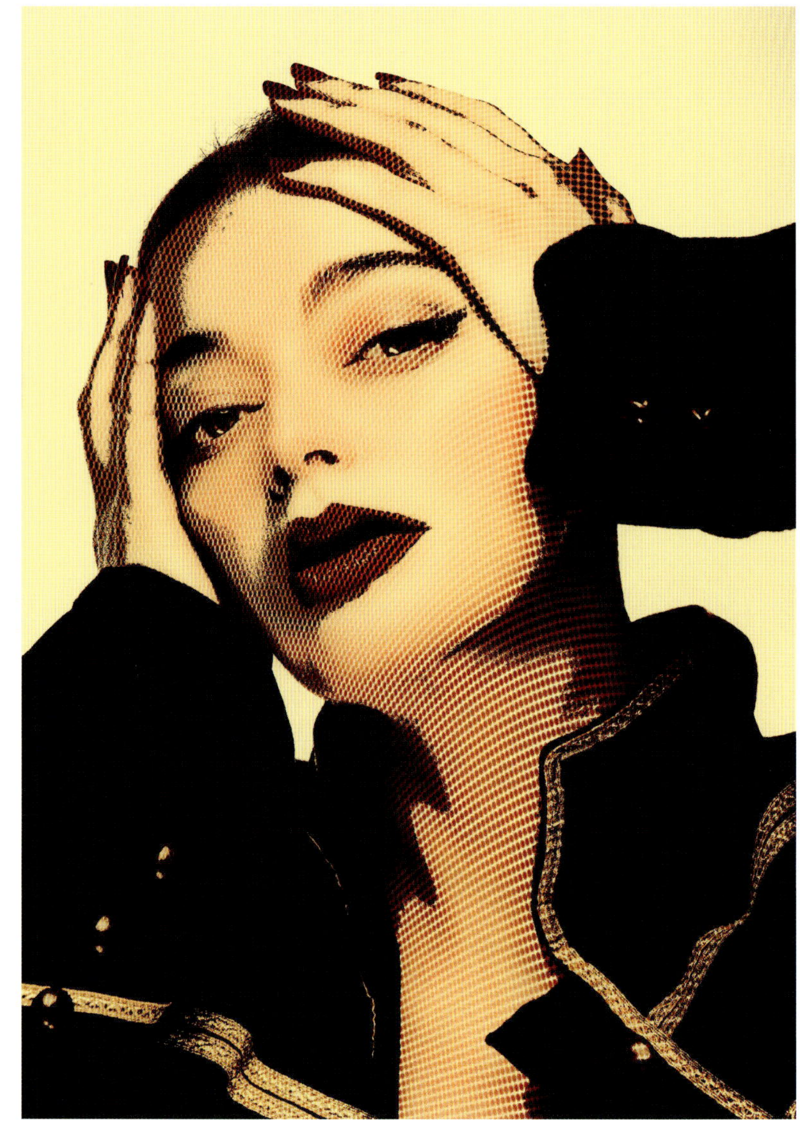

漫畫
The Comic by David Rutter FRPS

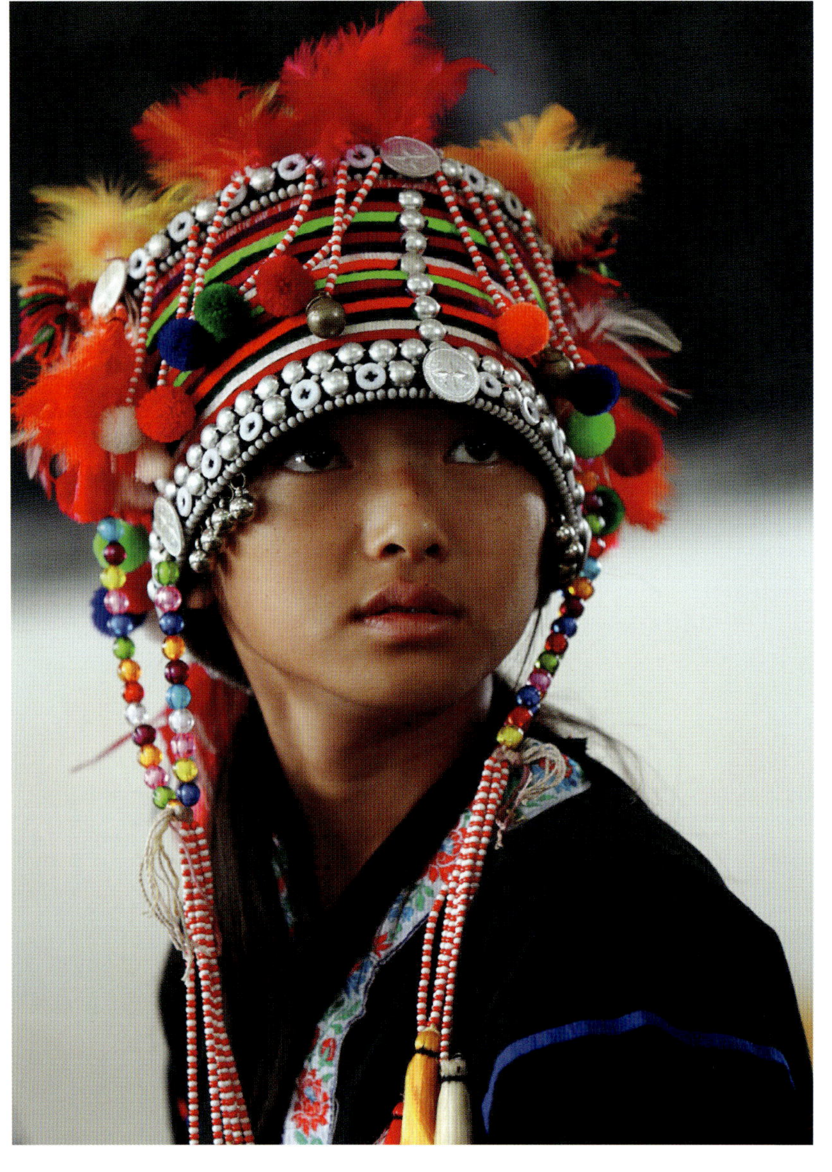

哈尼族小姑娘 / 攝影: 焦峰
Hani Girl by Jiao Feng

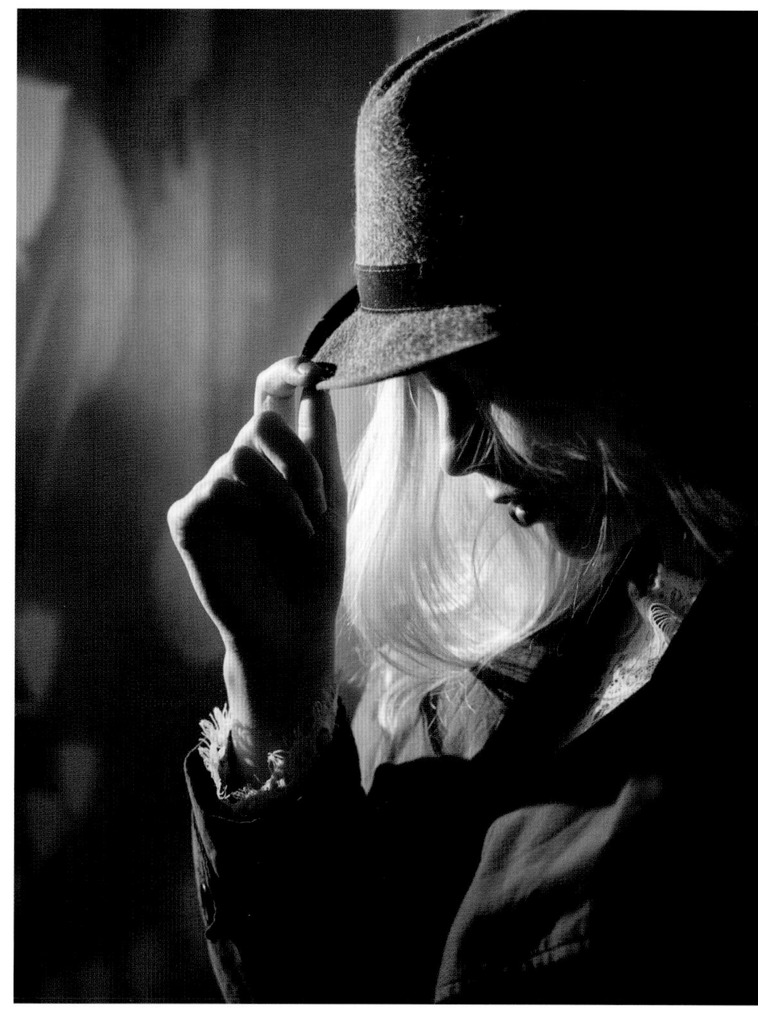

阿瑪利亞
Amalia by Jean-Michel O'Shea ARPS

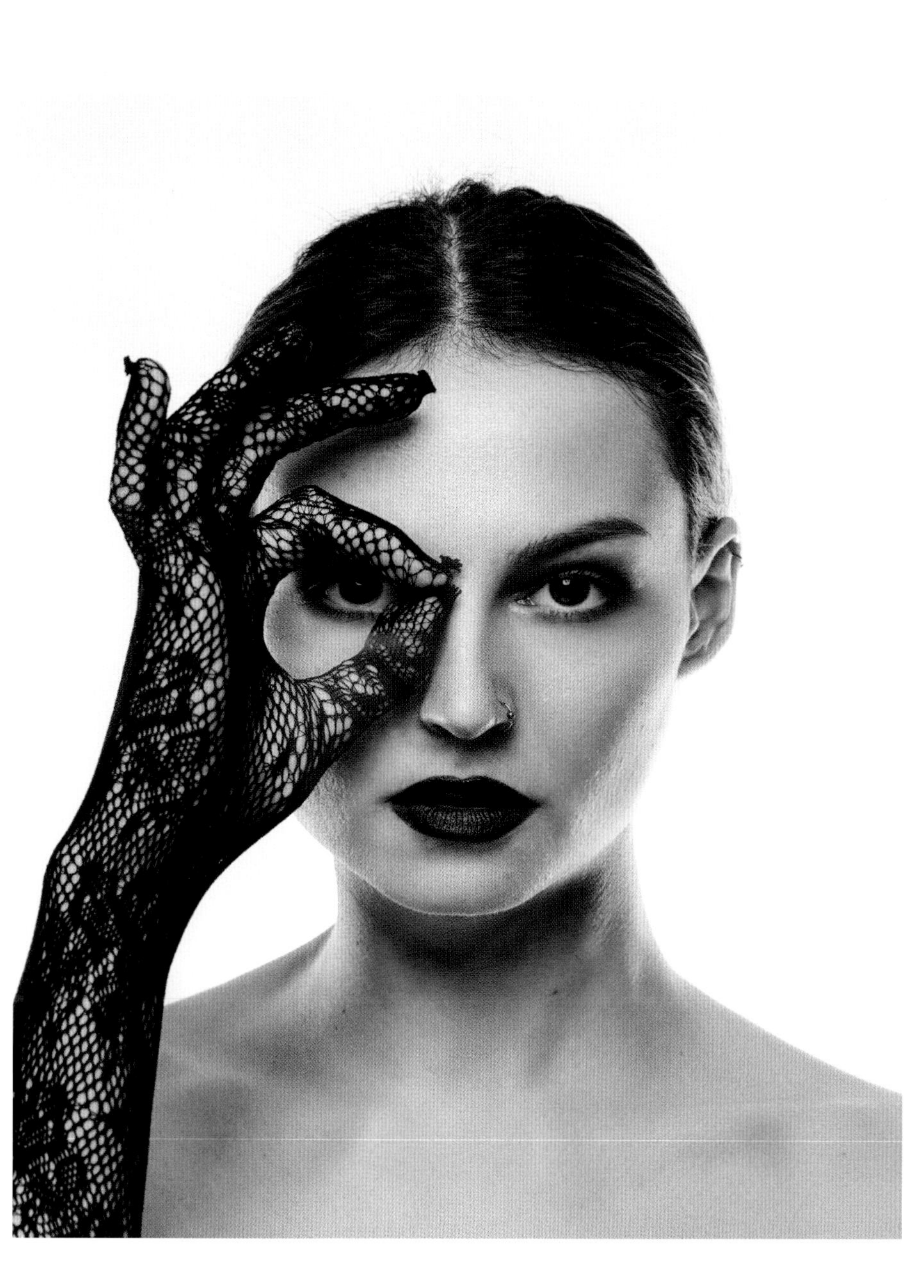

窺視
Peep by Kyle Tallett FRPS

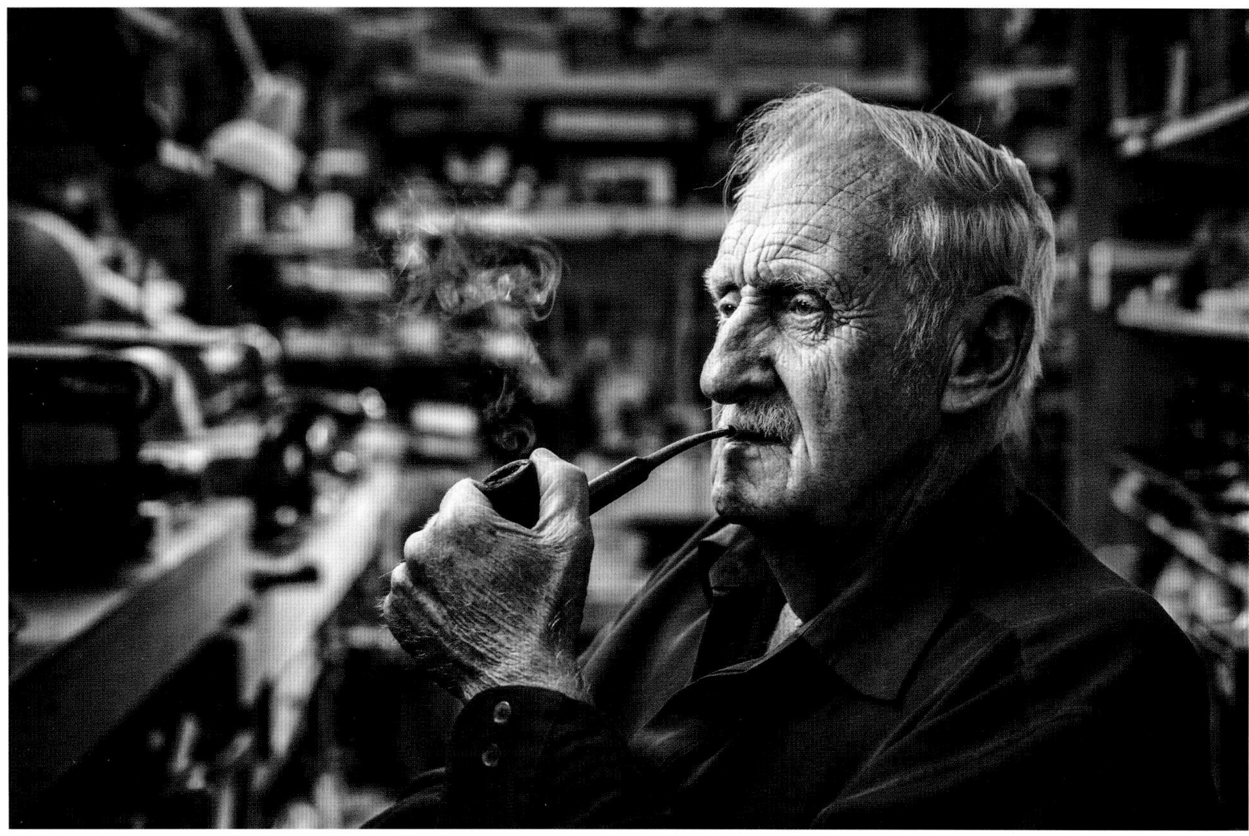

特雷弗・貝利斯
Trevor Baylis
by Colin Clarke ARPS

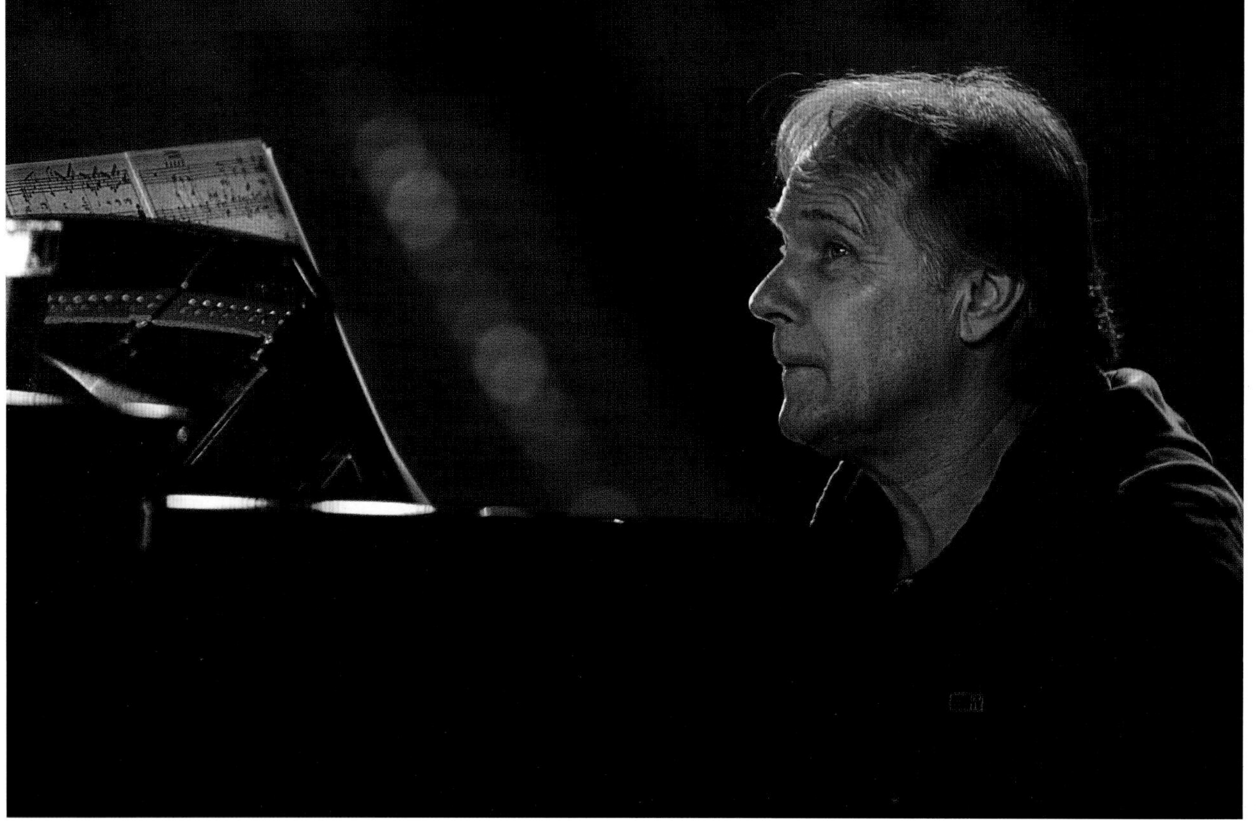

著名鋼琴演奏藝術家
理查德・克萊德曼 /
攝影: 石一
Famous Pianist
Richard Clayderman
by Shi Yi

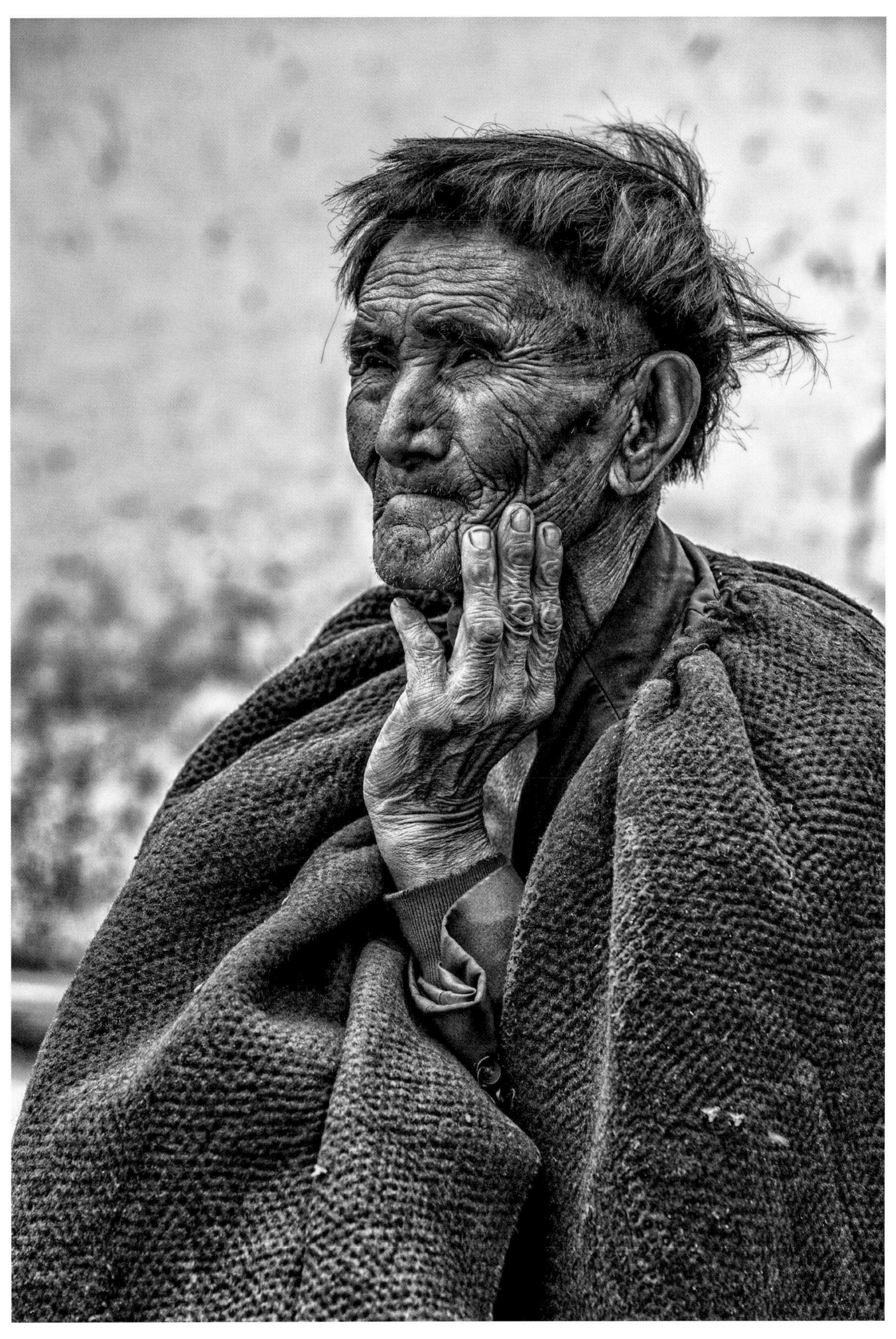

大凉山老人 / 攝影：焦峰
Old Man of Daliang Mountain
by Jiao Feng

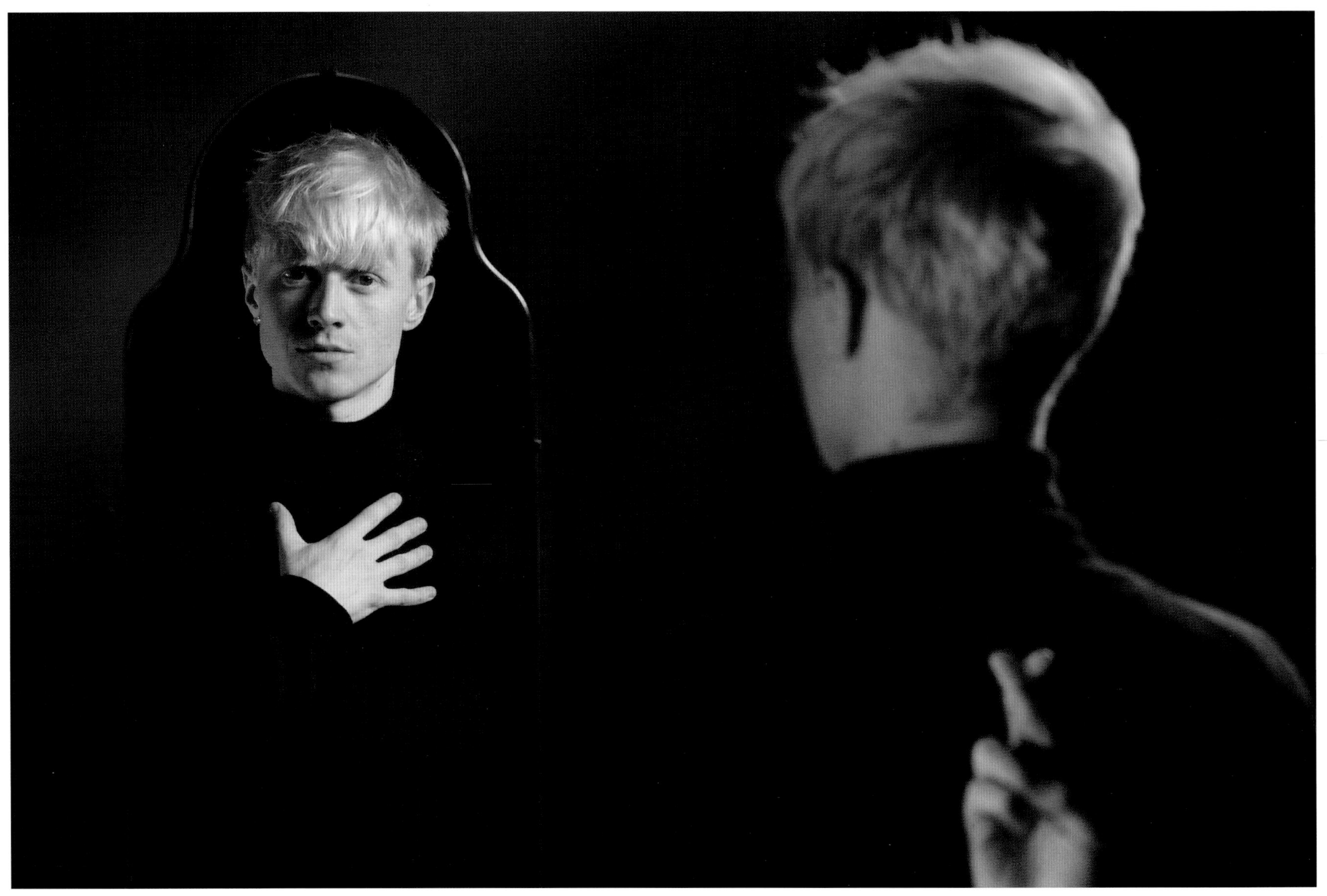

伊恩・伍兹
Iain Woods by Colin Clarke ARPS

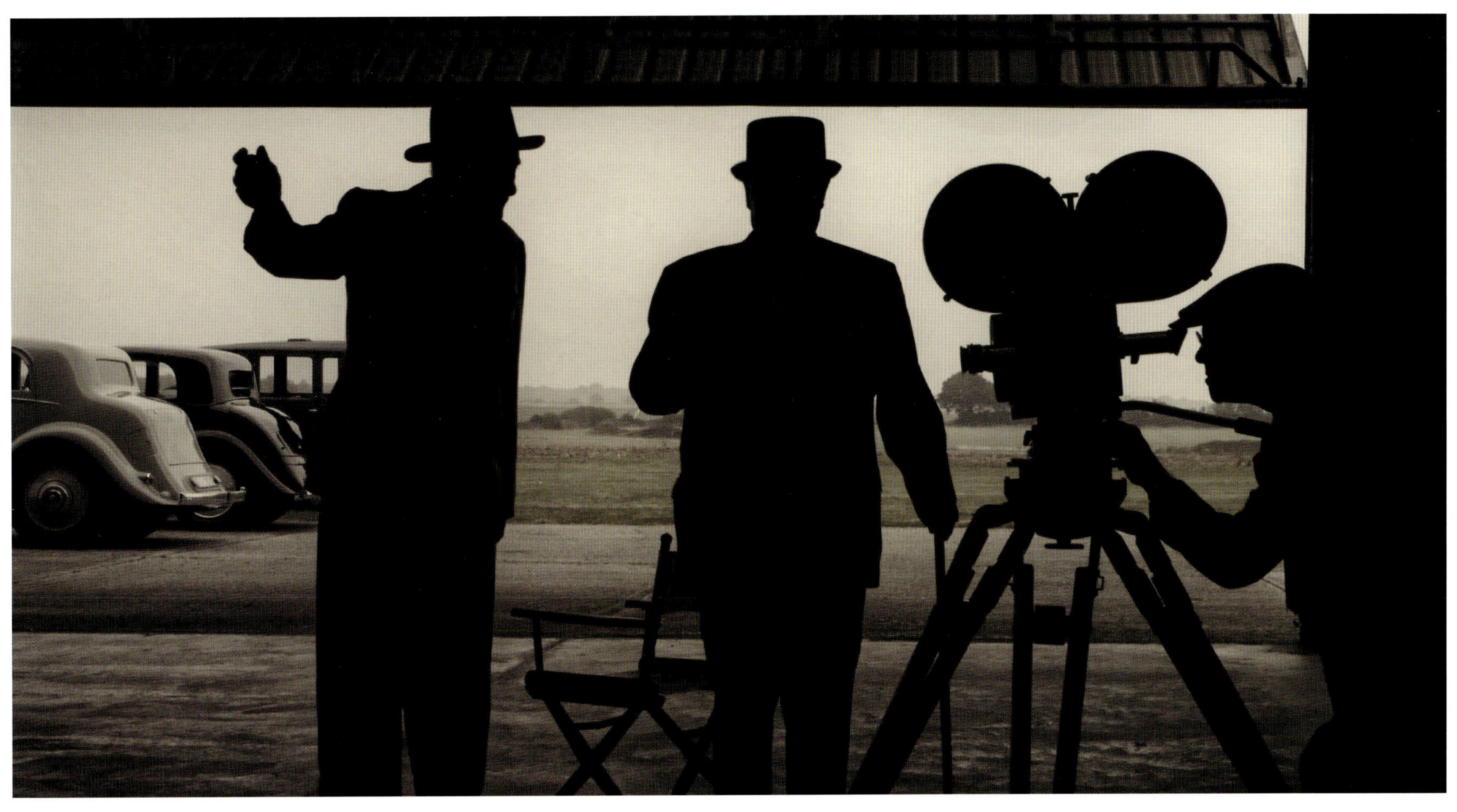

亞歷山大–科爾達向丘吉爾展示他的工作室
Alexander Korda Shows Churchill His Studio
by Colin Clarke ARPS

ORIGINALITY 創意

警戒，準備，進攻!
On Guard, Ready, Go!
by Nicholas Mackey

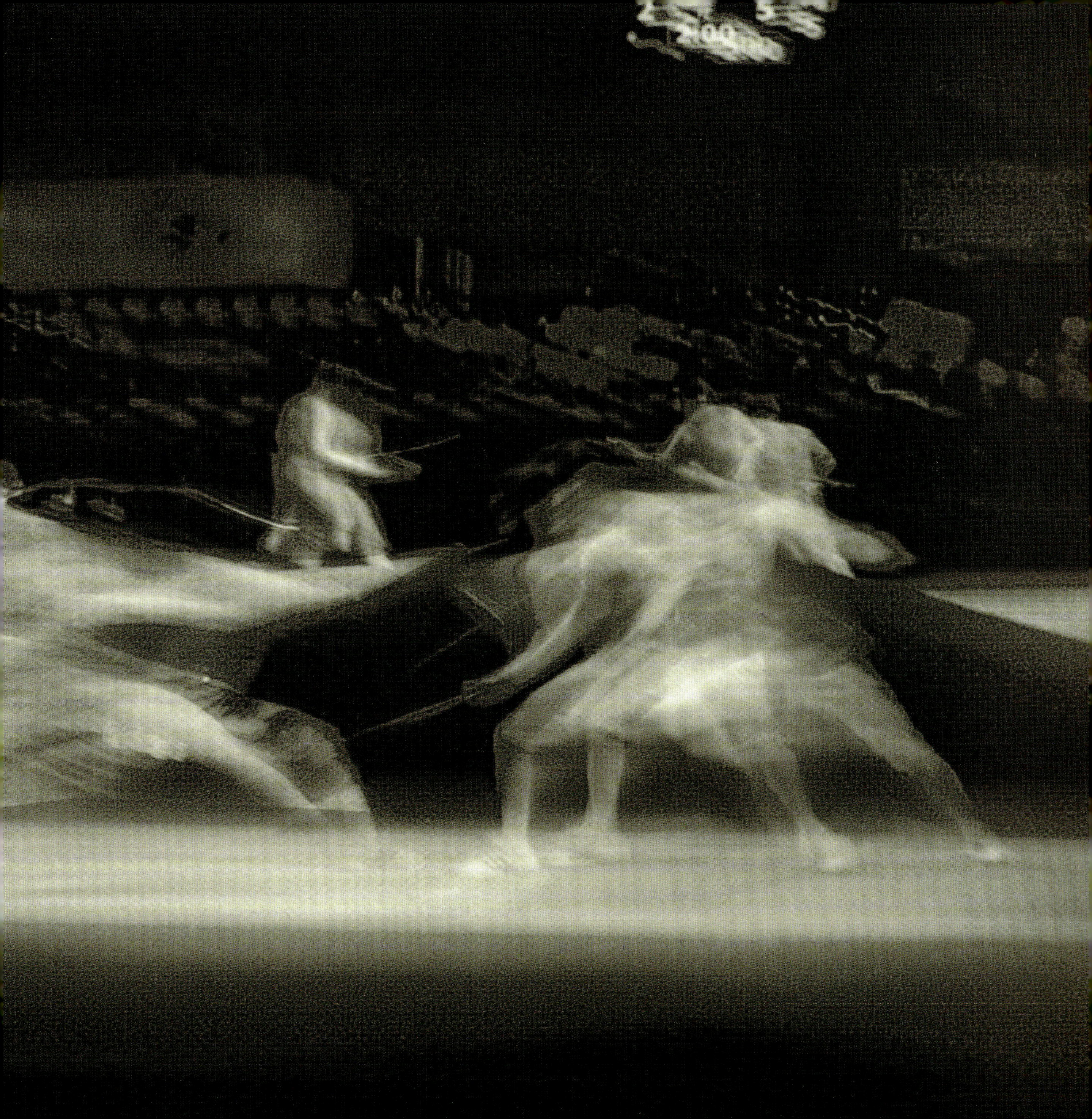

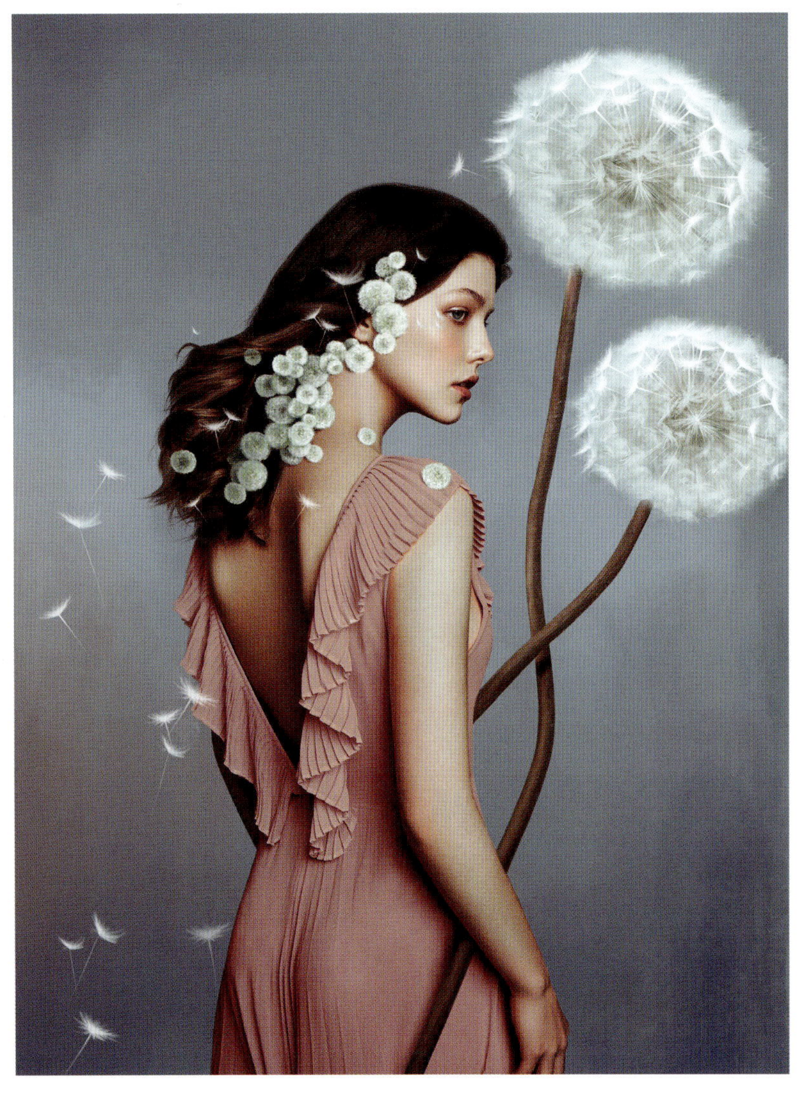

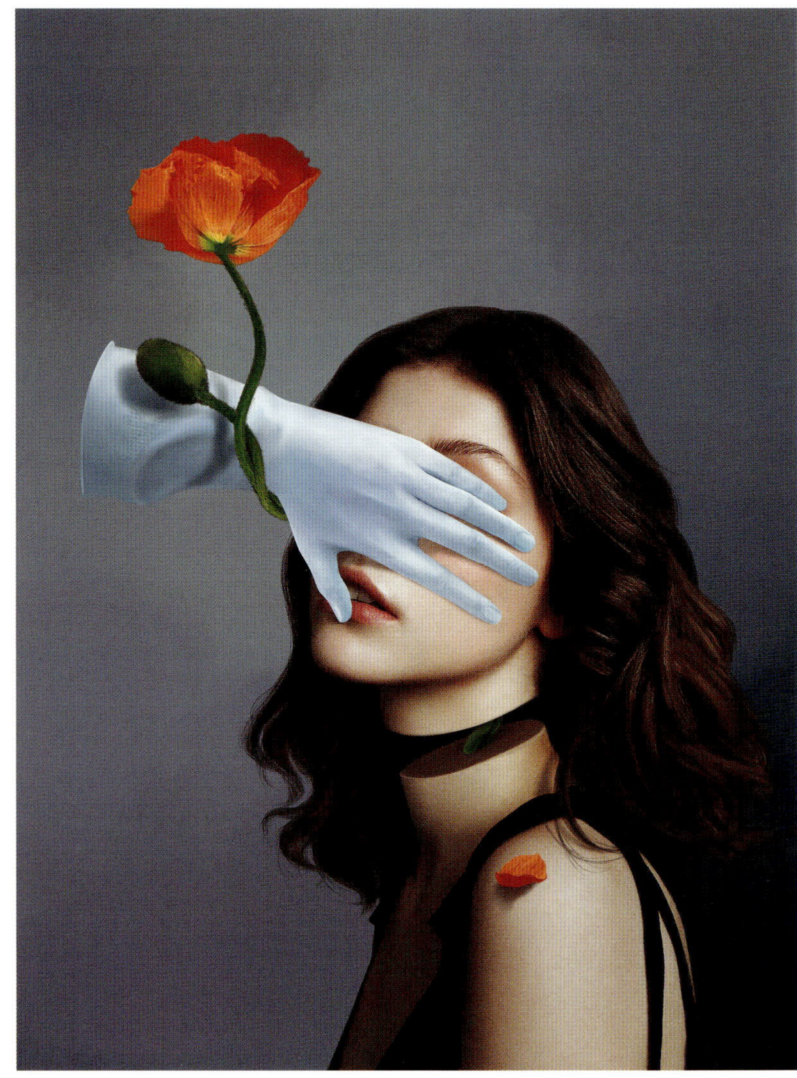

蘭心 / 攝影: 楊寒
Orchid Heart by Yang Han

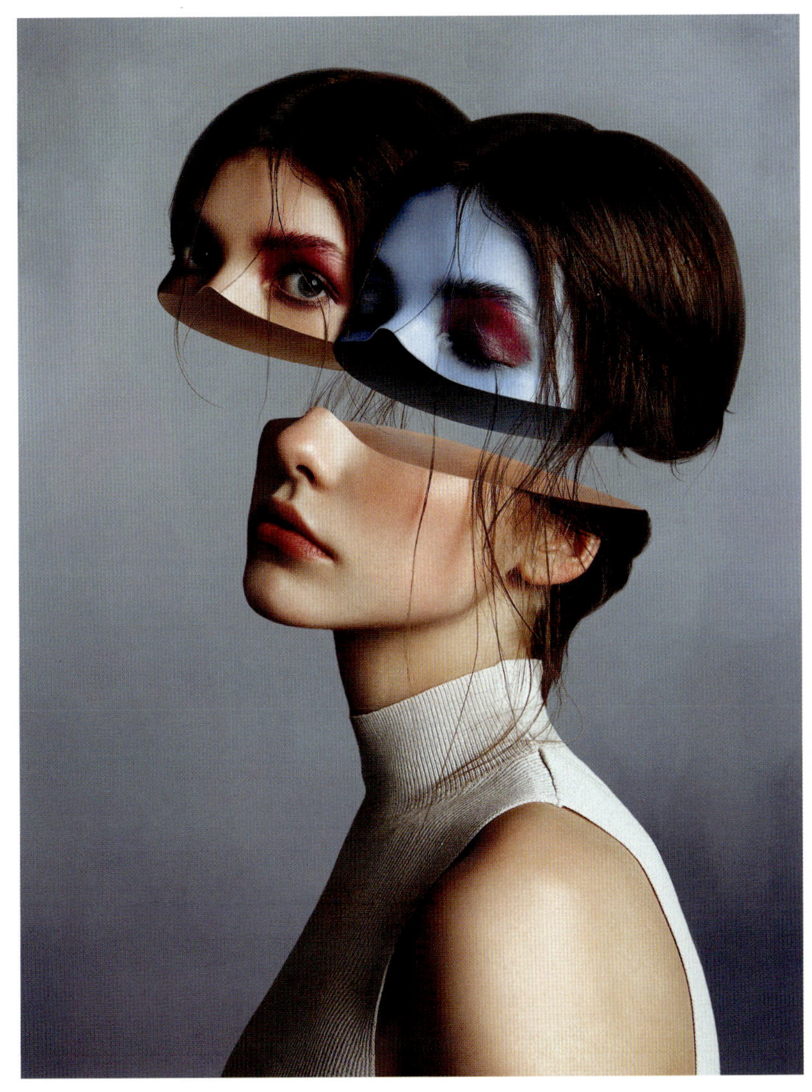

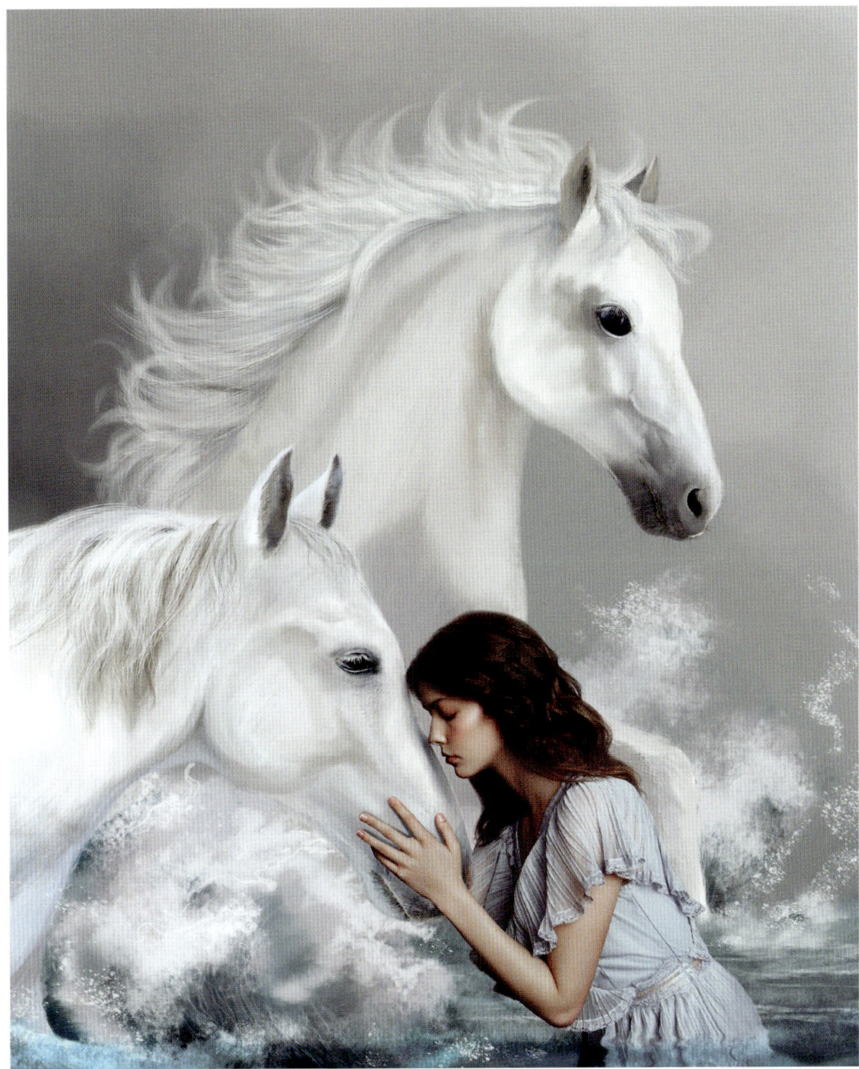

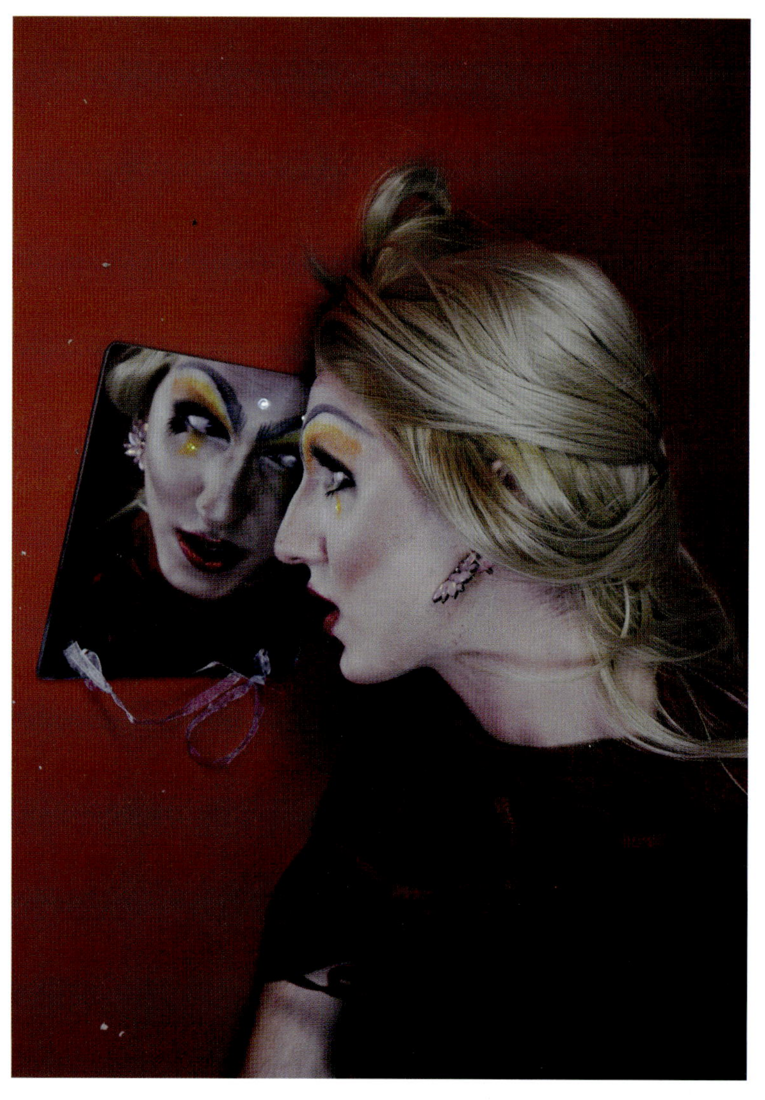

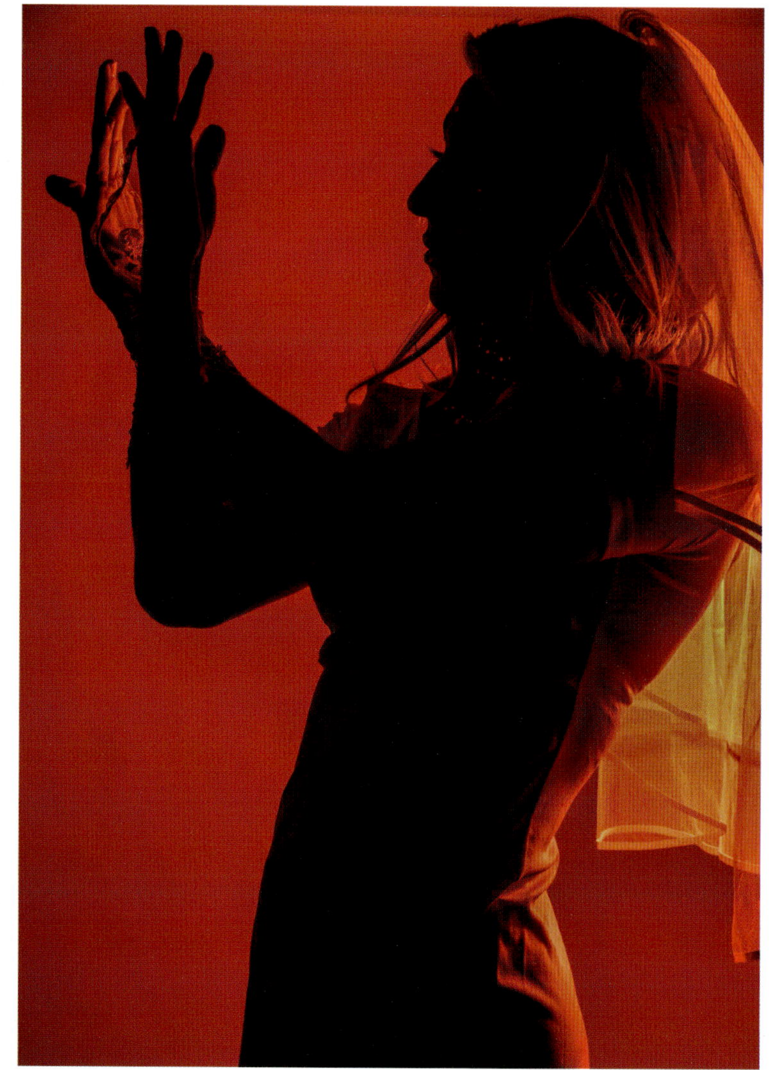

新娘 / 攝影: 劉思言
The Bride by Liu Siyan

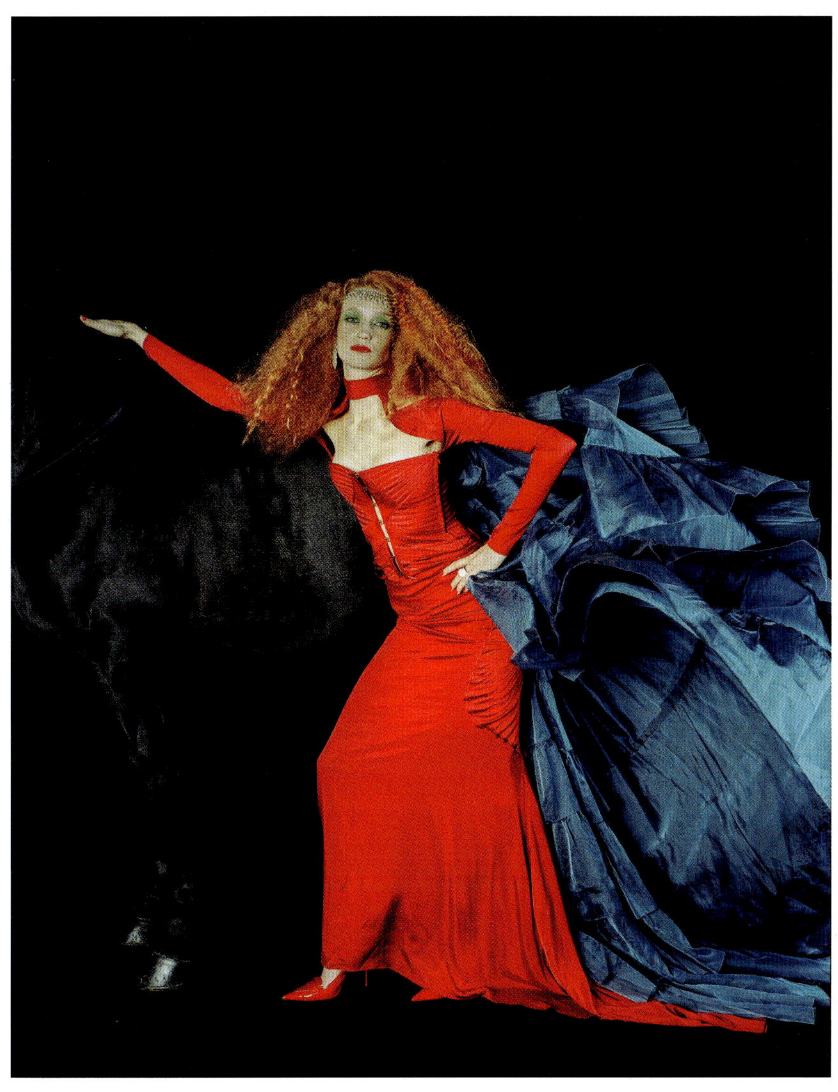

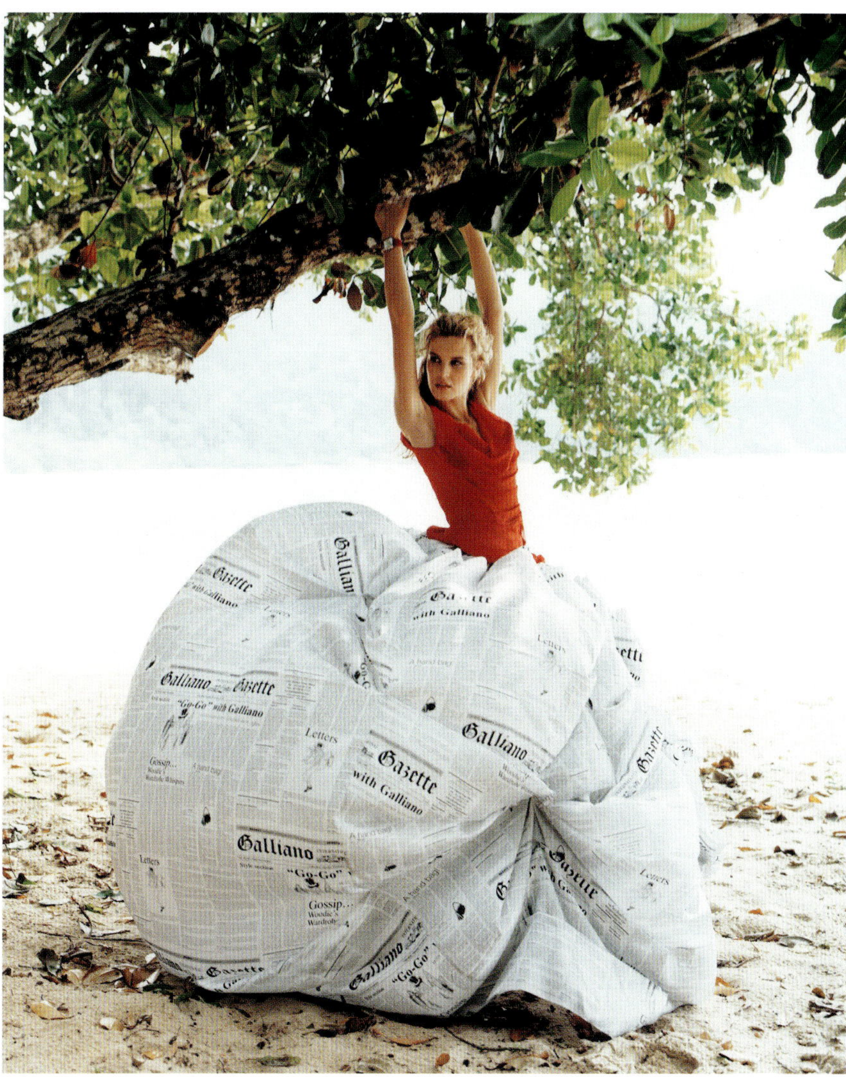

時裝
Fashion by Axel Bernstorff

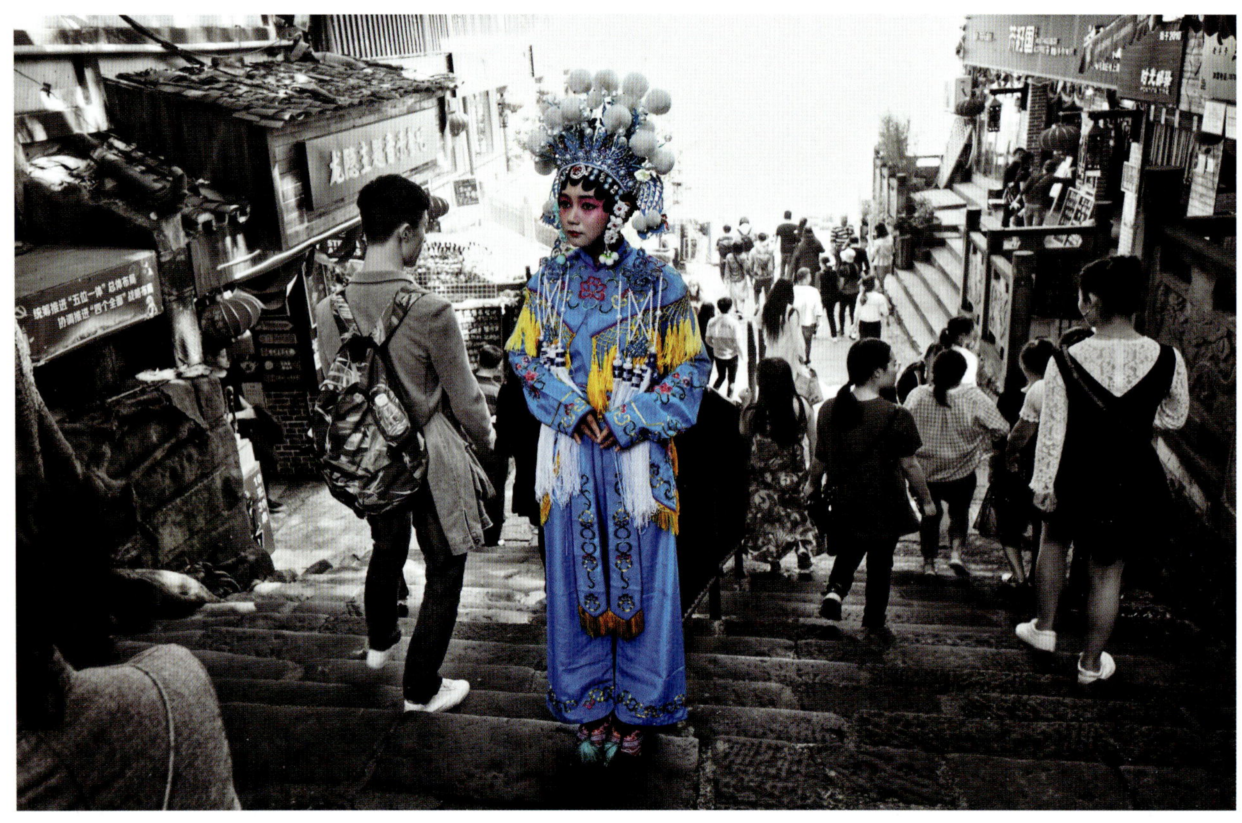

穿越來的小青 /
攝影: 郭大公
Xiao Qing from Time Travel
by Guo Dagong

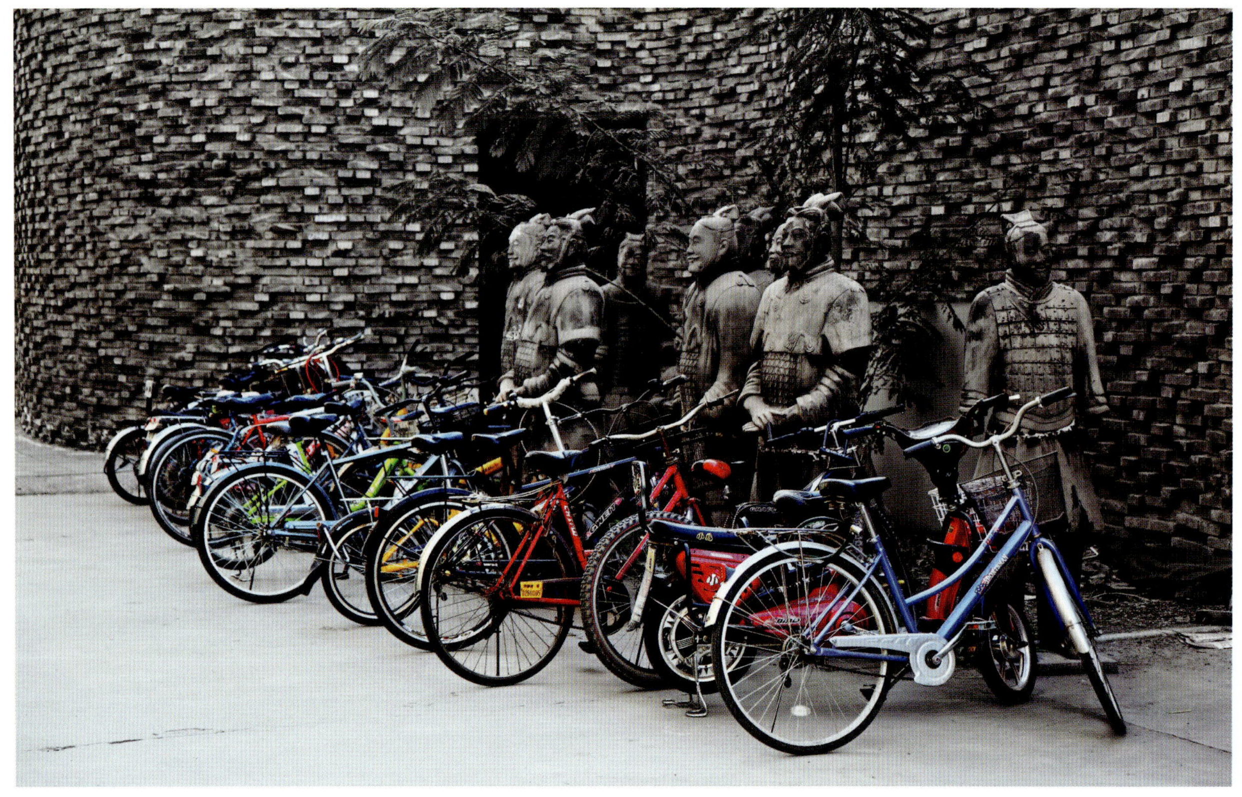

古今依存 / 攝影: 郭大公
Ancient and Modern Dependence
by Guo Dagong

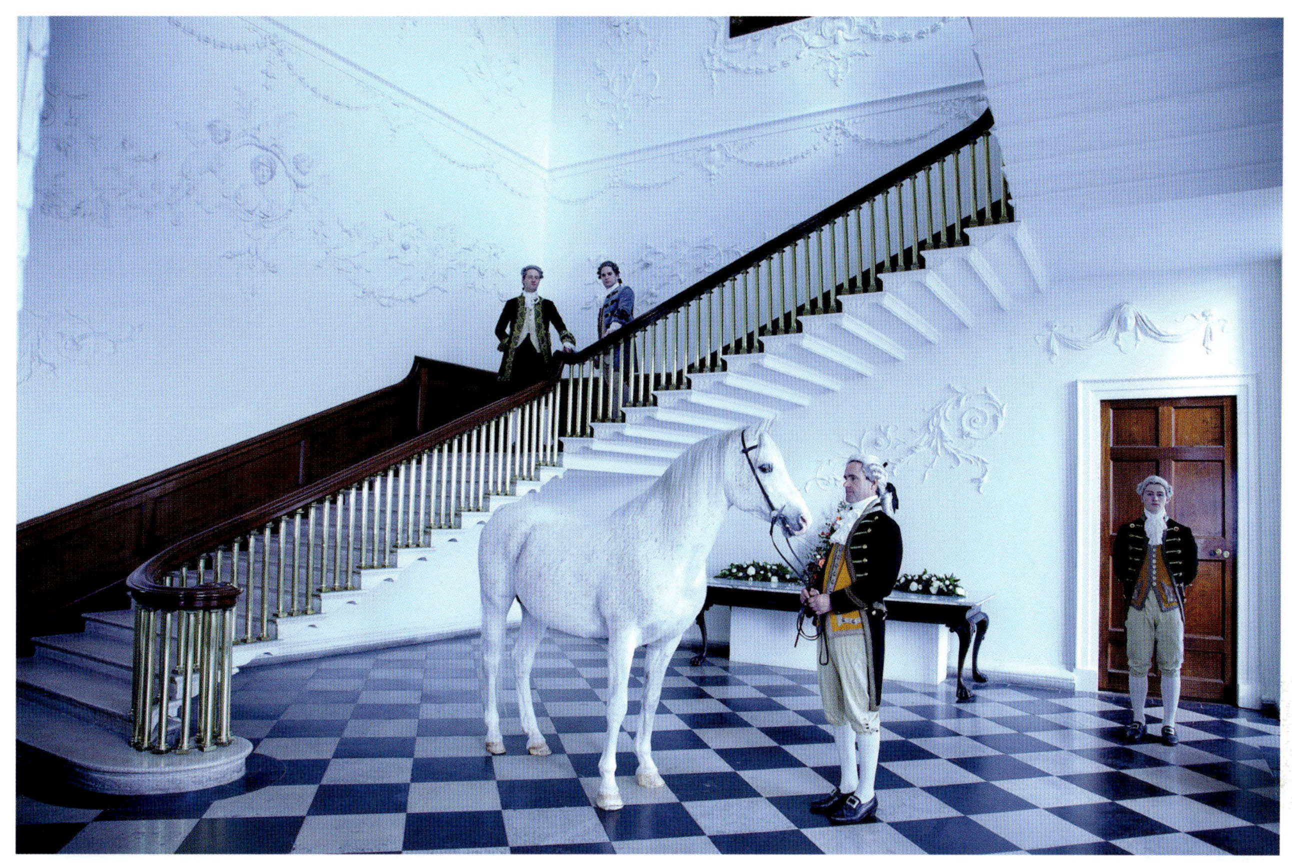

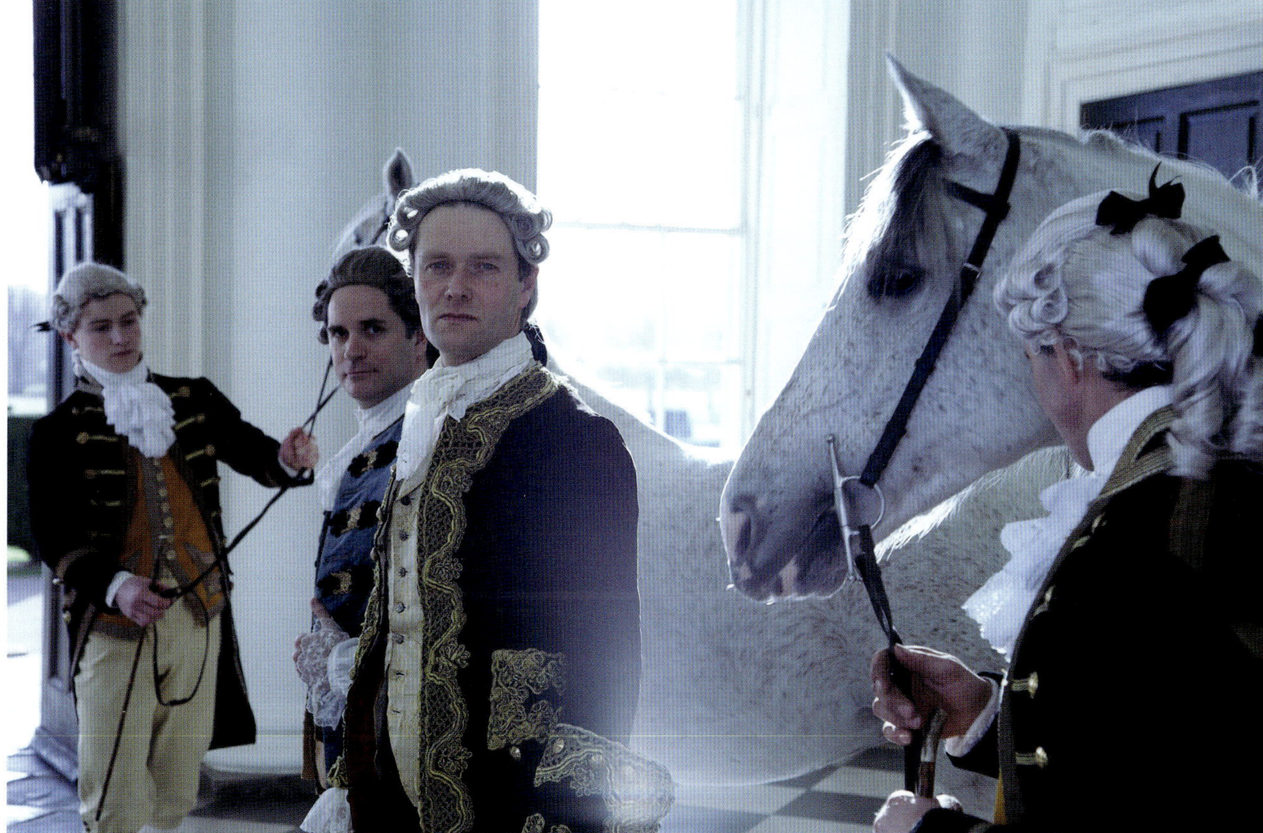

古裝戲
Costume Drama
by Axel Bernstorff

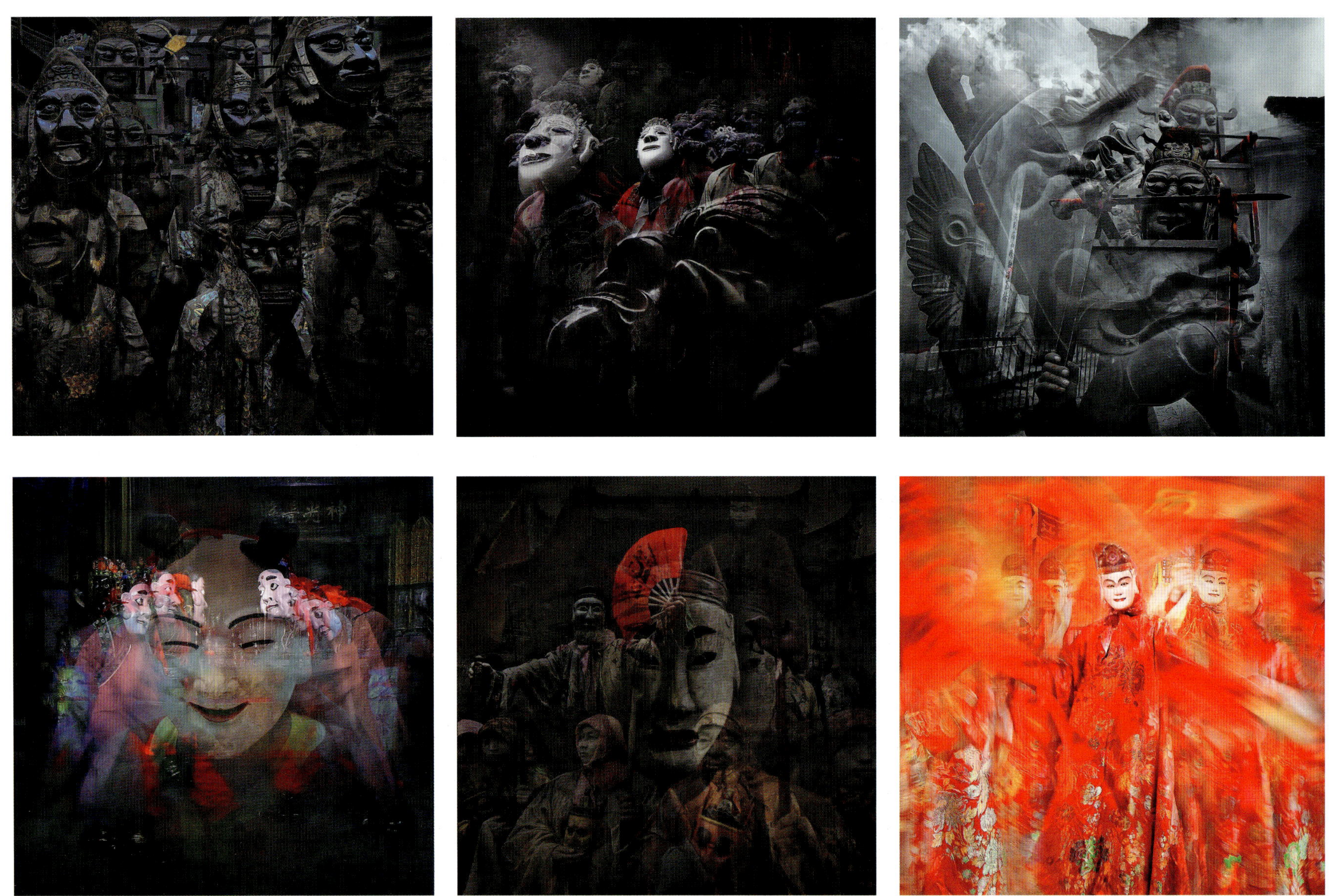

儺.探魅 / 攝影: 彭雪平
Discover by Peng Xueping

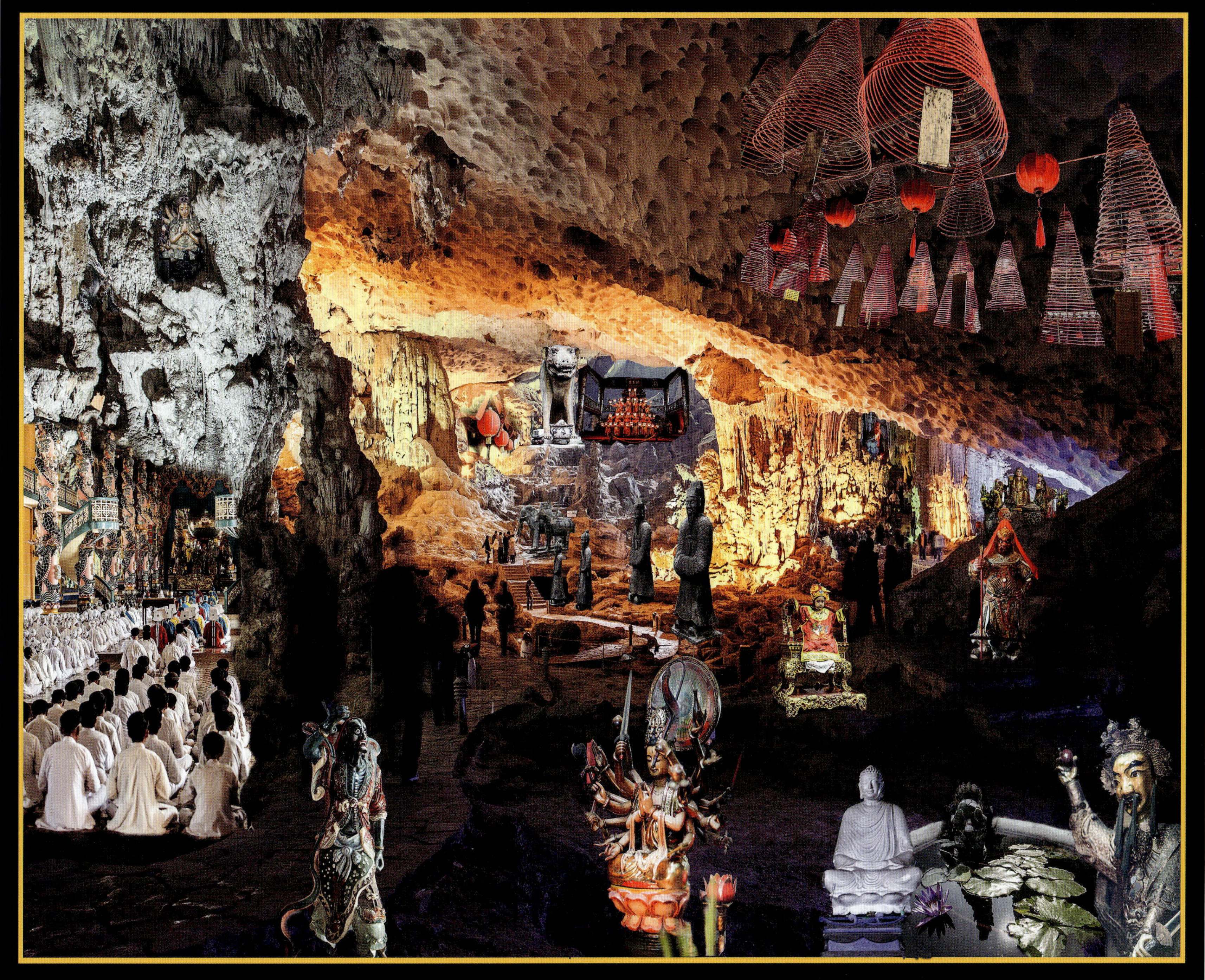

想像中的越南
Vietnam Imagined by Vince Harris

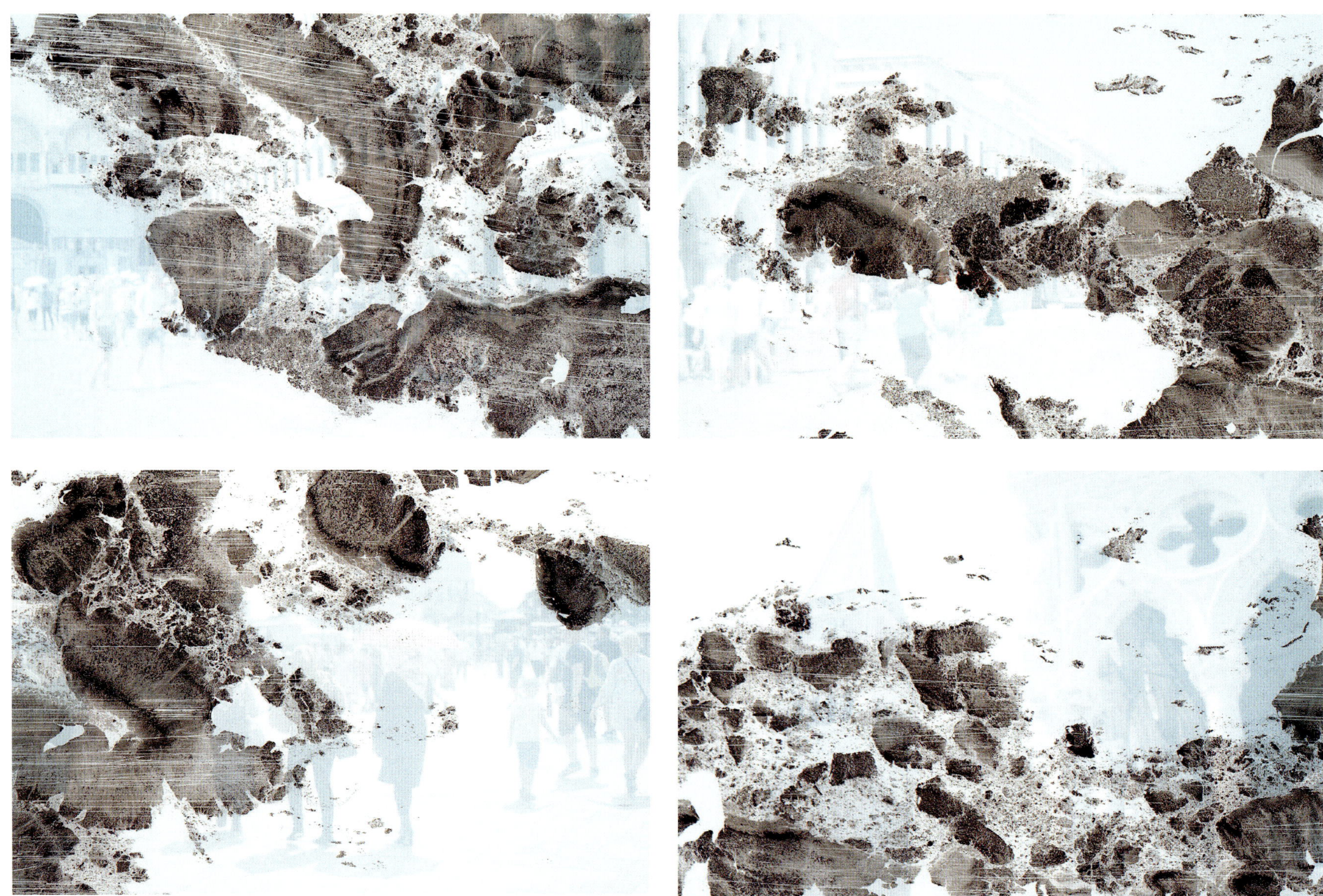

褪色記憶
Fade Memories by Aurelie Crisetig

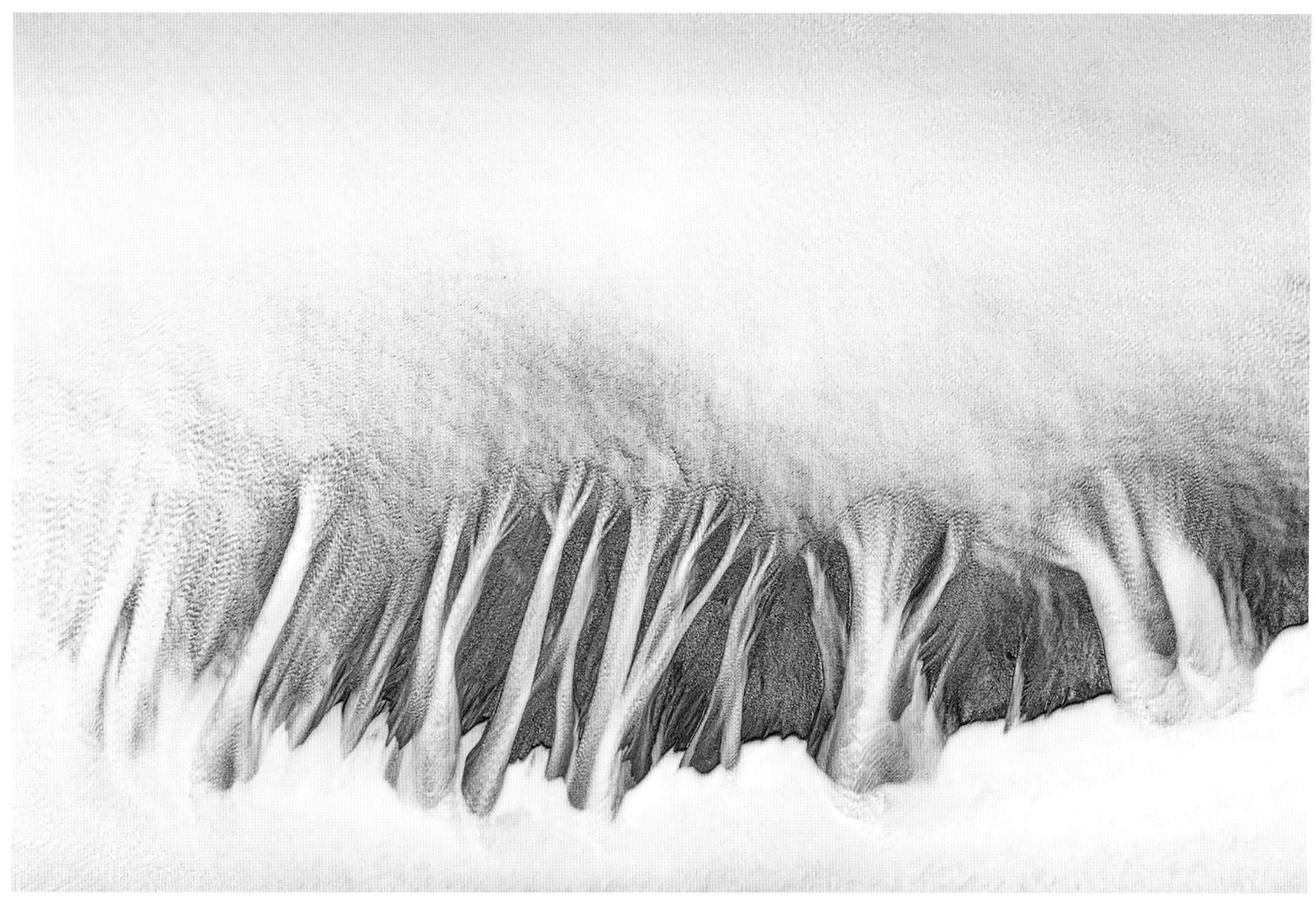

森林
Forest by Honey J Walker ARPS

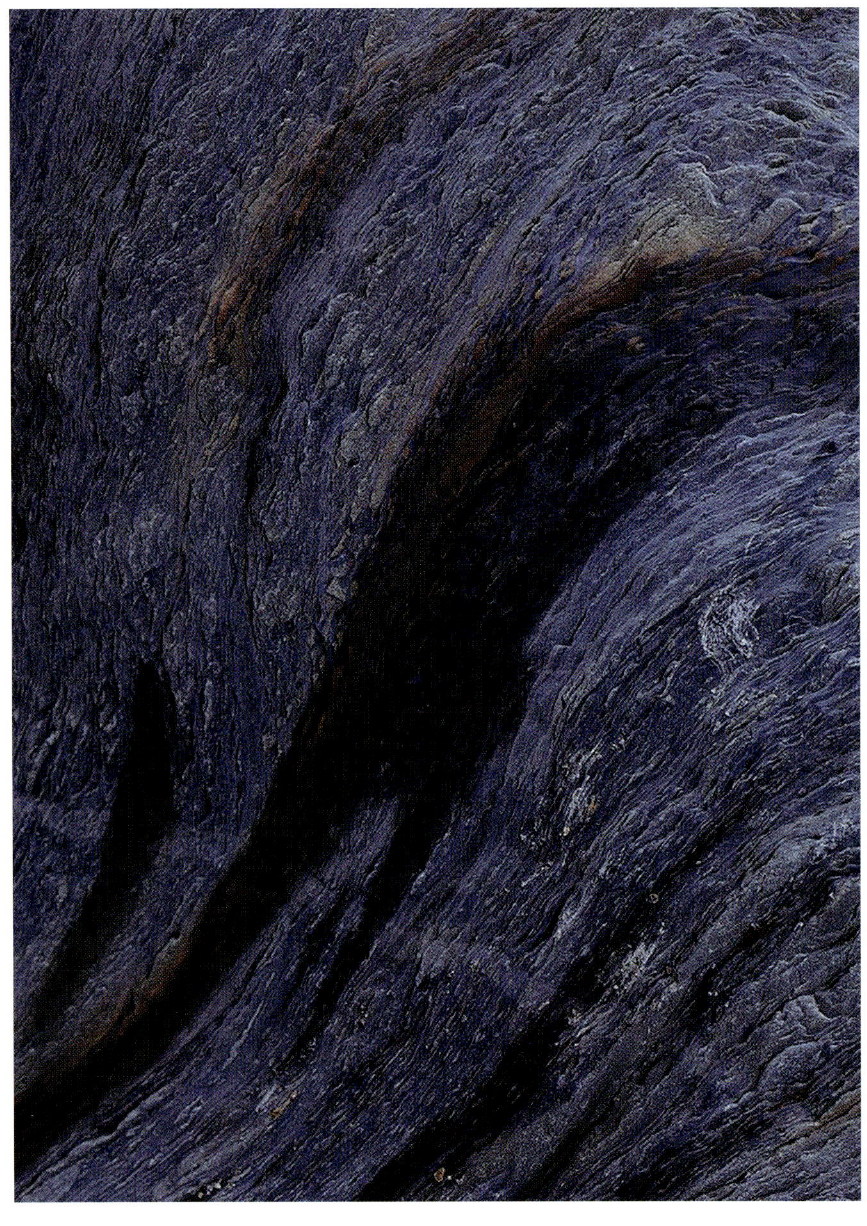

岩石上的瀑布形狀
Waterfall Shape on Rock
by Despina Kyriacou

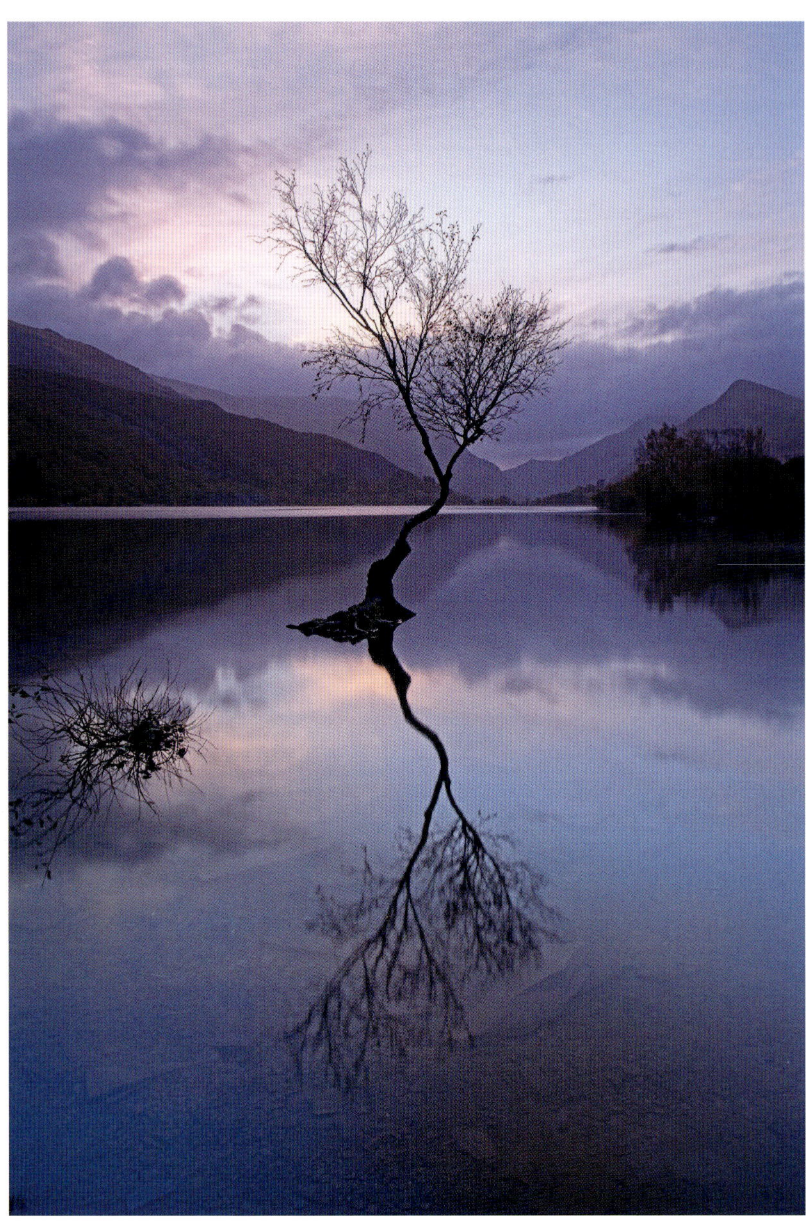

孤樹
Lone Tree by Carl Goodwin ARPS

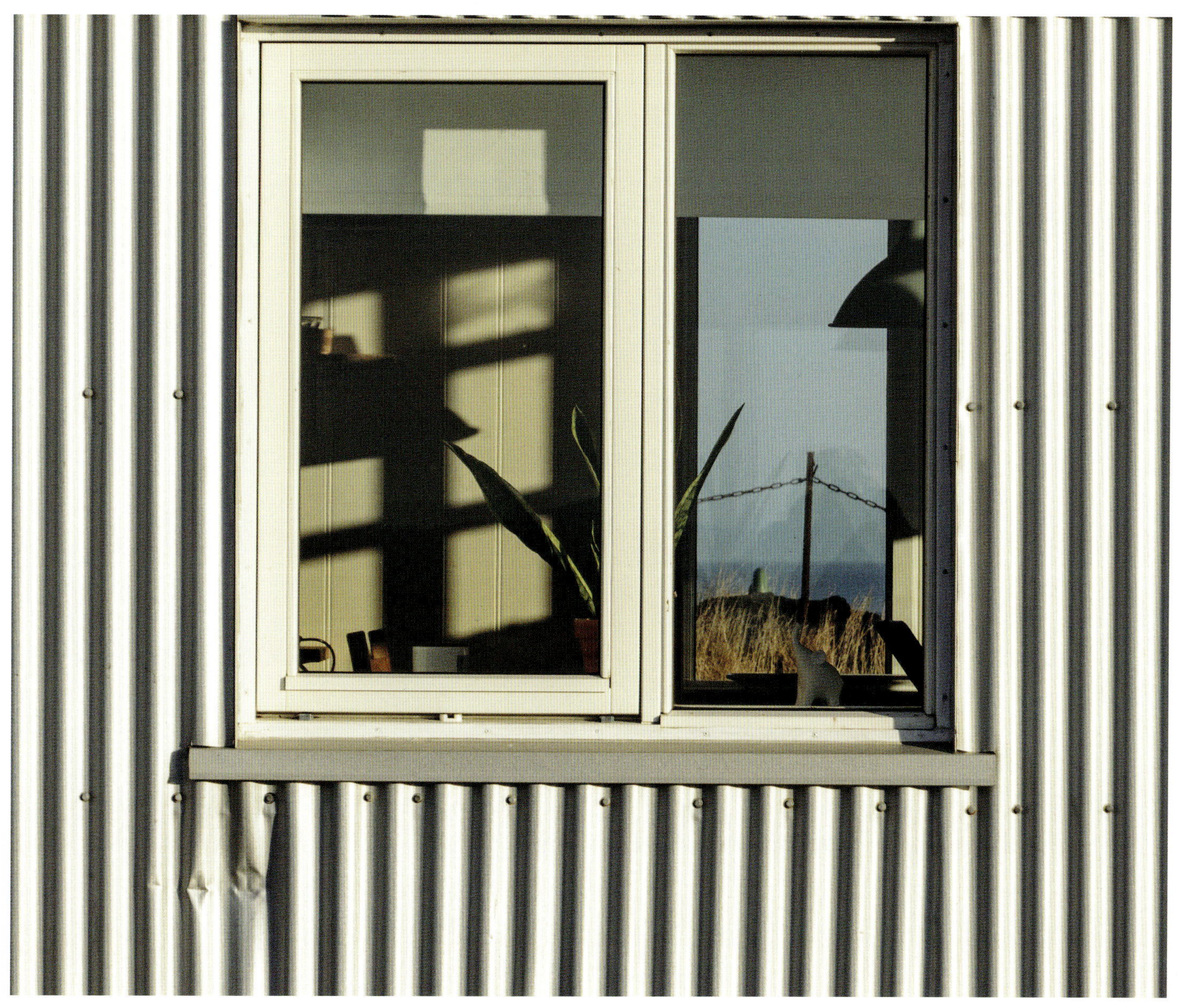

冰島的窗
Window on Iceland by Catherine Chetwynd LRPS

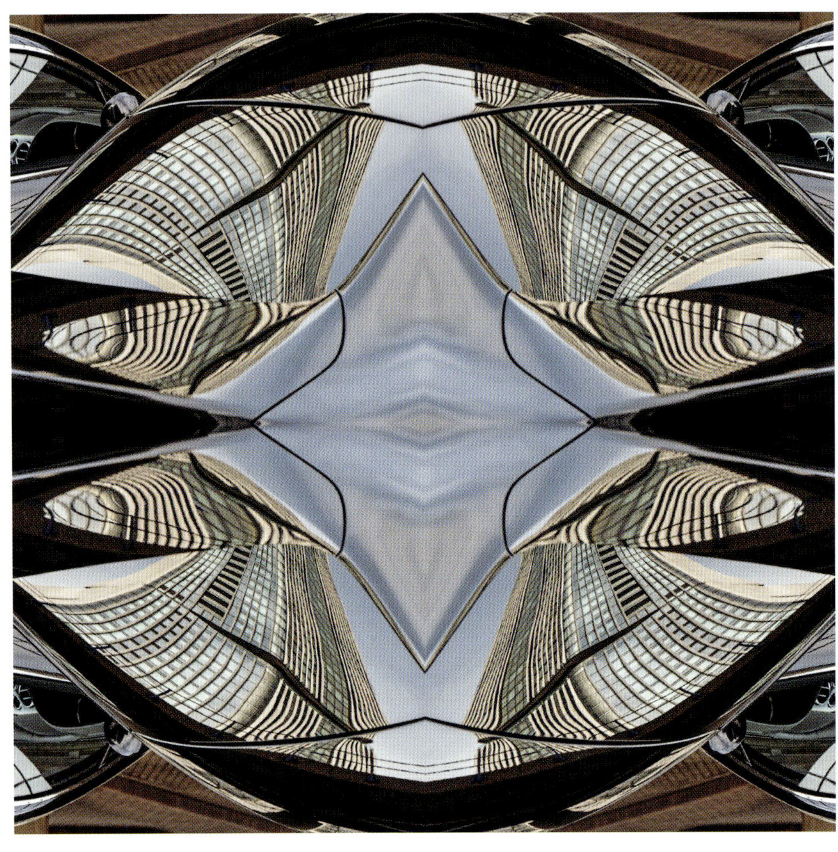

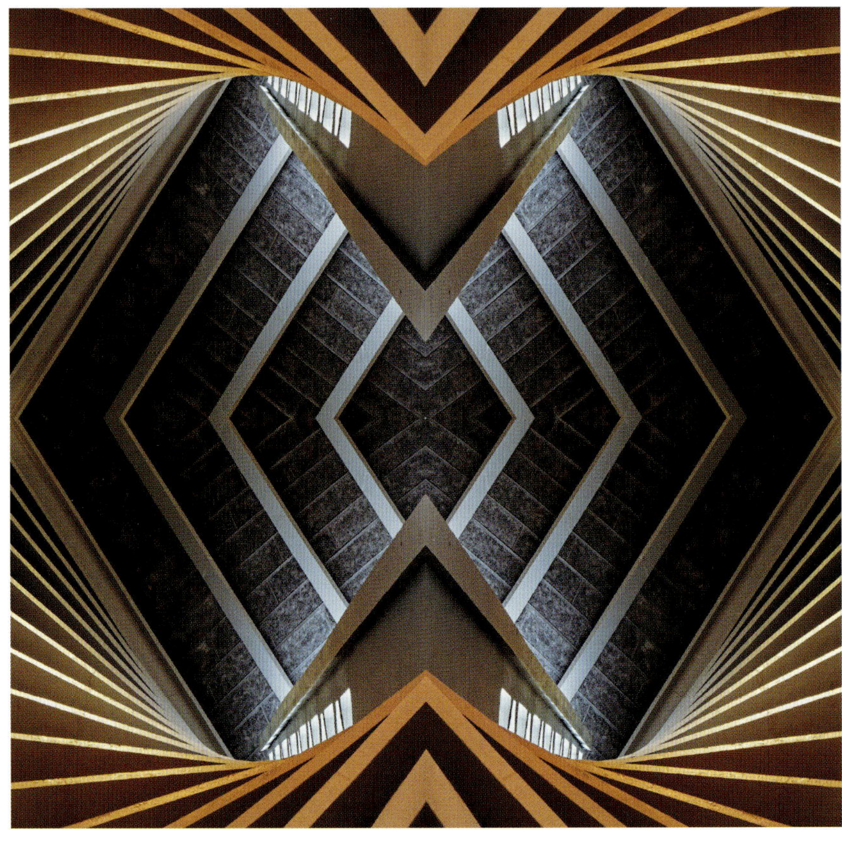

金絲雀碼頭的汽車反射
Canary Wharf Car Reflections by Fred Barrington FRPS, AFIAP

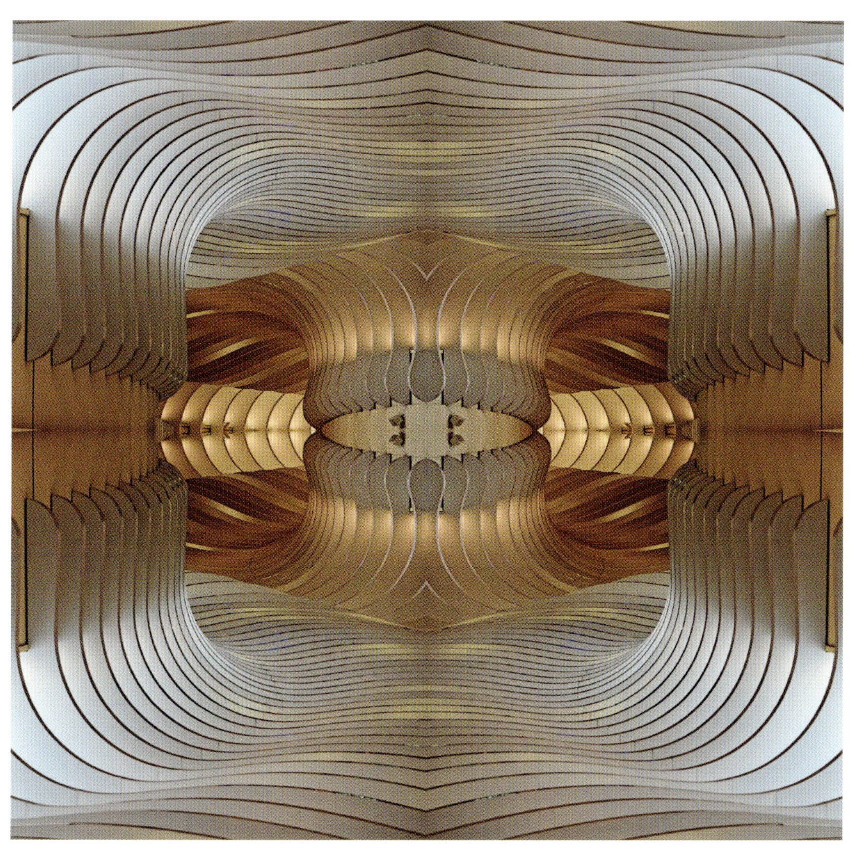

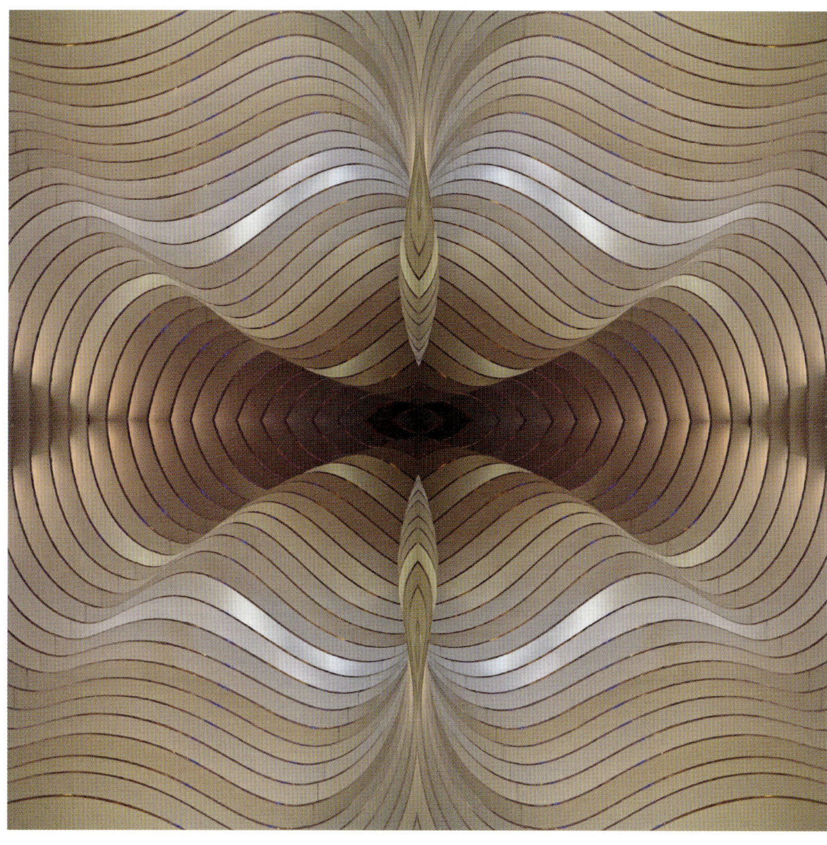

標志
Icon by Fred Barrington FRPS, AFIAP

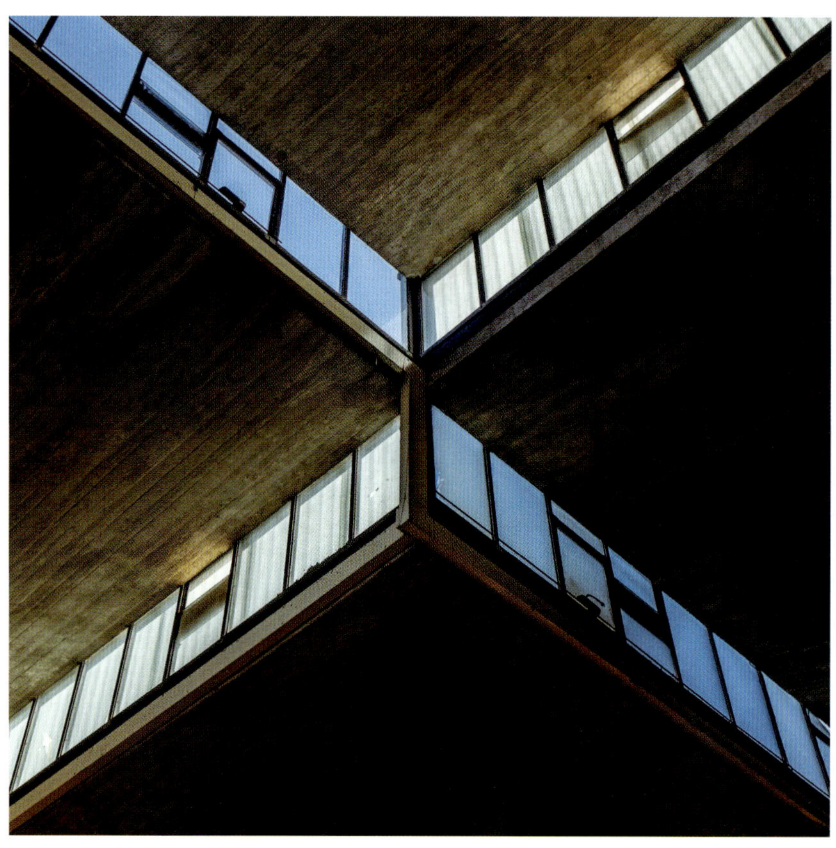

皇後門市場
Queensgate Market by Robin Maurice Barr

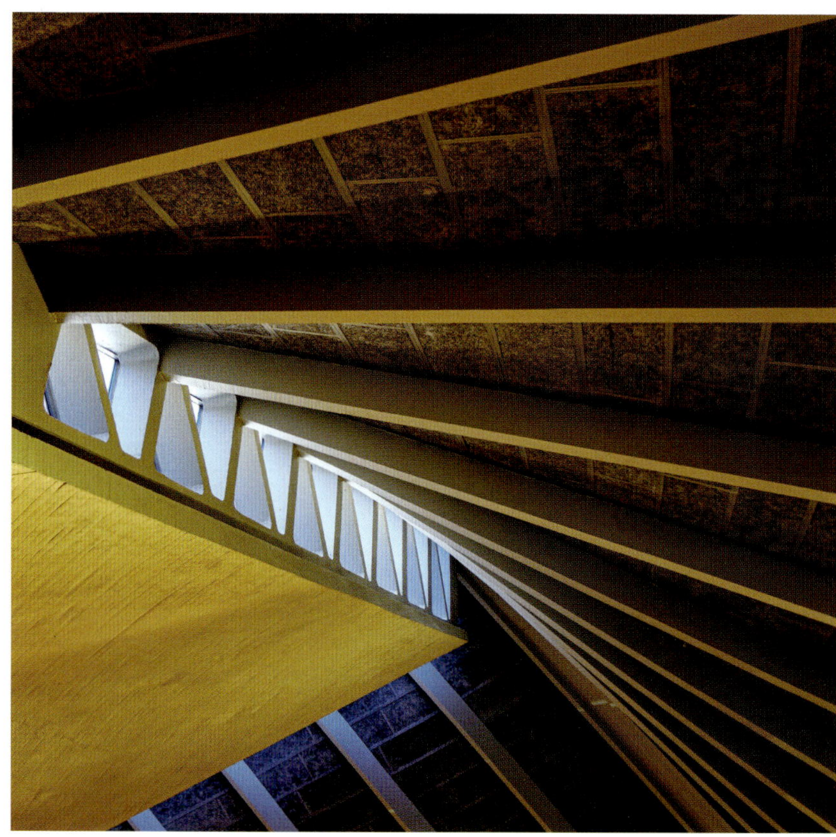

設計博物館
Design Museum by Robin Maurice Barr

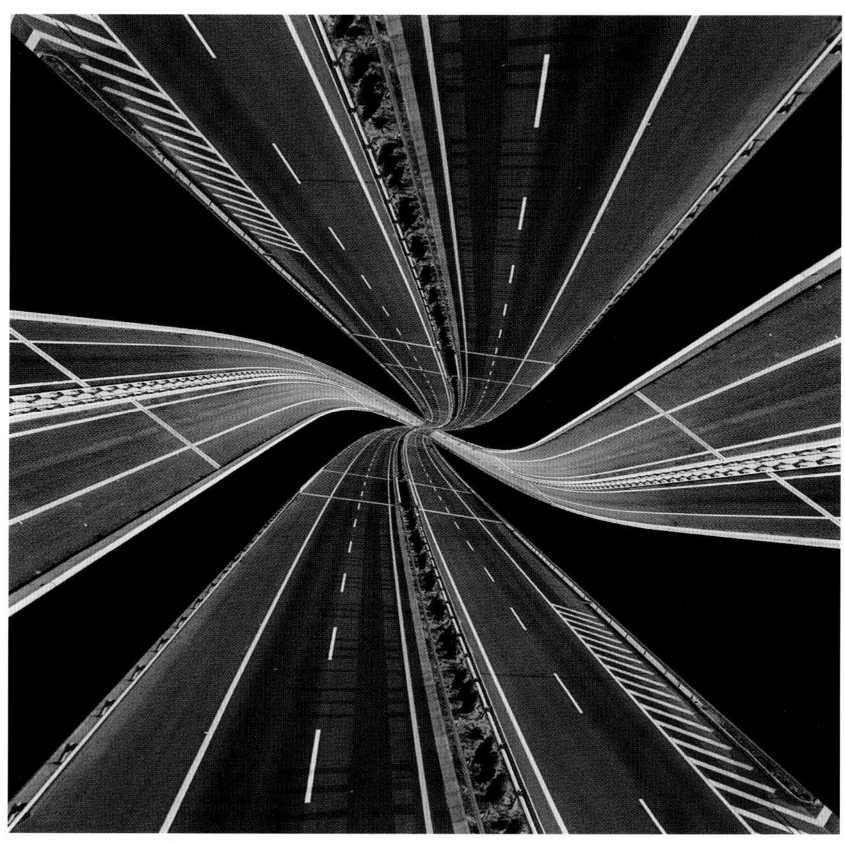

世紀歌舞 / 攝影: 成貴民
Century Song and Dance by Cheng Guimin

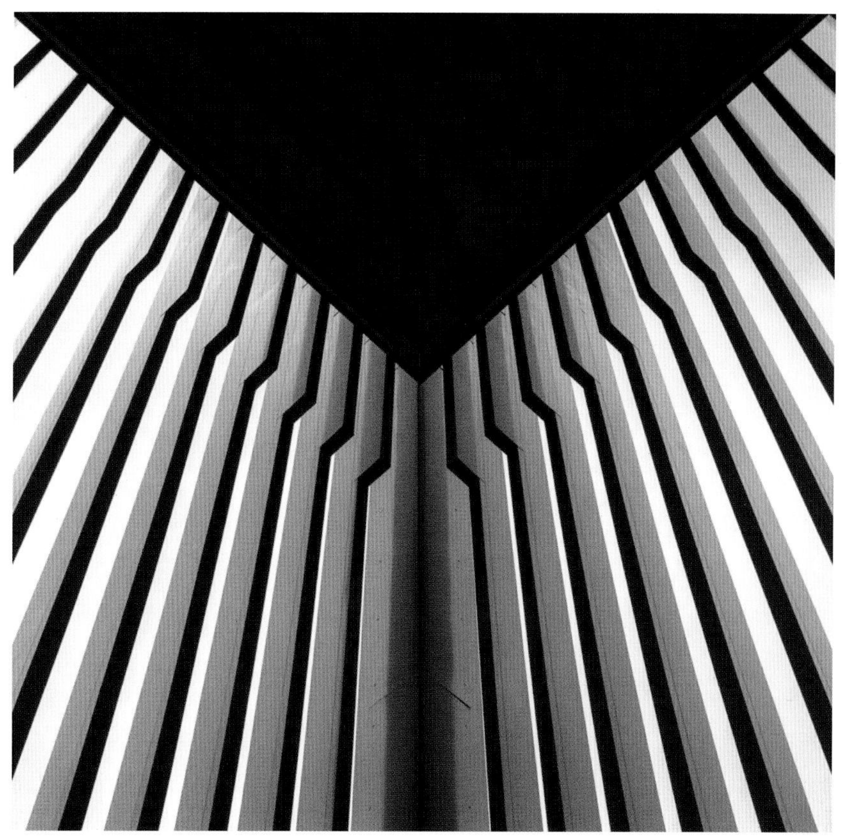

哈克尼威克
Hackney Wick by Robin Maurice Barr

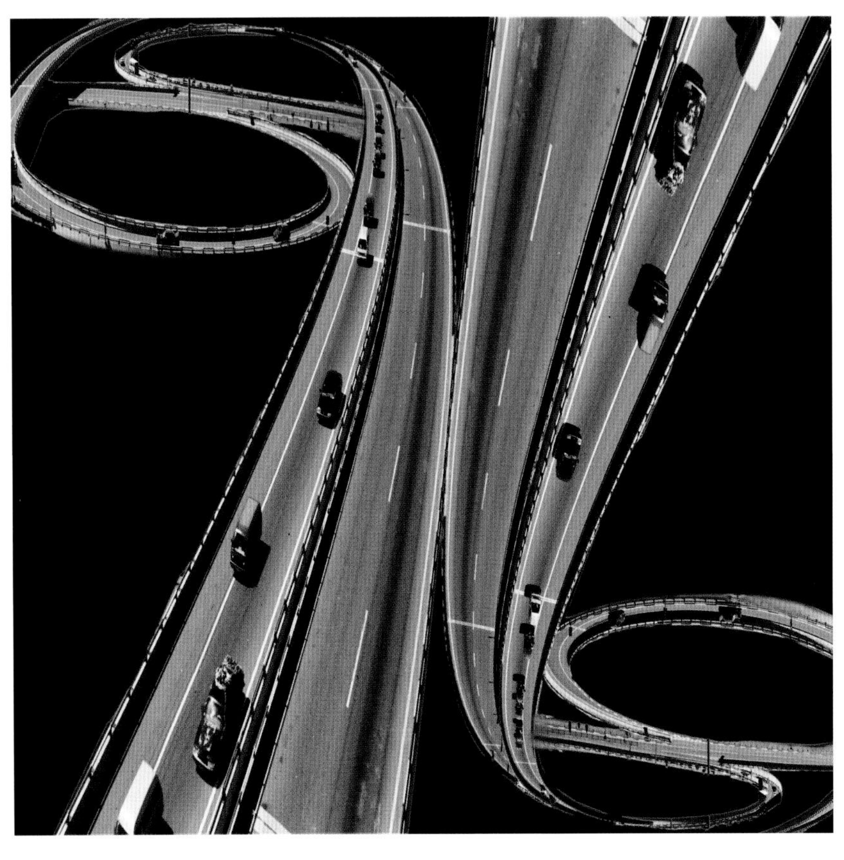

世紀歌舞 / 攝影: 成貴民
Century Song and Dance
by Cheng Guimin

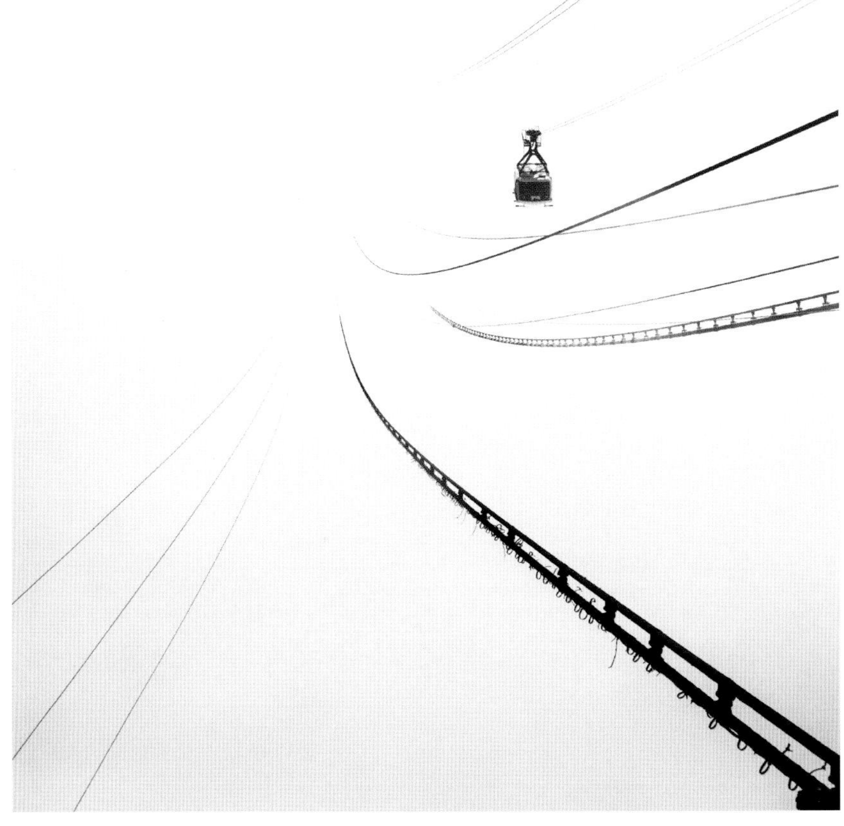

霧中的纜車
Cable Car in the Mist
by Fred Barrington FRPS, AFIAP

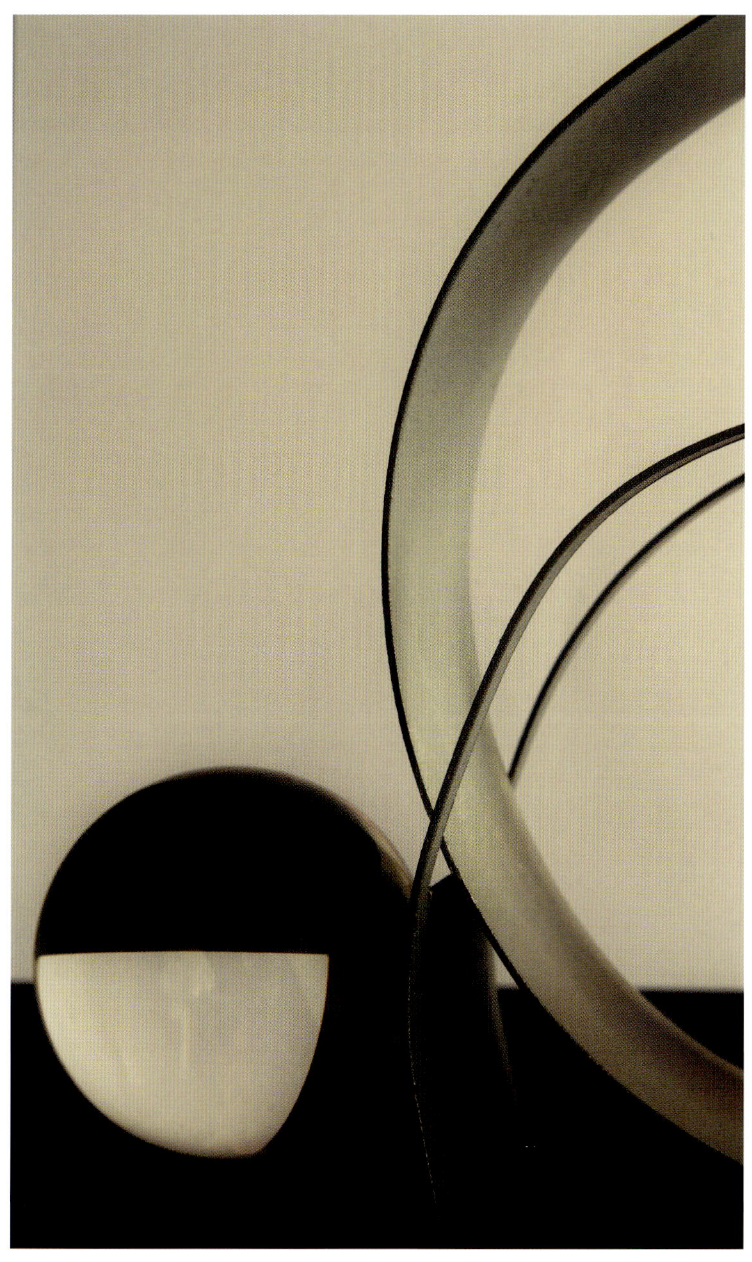

曲綫
Curves by Mary Davis

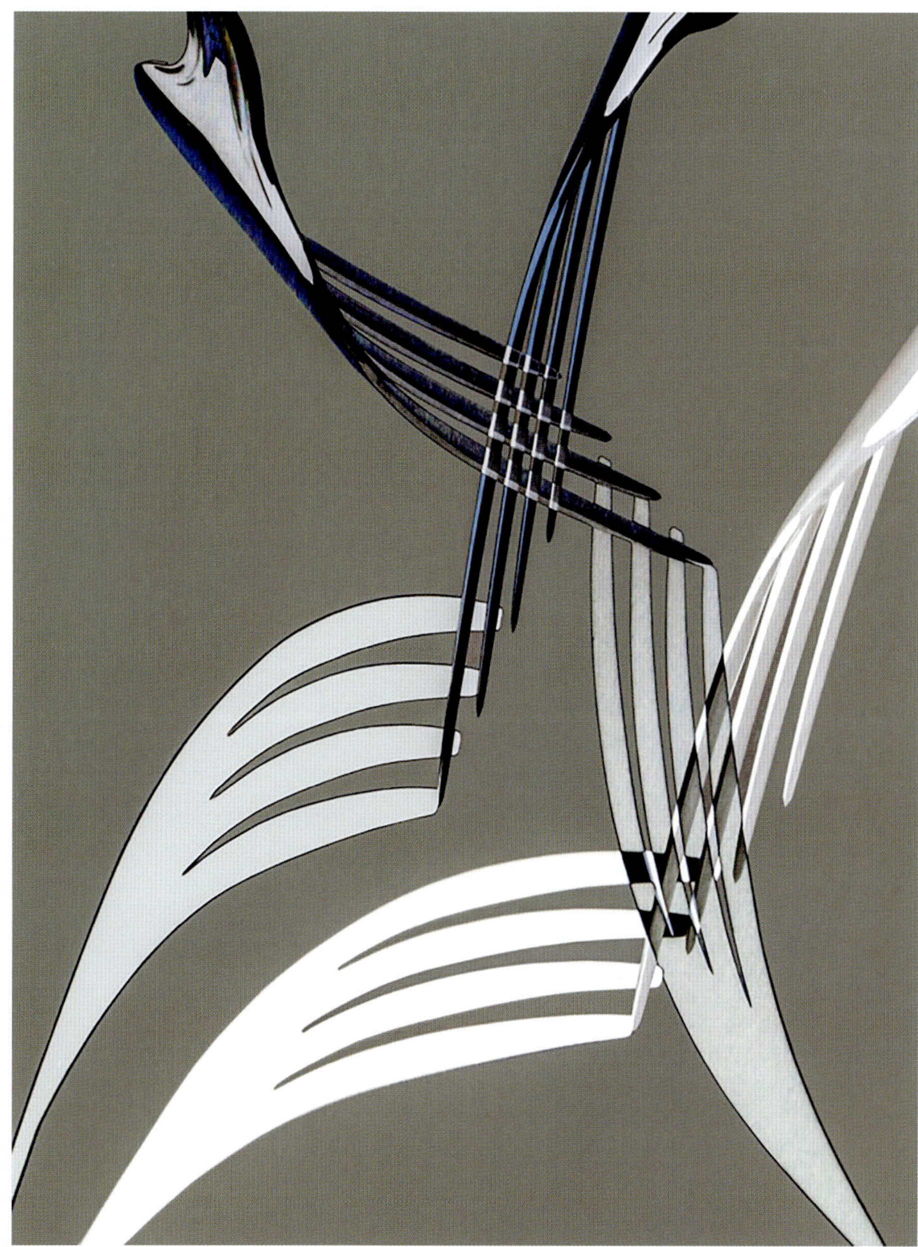

叉子和它的陰影
Fork and its Shadows by Gordana Johnson

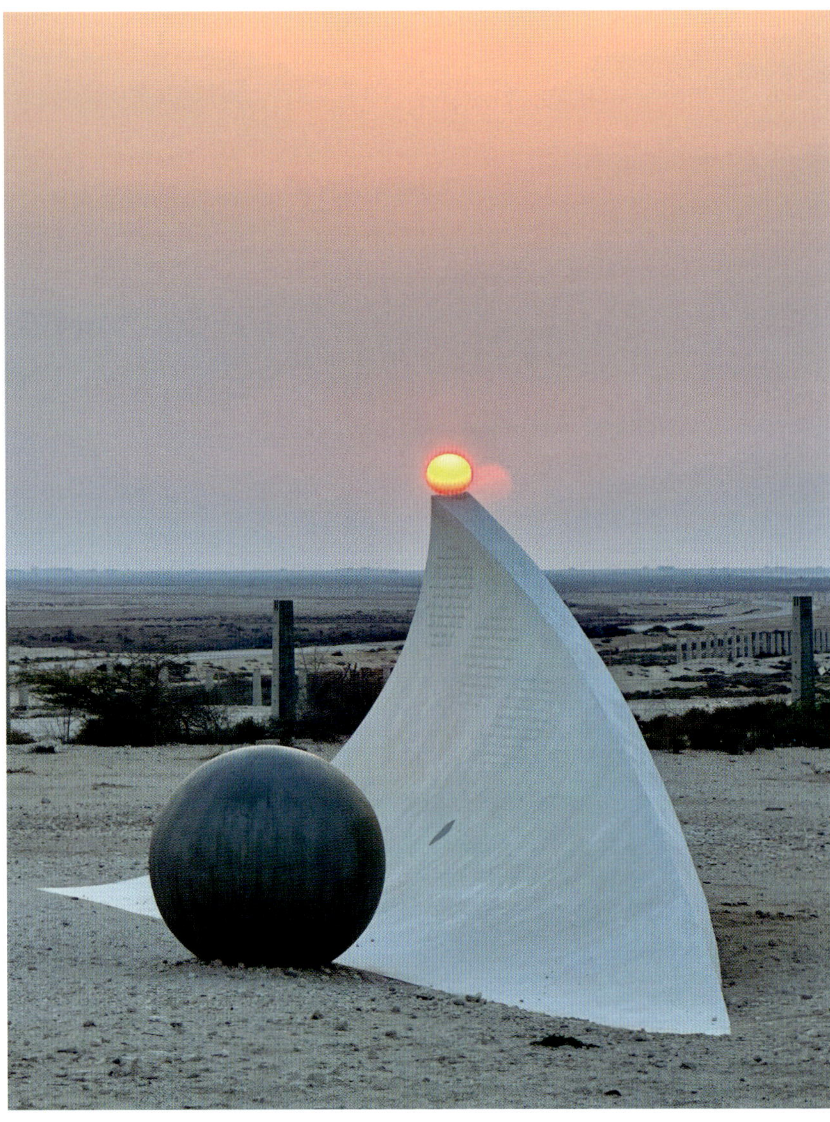

道遠日落 / 攝影: 鄧予立
Far Away Sunset by Tang Yu Lap

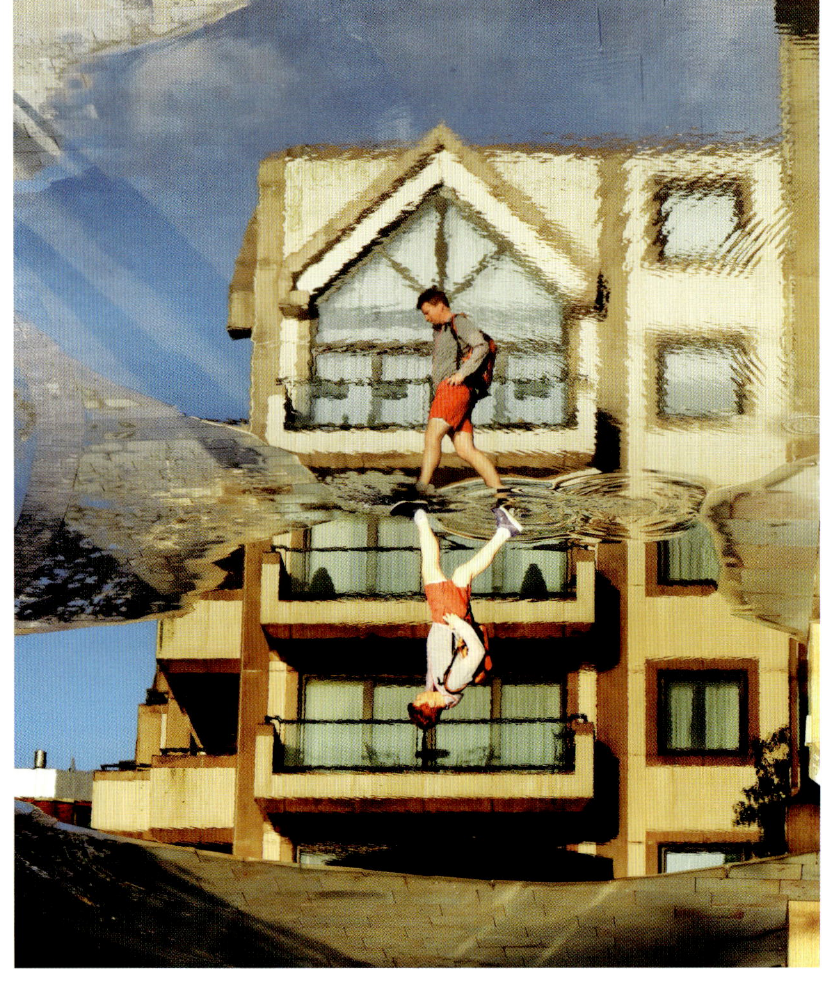

二元
Duality by Alex Flynn

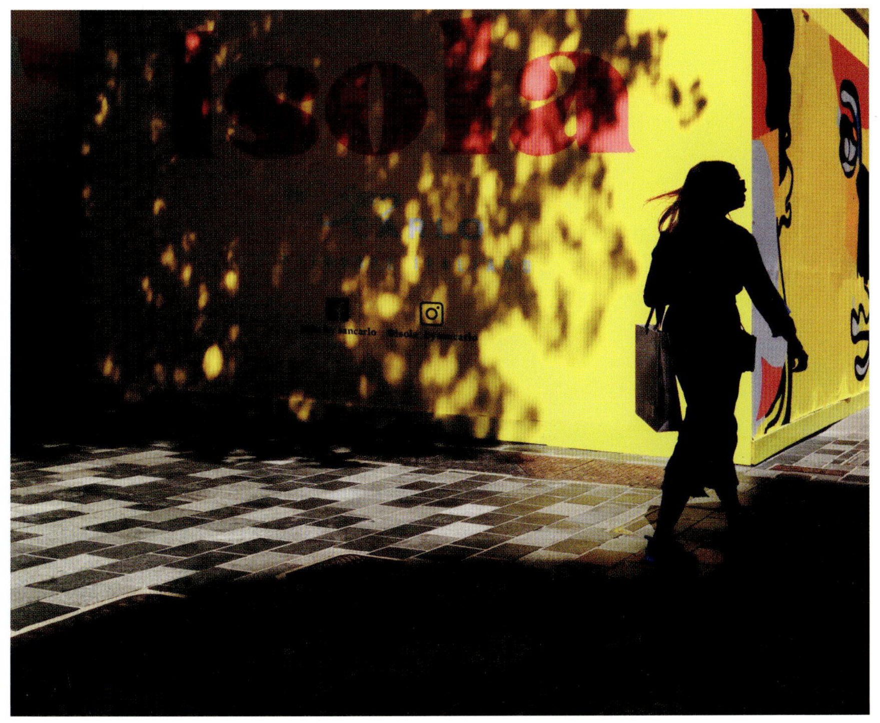

磯山村
Isola by Alex Flynn

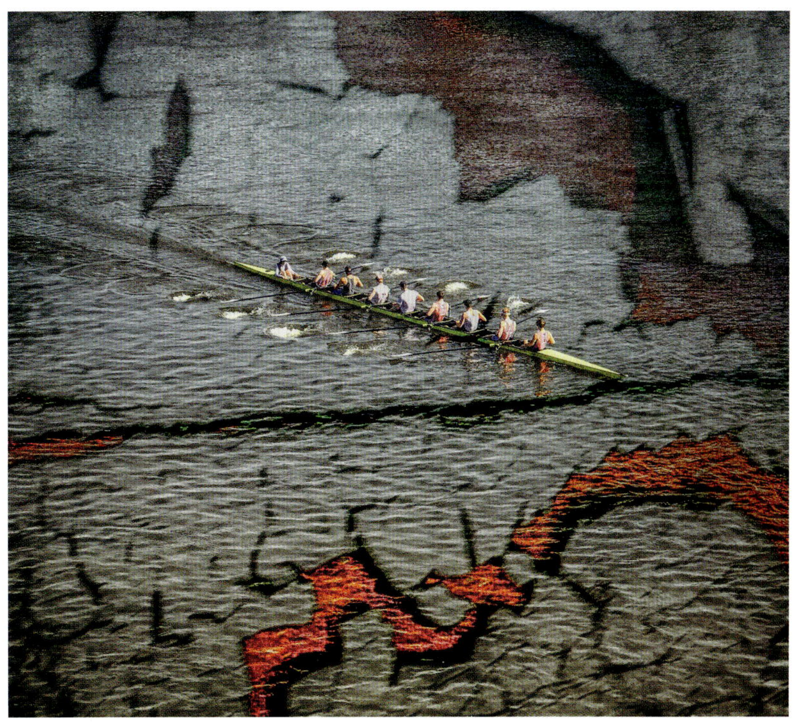

飛入
Fly Past by John Kelly LRPS, CPAGB

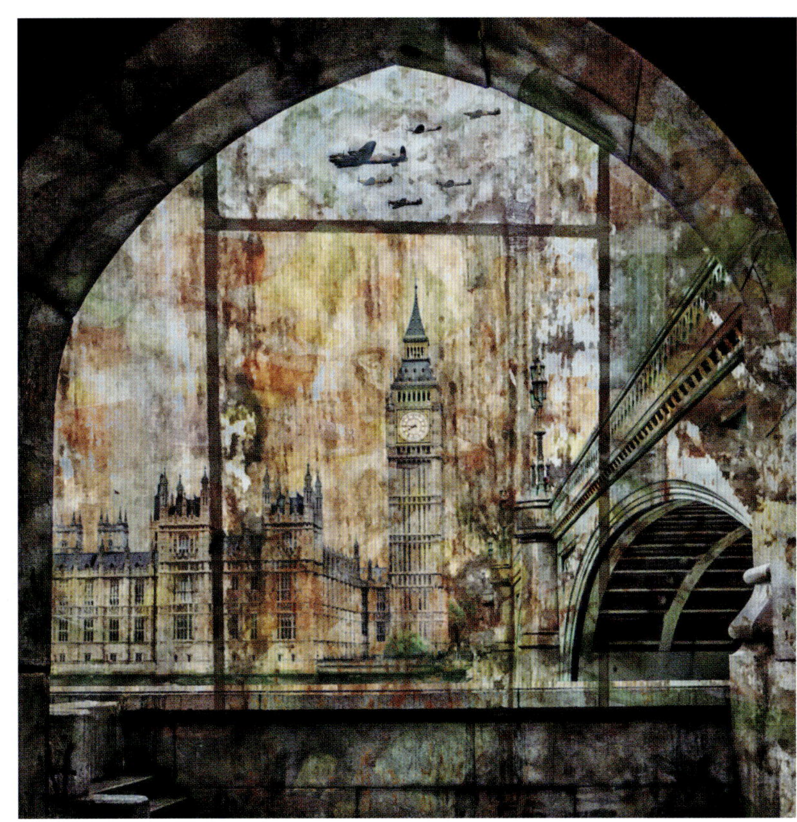

進入未知世界
Into The Unknown
by John Kelly LRPS, CPAGB

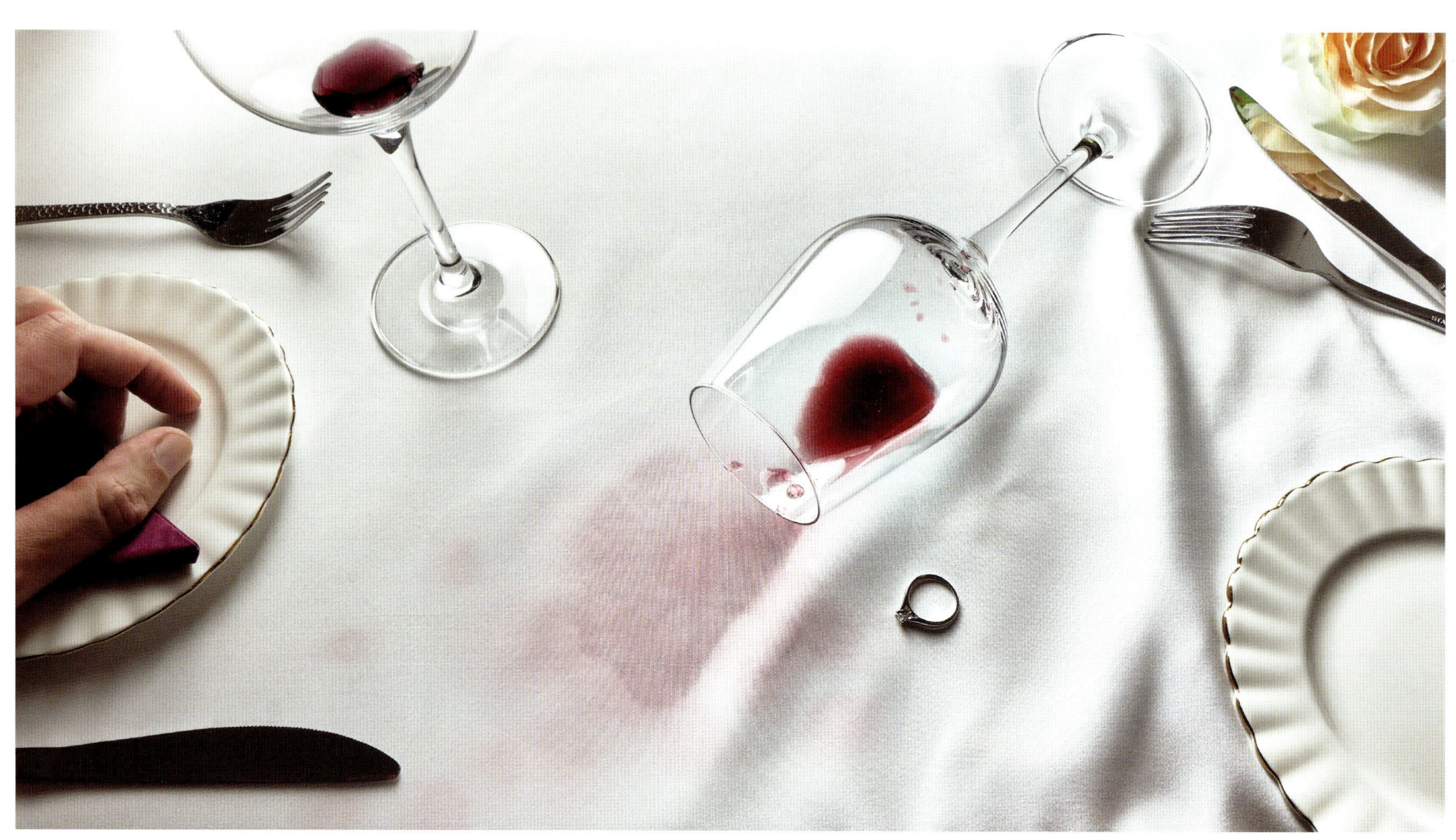

第一次再見
First Goodbye by Dain Evans LRPS

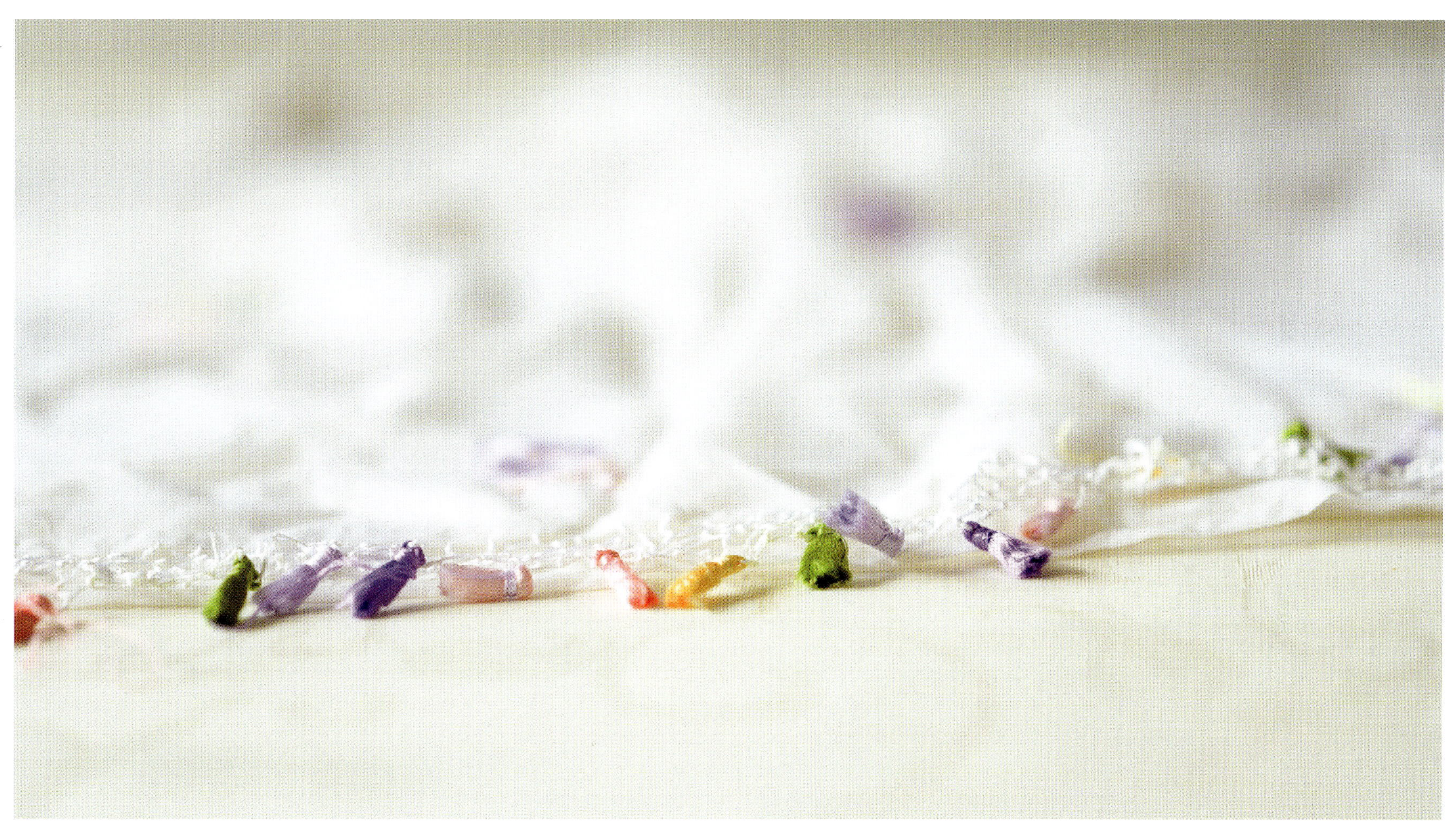

無聲之聲
Silent Voice by Bunshri Chandaria FRPS

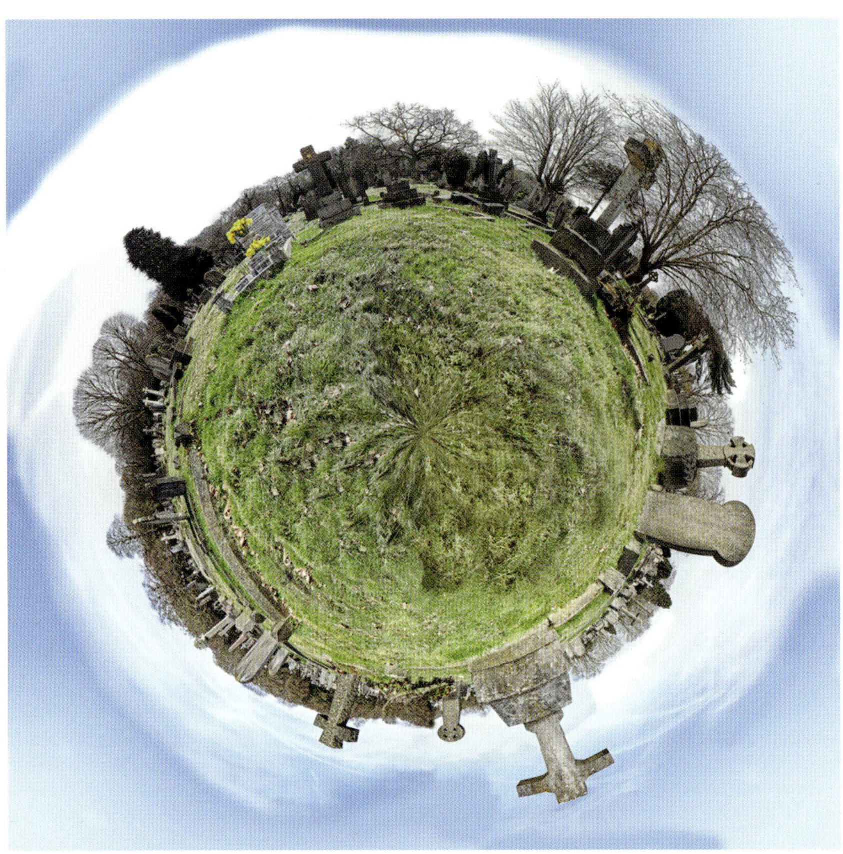

普特尼谷公墓
Putney Vale Cemetery
by John Kelly LRPS, CPAGB

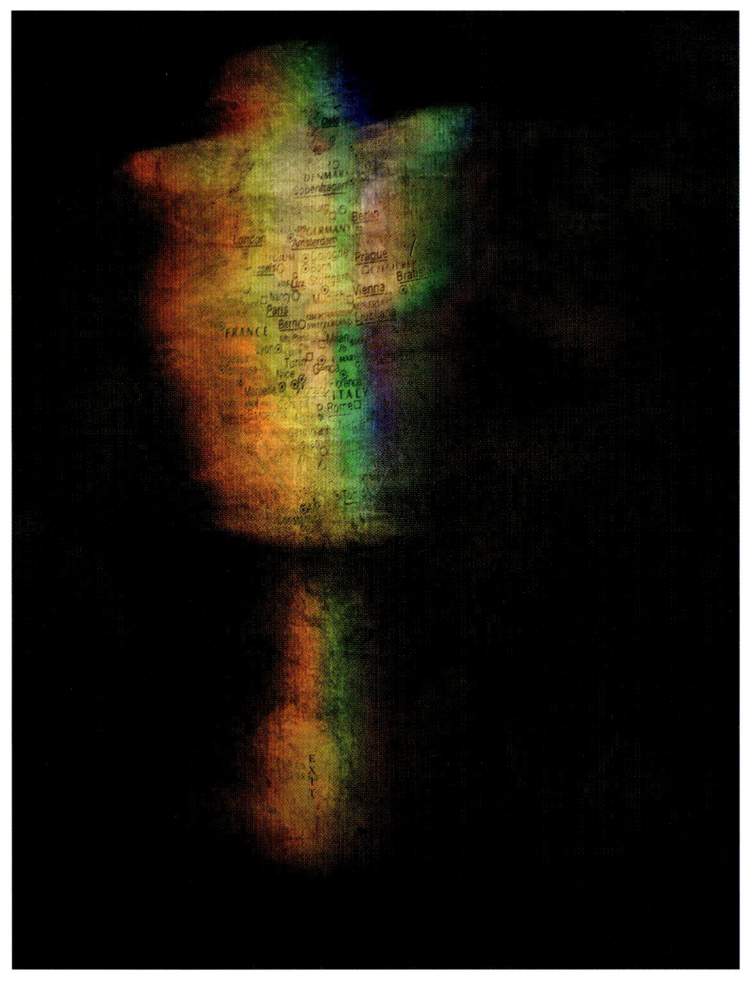

英國脫歐
Brexit by John Kelly LRPS, CPAGB

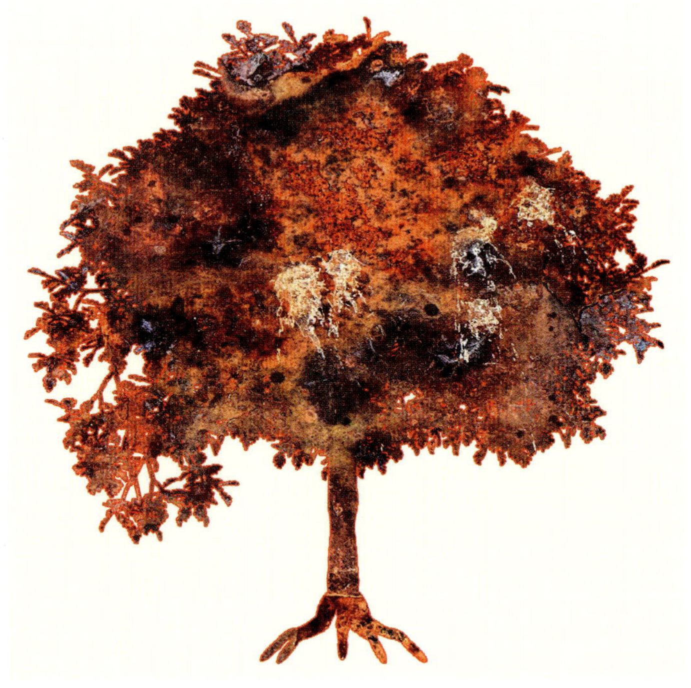

樸素的樹
Rustic Tree
by John Kelly LRPS, CPAGB

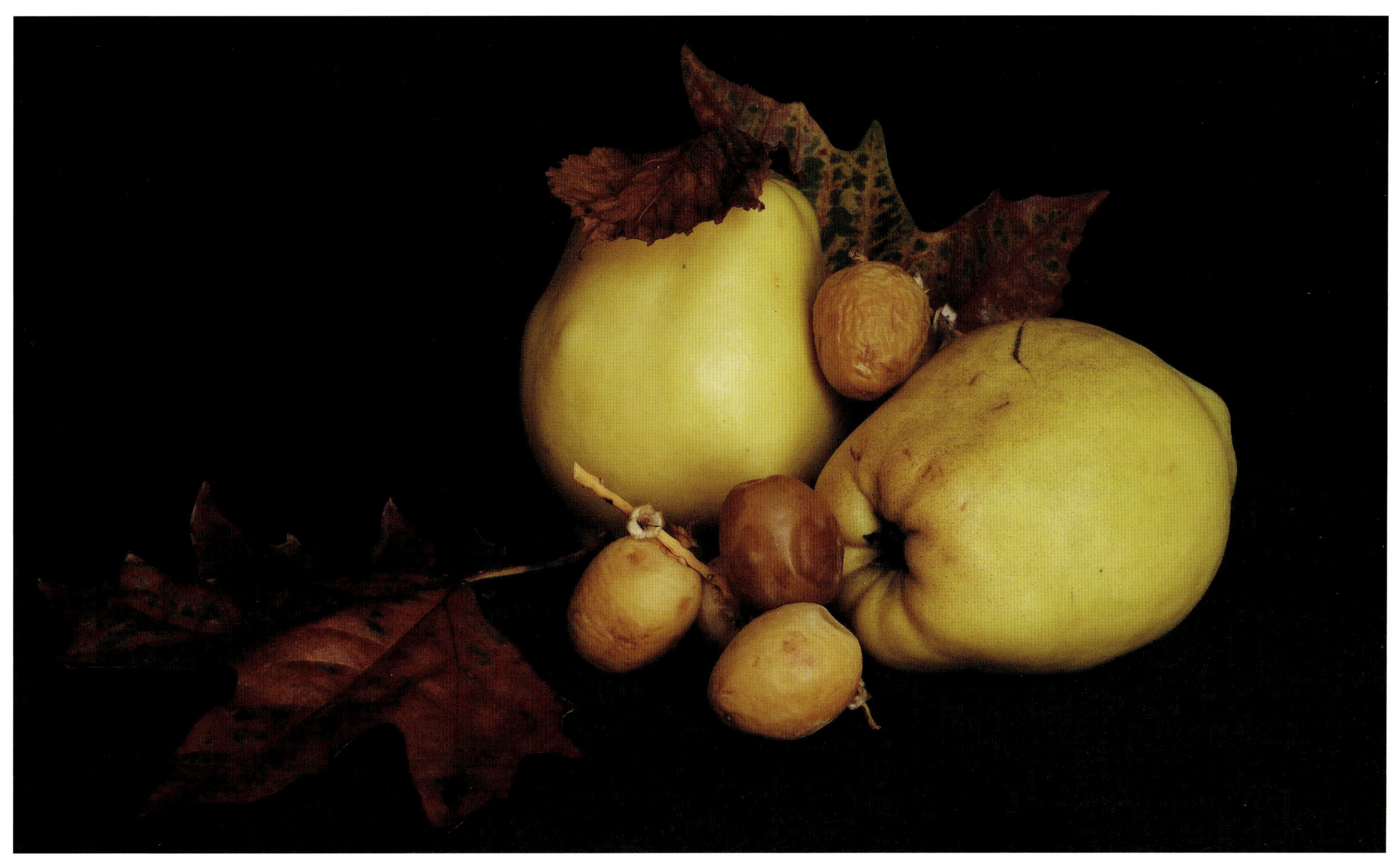

奎因和日期
Quinces and Dates by Petra Laidlaw LRPS

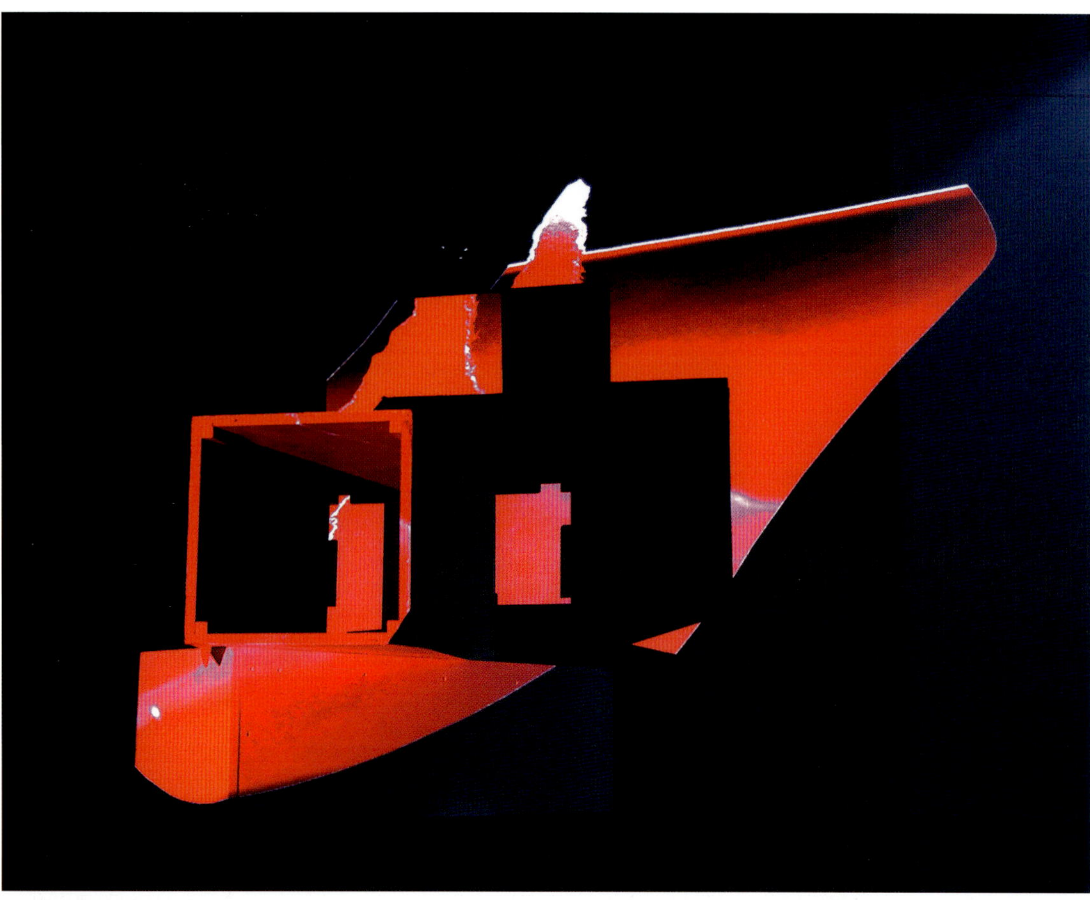

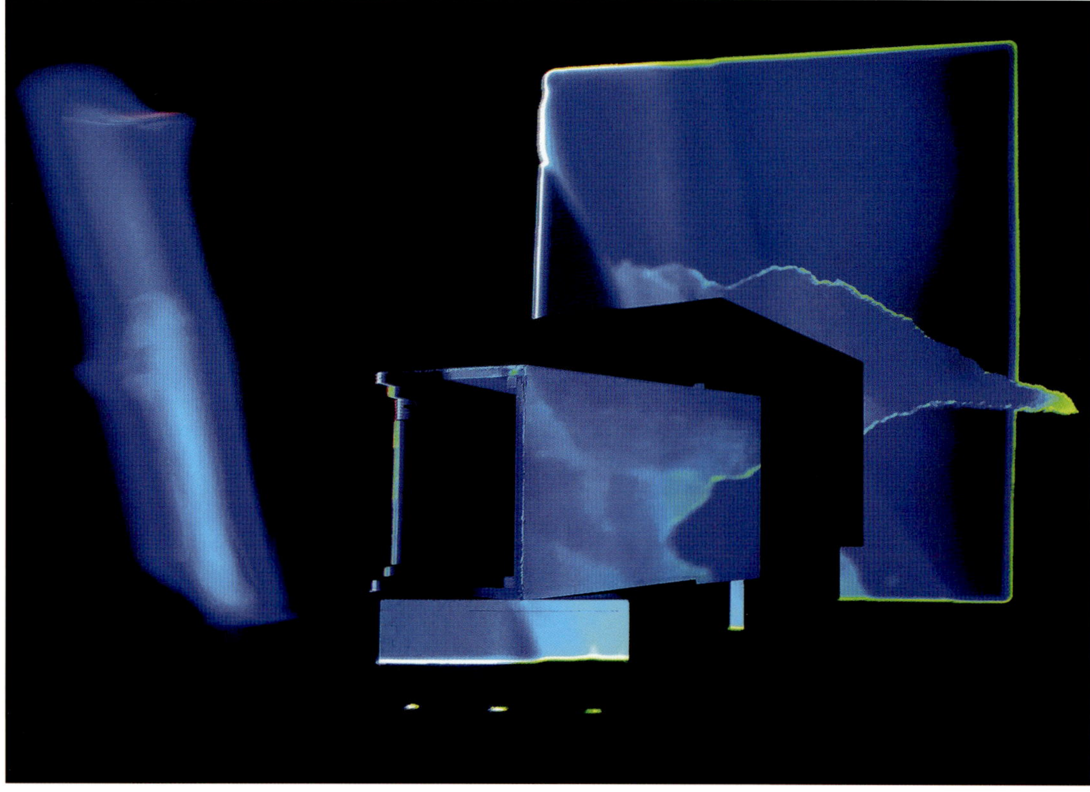

抽象
Abstract by Jake Bonnell

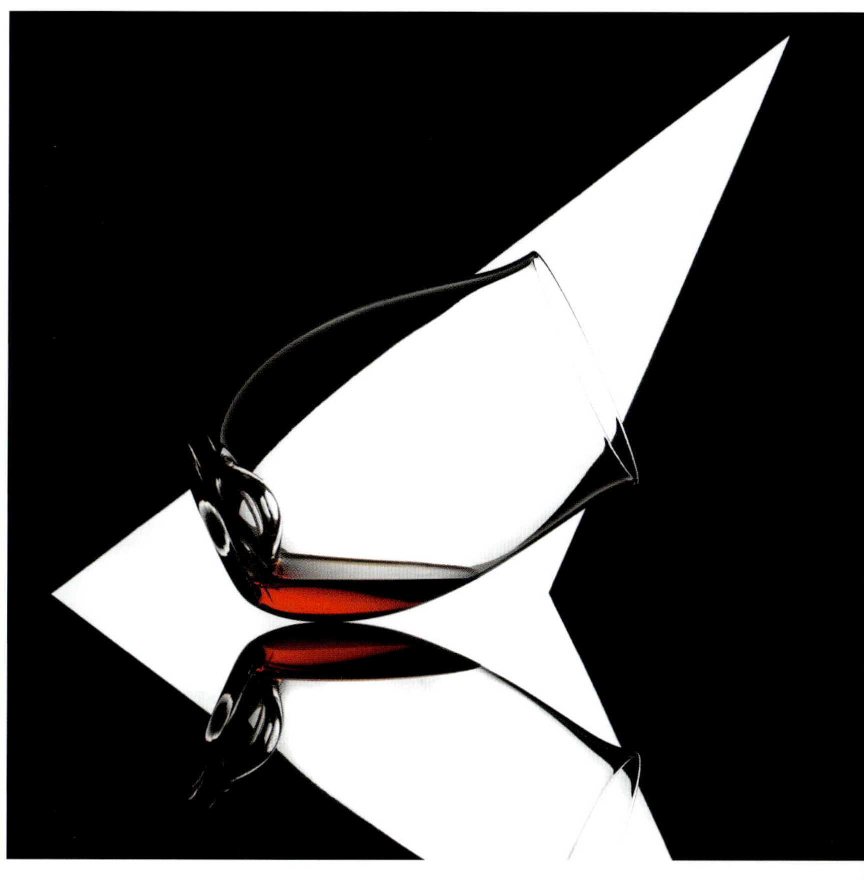

平衡
Balance by David Rutter FRPS

紅點2
Red Point 2 by David Rutter FRPS

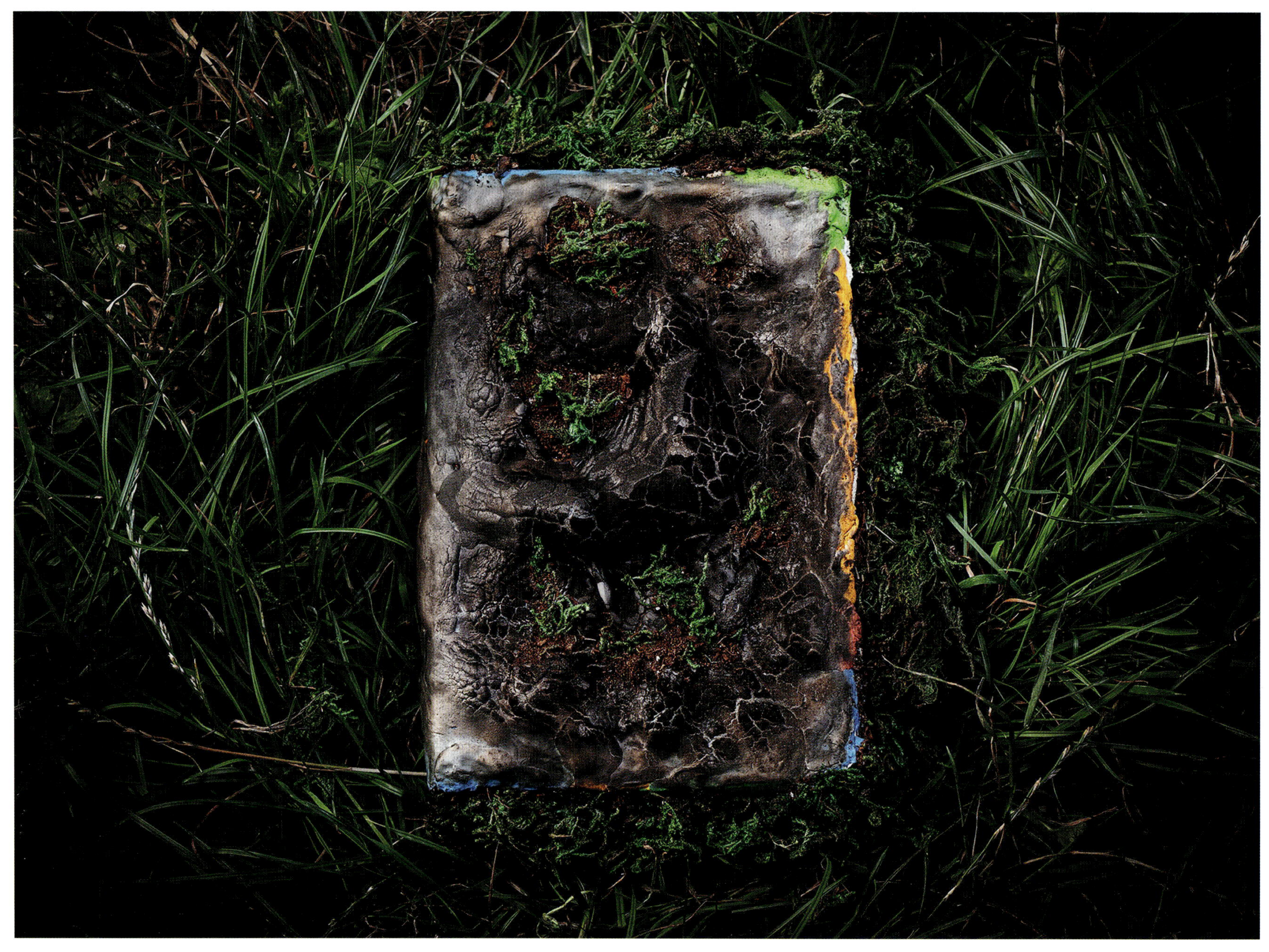

一則星球寓言 / 攝影: 梁藝寶
A Fable of the Planet by Liang Yibao

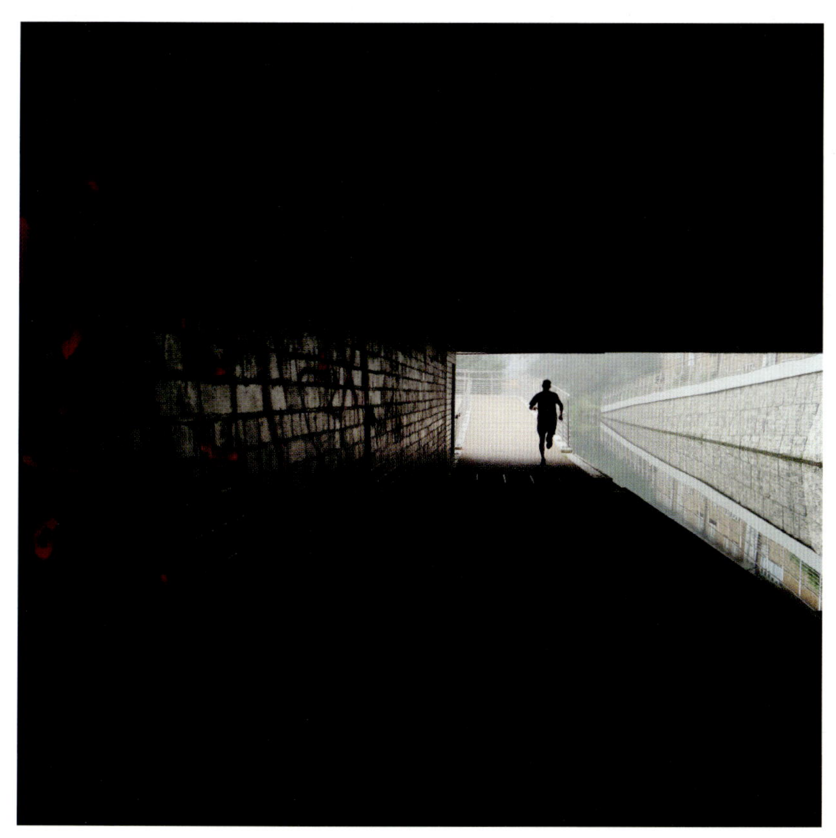

跑步者
Runner by Alex Flynn

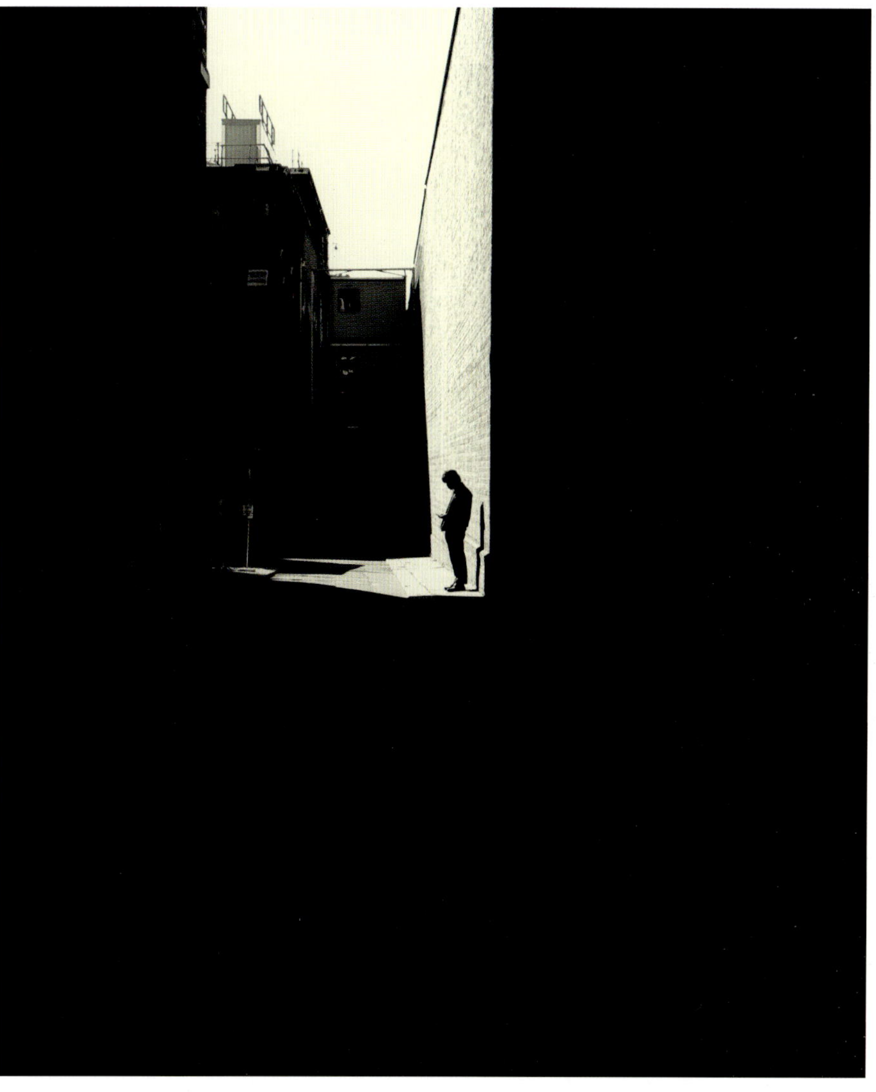

光軸
Shaft of Light by Alex Flynn

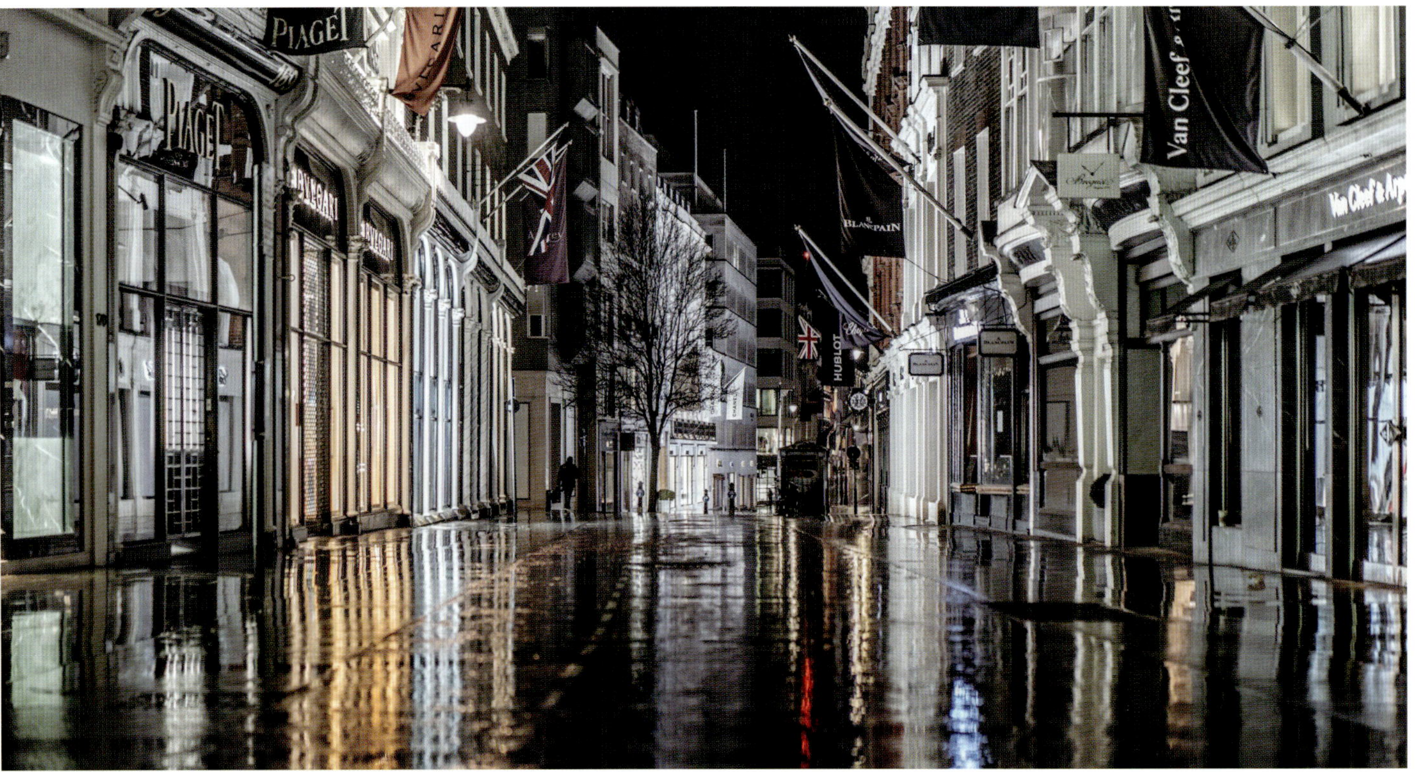
PIAGET
PIAGET
Van Cleef
HUBLOT

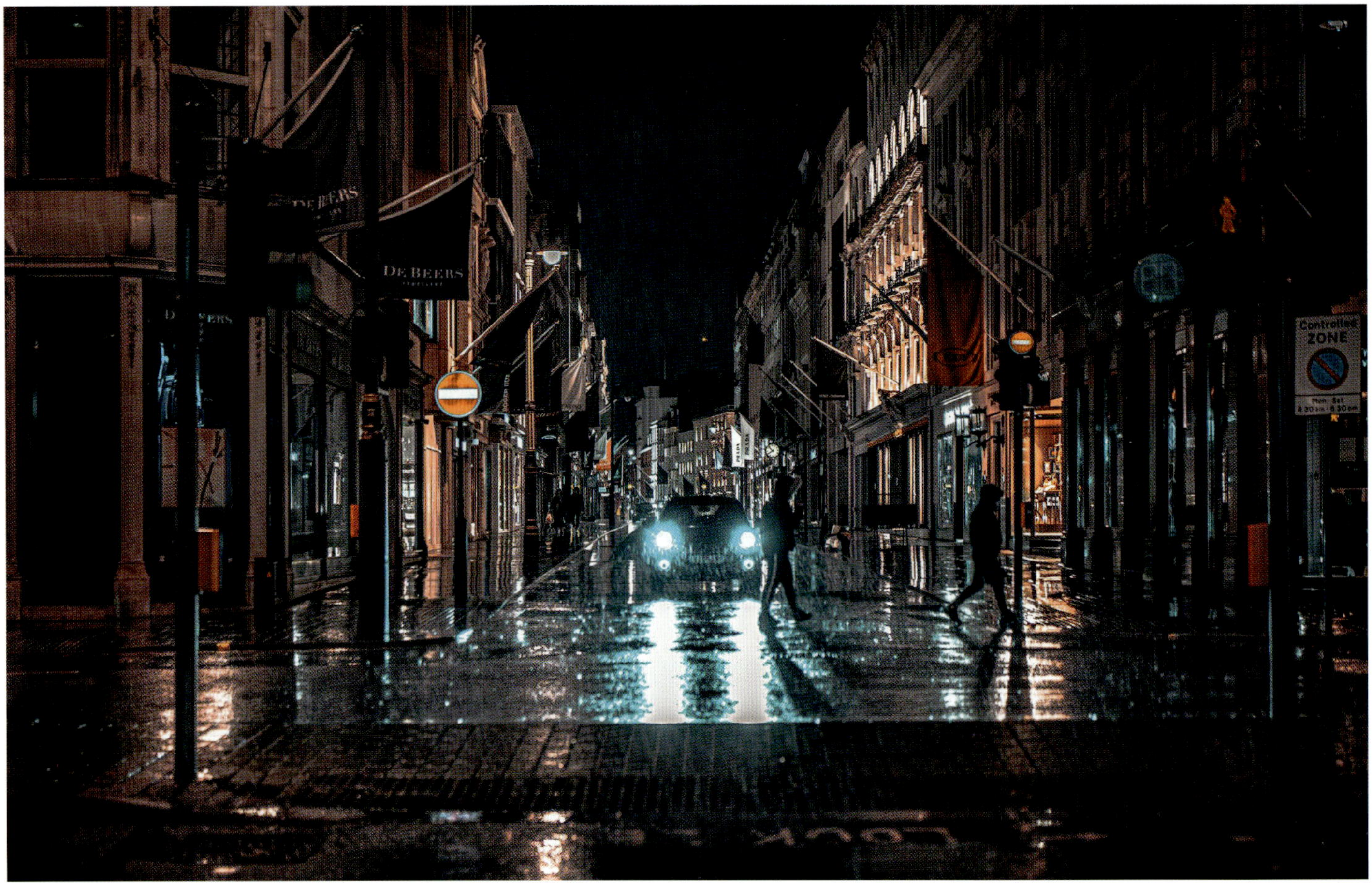

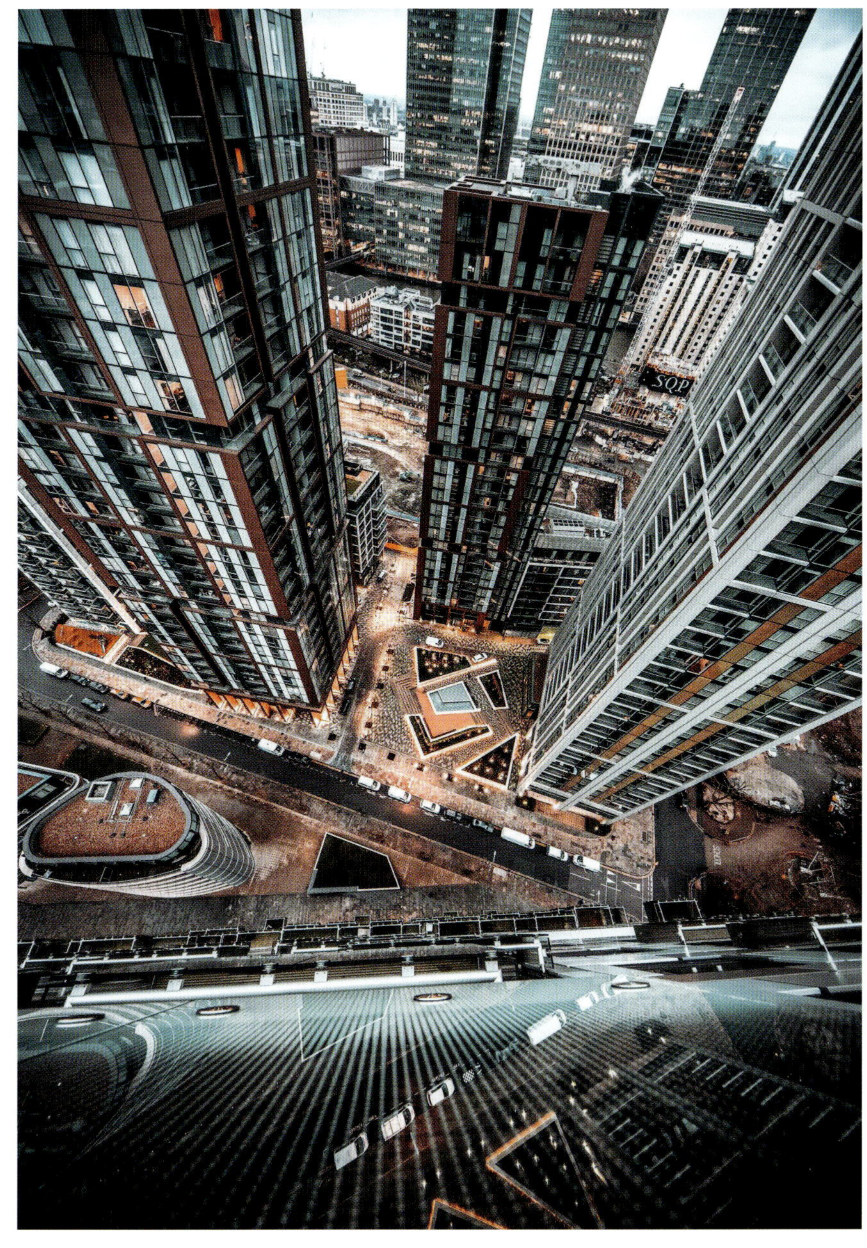

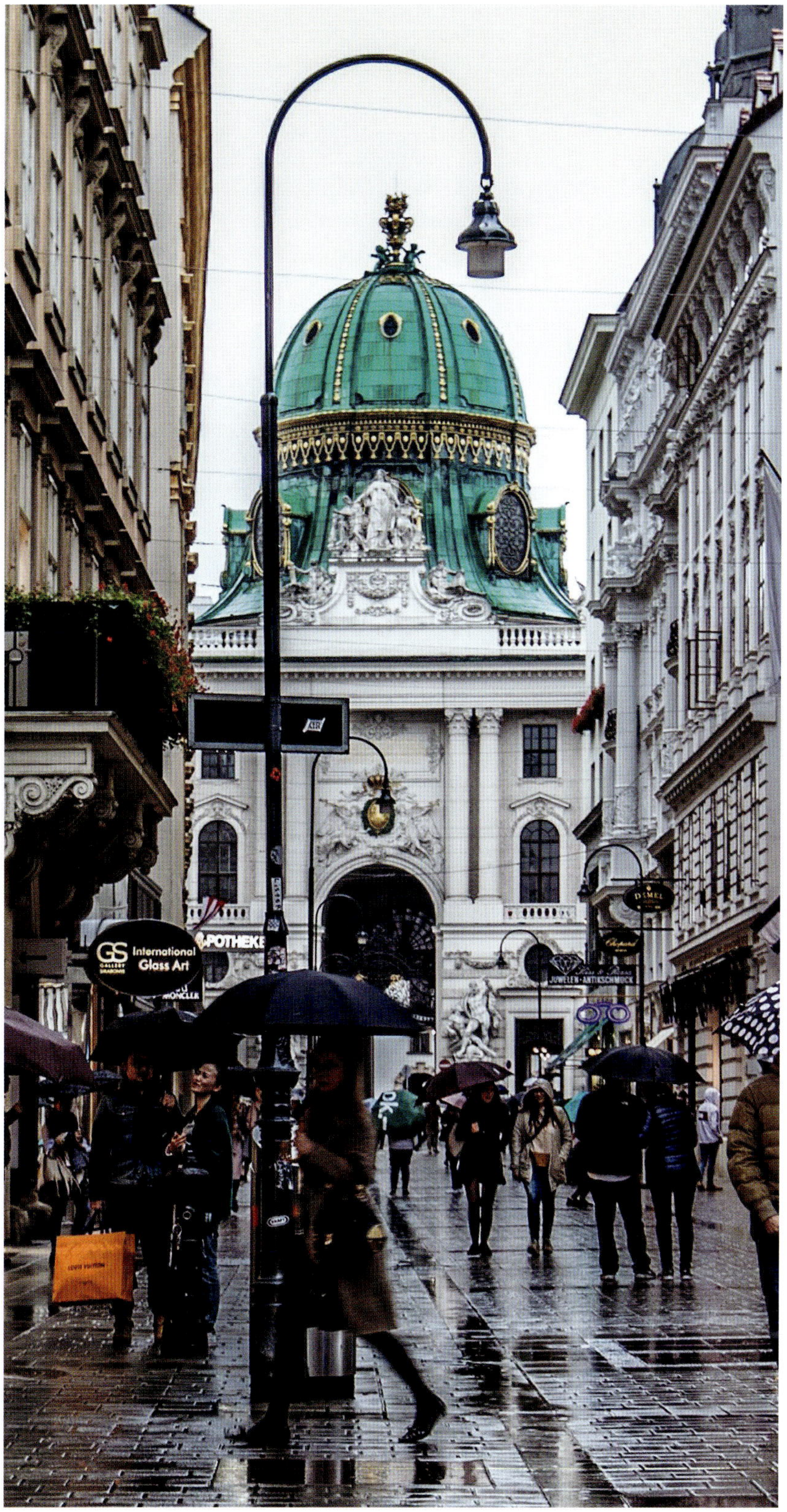

城市掠影 / 攝影: 農賀迪
City Snapshot by Nong Hedi

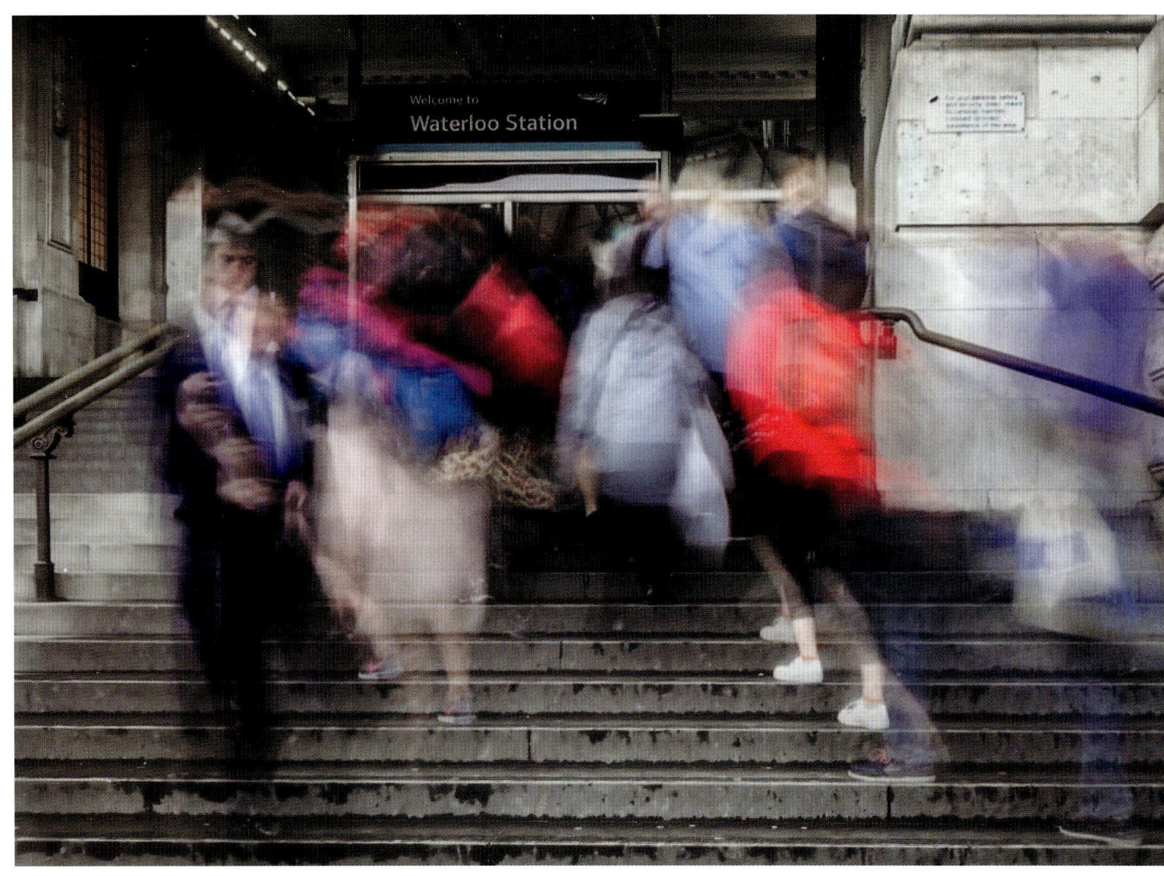

高峰期
Rush Hour
by John Kelly LRPS, CPAGB

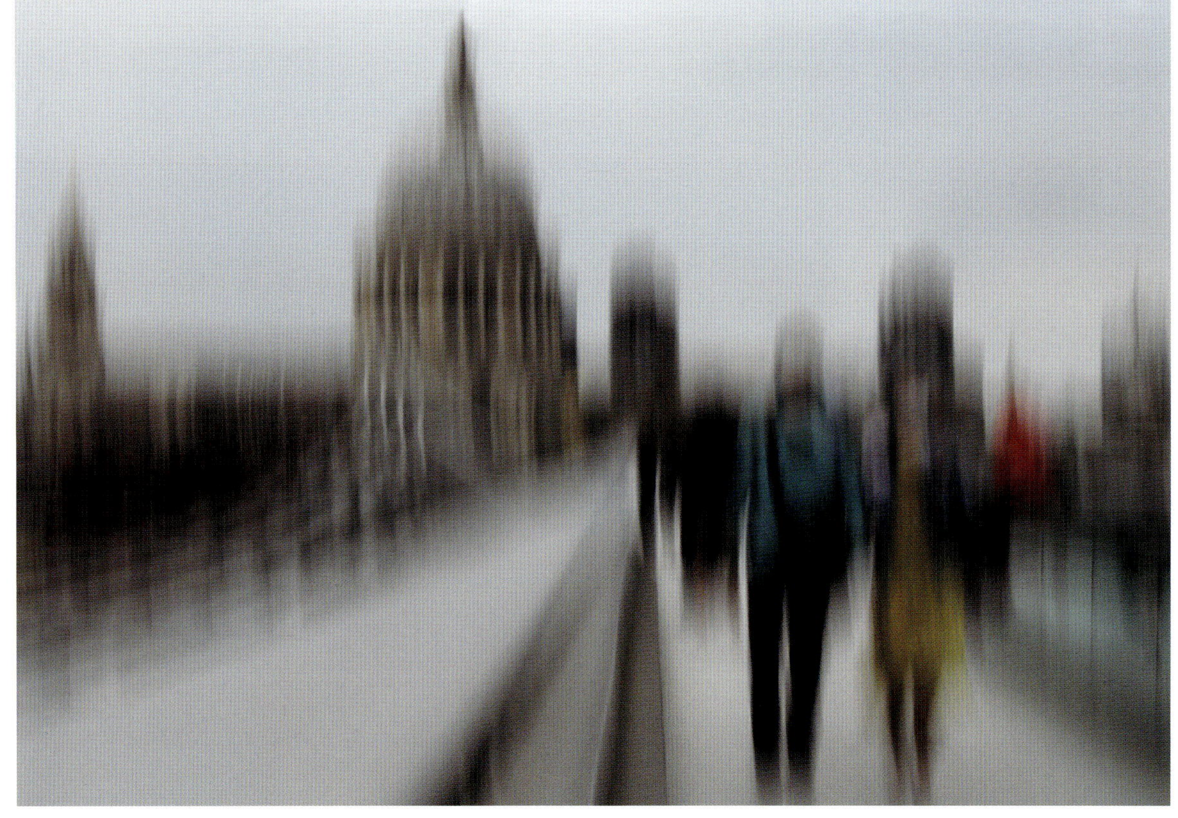

穿越千禧橋
Crossing Millennium Bridge
by Dawn Clifford LRPS

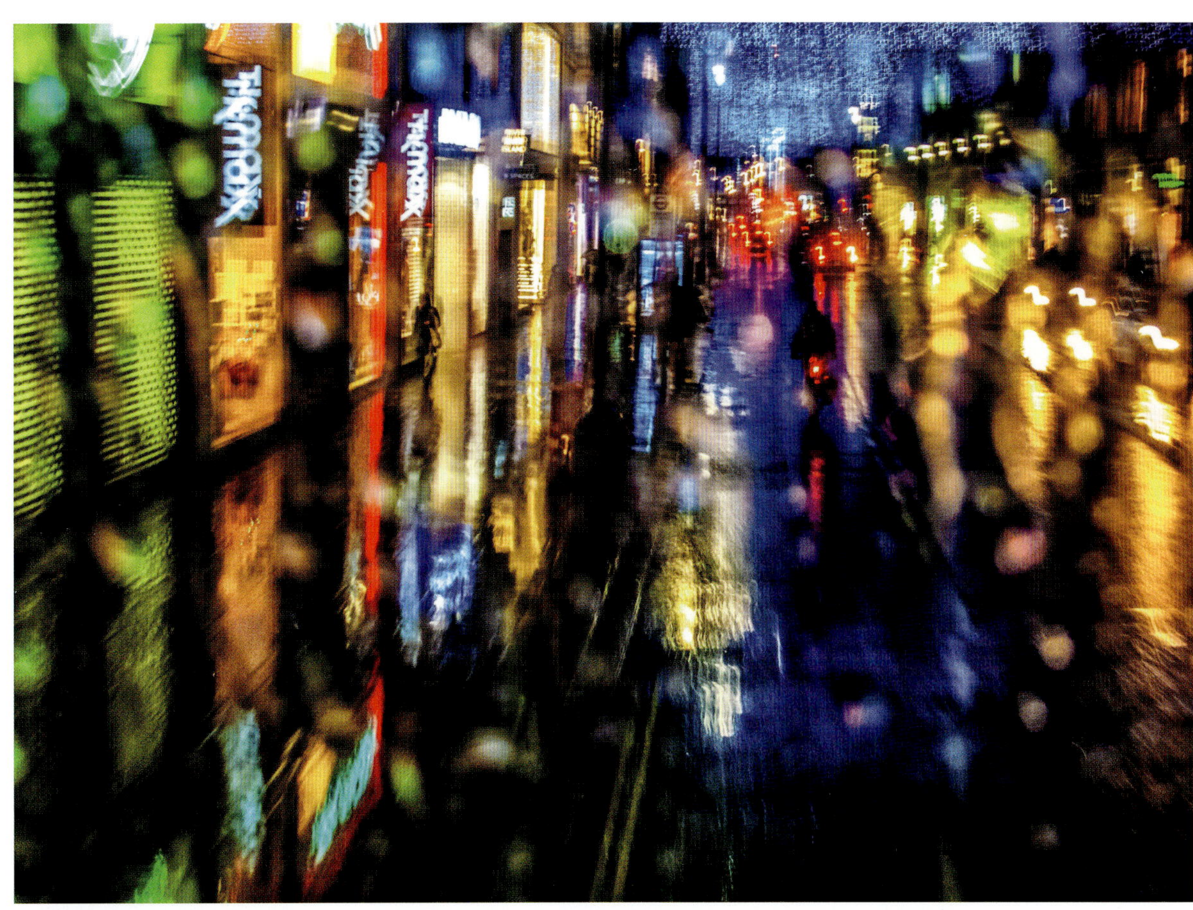

牛津街的反射
Oxford Street Reflection
by Chris Burrows

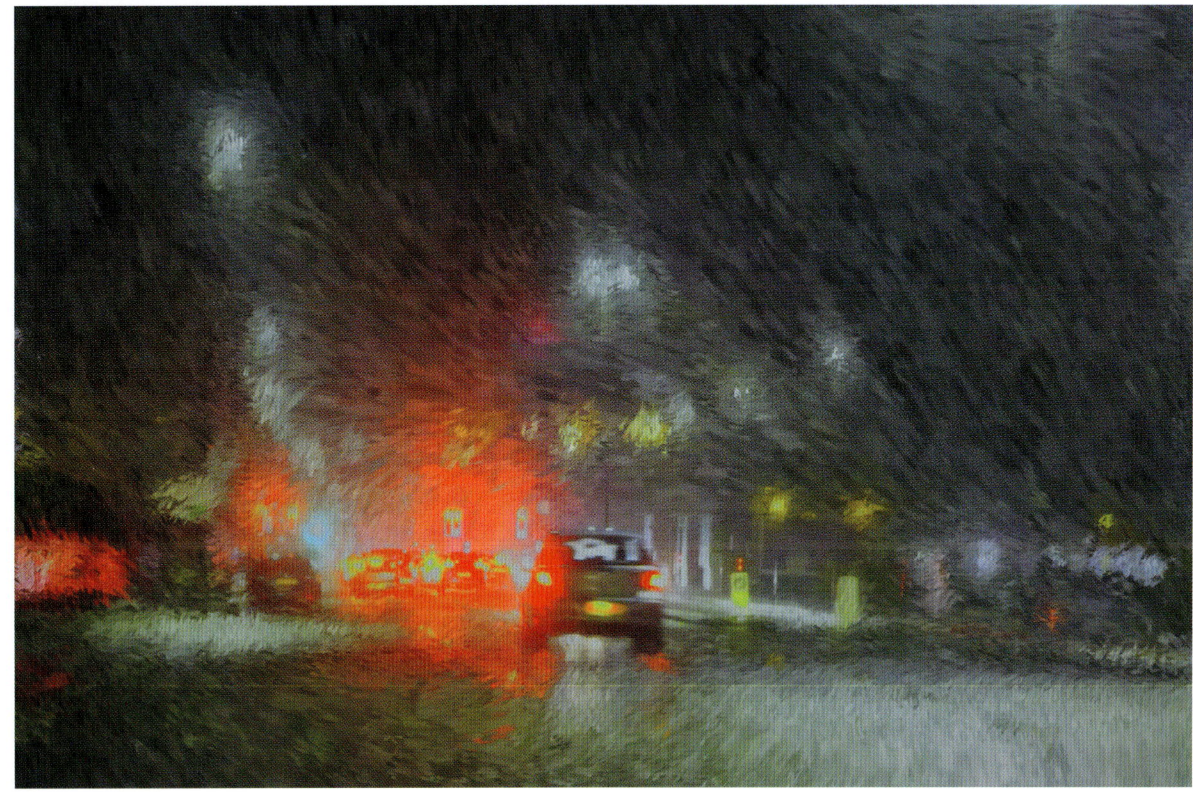

暴風雨的夜晚
A Stormy Evening
by Gerald Kitiyakara LRPS

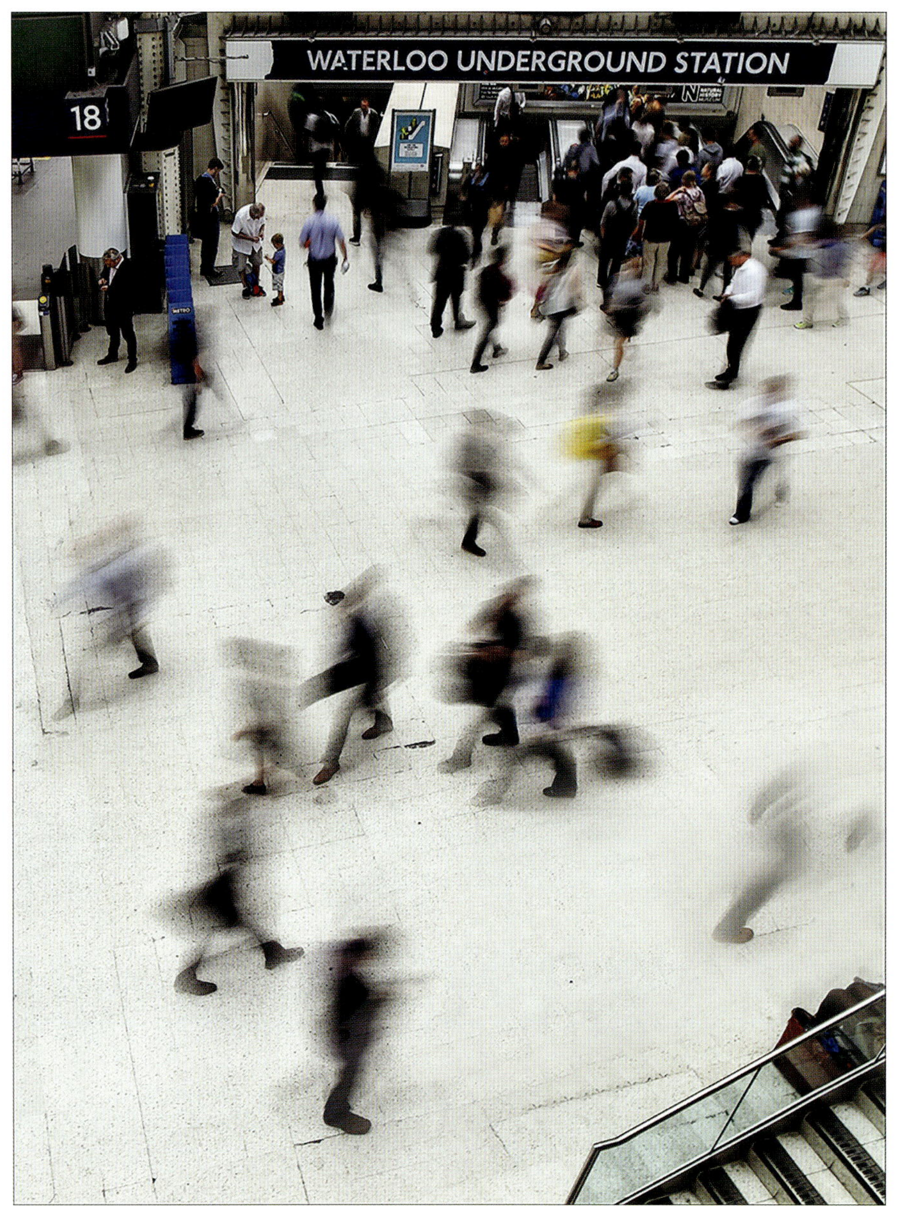

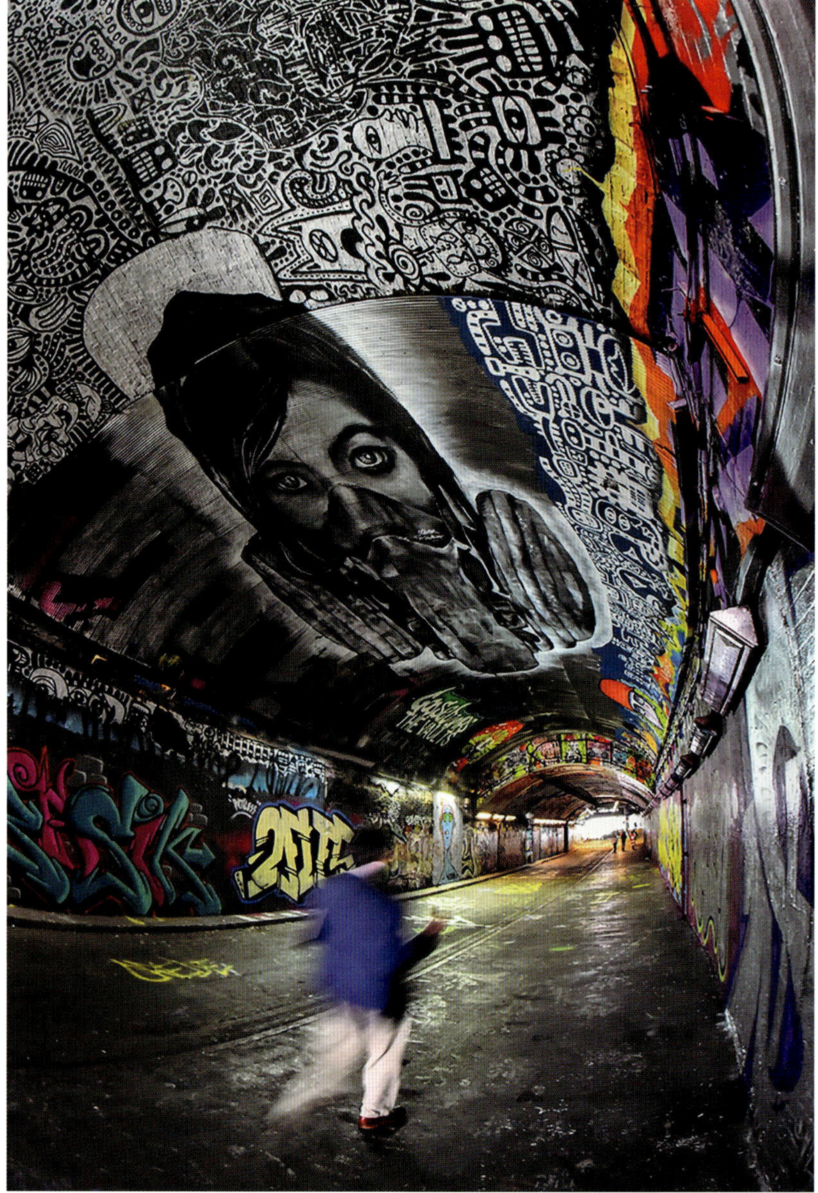

在滑鐵盧車站的瞬間
A Moment at Waterloo Station
by Peter Crane ARPS

迅速通過
Moving Through Quickly
by Peter Crane ARPS

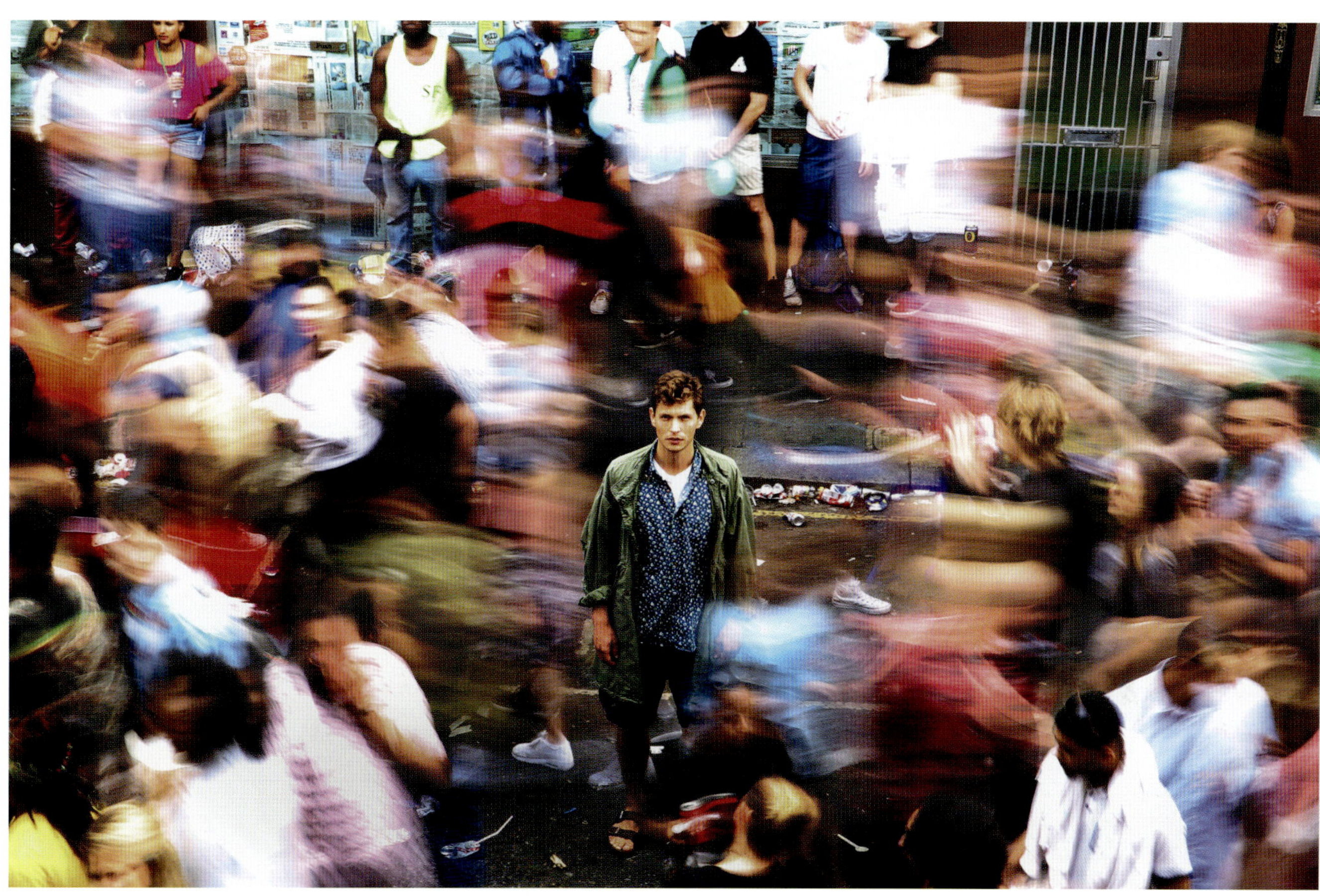

狂歡節人群中的塔達斯
Tadas in Carnival Crowd
by Chris Dawes

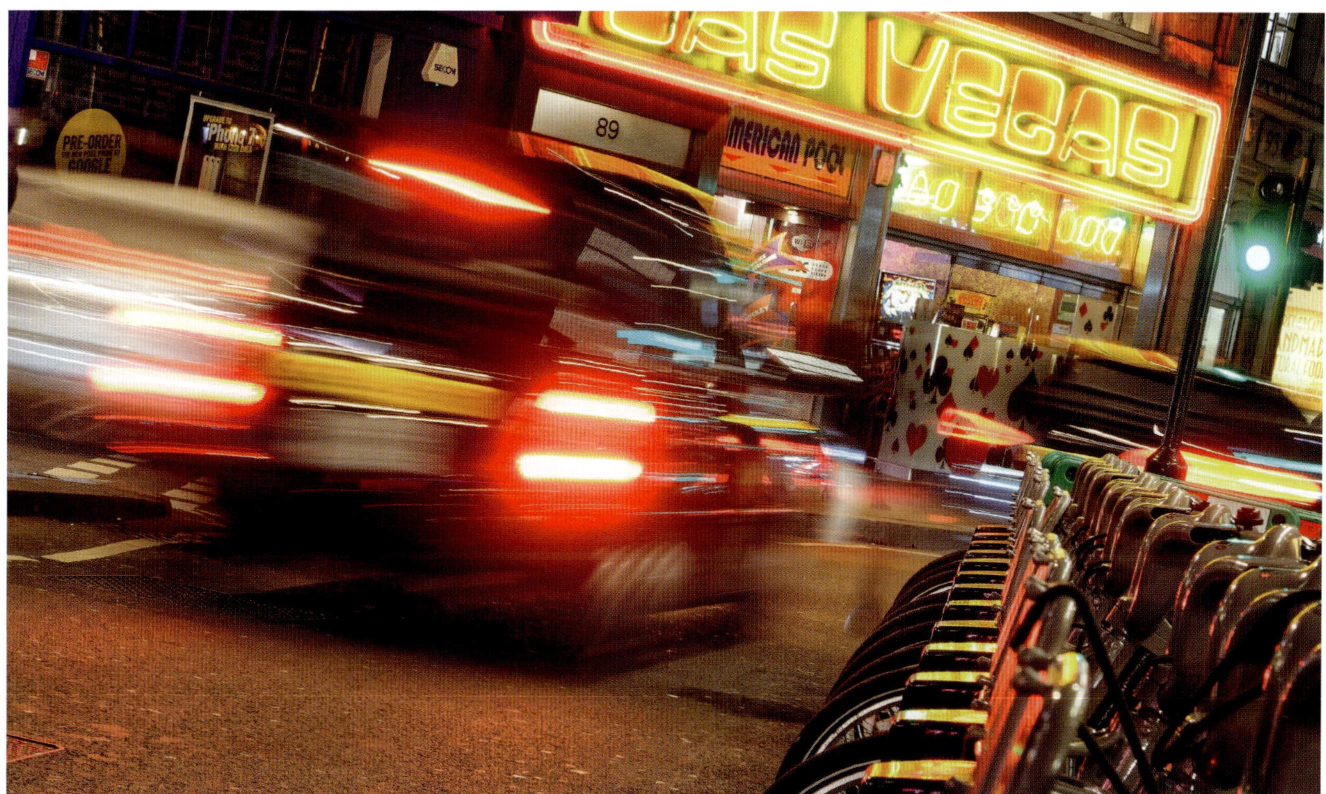

蘇活區的高峰期
Soho Rush Hour
by Michael Colman

COMPARING EAST AND WEST
東西方文化比較

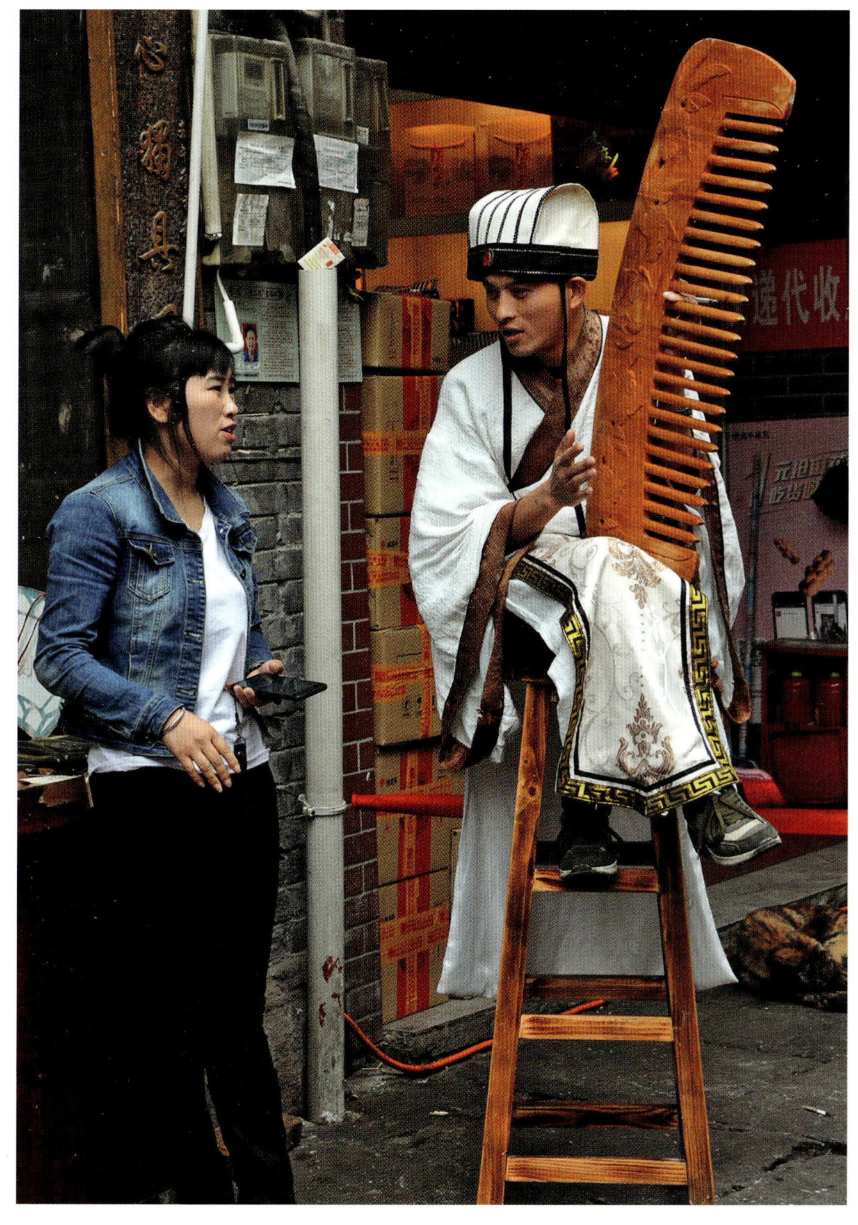

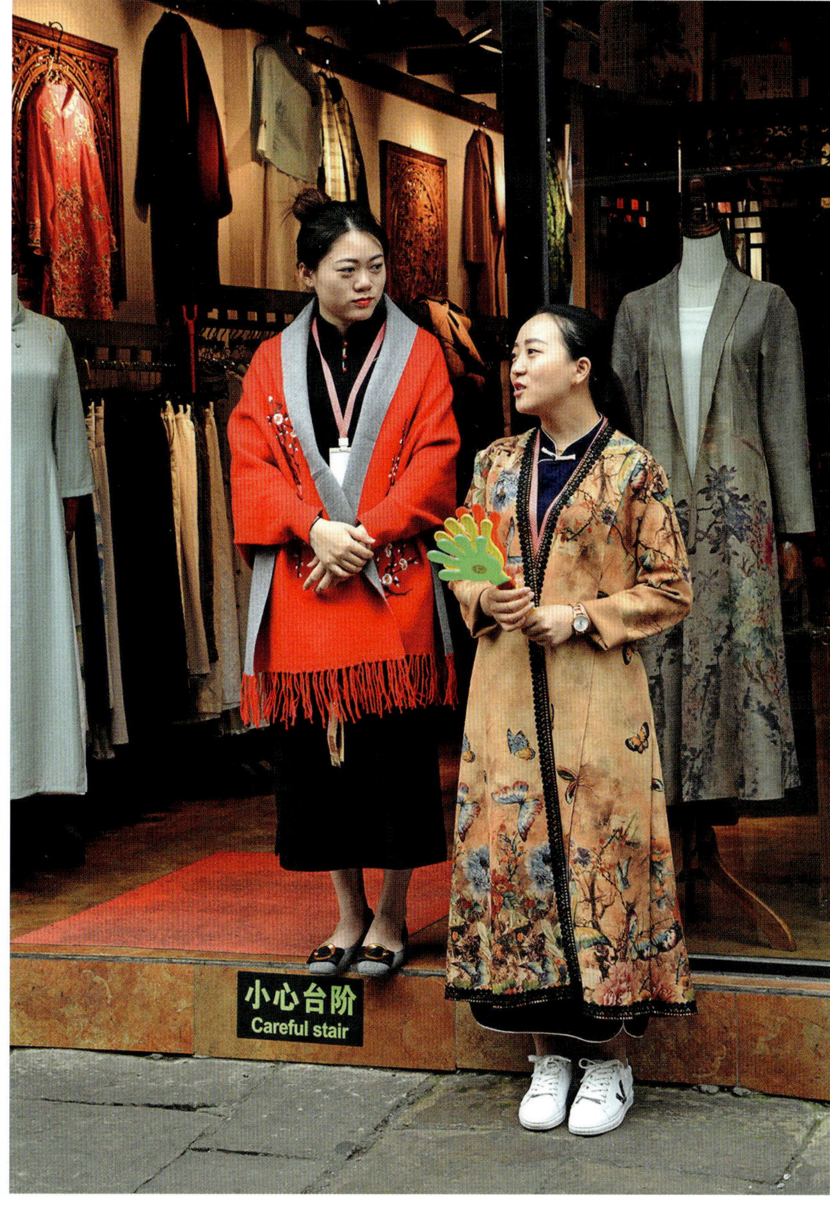

European Photographers in China
歐洲攝影師攝於中國
by Peter Crane ARPS

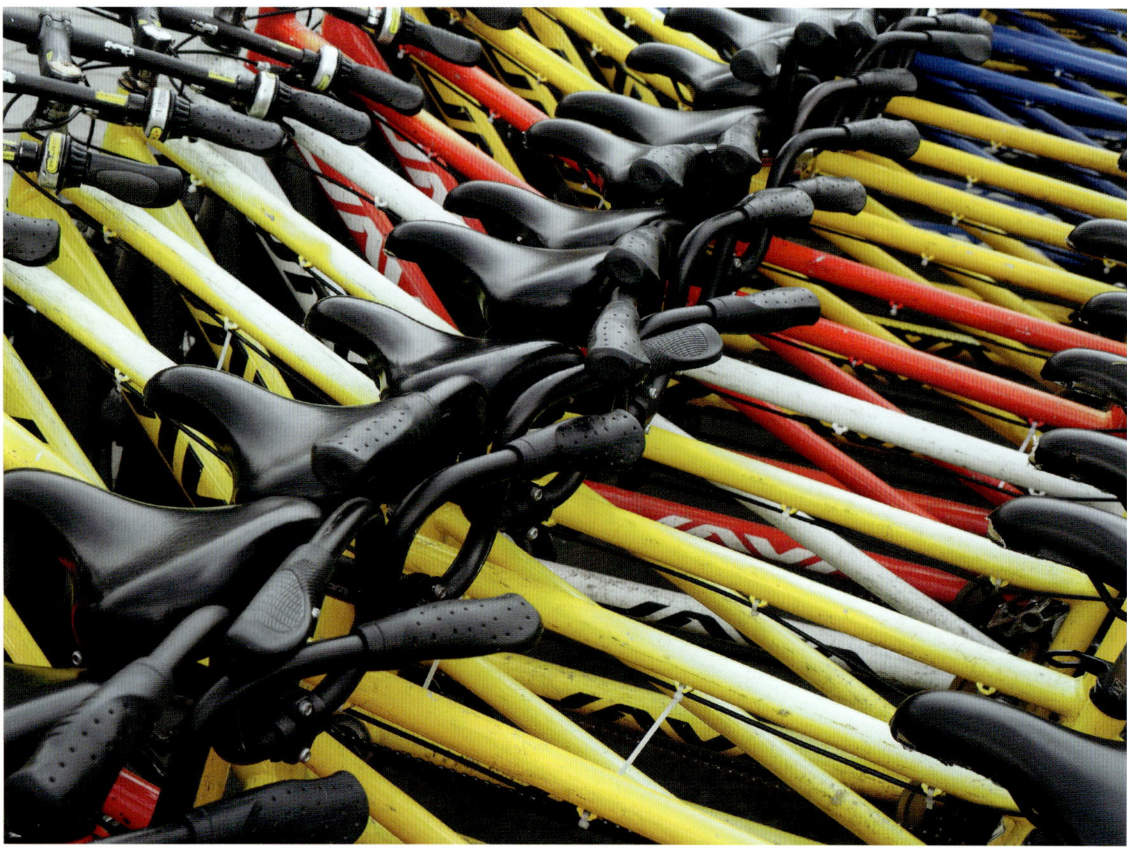

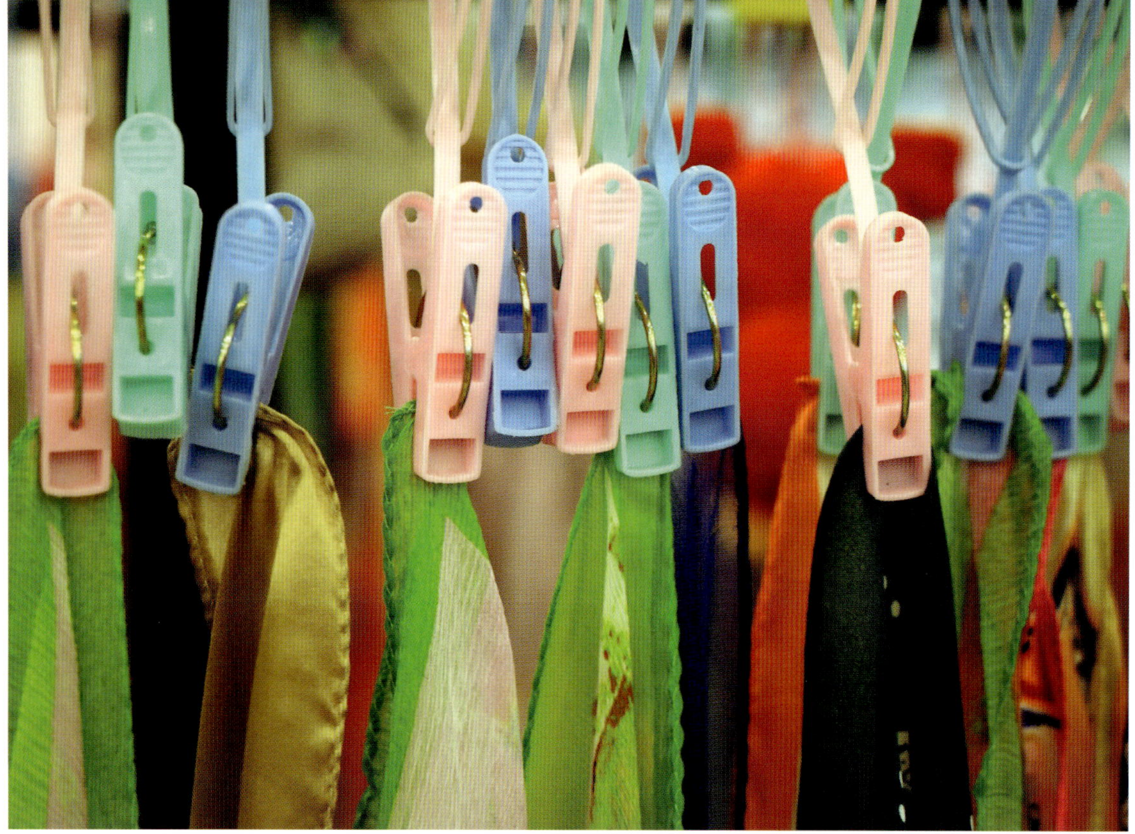

European Photographers in China
歐洲攝影師攝於中國
by Mike Longhurst FRPS

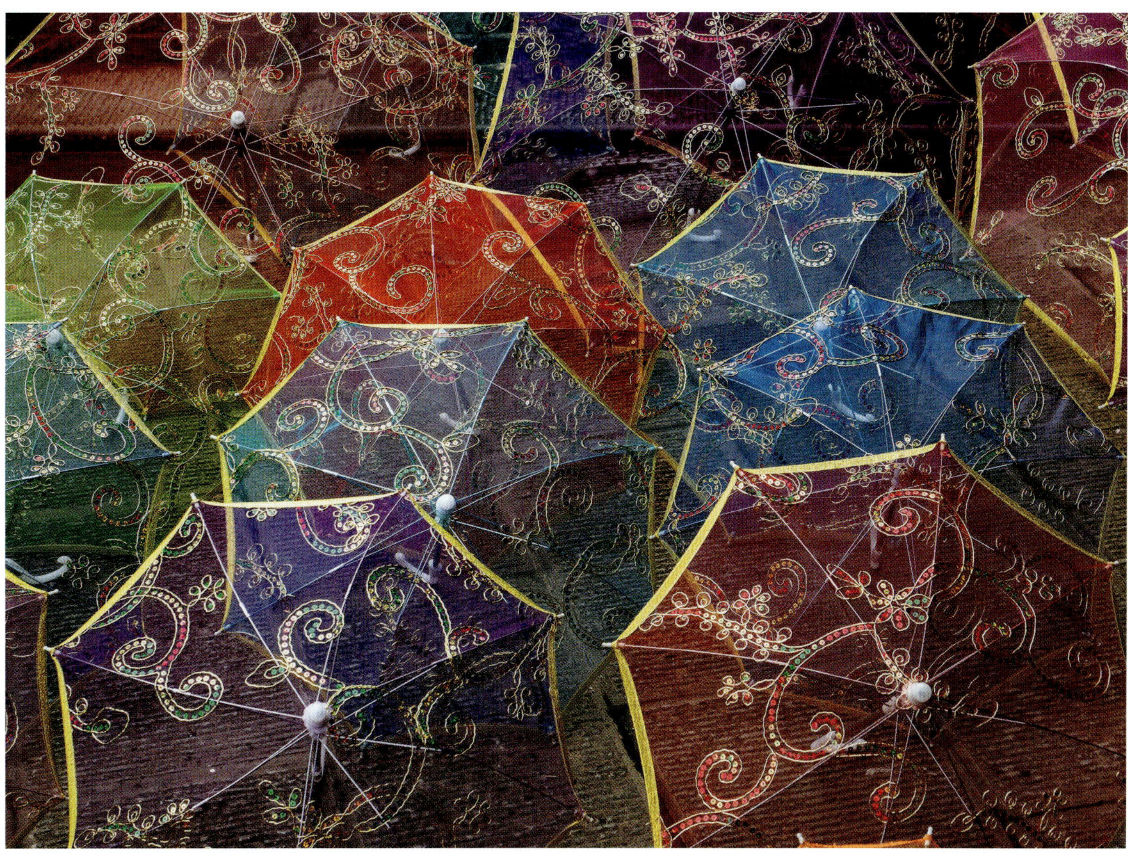

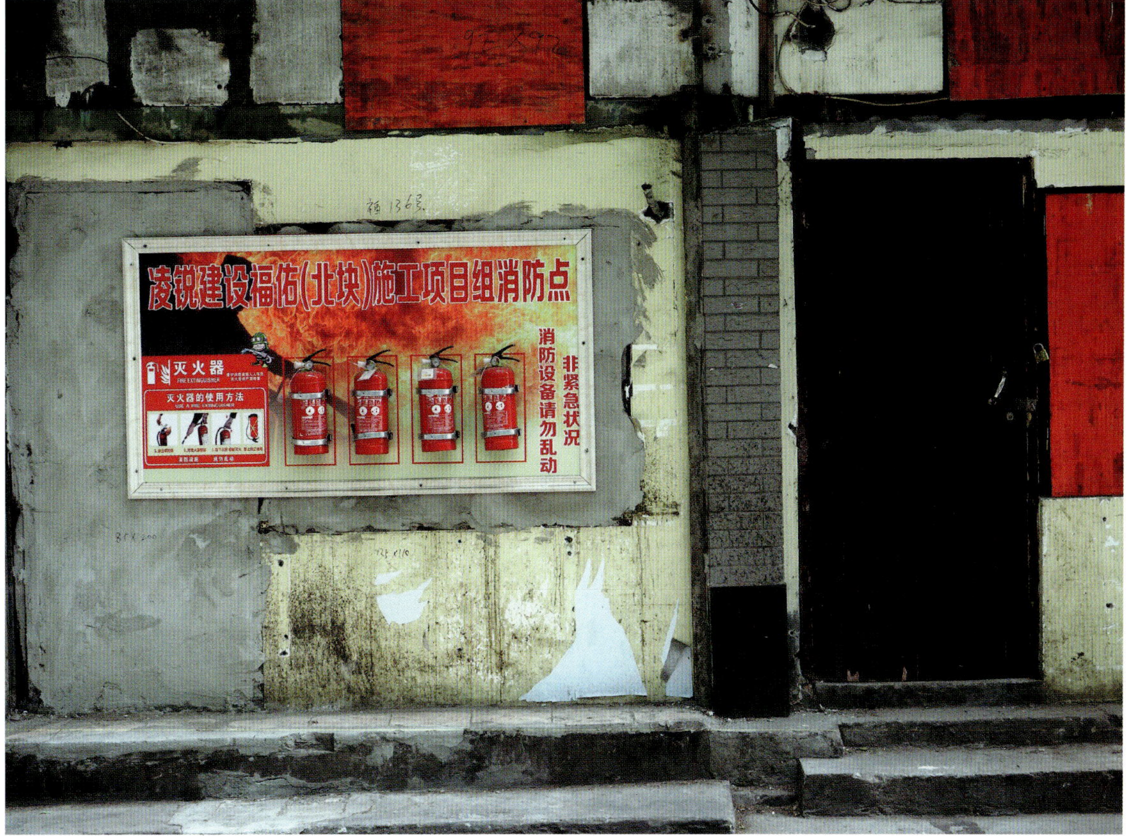

European Photographers in China
歐洲攝影師攝於中國
by Mike Longhurst FRPS

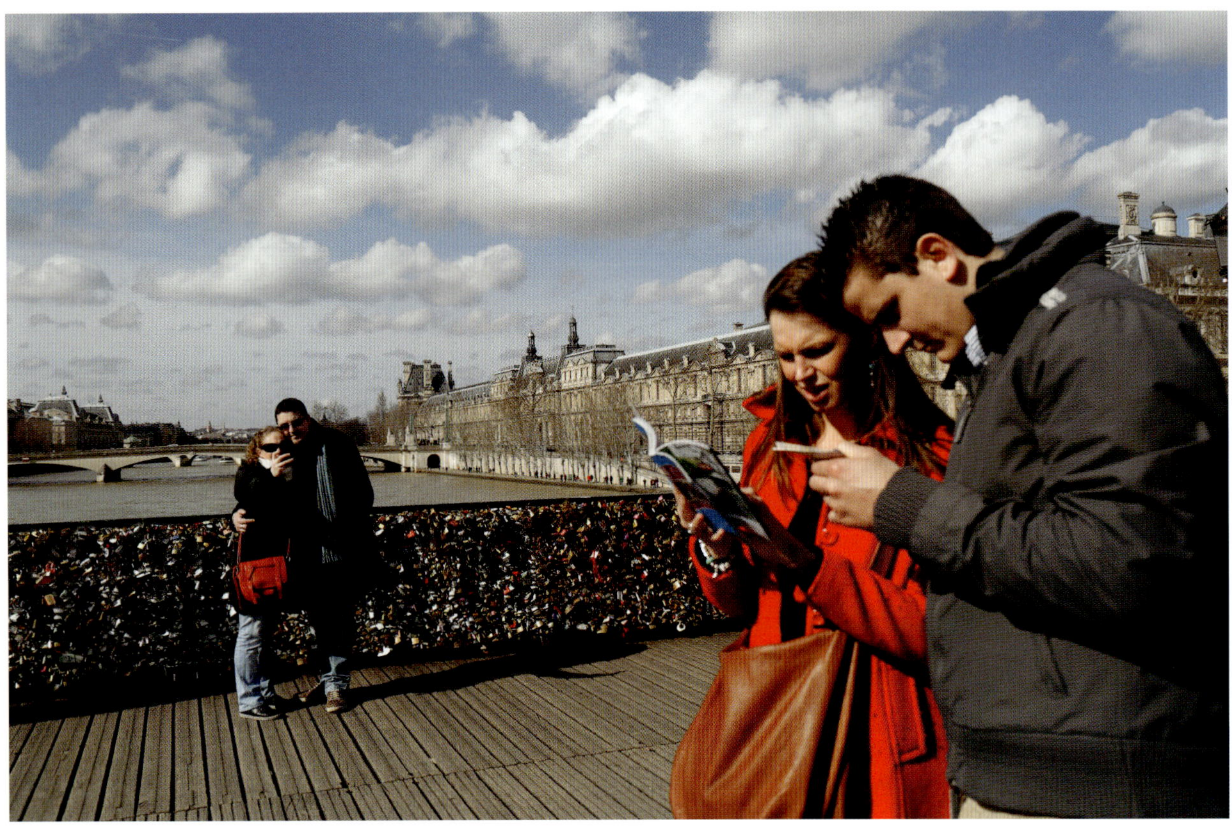

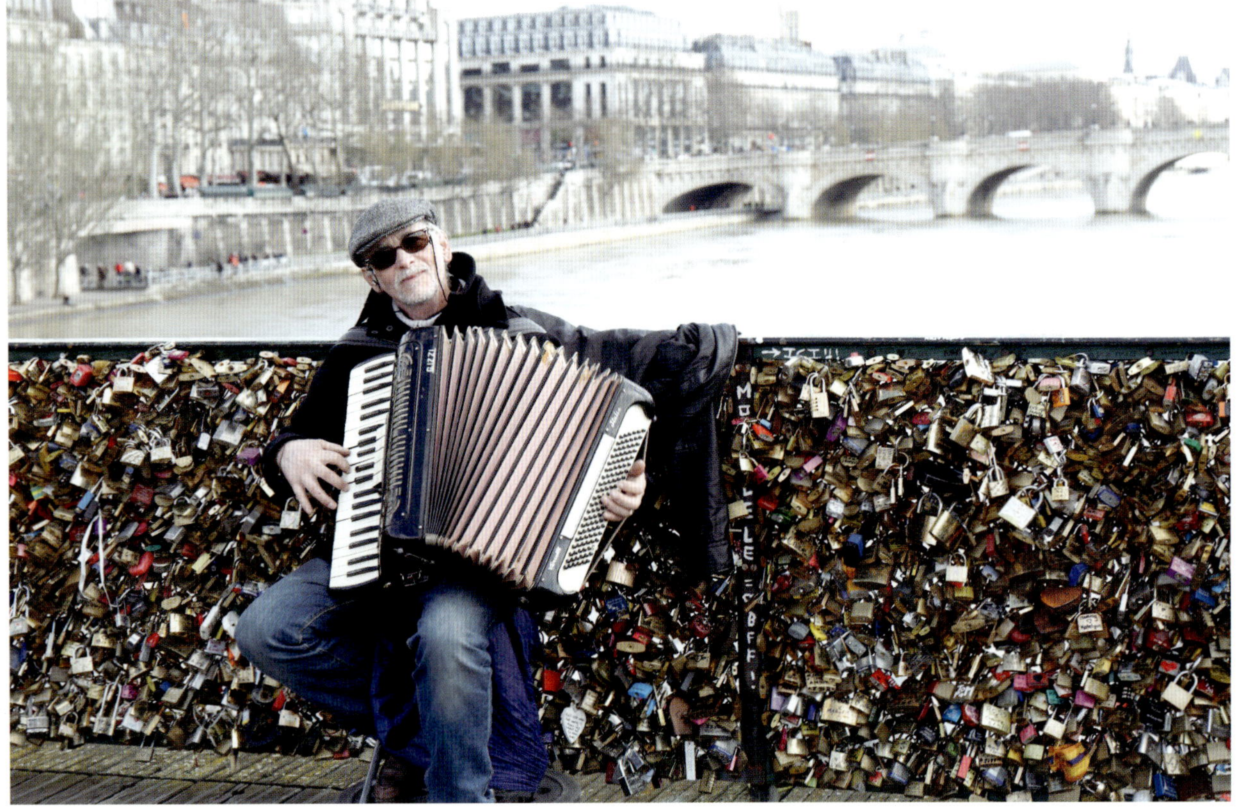

Chinese Photographers in Europe
中國攝影師攝於歐洲
by Huang Songhui FRPS 黄松辉

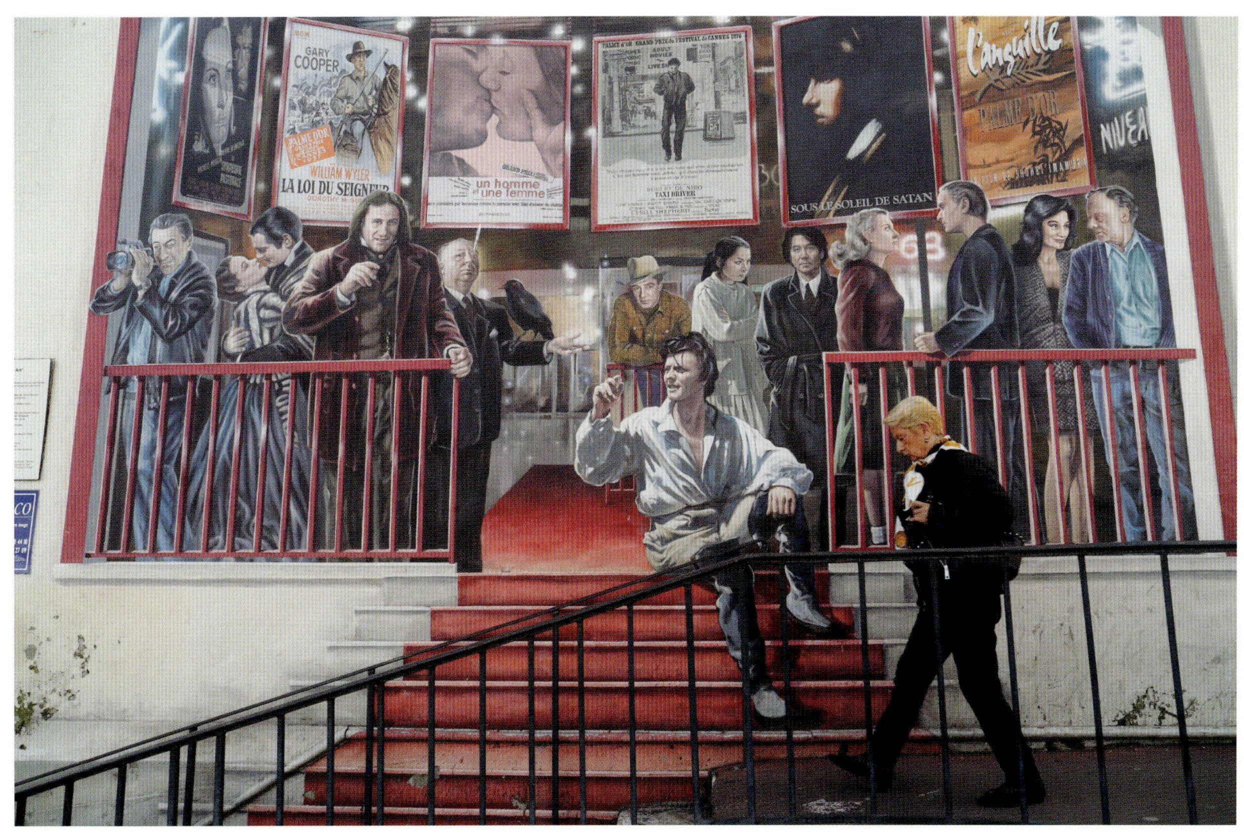

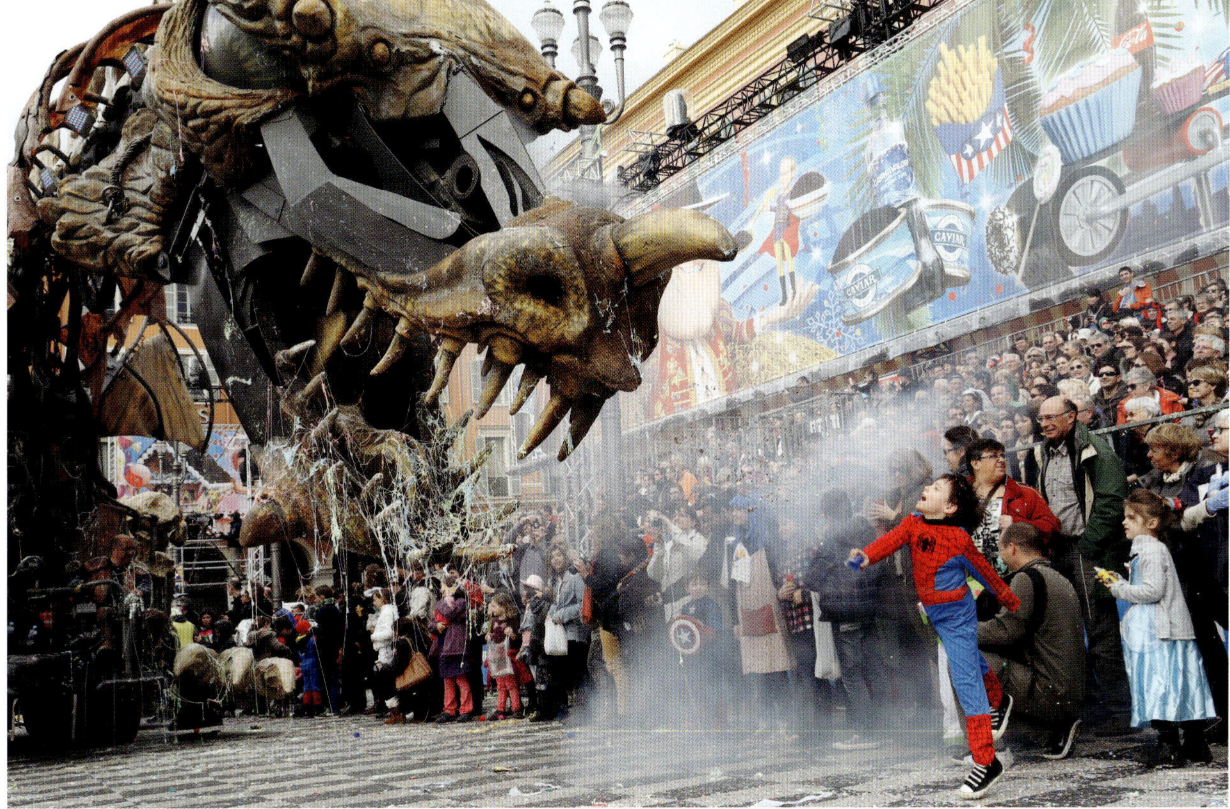

Chinese Photographers in Europe
中國攝影師攝於歐洲
by Huang Songhui FRPS 黃松辉

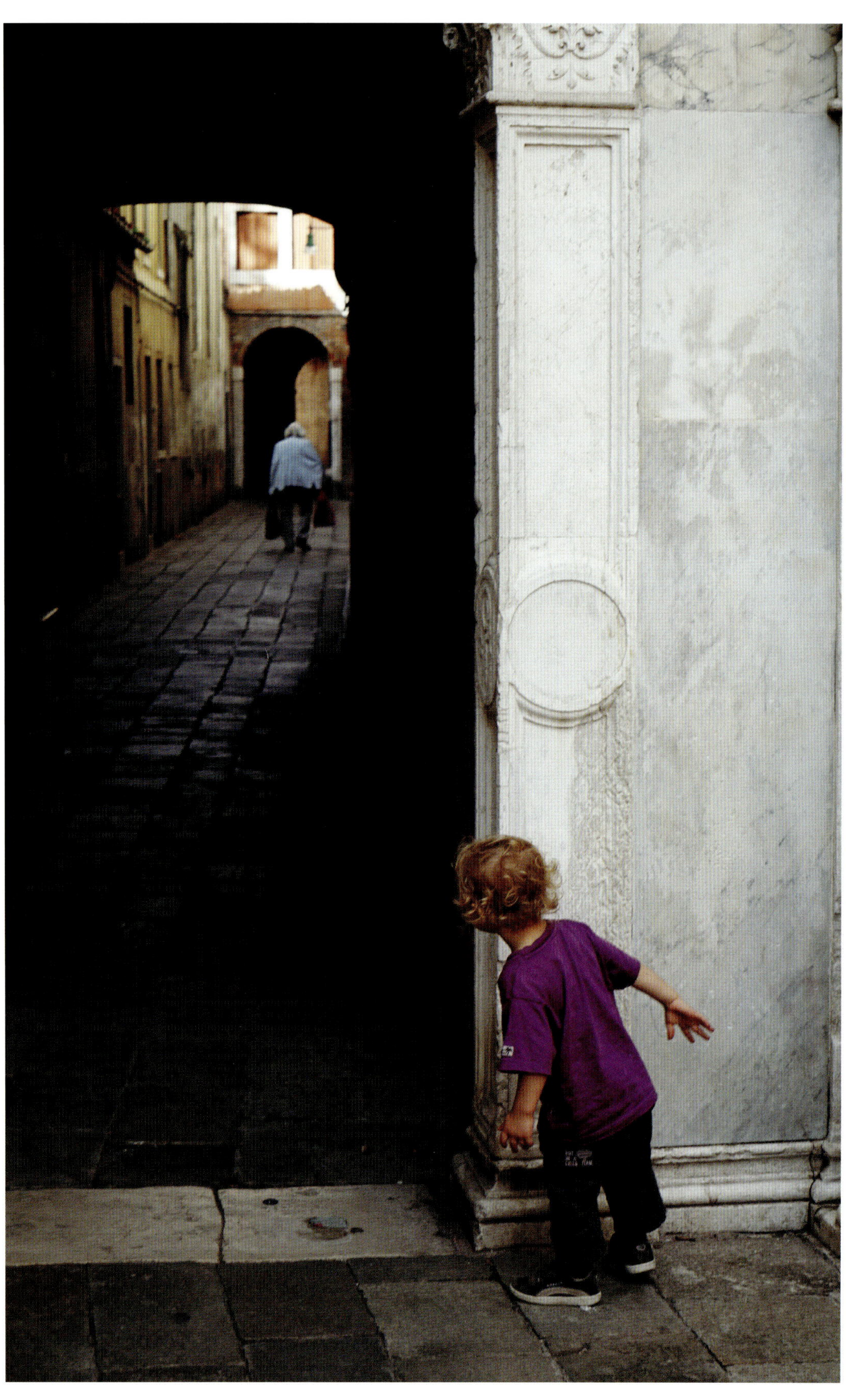

Chinese Photographers in Europe
中國攝影師攝於歐洲
by Huang Songhui FRPS 黄松辉

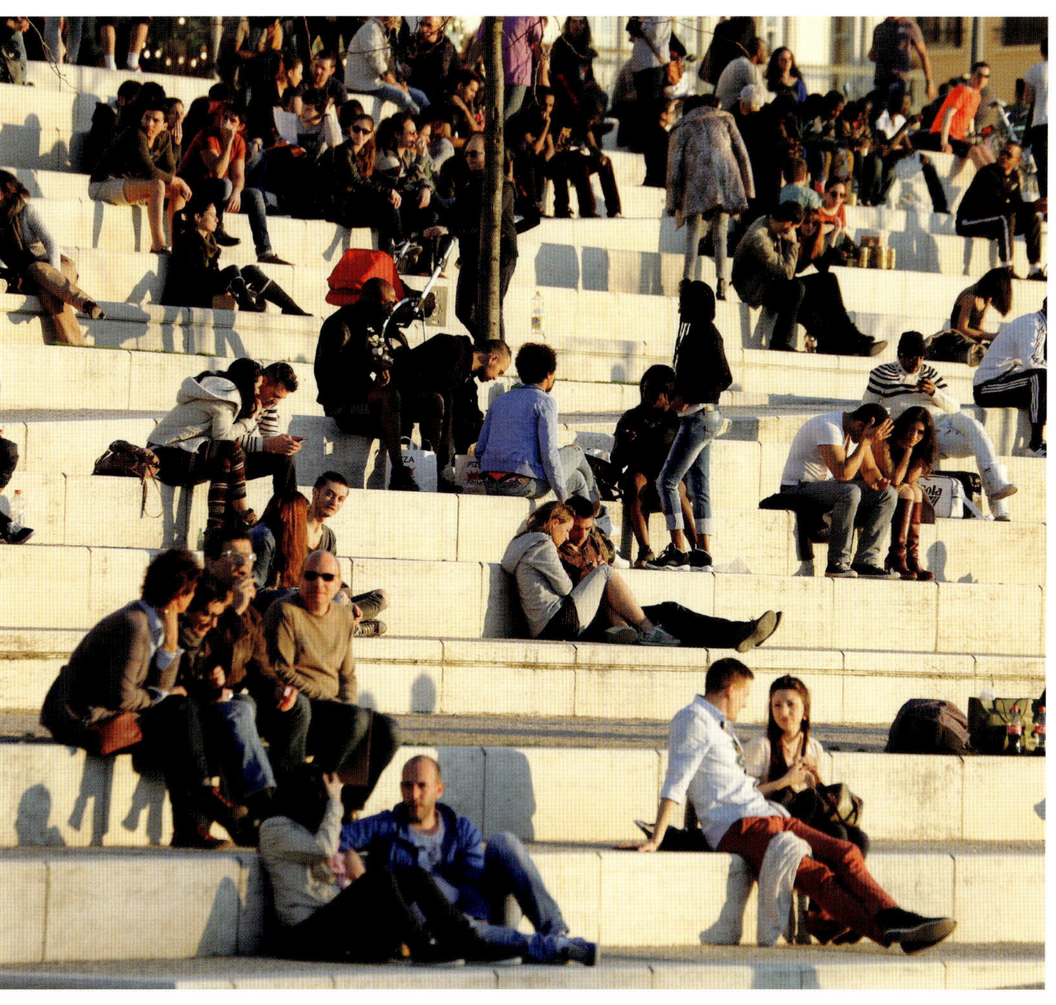

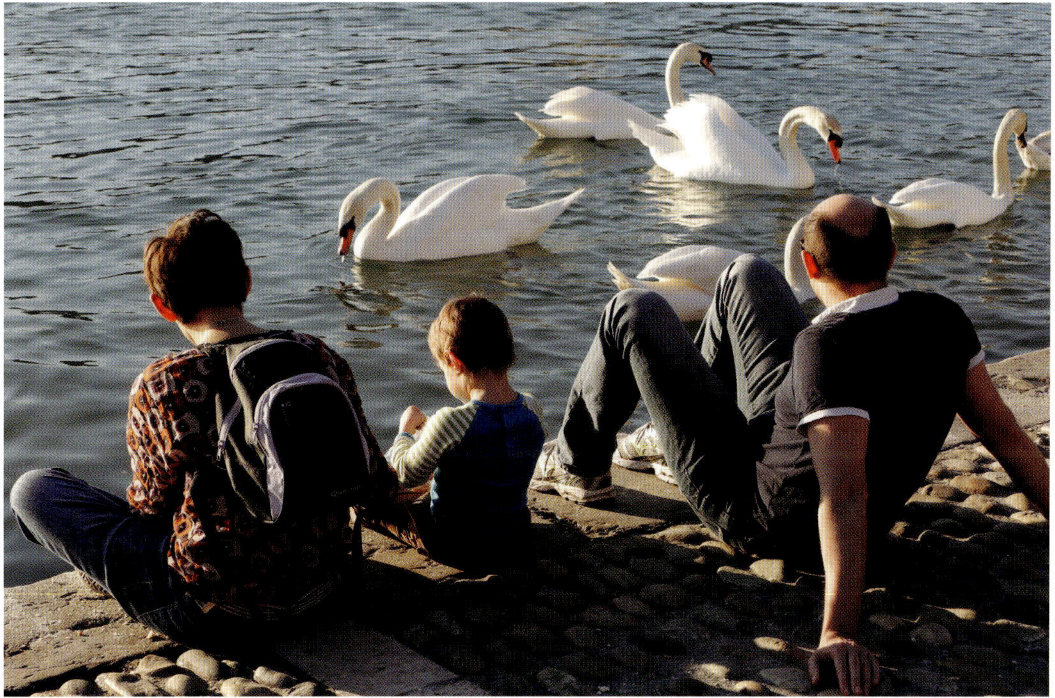

Chinese Photographers in Europe
中國攝影師攝於歐洲
by Huang Songhui FRPS 黄松辉

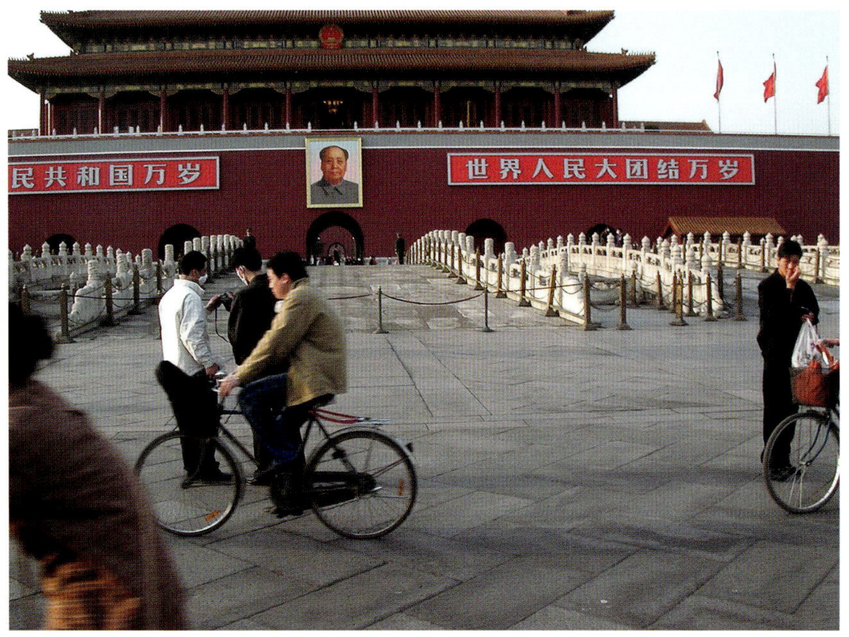

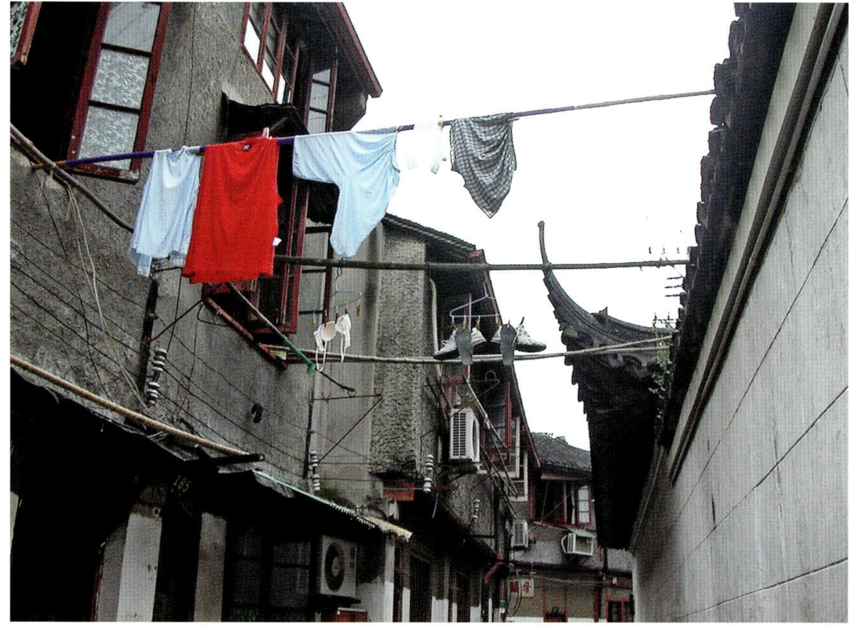

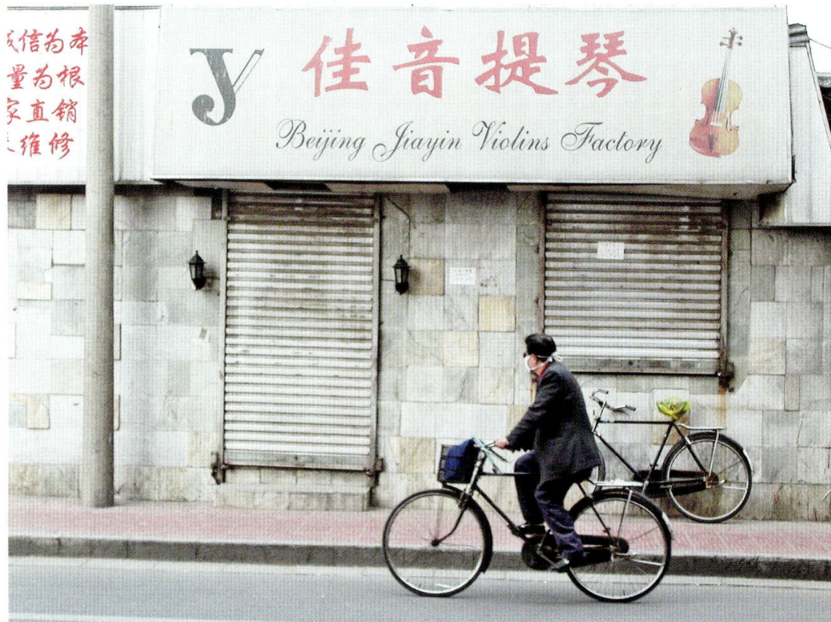

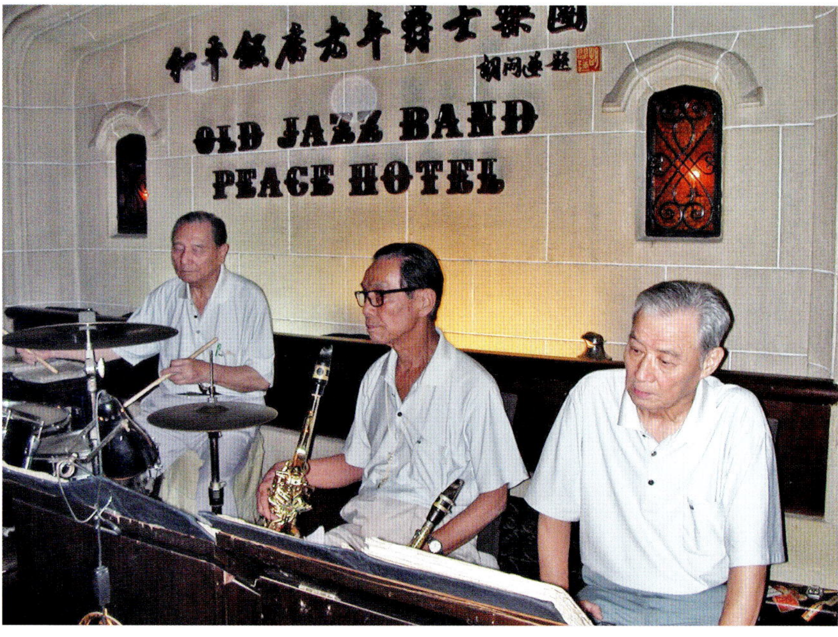

European Photographers in China
歐洲攝影師攝於中國
by David Reed

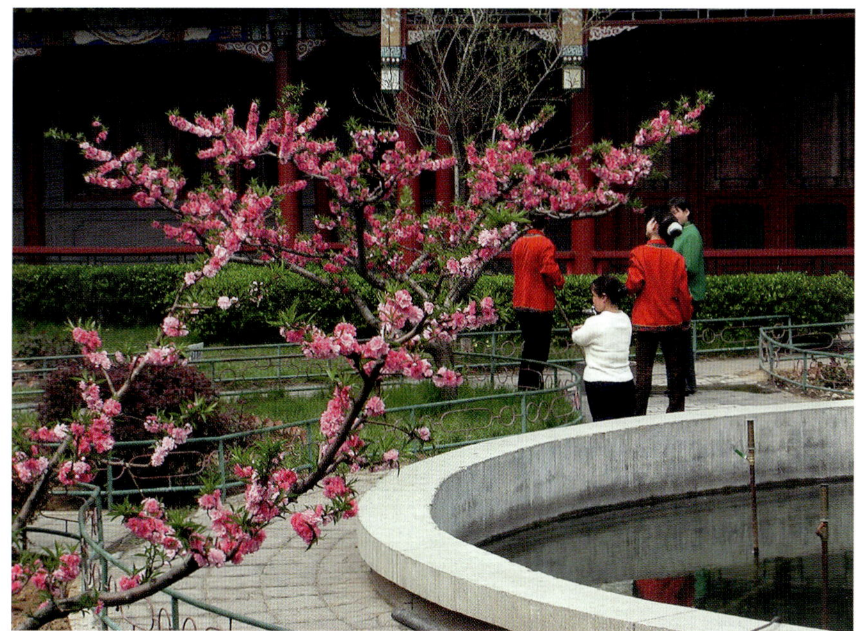

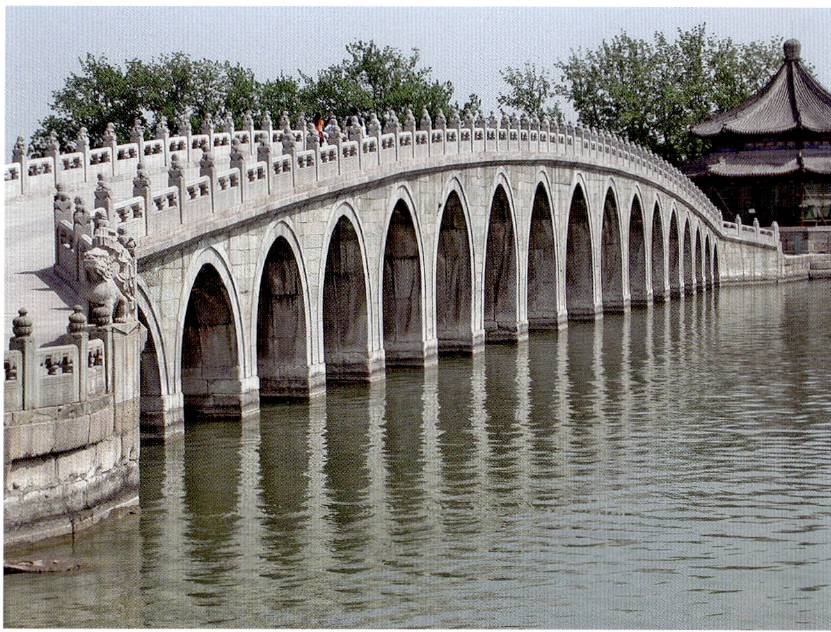

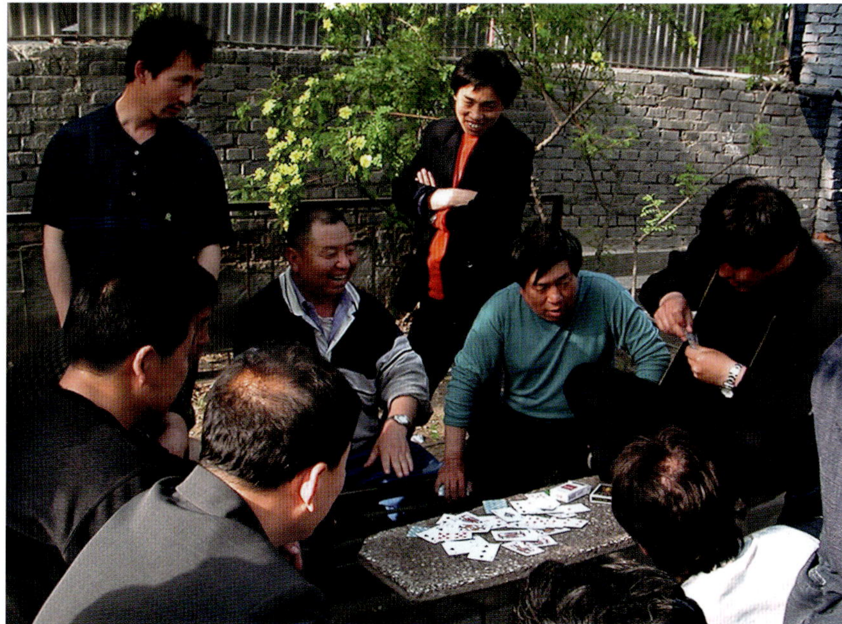

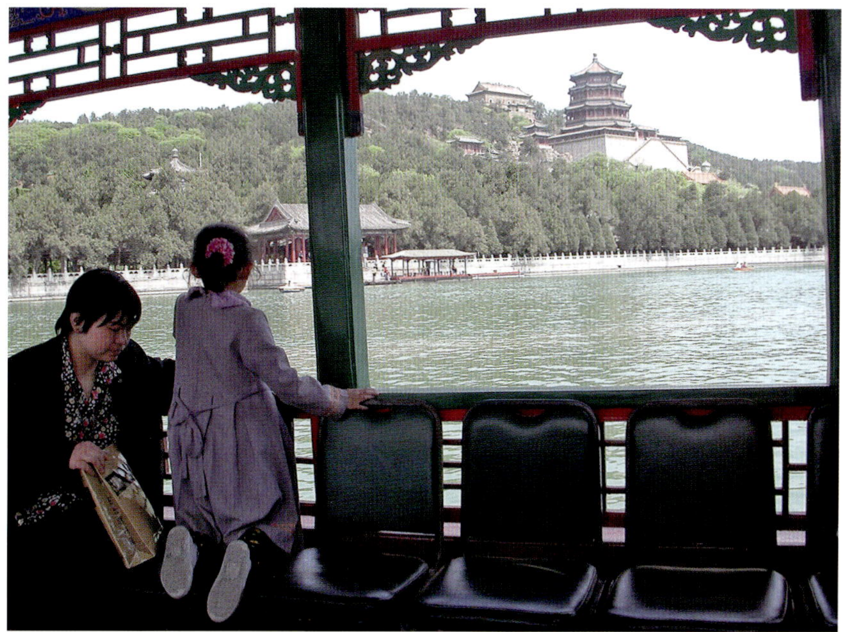

European Photographers in China
歐洲攝影師攝於中國
by David Reed

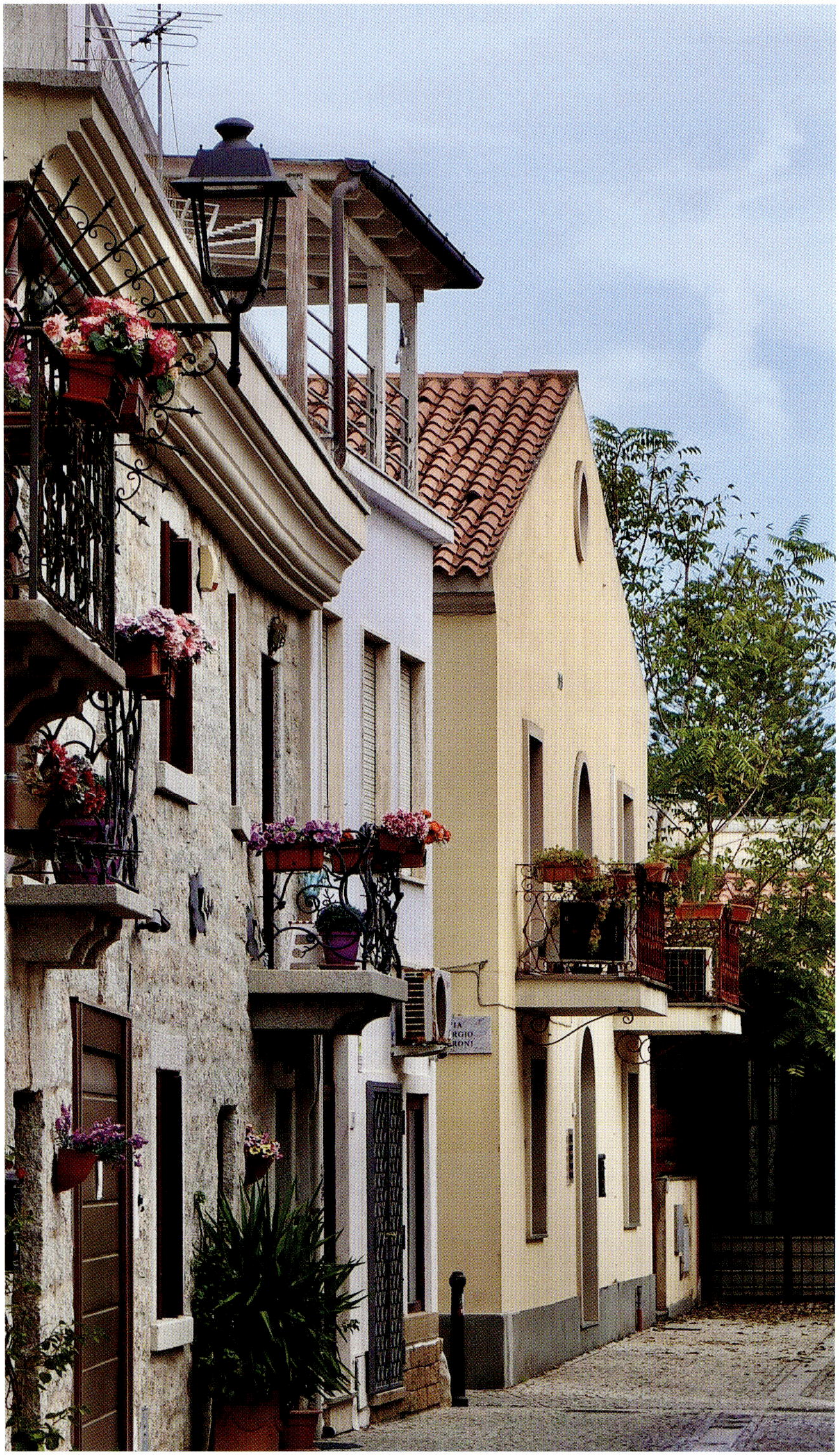

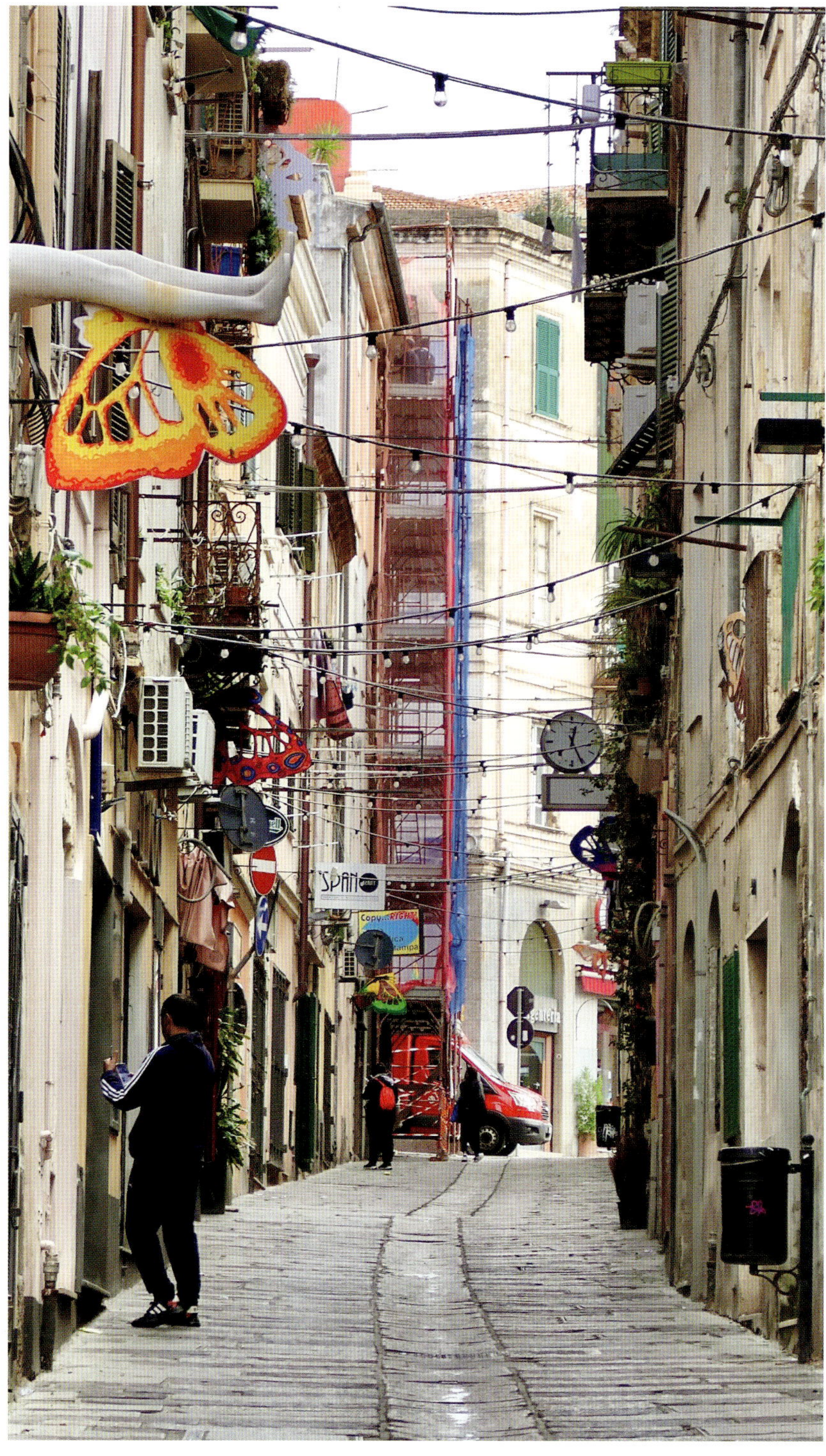

Chinese Photographers in Europe
中國攝影師攝於歐洲
by Tang Yu Lap 鄧予立

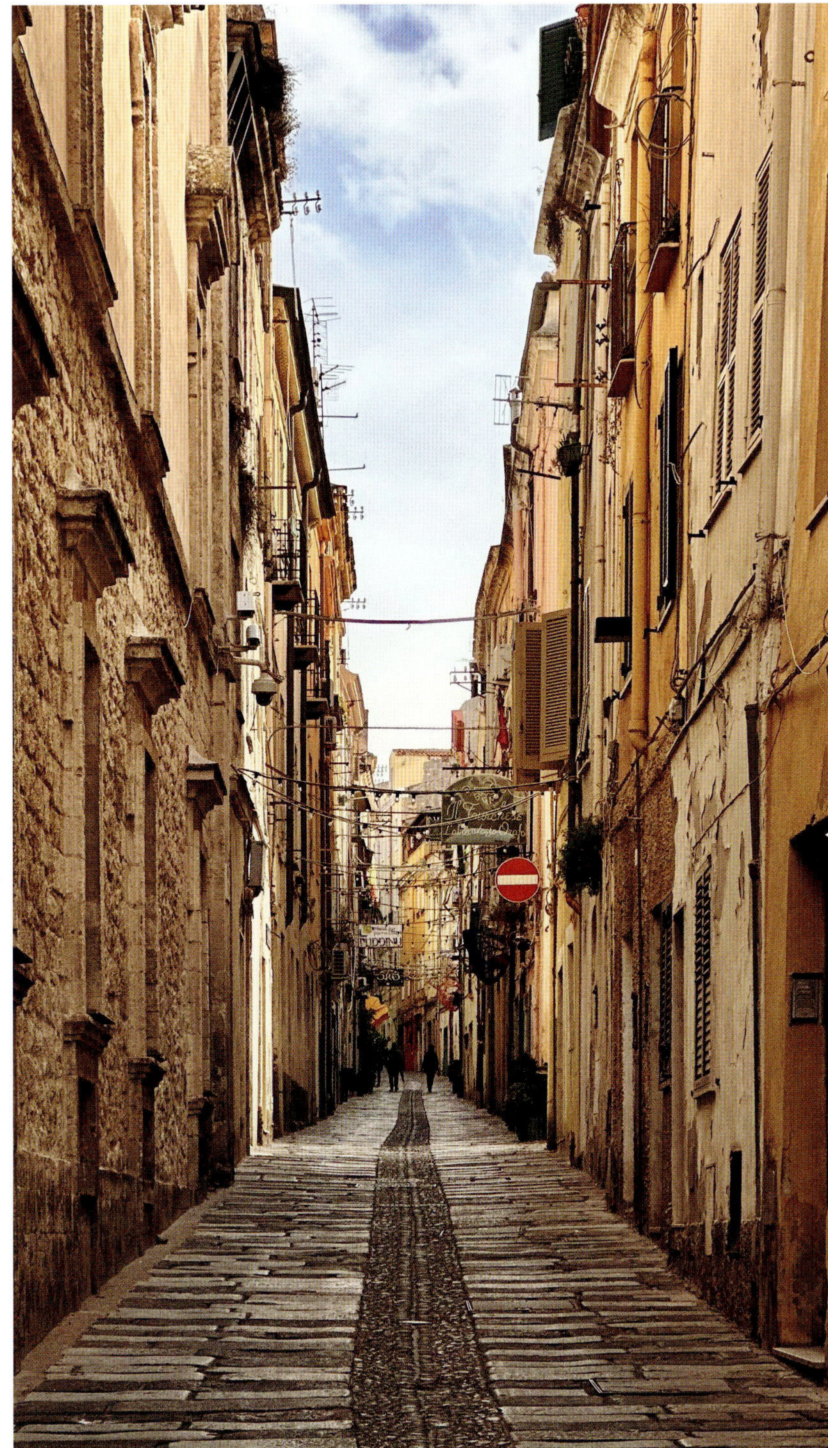

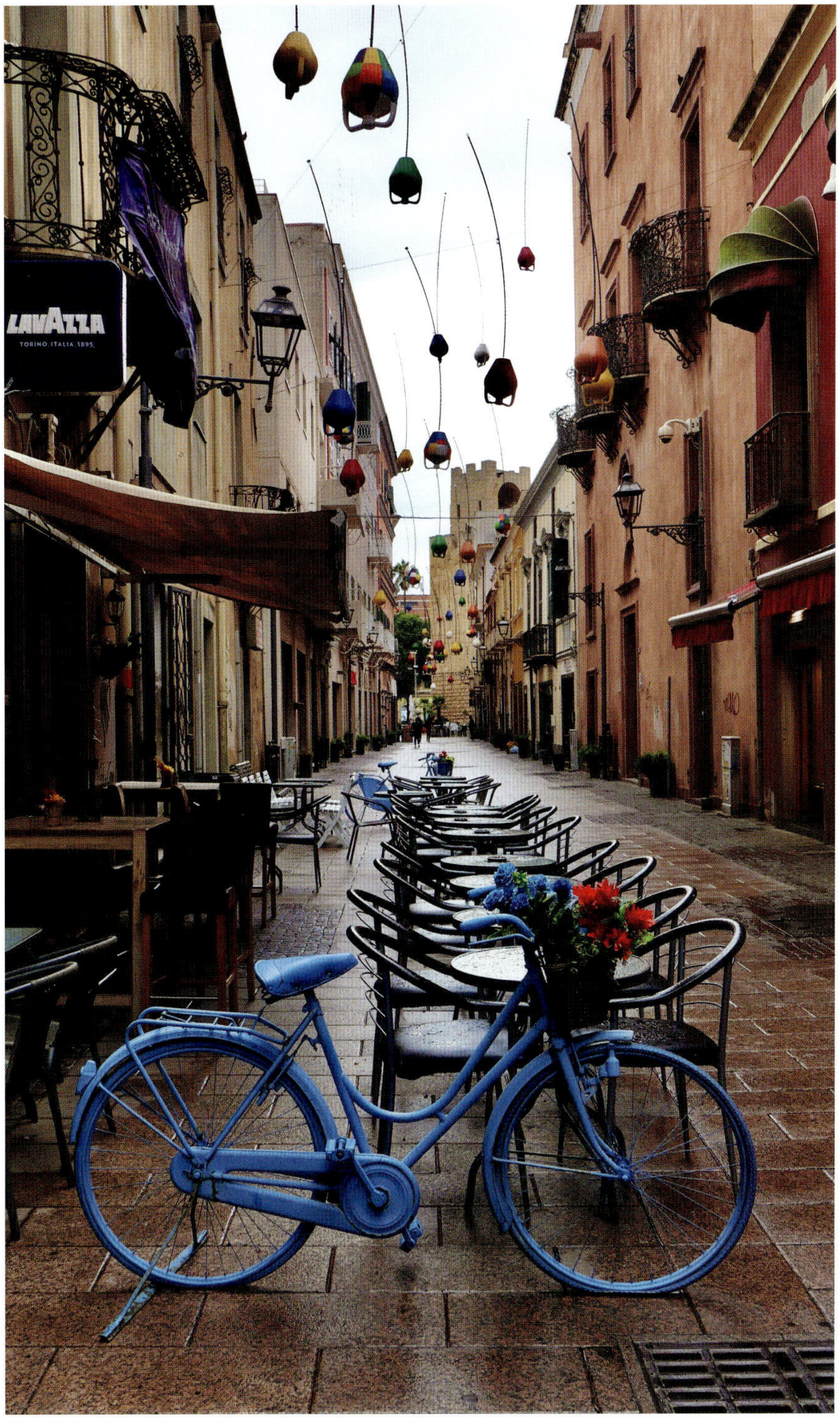

Chinese Photographers in Europe
中國攝影師攝於歐洲
by Tang Yu Lap 鄧予立

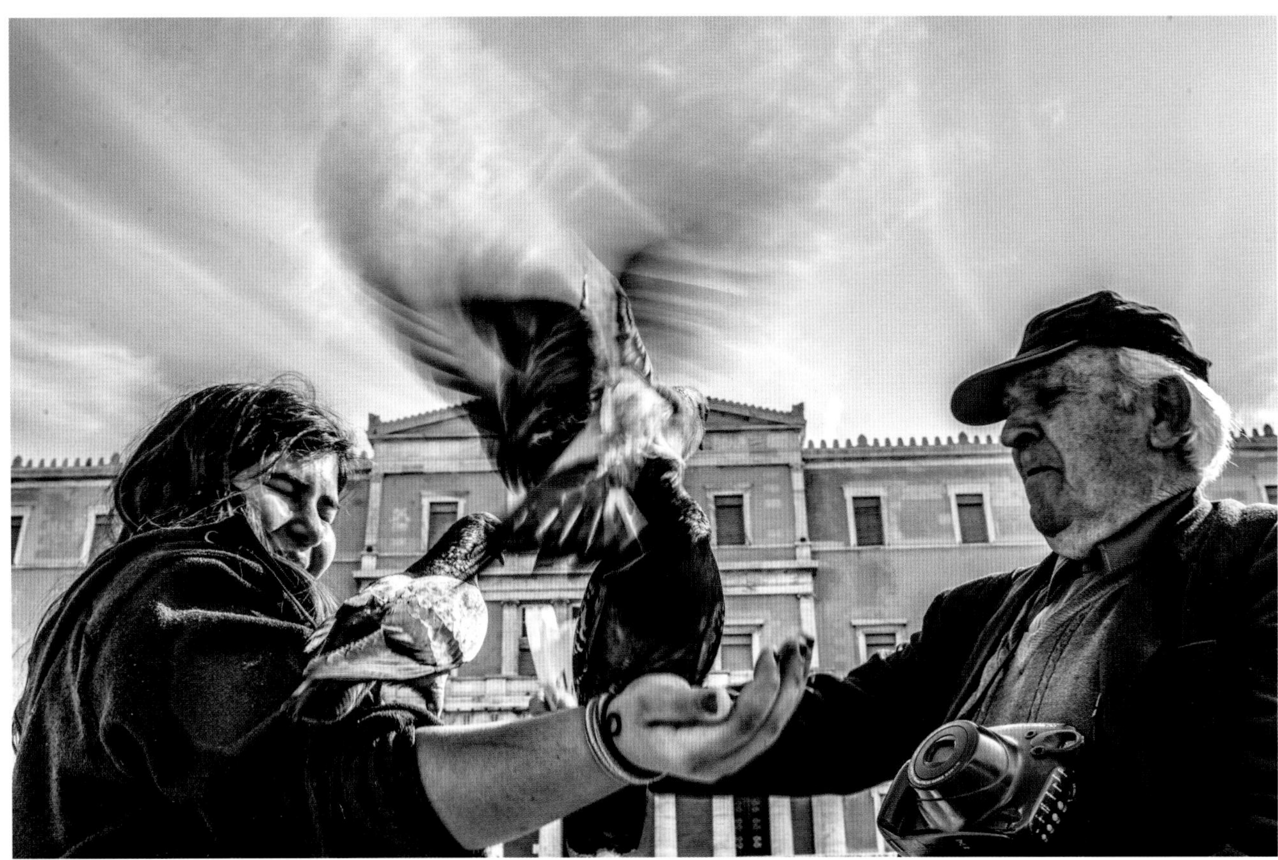

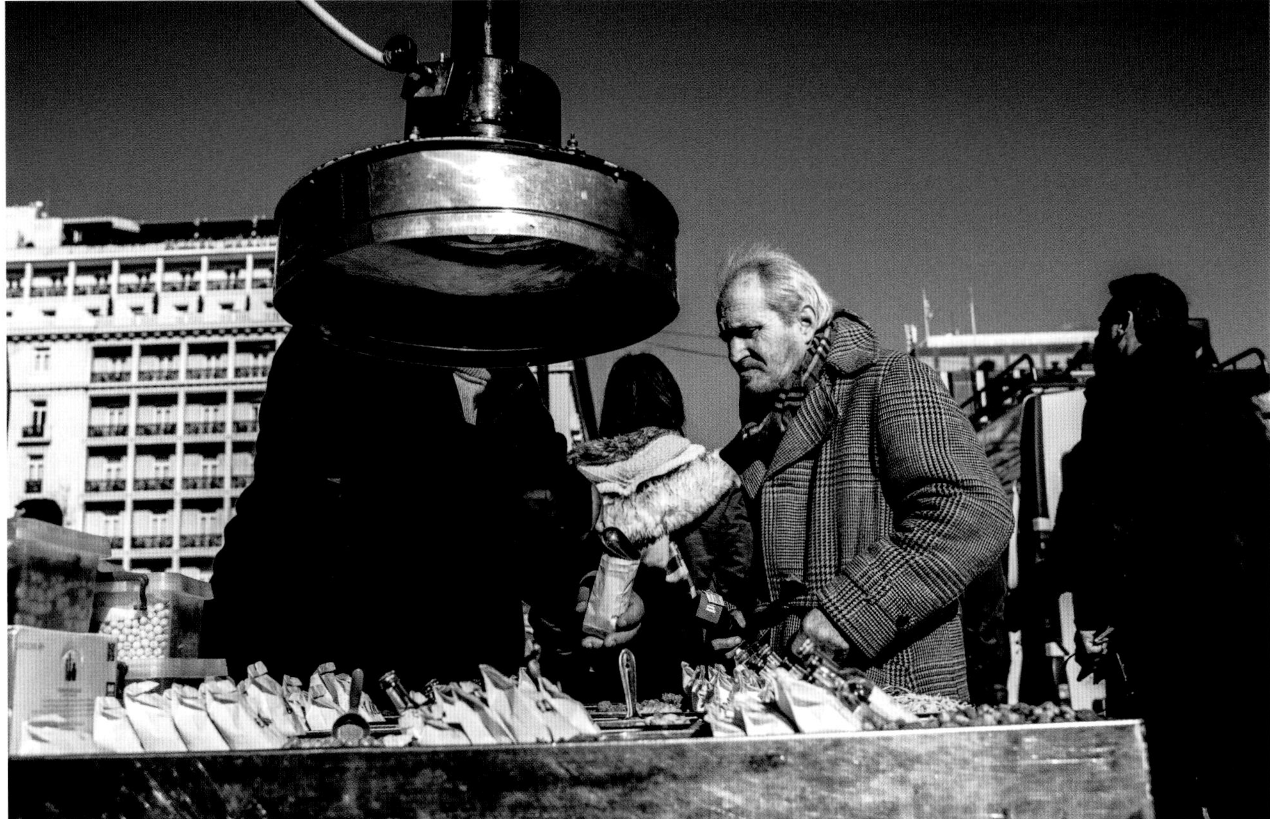

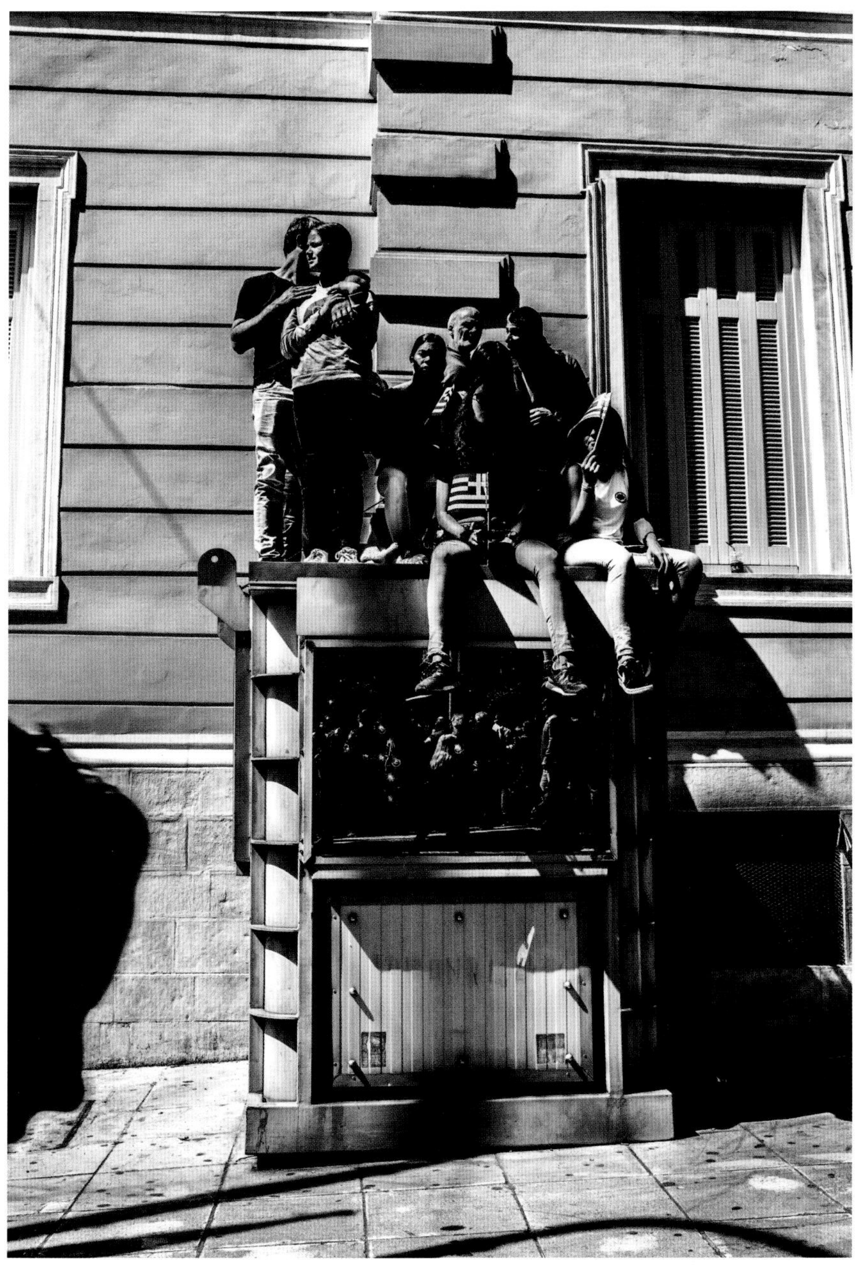

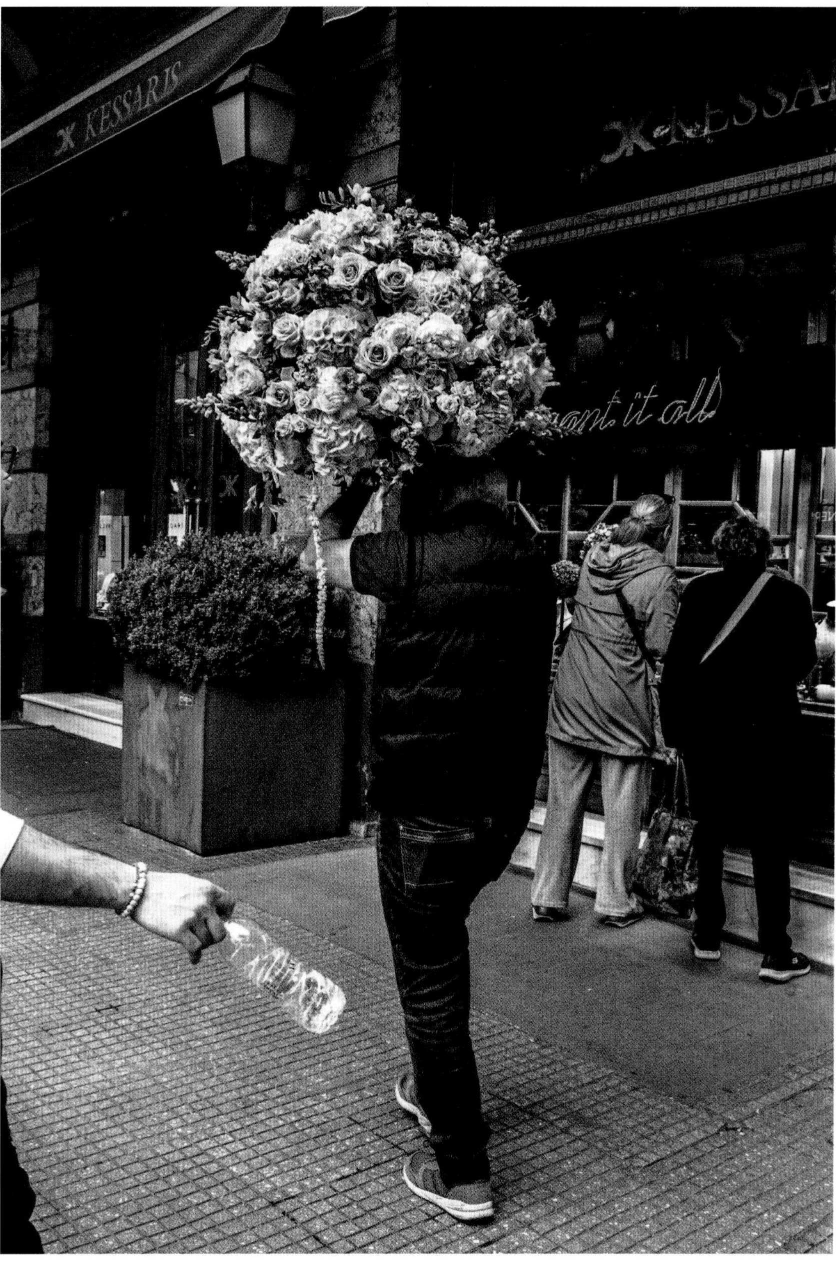

Chinese Photographers in Europe
中國攝影師攝於歐洲
by Huang Hua 黄華

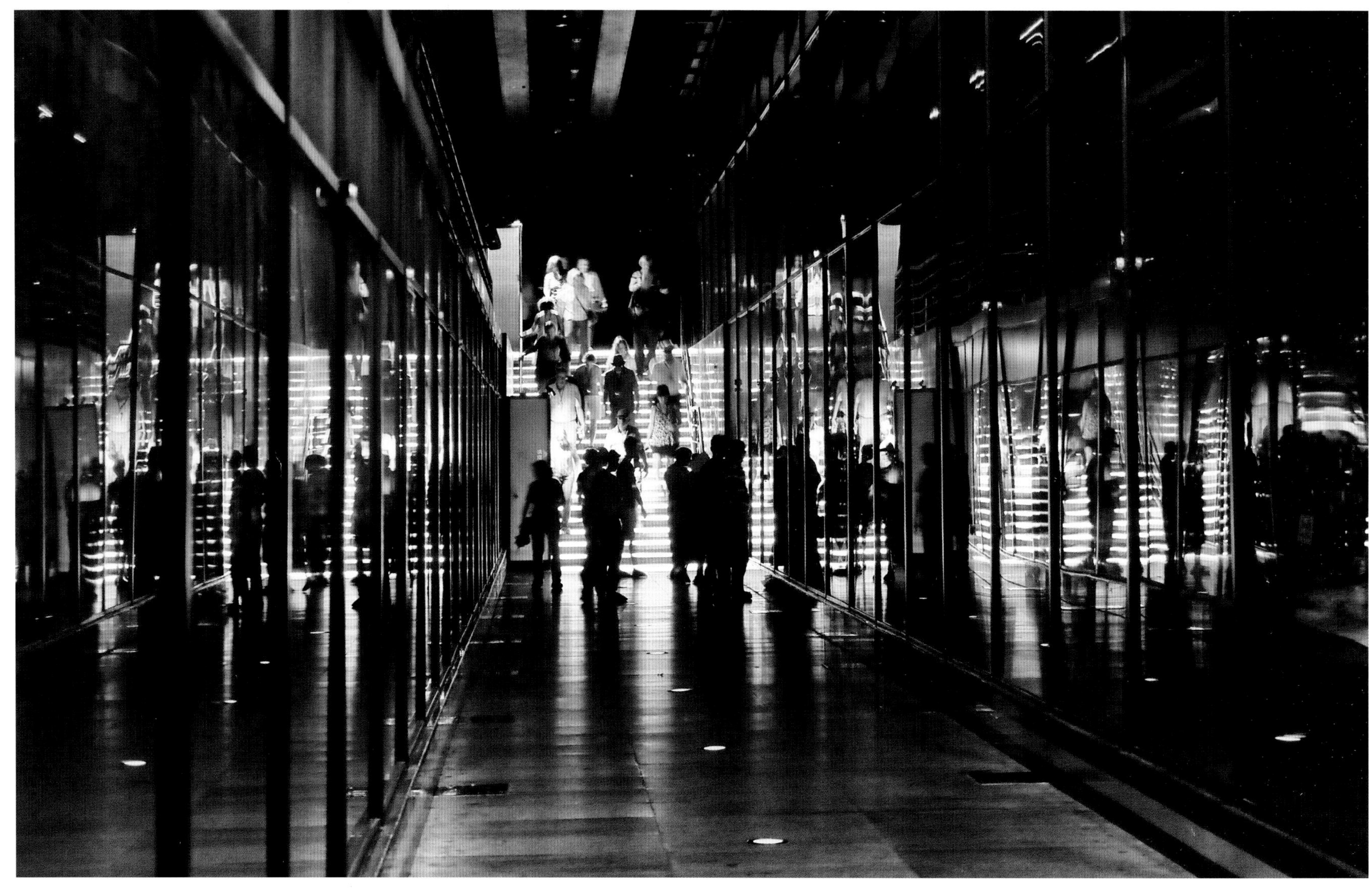

European Photographers in China
歐洲攝影師攝於中國
by Mike Longhurst FRPS

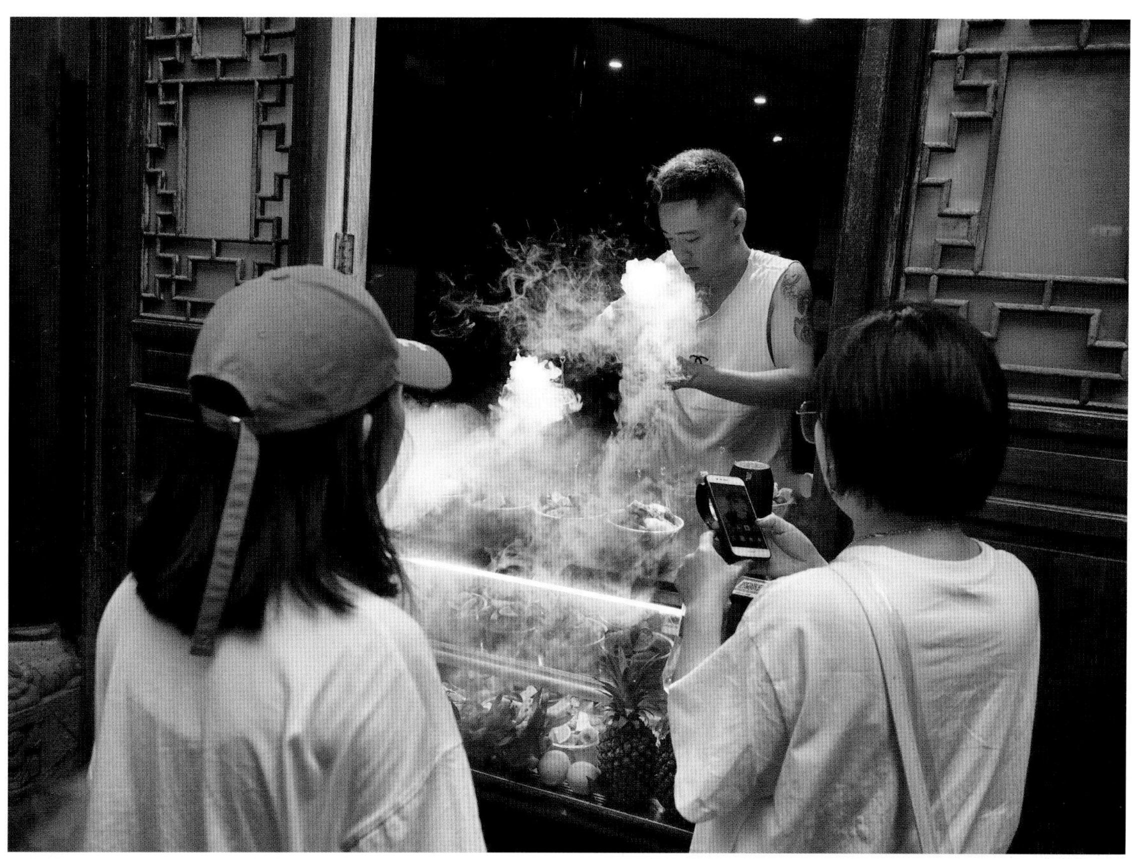

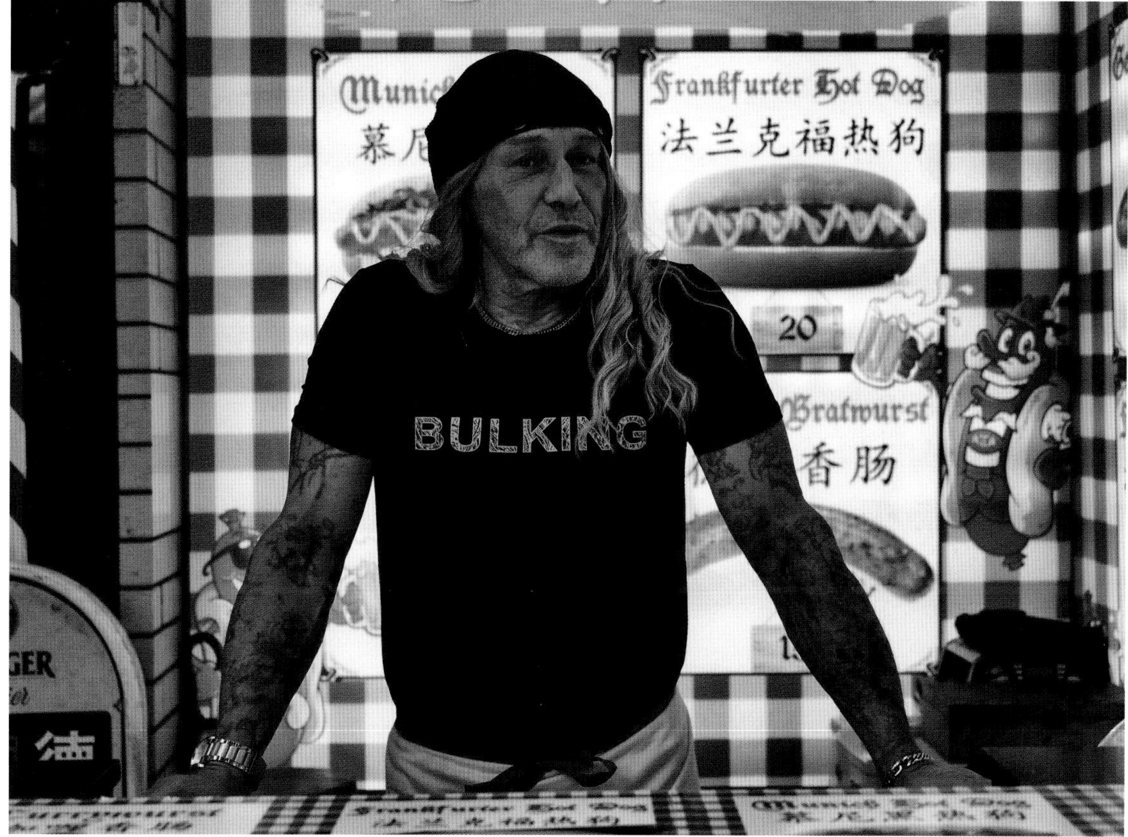

European Photographers in China
歐洲攝影師攝於中國
by Mike Longhurst FRPS

後記

《中國攝影藝術年鑒–歐洲卷》2022–2023是首卷，也是首次在英國倫敦出版，此卷的誕生可謂不易，遭遇了百年不遇的新冠疫情，歷經了國際的風雲變幻。在這艱難的歲月裏，它的誕生，純屬是一種挑戰，從構思、徵稿、編輯、設計到出版，千頭萬緒，一言難盡，無處不融入大量的心血。

攝影技術誕生于歐洲，至今近200年的歷史，從法國的路易・達蓋爾的銀版攝影法到英國的威廉・塔爾博特的人類歷史上的第一張黑白底片，從純機械技術到模仿繪畫直至二戰後的理念及當今的數碼創意，已經發展爲一門獨立的藝術學科。攝影最大的功能就是記録歷史，攝影是無聲的語言、符號的語言、象徵隱喻的語言，也是繪畫的延續。它具有文學性，却是没有語言的文學，除了語言以外的另一種交流方式。當社會進入了影像時代，繪畫不如攝影更能表現瞬間與細膩。攝影的本性是紀實，一旦走向藝術，必得經由攝影師的心靈借助鏡頭對世界的凝視與觀察、絮語與相擁、詩情與畫意。當代攝影從被動走向主動，進入主觀視角，嘗試、探索，産生了新的理念與方法。

本年鑒的目標是搭建東西方攝影家的對話平臺，架起東西方文化交流的橋梁。同時展現視覺藝術的魅力，分享捕捉瞬間之美，引起觀衆共鳴。爲更全面地記録中歐攝影藝術現狀，促進中歐思想交流，發揮其在東西方藝術文化領域的紐帶作用。正值中英建立大使級外交關系50周年之際，在這個重要的歷史時刻，我們隆重地推出《中國攝影藝術年鑒- 歐洲卷》。這本年鑒匯集了來自中國和歐洲的 150 多位攝影師的作品，旨在匯集多種視角對周圍世界的不同看法，這對進一步促進雙方的溝通和了解，將産生深遠的影響。

早在中英兩國建立大使級外交關系45周年時，我曾受中國美術家協會委托，在倫敦策劃了一場盛大的“首届北京國際美術雙年展英國巡展”，名爲“藝術與和平”中國當代藝術作品展，看來致力于促進東西方文化藝術交流是我們義不容辭的責任和時代使命。

此卷攝影作品系列，各種流派紛呈，主題和風格迥异。既有壯觀的自然風光，鮮活的野生動物，又有真實記録人類社會瞬間的人文影象和栩栩如生的人物肖像，不僅具有巨大的視覺衝擊力，同時還對東西方攝影師的視覺文化進行對比，窺視不同文化背景下雙方的思維方式和視覺意識，表達出攝影師深沉幽遠的思想和情感。人類無法阻止時光的流逝，但可藉由相機留住瞬間，這不僅承載了時代的風起雲涌，也展現着生活中平凡的瞬間，讓之永恒，爲史作鑒。

在這《年鑒–歐洲卷》首卷出版之計，思緒萬千，浮想聯翩，絮絮不休，由于篇幅有限，就此擱筆。

在此，由衷感謝《中國攝影藝術年鑒》主編高建生先生的信任和授權，感謝中國駐倫敦旅游辦事處、英國皇家攝影學會和漢普斯特德攝影學會的支持，以及各國攝影師的貢獻和編委會成員的配合。

主編：牟樺 女士
《中國攝影藝術年鑒–歐洲卷》
寫于2022年12月30日英國倫敦

POSTSCRIPT

This *European - Chinese Photographic Art Yearbook 2022-2023* is the first volume and it is also the first time the Yearbook has been published in London, UK. Its creation was not easy. We had to work on the book as the unprecedented first worldwide pandemic in a century heavily impacted both countries, and we also encountered major international changes in these difficult years. Consequently, its creation was a major challenge, and the journey from inception, call for entries, editing and design to final publication, was an intricate one that involved a lot of hard work along the way.

Photographic technology was born in Europe and has a history of nearly 200 years. The mid-19th century saw the earliest developments: Louis Daguerre's daguerreotypes in France and William Henry Fox Talbot's first black-and-white negatives in England. In the decades following, these ideas were developed from purely mechanical technology to imitate the creativity of painting. Developments have continued since World War II and on into today's digital world which has resulted in an independent and highly creative artistic discipline. The greatest function of photography is to record history. Photography is a silent language, a language of symbols, a language of symbolic metaphors, and it is also an extension of painting. It is literary, but it is literature without language, another form of communication besides language. When society entered the age of recorded images, painting was found to be inferior to photography at capturing precise moments and delicate details. The nature of photography is documentary. Once it becomes an art, it must encounter the photographer's mind and lens to gaze and observe the world, talk and embrace, create poetic and picturesque situations. Contemporary photography has moved from passive to active, entering a subjective perspective, trying and exploring, and producing new ideas and methods.

The goal of this yearbook is to build a platform for dialogue between Eastern and Western photographers, and to build a bridge for cultural exchanges between the East and the West. At the same time, it showcases the charm of visual art, shares the beauty of capturing moments, and resonates with the audience. In order to more comprehensively record the current situation of photographic art in China and Europe, promote the exchange of ideas between China and Europe, and play its role as a link in the field of art and culture between the East and the West, on the occasion of the 50th anniversary of the establishment of ambassadorial diplomatic relations between China and the UK, in this important historical moment, we solemnly launch the first European volume of *Chinese Photographic Art Yearbook.* This annals brings together the works of more than 150 photographers in the world and aims to bring together their various perspectives on the worlds around them.

As early as the 45th anniversary of the establishment of diplomatic relations at the ambassadorial level between China and the UK, I was entrusted by the Chinese Artists Association to curate a grand UK Tour of the First Beijing International Art Biennale in London entitled *Art and Peace* - Chinese Contemporary Art Works Exhibition. I am proud to accept my inevitable responsibility and the mission of our times to be committed to promoting the exchange of Eastern and Western culture and art.

In planning for the publication of the *European - Chinese Photographic Art Yearbook* in 2022, there has been a lot of thought, imagination, and endless debate. Due to limitations of space not everything can be described here.

Here, I sincerely thank Mr. Gao Jiansheng, editor-in-chief of *Chinese Photographic Art Yearbook* for his trust and authorisation, and thank the Chinese Tourism Office in London, the Royal Photographic Society and the Hampstead Photographic Society for their support, as well as the contributions of photographers from various countries and the full cooperation of editorial board members.

Editor-in-Chief : Suzanna Mu
European - Chinese Photographic Art Yearbook
December 30, 2022, London, UK
admin@sinoeuropeanarts.co.uk
www.sinoeuropeanarts.co.uk

索引 INDEX

致謝

我要感謝每一位攝影師分享他們的作品，我還要感謝給予了我極大幫助的我的家人和朋友,《中國攝影藝術年鑒–歐洲卷》編輯委員會全體成員的配合以及那些幫助我完成本書的所有人。

高健生
薛伶
朱憲民
王玉文
王悦
徐偉浩
黄松辉
農賀迪
鄭啓東
魏德華

邁克爾・普裏查德
朱迪・希克斯
朱利安・勞斯
大衛・希克斯
文斯・哈裏斯
亞歷克 ・ 斯弗林
大衛・裏德
梁藝寶
杜海東
陳秀慶

斯特拉斯卡倫勛爵
馬特・康威
格雷 ・ 厄姆基爾
克裏斯 ・ 戴
奈杰爾・麥金利
保羅・康威
劉金城
約翰 ・ 加拉德
戴夫 ・ 甘加丁
喬仲林

我認爲整個項目是真正的團隊合作。因此，盡管我嘗試盡可能多地提及一些人，但今年的篇幅特别有限，如果我漏掉了任何人，請原諒我，我感謝你們每一位以某種方式做出貢獻的人。

主編: 牟樺女士
《中國攝影藝術年鑒–歐洲卷》編輯委員會

ACKNOWLEDGEMENTS

I would like to thank each of the photographers who have generously shared their images in this book. I'd also like to thank my family and friends, The Team of the E*uropean-Chinese Photographic Arts Yearbook* Editorial Committee UK and those that have helped to make this book possible.

Gao Jiansheng
Xue Lin
Zhu Xianming
Wang Yuwen
Wang Yue
Xu Weihao
Huang Songhui
Nong Hedi
Zheng Qidong
Wei Dehua

Michael Pritchard FRPS
Judy Hicks LRPS
Julian Rouse LRPS
David Hicks
Vince Harris
Alex Flynn
David Reed
Liang Yibao
Du Haidong
Chen Xiuqing

Lord Strathcarron
Matt Conway
Graham Kill
Chris Day
Nigel Mckinley
Paul Conway
Liu Jincheng
John Garrad
Dave Gangadeen
Qiao Zhonglin

I emphasise that this whole project is truly a team effort. So while I try and mention as many people as I can, and with particularly limited space this year, please forgive me if I've missed anyone and know that I thank each and every one of you who has contributed in some way.

Ms. Suzanna Mu, Editor-in-Chief
European - Chinese Photographic Art Yearbook Editorial Committee

SUPPORTED BY:

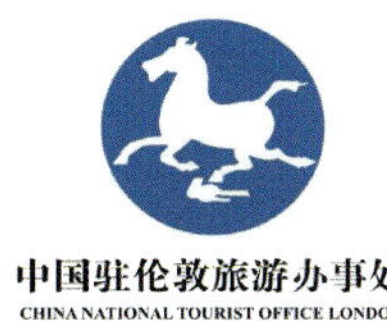

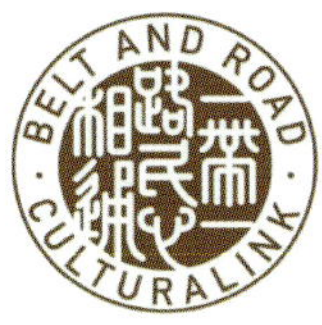

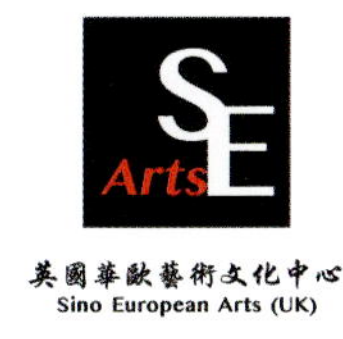

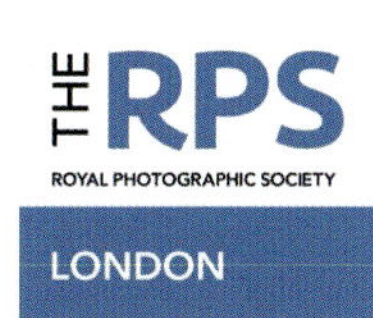

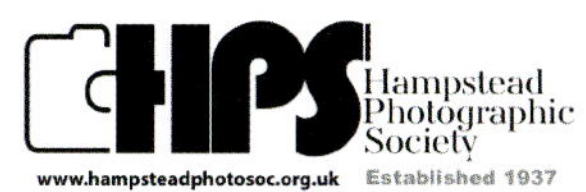

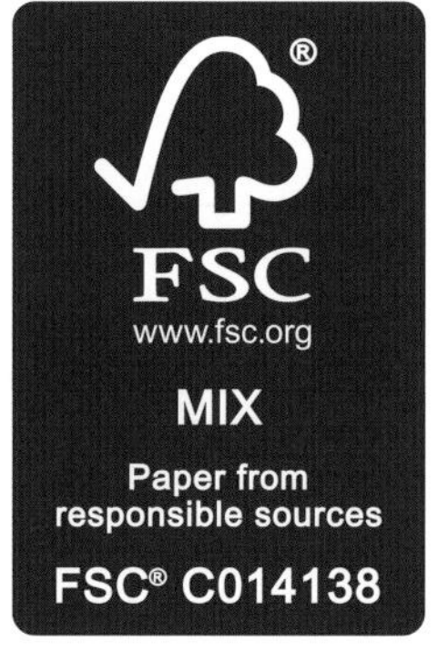
FSC
www.fsc.org
MIX
Paper from
responsible sources
FSC® C014138